LEON URIS

Leon Uris in Copenhagen, in front of an SAS sign as he transfers planes en route to Israel to research Exodus, *April 1956.*

Jewish History, Life, and Culture
Michael Neiditch, Series Editor

IRA B. NADEL

LEON URIS

LIFE OF A BEST SELLER

UNIVERSITY OF TEXAS PRESS AUSTIN

The Jewish History, Life, and Culture Series is supported by the late
Milton T. Smith and the Moshana Foundation, and the Tocker Foundation.

Additional support for this publication was provided by Sander and
Lottie Shapiro.

Unless otherwise indicated, all photos are from the Harry Ransom
Humanities Research Center, the University of Texas at Austin.

LIBRARY OF CONGRESS CATALOGING-IN-PUBLICATION DATA

Nadel, Ira Bruce.
    Leon Uris : life of a best seller / Ira B. Nadel. — 1st ed.
        p.   cm. — (Jewish history, life, and culture)
    Includes bibliographical references and index.
    ISBN 978-0-292-70935-5 (cloth : alk. paper)
    1. Uris, Leon, 1924–2003.   2. Authors, American—20th century—Biography.   3. Jewish
authors—United States—Biography.   I. Title.
    PS3541.R46Z79   2010
    813'.54—dc22
    [B]
                                                                        2010019951

I feel that if I have any gift as a writer at all it is to communicate my inner thoughts to the average man. Not to elevate him . . . or to educate him . . . but to paralyze him with a story he cannot put down.
—LEON URIS, 10 JULY 1957

Have to run. Just about to start my new novel and once again save mankind.
—LEON URIS, 17 AUGUST 1981

CONTENTS

ABBREVIATIONS

AGR   *A God in Ruins.* New York: HarperCollins, 1999.

AH   *The Angry Hills.* New York: Random House, 1955.

AR   *Armageddon: A Novel of Berlin.* Garden City, N.Y.: Doubleday, 1964.

AUTO   Unpublished autobiography by William Wolf Uris, 1975.

BC   *Battle Cry.* New York: Putnam, 1953.

EX   *Exodus.* Garden City, N.Y.: Doubleday, 1958.

EXR   *Exodus Revisited.* Photographs by Dimitrios Harissiadis. Garden City, N.Y.: Doubleday, 1959.

"HI"   "Hellenic Interlude." Unpublished, 1954.

HJ   *The Haj.* Garden City, N.Y.: Doubleday, 1984.

ITB   *Ireland: A Terrible Beauty.* With Jill Uris. 1975. New York: Bantam, 1978.

JSS   *Jerusalem: Song of Songs.* Photographs by Jill Uris. Garden City, N.Y.: Doubleday, 1981.

M18   *Mila 18.* Garden City, N.Y.: Doubleday, 1961.

MP   *Mitla Pass.* Garden City, N.Y.: Doubleday, 1988.

OHC   *O'Hara's Choice.* New York: HarperCollins, 2003.

QBVII   *QB VII.* Garden City, N.Y.: Doubleday, 1970.

RD   *Redemption.* New York: HarperCollins, 1995.

"SFI"   "Secrets of Forever Island." Illustrated by Channing Thieme. Unpublished, 1990.

TP   *Topaz.* New York: McGraw-Hill, 1967.

TR   *Trinity.* Garden City, N.Y.: Doubleday, 1976.

ACKNOWLEDGMENTS

T HROUGHOUT THE COURSE of this project, many have shared with me their experiences of Leon Uris, from a Chilean doctor who read *Exodus* at thirteen to a woman who toured Ireland using *Trinity* as a guide. This narrative reverses the process, telling the story of Leon Uris's life in order to share it with his readers. Three people have been especially important in its writing: the first is the late Milton Smith, a Texas philanthropist and businessman who was instrumental in facilitating the acquisition of the Uris archive for the Harry Ransom Humanities Research Center at the University of Texas at Austin. Matching his enthusiasm for this account of Uris was his energetic and persistent encouragement. Only just before his death at ninety-five did he grudgingly admit that "he did not have life by a long string," urging me not to waste time. The Moshana Foundation, which Smith founded with his wife Helen, has been, and continues to be, an active sponsor of cultural activities throughout Texas and beyond. Their support of this project is graciously acknowledged. Lonnie Taub, the current director of the Moshana Foundation and Milton Smith's daughter, has maintained her father's passion for the subject.

Mark Uris, Leon Uris's eldest son, was also a remarkable resource and support. His candidness in sharing details about growing up with his father and the adventures of travel, research, and skiing—a Uris passion—was highly valued. His generosity was constant and deeply appreciated. Mark's memory of the family's dramatic departure from Israel in 1956 during the Suez crisis is a keynote in my recounting of Uris's eight-month stay in the country. Additionally, his research into sources, stories, and documents wonderfully augmented my own investigations. In a spirit of cooperation, he offered letters, photographs, and information. His death from cancer in 2007 was as unexpected as it was tragic.

Jill Uris is the third figure without whose help this book would not possess any of its detail or possible merit. Her early and welcoming response, plus repeated encouragement, was matched by her kindliness in answering queries, confirming dates, and offering the names of additional Uris friends and associates who could clarify the story. Her gathering of many of Uris's friends at the Maroon Creek Club during my visit to Aspen in June 2005 was a remarkable moment, and I am grateful. Meeting Marti and Ken Sterling, Walt Smith, and later Andy Hecht and Dr. Robert Oden was an important starting point for the narrative.

Others in Uris's family who helped include Essie Kofsky, Leon Uris's half sister. Her memories of Uris growing up in Norfolk, Virginia, and his steps to fame were vivid, as was her recollection of her mother and family life. Idalea Kofsky Rubin, Essie's daughter and Leon Uris's niece, was also helpful in clarifying family connections. Additionally, Karen Uris, Leon Uris's oldest daughter, was an important source regarding family life, offering insights, especially about her mother, Betty, and photographs. Pat Uris, wife of the late Mark Uris, also provided useful details of the family's early years. Rachael and Conor Uris, the youngest children of Leon Uris, kindly offered comments and memories of life with their father in both Aspen and Shelter Island, New York.

Herschel Blumberg, Uris's cousin, met with me in Chevy Chase, Maryland, to review the early and the last days of Leon Uris. Herbert Schlosberg of Sherman Oaks, California, was gracious in letting me spend an afternoon with him as he recounted meeting Uris for the first time and the challenges of remaining his business agent, lawyer, and general manager for some forty years. His own career in the marines, including the assault on Iwo Jima, was one of courage and bravery.

Through the help of my son Ryan Nadel, then in Israel, I was fortunate enough to locate Ilan Hartuv, who had served as guide, assistant, and general pathfinder for Uris when he was researching *Exodus*. Hartuv's own life—as a diplomat, an ambassador, and then, frighteningly, a hostage at Entebbe who was rescued by the Israeli commandoes in July 1976—nearly overshadowed his many adventures with Uris during the research for both *Exodus* and *Jerusalem: Song of Songs*. He was precise as he recalled incidents and people whom Uris had met, and recounted the later challenge of working with Otto Preminger. Rochelle and Garry Mass of Gan Ner, Israel, were wonderful hosts, encouraging supporters, and able translators.

Oscar Dystel, the former president of Bantam Books, was a remarkable figure who, with Esther Margolis, the founder of Newmarket Press and a former publicist at Bantam, collectively brought to life the impact of Uris's writing on the popular-book trade. To listen to them was an education in the promotion, marketing, and selling of books during a time when the viability of the paperback was emerging. Michael Neiditch of Washington, D.C., was a constant source of Uris details, having befriended him in New York after Uris moved there in 1988 and later traveling with him in Russia. Micky was a source of facts, anecdotes, and events that helped me define the character of Uris and his commitment to Jewish social and political values.

Michael Remer and Lee Snow, attorneys in New York, took time from their busy practices to answer questions and smooth the way. Nancy Stauffer, Uris's former agent, met with me at Uris's favorite New York hotel, the Algonquin, and kindly shared with me details of his later career. Channing Thieme Penna was especially helpful in providing details of Uris's life in New York and Shelter Island. Her description of Uris's commitment to the theatre and renewed interest in writing, first a children's story and then his last novels, illuminated his late style for me.

In Austin, Thomas F. Staley, the director of the Ransom Center, remains a catalytic figure who ignites new projects and guides authors new and old with eagerness and enthusiasm. His professionalism and friendship is infectious and undiminished. As friend and guide, he has both nurtured and propelled this study. Tim Staley, formerly at the University of Texas Press, was also an early and continuous supporter of the book who, in its early stages, managed its progress through administrative and other challenges. Joanna Hitchcock, the director of the press, was also a helpful and encouraging voice, while Jim Burr, humanities editor, has proved to be an able and supportive guide as well as an excellent critic.

Liz Murray, an archivist at the Ransom Center, remains the best-informed and most helpful scholar of the Uris archive and was a constant source of new details, locating sometimes-misplaced documents, while being a wonderful booster of the project. Her skill in identifying important materials is exceeded only by her efficiency and availability. Others at the Ransom Center who assisted include Joan Sibley, Pat Fox, and Alex Jasinski (who is especially knowledgeable about military matters). Thanks also to the staff members of the Ransom Center's Reading Room, who by now know how to parry frequent requests for longer hours, more time, and no holiday breaks.

Aaron Zacks, at the Department of English at the University of Texas, Austin, and the Ransom Center, was an outstanding research assistant who, even when I could not be on site, managed to conduct important forays into the archive. Alan Friedman and Elizabeth Cullingford generously shared with me not only their wide knowledge of modernist writing but also their home. Every trip to Austin was an opportunity to renew a longstanding friendship for which I am grateful.

Additional help came from Uris's various research assistants, Marilynn Pysher and Diane Eagle in particular. Marilynn was an informative guide to Shelter Island, making sure I understood its history and culture. Diane helpfully told me how Uris worked and the challenges he presented daily. Evelyn Englander, formerly the librarian at the U.S. Marine Corps Historical Center Library at the

Navy Yard in Washington, was also an important resource. Glenn Horowitz has again been a stimulating voice, one always in tune with the changing tempo of New York book life. Donald MacDonald, an architect in San Francisco, was immensely helpful in introducing me to Larkspur, as was the staff at the Larkspur Public Library. Also to be thanked is Patty Raab, a public safety records specialist for the Aspen Police Department in Aspen, Colorado.

On a more personal level, my son Ryan Nadel assisted in Israel with translation, travel, and transitions from one culture to another. He was also able to locate and provide me with a set of Hebrew editions of Uris's work, and he discovered Ilan Hartuv. My daughter Dara, having herself just completed a year at Hebrew University, provided further insight as she read through several Uris novels and posed probing questions from Israel and Montreal. Anne MacKenzie continues to be a marvelous companion and support, providing balance and style to a life that can be too easily spent in the study or the archive.

LEON URIS

PROLOGUE
"AMERICAN MARINE, JEWISH WRITER"

Q UANTICO NATIONAL CEMETERY, just south of Washington, contains more than 23,000 military graves on 725 acres. On a gently sloping hill facing Thomas Jefferson Road, several hundred gravestones of equal height stand in quiet formation. One, near the bottom, is slightly more noticeable. Beside a soldier who died in Vietnam, and below a marine and sailor who fought in Vietnam and Korea, is the writer Leon Uris. Under a Jewish star, his name, rank, service, war action, and dates are followed by his own simple epitaph: "American Marine / Jewish Writer." The order of the words is telling: it underscores a self-image that this biography will alternately reaffirm and question.

Burial as a marine forms one bookend to his life. The other is his enlistment at seventeen, a month after Pearl Harbor. From discipline and self-reliance to patriotism and duty, the Marine Corps instilled in Uris a moral code and an American identity that defined his career. His outrage at injustice and persecution found reinforcement in the spirit of the corps and its commitment to helping liberty defeat oppression. "This is my war—personally," he proudly wrote in a letter of November 1943. He meant it. Underlining his devotion to the marines are his first and last novels, *Battle Cry* and *O'Hara's Choice*: both concentrate on the corps. There were other influences, of course, from his left-leaning father to his Hollywood screenwriting. But the marines provided the foundation of his life, and he was thrilled to be one of them.

Fame came suddenly. When *Exodus* appeared in 1958—Uris was thirty-four— it sold more copies than any other American book except *Gone with the Wind*, spending more than a year as a *New York Times* best seller, including twenty weeks at number one. *Exodus* has never been out of print. At one point, it was selling 2,500 copies a day. The advance printing for the paperback was 1.5 million copies. It was soon increased to 2.9 million. To date, *Exodus* has gone through eighty-seven printings and appeared in fifty languages.[1] *QB VII* stayed at the top of the best-seller list for nine weeks, selling over 300,000 copies in hardback.[2] *Trinity* held the number one position for thirty-six weeks, remaining on the overall list for seventy-three, the longest-running continuous fiction best seller of the 1970s (*Exodus* lasted a mere seventy-one weeks). At one point, *Trinity* was selling 10,000 copies a week. The doyen of popular literature, Uris reigned over the best-seller list, his works equal in sales to the combined total of John Hersey, James Jones, Norman Mailer, and Saul Bellow.

His decline was equally precipitous. After *Trinity*, the interest in Uris's work fell off, partly because of competitors and partly because he substituted research for action, detail for drama. *The Haj* was too partisan, *Mitla Pass* too indulgent. *Redemption*, his longest novel, never found its audience. Later titles like *A God in Ruins* and the posthumous *O'Hara's Choice* similarly disappointed. But at his height, David Ben-Gurion, Israel's first prime minister, as well as Bobby Sands, the imprisoned Irish Republican Army supporter, admired his work. The heiress Barbara Hutton was photographed carrying a copy of *Battle Cry*, while a long-legged chorus girl on *The Ed Sullivan Show* was shown leaning against a television camera, engrossed in a paperback of the same novel. Joe DiMaggio owned a copy of *Exodus*, as did President Truman. A future prime minister of Ireland—Charles J. Haughey—praised *Trinity* at the time of its publication.

What explains this popular success? How did this high school dropout, exmarine, screenwriter, and talented author become an international sensation who was read by prime ministers and prisoners, socialites and showgirls? Such questions led me to write this book, which, as it unfolded, became the story of the rise of American popular fiction, mass-market paperback publishing, celebrity authorship, and authors' ways of making a living. Uris's impact intrigued me: how could one who wrote so ineptly still find such a wide and persistent audience? How did he succeed when greater writers did not, if success is measured by sales, readership, and public attention? Uris drew crowds; Faulkner did not. How did he achieve international recognition when more adventurous and artistically important writers did not?

This biography is also the story of what happens when popular culture collides with critical opinion. Few critics thought of Uris as a major writer, but many recognized his power as a storyteller whose subject was history. Few critics praised his literary skills, but readers did not care. His books were worldwide sensations that fueled a dazzling life of first-class travel, an estate on a mountainside in Aspen, Colorado, and marriages to a series of beautiful wives. The self-dramatizing writer Felix Abravanel in Philip Roth's *The Ghost Writer* comes to mind, although Uris seems to exceed even his narcissistic excesses.

Part of the explanation for Uris's success lies in the nature of postwar popular writing: realistic, genre-based fiction that never disappointed its readers. Its heroes triumphed as they vanquished evil in the pursuit of justice. The writing style was conventional, and the form repeated itself to duplicate earlier pleasures. Uris followed the practice, relying on dramatic presentations of recent history built around the exploits of larger-than-life figures and set in vaguely understood but exotic locales: the Pacific, Greece, Israel, Poland, Germany, Ireland, New Zealand. The western—he wrote the screenplay for *Gunfight at the O.K. Corral*—was also a critical influence, partly because it pitted good against evil, right against wrong, while showing how violence threatened domestic life.

Transferred to twentieth-century historical fiction, such writing provided a formula for success while repeatedly proving Uris's financial and literary worth. His heroes—from Ari Ben Canaan in *Exodus* to Conor Larkin in *Trinity*—consistently triumph. Uris and his protagonists, however, did not have time for introspection; they concentrated on action, plot, and movement. Psychological reflection was a distraction. His work, anticipating that of both Irving Wallace and Tom Clancy, was instructive and entertaining, blending information with romance. The public loved it.

"Research to me is as important or more important than the writing," Uris said just before *Redemption* appeared in 1995.[3] The comment is apt because it identifies his skill but also his weakness. His early novels established their authority through detailed research, but it was often subordinate to, or at least in competition with, character and drama. This is clear in *Exodus*, *Mila 18*, and *Trinity*. But with his later work, notably *The Haj* and *Redemption*, Uris's research dominated narrative and plot, inflating the story. At 827 pages and ninety-one chapters, *Redemption* is Uris's longest work. But its anticipated success never materialized, and he became caught in a cycle of money woes and debt.

But Uris was part of another phenomenon: the growing adaptation of novels into movies or television miniseries. James Jones's *From Here to Eternity* set the pattern for such treatments of popular writing in the movies, becoming an Oscar-winning film. *Battle Cry*, *Exodus*, and *Topaz* (directed by Alfred Hitchcock) are Uris examples. Uris's *QB VII* (1970) became the first television miniseries and the winner of six Emmys. It was seen by millions of viewers over its two-night showing in 1974, which boosted sales of the book dramatically. Uris was also part of the postwar fiction boom that responded to a public eager to understand the immediate past through storytelling. Fiction could make that past both more comprehensible and more exciting than straightforward historical accounts. Uris quickly discovered a formula that was later adopted by authors such as Joseph Heller (*Catch-22*), William Styron (*Sophie's Choice*), Alan Furst (*Dark Star*), and Louis de Bernières (*Corelli's Mandolin*). He also pioneered the popularization of novelists through talk-show appearances, author signings, book tours, and media features. He was on *The Ed Sullivan Show* and featured in *People Magazine*. It seemed absolutely right for Uris to appear in a photograph with Jacqueline Susann, each holding the other's best seller: Susann confidently gripping *Exodus*, Uris nervously holding *Valley of the Dolls*.

Financially, Uris benefited from the attention. He became one of the wealthiest writers in America. He traveled around the world to research new works, meet readers, and parade his wives. His second marriage made front-page, banner news in the *Los Angeles Times*. His third was a society story in New York, the wedding heralded as one of the most important held at the Algonquin Hotel, de facto headquarters of the New York literary world. It was the site of the Algonquin Round Table, a noted and daily gathering of literary notables during the twenties. When he faced libel charges in England in 1964, in what was then the longest libel trial in English history, the case made international headlines; when he went to Russia in 1989, he was mobbed.

But who was this man and why was he such a sensation? Did Uris remake the mold of the popular writer? And how did he fit in with the growing popularity and promotion of writers such as James Michener, Herman Wouk, Norman Mailer, and Irving Wallace? His novels changed the popular perception of Israel and Ireland—but how? Did publicity shape his career when criticism did not? These are some of the questions that engaged me during the course of the research, travel, and interviews that provided the material for this book.

Uris was never ambiguous about his aims. In a 1957 letter to his father, written while working on *Exodus*, he outlined his approach to winning readers: "I thoroughly disagree that the 'duty of the literary writer is to elevate the taste artistically and literarily and not lower the taste of the uncritical reader.' . . . The duty of a writer is to translate life as HE SEES IT."[4] A week later, he wrote: "The most important function of a writer is as a chronicler of his times."[5] Uris was not ashamed to write for a living. In fact, he saw it as a noble cause: "Writers who 'intentionally' try to reach for 'immortality' generally fall flat on their faces such as Wouk in *Morningstar* and Steinbeck in *East of Eden*. I find absolutely nothing dirty about a writer, musician or painter making a living . . . although, in some quarters this is looked upon as a weakness."[6]

Uris adopted William S. Burroughs's neat prescription for best sellers: "write something that people know something about and want to know more about."[7] Uris knew how to expand history and translate it so that ordinary readers could understand it. He also sensed a postwar interest in the recent, though incompletely understood, events that had occurred in Europe and the Middle East. This made his fiction compelling. With his ability to condense history into a single paragraph or page, and his remarkable narrative skills, he emotionally engaged his readers in his stories when mass-market paperbacks were finding a wide audience and movie tie-ins and celebrity author tours were starting. Uris took full advantage of all these developments. As a self-promoter and celebrity, he was invited to appear on television shows as well as at graduation ceremonies, conventions, and fund-raising events. He also understood the value and appeal of the movies, and from his experience as a screenwriter, he adopted techniques that would shape his books. Uris also made headlines by negotiating some of the most lucrative book and film contracts of his day.

Uris was a mythmaker who redefined the cultural status of the Jew for North Americans. Coming from the South—he was born in Baltimore and spent his youth in that city and in Norfolk—he understood what it meant to be an outsider. Prejudice was a reality, as was failure. Uris witnessed his father's failure at numerous careers. The experience turned Uris into an activist determined to present "tough Jews" who succeed. His father's activities in leftist groups reinforced his motivation to improve his condition. Uris's Jewish heroes strenuously reject Shylock's belief that "suff'rance is the badge of all our tribe."[8] For Uris, the badge was a gun. His heroes are unafraid. His iconic image of the Jewish freedom fighter, represented on the cover of *Exodus* and the wrought-iron fence at his Aspen home, symbolized his stance, in both his own aggressive nature and in his fiction. His experiences in the marines proved to him that Jews could be fighters and be accepted as such. He also recognized this quality in himself, candidly admitting that he once thought of himself "as a very sad little Jewish boy isolated in a Southern town, undersized, asthmatic [but] when I read all my correspondence again, I realized I was a hustler. I was tough. I used everything to my advantage. I could be ruthless."[9]

The social function of literature dominated Uris's idea of the author. He rejected the personal as a literary indulgence: "Too many writers today serve personal manias rather than a cause. They spend too much time psychoanalyzing themselves in print. Great writers in the past were aroused by social causes—*The Grapes of Wrath*, *The Wall*. I prefer to write about people caught up in the tides of history."[10] But as part of this, a writer needed to be angry. This, for Uris, meant "having strong motivation. Something must be driving you to make this maniacal commitment to that torture machine the typewriter."[11]

For Uris, the anger that gave a writer purpose appears to have originated in personal sources, although he rarely acknowledged them. Rather, he transferred them to, and wrote about, history, but always as a struggle. His criticism of Jewish writers who turned their lives into their fiction was a reaction to his own fear and avoidance of such subjects—although by *Mitla Pass* (1988), Uris was willing to acknowledge them, at least in fictional form.

The origin of Uris's personal anger may well have been his father's failures, which were projected onto his son as constant pressure to succeed. The repeated prodding of his son to write better masked the father's own shortcomings and potted education, which was more political than historical. He relentlessly criticized Uris, mixing advice with guilt: "God forbid I should tell you what to write. I am only offering a suggestion that should be carefully followed, FOR YOUR SAKE," a letter reprinted in *Mitla Pass* exhorts (*MP*, 24).

Whereas Uris's father's was candid, his mother was reserved. In addition, her distrust of love became a likely source of detachment and unhappiness, which drove Uris to present women unsympathetically in his fiction. The conflict he witnessed between his parents, leading to their divorce when he was six, also contributed to his aggressive posture, a defense against other threats to his emotional or personal security—he did not let anyone interfere with what he thought was right. Hence, his determination to leave high school to join the marines, a decision that was more personal than patriotic. He wanted to be independent and free of his family, even if doing so cost him his life.

Conflict—personal, social, political, and cultural—is the heart of Uris's writing. It could be between men in a marine squad (*Battle Cry*), between a plaintiff and a defendant (*QB VII*), or between England and Ireland (*Trinity*). For Uris, life, whether actual or fictional, consists of confrontation, which found early expression when he received the galleys of his first novel, *Battle Cry*. The publisher had removed the first-person narrator. Uris had to decide whether to accept the change, knowing that a refusal could have jeopardized publication. Defiantly, he stood his ground and refused to accept the modification, knowing that if he compromised, he could not go back. The publisher gave in.

Uris's interpretation of modern Jewish history confirmed his resolute and aggressive behavior. He believed that Judaism, and Israel in particular, had survived because adversity had made it tough. The Jew was a fighter who challenged social injustice despite often insurmountable odds. Although not the first to express this position, Uris was the most vocal writer to advance this view, not only in his characters, but also in lawsuits and other battles involving his books. Uris had heroes: Theodore Dreiser, John Dos Passos, Ernest Hemingway, and John Steinbeck. He placed himself squarely in a tradition of American social fiction, although he shifted the arena to Europe or the Middle East with heroes who were Israeli, Polish, or Irish. Or if they were American, like Major Huxley in *Battle Cry* or Abraham Cady in *QB VII*, they seemed more at home in foreign countries.

Uris's aggressiveness synthesized resentment against his father's weaknesses, and his status as an outsider reinforced his determination to succeed as a novelist. From the start, he aimed to write best sellers, and *Battle Cry* (1953) did not disappoint: it went through two printings before publication and was one of the most successful titles ever published in hardcover by Putnam. Its appearance in paperback, a month or so before the release of the 1955 movie staring Dorothy

Malone, Aldo Ray, Van Heflin, and the young Tab Hunter, ensured even greater sales. His second novel, *The Angry Hills*, although a constant seller, had less startling success, but his third, *Exodus*, was an international hit with over twenty million copies in print.

Uris appeared at a time when blockbuster novels were shaping the best-seller list. Big subjects in big books by name authors were beginning to control the list in the fifties and, most importantly, were being read by men as well as women. Historical romances no longer dominated. At the same time, being Jewish was becoming mainstream: Uris, Norman Mailer, Herman Wouk, Meyer Levin, Jerome Weidman, Harry Golden, and Saul Bellow were leading the way, followed by a younger set that included Bernard Malamud, Philip Roth, and Joseph Heller. Mass-market sales of paperback books were also taking off, so print runs in the hundreds of thousands for major titles like *Marjorie Morningstar*, *Exodus*, or *Dr. Zhivago* were not uncommon. Interestingly, the decade of the fifties began with a religious best seller as number one, *The Cardinal* by Henry Morton (1950), and ended with another, *Exodus* by Uris (1958).[12]

Setting, history, romance, and plots based on recent events (of which the public often had incomplete knowledge) led to Uris's success. Marketing, promotion, and film tie-ins also helped. *Topaz* (1967) is representative. Drawing on the Cuban missile crisis of 1962, Uris, who did extensive research and had the assistance of the former head of French intelligence in Washington, pits the Soviet Union and the United States against each other in a Cold War confrontation. The polarities of communism and democracy result in a characteristic struggle of a formulaic kind, rendered vivid by inside information of actual espionage operations. Reviews were mixed, a number of them referring to the work as a "non-fiction novel" or an example of the "Uris School of Non-Fiction Fiction." But even a virulent review in the *New York Times*—Uris takes "130,000 words to display his incompetence"—did not deter readers.[13] They loved the book and its combination of espionage, contemporary history, and romance. It remained on the best-seller list for forty-eight weeks and had a new burst of sales when Hitchcock released his film of the novel.

Uris's appeal also came from the moral intensity of his writing, which was propelled by hatred of injustice and abuse. Part of this originated in his father's radicalism and political involvement and in his mother's support for such causes. There is an urgency to his style and characters that makes his work both gripping and awkward. Stylistically, Uris is often melodramatic and mannered, matching clichés with stereotypes. Yet his narrative skill pulls readers into his stories, forcing them to overlook the repetitious phrasing, unimaginative language, and clumsy syntax. And he offers readers an emotional, though not always authoritative, sense of experience, which originated in his Hemingwayesque need to experience the events he described. Uris became a hero to himself as well as to his public. The author photo on the rear jacket of *Exodus* says it clearly: Uris stands in fatigues next to a military jeep while on patrol in the Negev, his left hand on its MG 34 machine gun, which is pointed skyward. The message is clear: here is a writer willing to challenge danger and do battle—for a country, himself, and literature. Hemingway, not Henry James, was his model. This naturally led to socially engaged, politically alert, morally aware fiction filled with macho action at the expense of emotion and complexity.

Uris's life constantly proved to be his best text, beginning with his war experiences in the Pacific (*Battle Cry*), his dangerous travel in Israel (*Exodus*), his visit to communist Poland (*Mila 18*), his trips to occupied Berlin (*Armageddon*), his libel trial in Britain (*QB VII*), eight months in fractious Northern Ireland and the Irish Republic (*Trinity*), and reliving the history of the marines (*O'Hara's Choice*). The list highlights only a few of his adventures, overlooking a secret flight to Iran to bring Yemenite Jewish refugees (who had fled there) to Israel, threats on his life by the French intelligence service as a result of *Topaz*, and a dangerous trip to the Soviet Union in 1989, where he received an underground copy of *Exodus*.

Uris also realized that his subject matter suited his style, which is overheated, expository, and dramatic. His uncompromising nature and behavior, in turn, fashioned his essentialist presentation of history: Arab versus Jew, English versus Irish, and culture versus anarchy were his unwavering dichotomies. History for Uris was never gray; it exhibited an exhilarating moral clarity that appealed to his readers.

Realism infused with romance characterizes his aesthetic. Such a style often sacrificed accuracy, but his readers rarely complained. Story demanded the alteration of facts. For example, few took issue with his rewriting the history of the ship *Exodus*, which in reality never transported a cargo of children from Cyprus to Israel. The actual ship, the former Chesapeake Bay steamer *President Warfield*, had to unload its European refugees—who had been picked up in France, not Cyprus—onto British prison ships after two British destroyers rammed the boat as it tried to land in Israel in July 1947. The British then sent the refugees not to Cyprus, as originally promised, but on a return voyage to France, and then to Germany.

For Uris, the more tangible the source material, the better the imaginative possibilities. Reference books, maps, autobiographies, letters, histories, journals, government documents, travel brochures, and even issues of *National Geographic* provided inspiration. The result was the kind of exactitude valued by Hemingway. At the end of *A Farewell to Arms*, he writes: "Abstract words such as glory, honor, courage, or hallow were obscene beside the concrete names of villages, the numbers of roads, the names of rivers, the numbers of regiments and the dates."[14] Uris understood this. He filled his novels with information, and his characters with knowledge, that often seems remarkable. His public responded, making his sales among the largest ever recorded in bookselling. Criticized for sloppy writing, one-dimensional characters, and wooden dialogue, Uris was nonetheless one of the most popular and successful novelists in America, perhaps in the world, for almost thirty years. He was often the envy of others, as he sensed in 1967: "It seems that I have committed a cardinal sin in my profession—I have become a success."[15] This biography will examine how he achieved that status and at what cost. It will also explore what success meant during the emergence of the best seller and how publishers helped shape such a career.

The title of this book confirms the transformation of Uris into a celebrity, something new for writers of the fifties and sixties. He did this partly through promotion and the projection of himself as a romantic figure who traveled the globe to write. A photo of him preparing to board an SAS flight from Copenhagen to Rome en route to Israel to begin *Exodus* illustrates this clearly. Dressed in a leather jacket with a shoulder bag and a carry-on, the youthful writer is exuberant. His smile is infectious. The entire world is before him: "Scandinavia, Europe, Far East, Asia-Africa" reads the sign next to him. There is a sense of adventure in the journey, of expectation and confidence best summarized perhaps in the phrase "foreign correspondent."[16] The photographs of Uris that appear on the backs of his novels enlarge the idea of the author as explorer. For Uris, image and author are one. Both are best sellers.

"THE TRUTH WILL RISE"

Thank God English and writing have little to do with each other.
—LEON URIS, IN A 1959 INTERVIEW

THAT RESPONSE TO A NOTE sent home after he failed English for the third time in high school unmasks Leon Uris's love of writing. In his novels, speeches, lectures, and essays, he understood that words could change the way people act. But you had to be on guard against rhetoric, which deceives, as a paragraph written in high school and titled "The Truth Will Rise" makes clear. In it, Uris is skeptical about public language: in America, he writes, "we get handmade, lie-riddled news that fears telling the truth . . . We are being blinded to the facts and bullied into another war."[1] Other early documents match this in intensity and protest. A student poem indicts the lynching of a black man, and a second text opens with a chained fighter of the working class but ends with a stanza imitating the Communist Party's "Internationale."[2]

The tone of complaint and the voice of politicized, assured youth, mixed with exhortation, anticipate Uris's later anger at and censure of personal abuse, political mistreatment, and the exploitation of individuals by governments and the law. The prose passage also anticipates his own choleric nature, which resulted in fractious relationships and lawsuits. Otto Preminger, Alfred Hitchcock, and various publishers were among his targets.

Liberation, politics, and protest—the features of these early works—reveal the deep-seated character of Uris's drive for social action, which would express itself in works like *Exodus* and *Trinity*, novels in which national and personal freedoms intersect. His early writing, whether criticizing workers' lack of rights or the absence of free speech, contains the seeds of Uris's later support of and determination to aid Russian refuseniks, Jewish immigrants, and history's victims.

The source of Uris's persistent outrage at injustice was his family, more specifically the political ideals and actions of his father. Wolf Yerusalimsky, later known as Wolf Yerushalmi (man of Jerusalem), and then, in America, as William Wolf

Uris, was an impassioned, restless, left-leaning activist who constantly challenged, angered, and upset his son. But Uris could not shake him: Uris wrote in detail to his father about his war experiences, the progress of his writing, his success (and failures) as an author, and his personal upheavals. History, especially that of Israel, was a constant topic between them, as was the unfair reaction of critics to Uris's work. Guilt was another part of Uris's persistent reports: should letters fail to appear regularly, the father would berate the son and complain of his neglect. Uris's urge to publish was partly an attempt to gain his father's respect for his career as a writer, as if he were responding to the remark made by Saul Bellow's father when he learned his son wanted to be an author: "You write and then you erase. You call that a profession?"[3]

WILLIAM WOLF URIS

A remarkable document details the life of Wolf Yerushalmi: a 1975 autobiography written at the urging of his wife, son, and stepdaughter. It begins with a chilling dedication: "To the memory of my mother Lea and my sister Luby who were murdered by the Nazis in Treblinka in 1942" (AUTO, n.p.). Wolf was born on 25 April 1896 in the city of Novogrudok in White Russia (now Belarus), the oldest of seven children. He began school at age five; by twelve, he was fluent in Hebrew and Yiddish and had begun to study Russian and math. But he also began to rebel and refused to continue at the cheder, or religious school, becoming a messenger for a loan association. After he threatened to move out of the house if forced to continue at the Hebrew school, Wolf's parents agreed to send him to a modern orthodox school in Lida, which was headed by the founder of the Mizrachi (religious Zionism) movement, Rabbi Reines. He stayed at the threadbare school, supported by the son-in-law of the supposed tea baron of Russia, Visotzky, and the Jewish banker Baron Ginzburg from St. Petersburg, for a year.

Bar mitzvahed on 25 April 1909, Wolf still rejected a religious career. Nonetheless, he studied the Talmud for two hours a day with his father, continuing with Russian as well. One of his closet friends was an uncle (only two years his senior) who was the leader of the young "bund" in Novogrudok, the Jewish Social Workers Party. This was his introduction to politics and Zionism, which would shape his early life even after his immigration to America.

The First World War and political change in Russia forced Wolf's move to a semiunderground existence. Working in Minsk, he soon joined the Poale Zion (Labor Zionists), actively attending lectures and meetings. His father, hearing of these activities, resented his son's freethinking and independence, but the active cultural life of Minsk, with its many institutions of Jewish learning, stimulated

Wolf, who began to read avidly works in Russian and Yiddish, including those by Leo Tolstoy, Fyodor Dostoevsky, Aleksandr Ostrovsky, Isaac Peretz, Mendele Mocher Sforim, Shalom Aleichem, and Sholem Asch. He began to think of immigrating to Palestine.

But he also became enamored of the theatre and joined a group of young men and women interested in drama. Using an abandoned cinema in Bialystok, Poland, they attempted to put on a program once a month (AUTO, 37). A professional actor was the artistic director for what became an immensely popular event. Wolf happily joined this troupe, anticipating his son's early interest in drama. On his enlistment form for the marines in January 1942, the young Leon Uris listed "playwriter" as his occupation.

In April 1920, Wolf began to make plans to immigrate to Palestine, seeing no future for himself in anti-Semitic Poland. His father, an ardent Zionist, was pleased, as was the Polish government, which was glad to get rid of Jews. It offered transit papers to any Jew who requested them. A special committee from Palestine, in fact, set up an office in Warsaw to regulate emigration from Poland. A day before his departure, a picture was taken with a group of *chaverim*, or Hebrew students, outside the house of a friend. Only five in the photo survived the Holocaust, Wolf Yerusalimsky among them.

Wolf's arrival in Palestine was antiromantic—he had been ill on the journey and suffered recurrent bouts of sunstroke after he arrived—in stark contrast to the arrival of the ship *Exodus* in Uris's novel, when some twenty-five thousand people crowded the dock as the Palestine Philharmonic played "Hatikvah," soon to become the Israeli national anthem. And unlike the characters in Uris's novel, who sustained their excitement and hope after arriving in their new home, Wolf soon met with disappointment. In fact, illness, little work, unhappiness, and political unrest marked Wolf's stay. Zionism, the operative philosophy, could provide neither employment nor comfort. Whether working as a night watchman or building roads, he found little satisfaction, his Zionist leanings contradicted by the harsh reality of the land.

But he did pursue culture, joining the Borochow sports club, attending lectures, enjoying cultural evenings, studying Hebrew, and organizing a singing group. He soon became known for his recitations of Aleichem, Sforim, and others. At the time, he rented a room in the Neve Shalom neighborhood, where the Levenstein-Shulman candy factory employed Arab women at the lowest possible wages. The Histadrut (federation of labor) tried to get the Arab women to organize the shop and to hire Jewish workers. One day, the federation called a general strike to support the movement, an act Wolf supported. A few days later, a fight broke out at the Krinitzky furniture shop when the owner would not let the workers strike. The police severely beat one striker, and when Wolf and a male nurse ran to help the fallen Arab worker, Wolf was hit with a club and ended up in the hospital. The strike and the confrontation with the police left a lasting impression on Wolf and the workers throughout the country, while reaffirming his commitment to social protest.

But nothing seemed to be taking hold: he was without a career, although he remained enthusiastic about a Jewish Palestine. At this time, he changed his surname from Yerusalimsky to Yerushalmi, "man of Jerusalem."

By chance, he wrote to an Aunt Keile (Kathy) in America, and two months later he received a letter from her along with a ten-dollar gold piece. In the letter, she offered him whatever help he needed to emigrate. Wolf began to reconsider his future in Palestine, recognizing that his dream of becoming a member of a kibbutz would not be realized. He also had no experience in the business world, and although he loved Palestine, the harsh realities of his life outweighed his idealism (AUTO, 66–67). He needed to find security. Nevertheless, he explored the country, visiting Lebanon and Jordan also, but on the return from one of his journeys, he found a letter from Aunt Keile, inviting him to the United States. He had a large family there: four of his father's brothers, his aunt, and three brothers of his mother were in Pittsburgh. He would go.

Two months later, he received an affidavit with a sum of money guaranteeing his passage. After applying for and receiving the necessary visas in Jerusalem, he began his journey in February 1921, although he visited his grandmother's grave before he left. She had died in Palestine in 1915. His voyage took him across the Suez Canal to Ismail, Egypt, and then by train to Alexandria and boat to Marseille. From there he went to Providence, Rhode Island.

Wolf arrived in New Haven, Connecticut, on 2 April 1921 and then traveled on to New York and Yonkers, where he was met by Aunt Keile and others, who shortly after decided he should go into the garment trade and become a cutter. Oscar Schiller, a relative, lectured him on America as the land of opportunity but told him to expect no favors; he eventually found a job for him with a manufacturer of ladies blouses. No sooner had he started, however, than Wolf discovered that he had been hired as a scab to replace a worker on strike. He looked for work elsewhere, renting a room in Harlem and doing little more than delivering samples to department stores. He continued his political activism, however, joining the Linke Poale Zion branch, which met on East Broadway, and visited the Wolkowysker Verein, a group from a city in Poland where he had lived as an adolescent. Occasionally, he went to a Jewish theatre or to a movie. Of more importance was his attendance at the free night school for new immigrants in a Harlem public school. He understood that education was crucial and hoped to become a teacher, but his dream did not last long, since he had to keep looking for new work. Most employment was temporary.

Two months after his arrival, when he applied for his first citizenship papers, Wolf formally changed his name. From the original "Yerusalimsky," altered in Palestine to "Yerushalmi," he chose "Uris" and replaced "Wolf" with "William." He took this step at the suggestion of a good *chaver*, or comrade, in the Poale Zion, over the objections of his uncles, who changed their names to "Sarinksy" and "Sarin" (AUTO, 83–84). His new name, "Uris," would sound more American and less foreign.

Work was still difficult to find, but the search did not cause William to lose his dignity. A job at a dye factory in Brooklyn at roughly fourteen cents an hour led to another protest. William threatened to expose the employer, a Mr. Horowitz, to his family, for his exploitation of workers. The owner relented and raised his pay. Other jobs included removing snow at the Metropolitan Museum of Art, working on a Jewish farm in New Jersey, and laboring in a factory in Brooklyn. Another uncle, Jack Kochin, a kosher butcher, invited him to try Pittsburgh, and there he met more family members, including his grandmother on his mother's side, who had immigrated to the United States before the First World War and had given birth to seventeen children (eleven died at birth or at an early age). Between his father's family in New York and New England, and his mother's in Pittsburgh, William had thirty-eight cousins.

In Pittsburgh he joined the Workers Party, the forerunner of the Communist Party in the United States. As the Labor Zionist movement faded in importance, membership in the Jewish Federation of the Workers Party increased. He also accepted a post as a Hebrew and Bible teacher at the school of Rabbi Kochin, his uncle. Pittsburgh soon became home, and Gold's restaurant became a magnet for young immigrants, Zionists, socialists, communists, and arguments. It was across the street from Rabbi Kochin's house.

In 1922, the Jewish Federation of the Workers Party began to publish a daily newspaper, *Freiheit* (Freedom), edited by a well-known socialist writer, journalist, and critic, Moissaye Olgin. A number of writers from *Forverts* (Forward), the mainstay Yiddish paper in New York, mostly left-wingers, departed to join the new daily Yiddish paper, which combined socialism with communism. Yiddish-speaking workers formed its readership, which found the paper the "nerve center of a Yiddish Left subculture" as well as a platform for some of the best Yiddish literature in the U.S.[4] *Freiheit*, however, seemed to be more under the control of communists rather than socialists. Gradually, the paper faced a crisis, and in the midforties it chose to be a Jewish radical paper rather than a communist organ. *Freiheit*'s stand on the formation of Israel actually led to its break with communism.[5]

One role of the Jewish Federation of the Workers Party was to collect money to sustain *Freiheit*. Leaders of his branch soon asked William Uris to manage the office of *Freiheit* in Pittsburgh, overseeing their fund-raising campaigns, collecting money from subscribers, obtaining local advertising, and summarizing the activities of the party for members of the movement in the area. As a manager, he automatically became a member of the executive committee and an elected delegate to the district committee of the Workers Party. He leapt at the chance: "Finally, I will have the opportunity to devote my energy to a 'great cause' to bring the working class the message of Marx and Lenin" (AUTO, 94).

For the next year or so, William devoted himself to building the circulation of *Freiheit* in Pittsburgh and the entire state, traveling to towns large and small to get subscriptions. Within a few weeks, he had established a well-paid, functioning *Freiheit* office and received a salary of $25 a week. But his personal life was stagnant—although he was occasionally harassed by the police because of his association with so-called extremists. He attended a summer high school and wrote an assignment on a bitter coal strike in favor of the strikers. One of his teachers, however, became enraged when he read the paper, screaming, "I will not allow radicals in my class." He then ran to the principal's office. The next day William was expelled (AUTO, 93). But he continued as an active member of the Workers Party, although he found their regulations strict and repressive. He could not, for example, travel from one city to another without party permission, and any "expression of dissent was punished with expulsion" (AUTO, 97). It was also considered unethical to associate with friends outside the party. Religiously observant people were not allowed in the party, and he was once reprimanded for attending a Passover seder instead of a farewell party given in honor of a minor party functionary. But despite his "naïve devotion to the party," William never denied or relinquished his identity as a Jew (AUTO, 97).

But persecution within the party continued: at one meeting he was accused of not only not attending but also observing religious customs, as well as of being anti-Leninist and anti-Marxist. He was found guilty, but not expelled, just "publicly criticized and warned in the future of any break in party discipline" (AUTO, 98). Nonetheless, his reputation in New York grew because of his success as a manager in Pittsburgh. After a year, he was offered the Philadelphia operation, which he accepted, although by now he realized that the Workers Party was actually run by the underground Communist Party. The leaders of the Jewish Federation, however, and the writers of *Freiheit* were mostly former members of the Socialist Party. Disputes over the organization of the party and the editorial policy of the paper continued.

William met his future wife in Philadelphia when he stayed at Mrs. Cohen's boarding house on 32nd Street in the Strawberry Mansion area. The home was a gathering place for Jewish radicals, and dinners there generally erupted into arguments over the Russian Revolution, socialism, communism, and anarchism.

One Sunday morning in July 1923, he met Anna Blumberg and her six-year-old daughter. Anna, a first-generation American born in Havre de Grace, Maryland, was a Jewish divorcée from Baltimore, "a beautiful, dark-complected woman" who was in Philadelphia to visit an uncle (AUTO, 104). William quickly fell in love with this self-educated woman who had a strong interest in music and reading; within five days of their meeting, they were married. He was twenty-seven.

Factional fighting in the Workers Party and at the paper, however, led Anna to suggest he find other work. He quit as manager of the paper, and they left Philadelphia for Baltimore, where she could work as a beautician while William looked for a new job. The move set a pattern: in six years of marriage, they relocated six times, from Philadelphia to Baltimore, Cleveland, Baltimore again, Pittsburgh, and finally to Philadelphia again. According to William, the reason for these moves was Anna's whimsical mood, her eagerness to fly from one city to another, although he, too, thought new opportunities would exist in a new locale. But by 1929, these moves and her displeasure with his constant lack of employment would lead to her permanently leaving him for her family in Baltimore.

During this period, William remained faithful to the Workers Party and "relentlessly supported the Russian Revolution" (AUTO, 105). Anna backed him and occasionally participated in some of the campaigns conducted by various radical organizations. When they first moved to Baltimore, they lived in her mother's home and William got a job canvassing door-to-door for a new insurance company, but was denied a state license because he was not yet a citizen. A sudden opportunity to manage the *Freiheit* operations in Cleveland, and take charge of all the Ohio subscribers, meant a move there.

William now had a press card and wrote regularly for the paper. He became something of a presence and often received "in-kind" benefits: for example, he and Anna saw seven productions of the Metropolitan Opera Company during its Cleveland tour in the winter of 1923. They heard the famous Russian bass Feodor Chaliapin and saw a performance of Eugene O'Neill's *The Hairy Ape*. And it was in Cleveland that Anna became pregnant with Leon, which caused them to move to a two-bedroom apartment on Kinsman Road and purchase new furniture on the installment plan. Essie, Anna's daughter, was now in the second grade, attending public school and a Yiddish school several afternoons a week. They also attended synagogue regularly.

Cleveland soon looked like the proper place to make their home. Good friends, a steady income, and proper medical attention: all was in place until Anna suddenly announced that she wanted to have the baby in Baltimore. She left in July with Essie, proposing to return after the birth of her child. William then writes: "August 3rd, 1924, I received a telegram that Leon was born [that day] (he is named after both our grandfathers—Leon, Marcus). It was (and it will be till my dying day) my happiest day in my life! My first born son!! I pitied myself . . . for not being able to be present at my son's 'bris' (circumcision ceremony). It was too expensive a luxury . . . to travel to Baltimore" (AUTO, 111).[6]

He excitedly prepared for the return of the family, but a few days later received from Anna a letter saying that she wanted to live near her relatives in Baltimore and would not return to Cleveland. She urged him to quit his job and join her, but he abhorred the idea of returning to Baltimore, living in her mother's crowded apartment, and knocking "on doors in search of a day's work." But he had no choice; Anna could not be persuaded—and he was too naïve to understand her motivation, that perhaps their life together was not bliss. But because he felt it was his duty and obligation to raise his son, he returned. Ironically, the birth of his son acted to divide husband and wife. As William noted: "I liquidated [note the highly politicized term] our household in Cleveland (lost everything I paid for) and came to Baltimore to be with my family" by mid-September 1924 (AUTO, 111–112). However, the emotional power of holding his three-week-old son overcame his anger at having to leave what had become a secure life.

William decided to learn a trade, partly for income and partly to identify with the working class: "What can be more appropriate for a good Communist than to work among the masses?" (AUTO, 112). He chose paperhanging because it was diversified and he could work part-time on weekends while fulfilling his apprenticeship. He and Anna rented a six-room house near East Baltimore Avenue and Bond Street in the southeast section of the city. Anna opened a beauty shop on the first floor. He was soon working for three dollars a week, although it was physically difficult; he then joined the union and got a two-dollar-a-week raise. Work became steady through a relative of the Blumberg family, who were real estate developers. In his spare time, William became active in the Jewish movement of the Workers Party. At this time, Essie, Uris's half sister, was "like a little mother to Leon" and virtually brought him up (AUTO, 113). And Jewish life in Baltimore at this time was vibrant: in 1924, the Jewish population was estimated to be 67,500, divided between German Jews (uptown) and Russian Jews (downtown and in East Baltimore).[7]

But William believed Pittsburgh offered more work, so he went there. Anna insisted they all go, and she closed up her hairdressing business and followed him two weeks later. He now worked full-time for a "sympathizer of the left-wing movement" and stayed almost two years before moving to Philadelphia and an apartment on Parkside Avenue (AUTO, 114–115). This time, he was determined to stay. He joined the only Jewish paperhangers union in the country, but it was still a difficult time, partly because he had debts from constantly moving from one city to another. But other issues began to emerge: "Had my family-life not been unhappy, I would be able to improve my financial conditions. But our relationship deteriorated" (AUTO, 114–115). This was in late 1929. Although frightened at the thought of separating from his son, he felt there was no other way than divorce to resolve his difficulties with his wife. One day he came home from work to find a note telling him that she had left with the children for Baltimore. He planned to visit the children frequently in Baltimore and did not want to initiate divorce proceedings, but a few months later, a friend sent him a clipping from a Baltimore newspaper: "Anna Uris got a divorce from her husband—the communist" (AUTO, 115).

Upset at the speed of the proceedings and his political (and now public) label, he traveled again to Baltimore to see his son. To his shock, William learned that Anna had left without leaving word of her whereabouts. He then writes that "the end of my marriage prompted me to intensify my activities in the Communist Party," which, since the 1920s, had functioned openly as a legal party (AUTO, 115). But this only masked his hurt. During the Depression, the little work to be found paid extremely low wages. He did manage to send a few dollars to Leon, however, care of his former mother-in-law in Baltimore.

William soon regretted having devoted so much time and energy to defending a cause that, under Stalin, brought so much misery and death to millions in the Soviet Union. He also criticized the rigid organizational structure of the party and its stringent rules and regulations governing personal life. But he still rose in the hierarchy, becoming an official in his union as well as a unit organizer and a member of the district control commission of the Communist Party. He also realized that his reason for participating in party activities "was to relieve my anxiety and longing for my son, and the inability to communicate with him," since Anna had disappeared with him (AUTO, 118). His economic situation was also dire: "The daily struggle for existence leads to extreme ideas and you respond readily to communist propaganda. [Yet] my sense of justice prevailed all my life"—an attitude inherited by his son (AUTO, 118). William particularly admired the support of the Communist Party for the rights of Negroes and civil rights in general, but the revelation of Stalin's repressive actions stunned him.

William's association with the Communist Party became increasingly fractious. He objected to Stalin's liquidation of members of the leadership of the Jewish section of the party in Russia but did agree with communist opposition to the Nazis. He also believed that Philadelphia was a Nazi center and wrote in his autobiography that the party was the first organized sector to demand that the government outlaw the Nazi Bund (AUTO, 124).

Radicalism generally did not have a foothold in Philadelphia, although mass meetings were popular.[8] At such a meeting in 1930, two of William's friends introduced him to Anna Rabinovitz, and a new relationship began. Divorced, she was the mother of an eleven-year-old son, Aaron, and a member of the Amalgamated

Clothing Workers of America. They married after a year of courting and remained together for more than forty-five years. But his happy marriage and involvement in the radical movement did not lessen his desire to be with his son. Yet he still could not locate him. Only when he met a friend of his first wife did he learn that she and the children were in Norfolk, Virginia. His second wife urged him to visit the city to find them.

Uris was six when his mother took him and Essie to Norfolk in 1930. Anna went to Norfolk because her first husband, who had run a department store, was from there, so she was familiar with its Jewish community. By 1930, Norfolk also was experiencing the radicalizing influence of the Communist Party and the Congress of Industrial Organizations (CIO); both made protest politics an everyday event. In the small but vibrant Jewish community of Norfolk, agitation and confrontation had the important effect of making the activist life the norm, something that Uris's early poetry about the condition of blacks and workers reflected.[9]

Immigrant Polish and Russian Jews in Norfolk brought with them strong communist and socialist ties. But the leftist community also brought culture; Uris later remembered the many theatre societies, reading groups, and recital associations in the city. In a July 2001 interview videotaped for his grandchildren, he recalled regularly attending the opera with his mother. "My education was both classical, in terms of music, and Jewishly political in terms of cultural," he recounted. But he was first moved by theatre, whose appeal would remain with him throughout his life.

In 1930, Uris began school at J. E. B. Stuart Elementary on Virginia Avenue, eight blocks south of the family's home on Massachusetts Avenue. Morris Cadyzynski's small Jewish bakery on Church Street, celebrated in *QB VII*, was a neighborhood attraction. The Jewish section of Norfolk, described in a long section in *QB VII*, started in the 100 block of Church Street and at St. Mary's Church and ran for seven blocks to the Booker T. Pharmacy, which marked the beginning of the Negro neighborhood. In the novel, Uris writes that it was a "tiny and close-knit" community that remained together, "unable to shake off all the ghetto mentality," although Morris Cadyzynski does shorten his name to the more Americanized "Cady" (an allusion to Howard Cady, Uris's early Doubleday editor; *QBVII*, 83). The Workman's Circle Hall was a fixture for the socially conscious in both the novel and actual Norfolk, as were the numerous small shops modeled on those in the old country. There was also "heated discussion in Yiddish where the two newspapers, the *Freiheit* and the New York *Forverts* vied for opinion" (*QBVII*, 84).[10]

The Jewish community, though not a village, gave the neighborhood an Old World resonance that Uris would not forget. Indeed, one of his later disappointments was his inability to write a novel about immigrant Jewish life in America. But there were also constant threats to Jewish life in Norfolk. It was, after all, in the South, and Jews were not easily, if ever, accepted. As the historian Eli N. Evans quipped, "Being Jewish in the South is like being Gentile in New York."[11]

A surprise visit to Norfolk by William in 1930 meant a surprised Essie, now thirteen, and a startled Leon, six, who did not recognize his father (AUTO, 121). His arrival was at first awkward, but William and his former wife came to an understanding, and he celebrated by taking the children downtown to buy Leon a suit and Essie a dress. Within a year, both children were visiting him in Philadelphia, spending the summer of 1931 with William and his new wife. Five years later, when Anna and the children moved back to Baltimore, Leon would come up by train to see his father in a complicated procedure. He would be put on a train by his mother, the conductor pinning a baggage tag on him so that a porter or steward would know to tell him to get off in Philadelphia when the train arrived. William was there to meet him; he would then signal Baltimore by phone that Leon safely arrived (AUTO, 122). They followed the procedure of the tagged child until Leon was fourteen. The only complication was William's occasionally shaky relationship with his second wife, because he was unable to establish a rapport with her son, Aaron.

Baltimore Jewish life offered a larger extended family for Uris, who returned there with his mother when he was eleven and his sister eighteen. He attended Garrison Junior High, where he first appeared in print, providing sports data for the school paper. He was a member of the drama club and starred in the school play, *The High School Mystery*.[12] He then attended Baltimore City College, actually a high school.

William continued to monitor Leon's development as the young boy made regular weekend visits from Baltimore to Philadelphia. He was a model student—at least until the age of fifteen, when he became withdrawn and even truant from school. When pressed, he told his father that he was upset with his mother and would like to come and live with him in Philadelphia. Arrangements were made for his legal transfer from his mother to father, and although the adjustment was not easy, his new stepmother made the change as easy as possible and he got on well with his stepbrother, who was six years older. He enrolled in summer high school to catch up on a subject he had failed in Baltimore and became an avid fan of books and plays, often staying up late to read. He also joined the New Theater Group, a Philadelphia gathering of amateurs and professionals interested in the stage. Occasionally, he wrote skits for them, the beginnings of his early and sustained interest in the theatre.

Uris's earliest writings were, in fact, dramas, first an operetta on the death of his six-year-old dog and then a series of plays recognized more for their effort than accomplishment. Favoring historical dramas of romantic distortion and intensity, he wrote *I'm in the City of London*, which was about the victory of the English over the French and involved two French spies and a princess. In his play *King Joe*, set in "any old time between 1400–1500," King Alex van Gerrie de Knacker, alias Joe II, holds forth while his daughter Esther exchanges bons mots with her admirer, David. At one point, he answers the question "Do you like to read books?" with "That's right up my alley. At the present time I am reading *Gone with the Wind*. Esther is reading *Romeo and Juliet*."[13]

He even tried opera. "FAIR IS MY GRACIA / ORIGINAL OPERA / plot by / LEON URIS" was written in January 1934, when Uris was ten, for Grade 3H–4L at J. E. B. Stuart Elementary. Uris wrote the music and words and fashioned the somewhat banal plot. His synopsis of the three-act opera emphasizes its romantic features involving love and marriage.[14] But for a youthful work, it has a strong sense of scene, action, and division of feeling. The themes of loss, death, and a broken home are also evident.

Several years later, on his Marine Corps enlistment form, Uris cited drama as his principal education, adding, "he has 4 years in dramatic school—did some professional stage acting and writing." Under additional occupations and hobbies, he lists "writing plays." Under the talent category, Uris again emphasizes the stage, while listing the piano as his musical instrument ("7 yrs. own amusement"), plus the glee club for two years and directing plays and acting. Track, tennis, and swimming were his sports.[15]

William's employment remained sporadic during this time, and he often thought of alternatives, including working for a brother-in-law in the poultry-processing business. However, his reputation as a radical forestalled that move, since there was fear he might try to unionize the employees. Nevertheless, he worked a night job at the plant, which meant he had little contact with fellow workers. Eventually, William went into the business himself, forming the Uris Poultry Company, and he was soon earning thirty-five to forty dollars a week. However, shady dealings by a New York poultry broker who never paid a large bill put William out of business. Owning a business was also frowned upon by the party: how could one so involved in the radical labor movement also be a boss? He went back to paperhanging.

Uris's early dislocated existence, during which he witnessed his father's lack of success, took its toll. Shuttling between Norfolk and Philadelphia, and then between Baltimore and Philadelphia, tagged as baggage, did little to aid his self-esteem. The six years he spent being shifted back and forth reinforced his great fear of loneliness and isolation, which late in life he would underscore through the writer Gideon Zadok in *Mitla Pass* (1988), his most autobiographical novel. Gideon's great fear is loneliness, compensated for by an aggressive determination to succeed, even at the cost of personal relations. During his youth, however, Uris also had a jaundiced view of success in America. With his father as an example, Uris saw only failure and discrimination as well as the exploitation of workers when they did not, or could not, improve their working conditions. Uris's resolve to become a successful writer may in part have originated in his objection to working for anyone other than himself and in his desire to find a platform to speak out against oppression.

A novel Uris read at about this time confirmed his negative view of his father's chance of success. *Jews without Money* by Michael Gold, which appeared in 1930, recounted the poverty and degradation of Jewish immigrants in New York's Lower East Side.[16] In the novel, Herman Gold's activities as a housepainter, the second or possibly third of his careers, at first brings hope to his family. His elevation to foreman ensures his success in America, but a fall from a scaffold and two broken legs prevent any further work. He withdraws into morbid despair and reluctantly turns to peddling bananas; his wife works in a cafeteria. Nevertheless, he lectures his young son Michael never to be poor and always to avenge injustice. Uris would soon adopt these attitudes himself, as well as the anger against oppression that Gold projects directed against discrimination toward and exploitation of the Jews.

To oppose wrongs became the young Michael Gold's purpose, as it would become Uris's, while Gold's encounters with Jews who were willing to fight for their identity reinforced a similar desire in Uris. Communism was the apparent way out of a morass of abuse and exploitation, and the narrator's exclamation at the end, "O Revolution, that forced me to think, to struggle and to live," echoes the young Uris's hope for social revolution, which was expressed in his earliest poetry and dramas.[17] He cites his mother's having read the book to him in *Mitla Pass* (MP, 385).

In 1988, Uris recounted the importance of *Jews without Money* in an address at the Smithsonian Institute in Washington, D.C., declaring, "it felt as though I were hearing the story of my own life, my relationships with my parents and what it mean to be a Jew."[18]

URIS AND STEINBECK

A month earlier, he had recorded the significance of another work read at this time: John Steinbeck's *Of Mice and Men* (1937). From "the characters of George and Lennie, I came to understand my own loneliness for the first time. From that moment on I never wanted to be anything but a writer." And from Steinbeck he "learned through writers that one man or one woman protesting injustice from his or her lonely room can have the power to make the world stop in its tracks and listen and even to change things. I never wanted to be anything but a writer again."[19]

Steinbeck's novella confronts isolation, nature, violence, and guns. In prose that seems transparent in its naturalness and in dialogue that is direct and unadorned, Steinbeck reveals the complex lives of itinerant ranch workers and the intense emotions of the simpleminded Lennie. The detailed style of the novel had lasting appeal for Uris.

The cinematic properties of such writing—a slow zoom takes the reader from the broad form of the building to the features of individual bunks in the opening passage—became part of a method that Uris imitated. *Of Mice and Men* remained a favorite of his, and he would often read passages to his own children when they were growing up. Later, he would cite *The Grapes of Wrath* and *Tortilla Flat* as influential works. He would also praise *In Dubious Battle*, Steinbeck's 1936 account of migrant workers taking on California landowners, in *Mitla Pass* (MP, 415).

Steinbeck, who researched his novels carefully—he spent long periods of time, for example, in the San Joaquin Valley of California, tracing the fate of migrant workers that would form the core of *The Grapes of Wrath*—and who was accustomed to public outcry over his work, became a model of how to be a writer for Uris. And Steinbeck's convictions demonstrated to Uris the importance of the writer's responsibility to his work and time. He would not allow changes to be made to his stories, although sometimes it happened, to his intense displeasure (as when Alfred Hitchcock altered important elements of his novella *Lifeboat*). Steinbeck would also not hide the truth or change his work for the sake of propriety. To Pascal Covici, his publisher and later editor, he said of *The Grapes of Wrath*, "I am not writing a satisfying story. I've done my damndest [sic] to rip a reader's nerves to rags. I don't want him satisfied."[20] Much the same can be said of Uris and works like *Exodus*, *Mila 18*, or *Trinity*, with their harrowing scenes of Auschwitz, the Warsaw Ghetto, or the violence of the Irish Republican Brotherhood. Steinbeck's convictions inspired Uris, who early in his career realized the importance of being true to one's artistic sense.

Steinbeck and Uris also shared an interest in the military and in film (Steinbeck had modest success as a screenwriter). In 1942, Steinbeck's account of the training of bomber pilots appeared as *Bombs Away: The Story of a Bomber Team*; the following year, he became an accredited war correspondent and went to England on a troop ship and then on to Algeria and Tunisia, filing reports. He later sent dispatches from the Salerno beachhead in Italy and participated in various operations off the coast of Italy, including the capture of an Italian island with a special operations unit. These actions paralleled Uris's in the marines during the Second World War and then in Israel before and during the Suez crisis in 1956. Both also wrote war novels (Steinbeck: *The Moon Is Down*, set in occupied Norway, and *Lifeboat*; Uris: *Battle Cry*, *The Angry Hills*, *Exodus*, and *Mila 18*); both published successful nonfiction books; both worked on screenplays of their own works (Steinbeck: *The Red Pony*; Uris: *Battle Cry*, *Exodus*, and *Topaz*); and both became celebrities (Steinbeck won a Pulitzer Prize and, in 1962, the Nobel Prize for Literature; Uris appeared at the top of best-seller lists); and both traveled widely and married often.

Steinbeck also became involved in politics, in 1960 joining an effort to draft Adlai Stevenson as the Democratic presidential nominee; in 1972 and 1976, Uris worked to support the presidential bid of Senator Henry "Scoop" Jackson for the Democratic nomination. Most importantly, however, Steinbeck had a social conscience: he not only stood up for the migrant workers of California but opposed injustice, writing, among other things, a defense of Arthur Miller in 1957, when he stood trial for contempt of Congress as a result of the McCarthy hearings. Steinbeck became a model for Uris, later sharing similar views of the critics. Shortly after he learned of his Nobel Prize, Steinbeck wrote to his Swedish friend Bo Beskow that he had had a long-term feud with the "cutglass critics, that grey priesthood which defines literature and has little to do with reading. They have never liked me."[21] Uris had similar views and grew increasingly to disregard critics, especially as his popularity increased.

The socially engaged fiction of Michael Gold and John Steinbeck set the tone for Uris's outlook, attitude, and style. Their writings outlined for him a way to confront and overcome his feeling of loss, isolation, and injustice.

LEON AND HIS PARENTS

As his father's politics changed—William's opposition to the communists grew as he learned of the Moscow trials, which targeted party leaders and generals, plus the silent disappearance of the Jewish Evske leaders (the Evsektsiia, the Jewish section of the Soviet Communist Party, was abolished in 1930)—there was an improved understanding between father and son. But Uris's relation with his mother became more troubled. He sought closeness with this self-educated woman who loved music and books, but her worrying, guilt-creating behavior and her misunderstanding of his artistic aspirations created distance. Even though he opposed his father's intrusive opinions and politics, the two constantly exchanged ideas and thoughts. But he could never do so with his mother, although in his early years in the marines, he would provide her with detailed reports of his activities. Some of his letters home are among the most thorough he ever wrote about his military training and romantic life, but they contain little or no emotion. Duty, not love, defined their attachment. She, in turn, showed little of the pride his father displayed in his son's achievements, whether in the marines or in the literary world.

Uris found the feminine love he missed from his mother in the affection expressed by his older half sister, Essie. The two were deeply attached to each other, and he confided much to her about his personal life. But to his mother, Uris provided only objective rather than intimate accounts of his activities, and rarely with any feeling. Yet he felt he had to prove himself to both parents, whether on the battlefield or the best-seller list.

Uris may have blamed the breakup of his parent's marriage on his mother, a belief that, in turn, may have affected his behavior with other women. Also, his belief that she had rejected his need for love may have contributed to his aggressive pursuit of it from others. His father's lack of affection may have been the catalyst for his economic and political ambition. But the divorce loomed large: if they loved him, it wouldn't have happened, he thought. In several of his later talks, Uris explicitly stated that writers write to gain (or regain) the love of their parents, although he purposefully avoided the indulgent autobiographical fiction he complains of in other Jewish writers like Herman Wouk, Meyer Levin, Jerome Weidman, Saul Bellow, or Philip Roth.[22]

Late in life, Uris still harbored resentment against his parents and emphasized the disagreements with his father in particular. In one interview, he referred to his father as a bitter man who went with the communists rather than the socialists when the break came in the 1920s in America: "The angrier the philosophy, the more attractive it was to him . . . It took me 60 years to have enough courage to go and look at this little boy I wanted to know something about."[23] In 1957, he summarized their relationship: "It seems that ever since I can remember we have been quarreling about one thing or another. We just have a personality clash and can't help but needle each other or explode on each other. It doesn't mean for one moment that I don't love you or anything could ever come between us. . . . So if our words get hot and heavy once in a while I wouldn't worry about it too much." He cannot resist adding, however, that "my feeling about the Soviet Union was and is so strong after going through the Sinai desert and seeing Stalin Tanks bent on the murder of Jews I could not contain myself, and . . . I suppose that it would be best if you and I never mention that again."[24]

William Uris died in July 1988 at age ninety-two, just before *Mitla Pass*, Uris's most autobiographical novel, appeared. He offered a critique of the book, which appears slightly revised as a letter from the protagonist's father to the son. The actual letter ends with "I have many, many, many more criticisms of which I will advise you in my forthcoming letters for only through criticism will you grow.

... God forbid I should tell you what to write. I am only offering a suggestion for that should be carefully followed FOR YOUR SAKE."[25]

In an interview the next year, Uris added, "He never told me I was good. He told me in essence that I exist to make him good."[26] When the interviewer asked whether relations with his father improved over the years, Uris denied it: "My relations with my father started out lousy and were lousy all my life and ended up lousy. I was existing as my father's alter ego. He was me and I was nothing, I was nobody."

Uris recalled letters he had read in preparation for writing *Mitla Pass*, and one, denying him a tuxedo for a school prom, was particularly distressing. The letter appears with little change in *Mitla Pass*, which has seven different narrators. Uris believed his father was basically a failure, a condition that formed his character and made him angry. Uris was determined not to suffer the same fate. Although he and his mother were distant, he credited her with teaching him an appreciation of the arts: "Her life was such that there was a heavy distrust of men in large part because of a very cruel father. We were essentially disinterested in each other. She was inside of her own head there somewhere."[27]

Uris described his mother as "very, very reserved. She was a woman who was a victim of a cruel Jewish husband and father. Her mother implanted in her a hatred of men which was well-founded because my Zaide was a shmuck. I had a loving Bubba who was the *Balabusta* and ran the family and when she died that family disintegrated and actually went into warring camps."[28] He added that what saved him was the marines: "The war came along at a time when I needed to go to war. My time had run out at being at home. The war worked into my life."

In his writing, Uris intentionally turned to history to avoid encountering the personal, rejecting any hint of autobiography until the late 1980s. History, he felt, was objective and clear and did not need to become confessional. This protection of the self may have colored his behavior with women, demanding commitment from them but believing that he was personally free to roam because they were, in all likelihood, not to be trusted. They certainly did not understand his devotion to writing, he believed. His dismissive and negative view of women—he rarely created sympathetic or complex women in his fiction (they are either sex goddesses or saints)—found resonance in his personal relationships with them. Uris seemed happiest when, as he wrote to his mother from New Zealand, "I'm ... drifting from skirt to skirt."[29]

On his military induction form, Uris (exaggerating as usual) listed eight years of grammar school in Baltimore and four years of high school in Philadelphia (at John Bartram High), noting that in addition to math, he took typing and scored fifty-five words a minute. Most interesting, in two places he indicated that he graduated high school; he did not. He also listed the Harding Conservatory and the New Theatre Group, both of Philadelphia, as sources of additional training, having completed the latter's program in 1941 with an emphasis on dramatics. A year earlier, in 1940, he had written to his mother to say that he was applying for a drama scholarship at the University of Pennsylvania and that he had dropped the play he was working on until Christmas.[30]

A further letter reports that he, his father, and his stepmother moved into Brantwood Apartments in Parkside and that he now had a room of his own with a comfortable chair and desk: "It is really the thing for me, quiet and I can do my work undisturbed." He was doing well in school: 100 in history, 95 in English, 83 in physics and chemistry, and 70 in algebra. He was also head of entertainment in the South West District. Importantly, "my new play is progressing very well. Although I think it's the poorest of my works, everyone says it's the best. It deals with the return of Christ to the earth with the *present situation*."[31]

But with the bombing of Pearl Harbor in December 1941, everything changed. Uris, three months from graduating high school, decided to enlist. His reason for doing so combined a sense of patriotism with a determination to fight oppression and a desire to escape a difficult, unstable family life.[32] But at seventeen and a half, he needed his parents' consent. Unexpectedly, one day in January 1942, Uris handed his father an application to join the U.S. Marines. William and his wife pleaded with him to finish school, and while the father admitted that he would be proud to have his son fight the Japanese and the Germans, he also admitted that he was too "weak, indecisive, and sentimental" to stop his son from going "prematurely to war" (AUTO, 136–137). But he also knew that his son would likely be drafted.

A determined Uris threatened to leave home and enlist in another city if his parents would not give their permission. William did not believe him, but Uris soon left for Baltimore. In the middle of the night a few days later, a neighbor called William to the phone (he didn't have one): it was Anna, crying that Uris had enlisted in the navy in Washington. William had to come to Baltimore at once to annul the enlistment. He left the next morning, but on the train he realized that he would have to give in to his son and that he, too, now wanted to enlist (AUTO, 137). At forty-six, however, he was too old. Uris greeted his father but would not change his mind. He was determined to do his patriotic duty (and escape his divisive family life). His father understood that his son's commitment to America and political justice, and his willingness to fight for them if necessary, overshadowed their fears. Nevertheless, it was a wrenching decision. Under pressure, his mother relented: a handwritten, penciled note on yellow paper from her reads: "For my son Leon to join the Navy if his father permits it."[33] The navy was his first choice because the marines were initially hesitant, for medical reasons (childhood asthma), to accept him.

Uris then wanted to switch from the navy back to the marines, so he drafted a letter to the commanding officer in Philadelphia, where he had originally tried to enlist, and another to the naval recruiting office in Washington. The spirit and heroism of the marines appealed to him; also, enlisting in that branch meant that he could leave from Philadelphia, where he still had friends. A few days later, he received a positive reply, and was ordered to report to the Marine Corps recruiting office in Philadelphia to depart for training camp.

On 19 January 1942, Uris officially enlisted in the marines, giving 4130 Parkside Avenue, Philadelphia, his father's address, as his legal residence; on another form, however, he listed 4916 Chalgrove Avenue, Baltimore, his mother's home, as his address. He listed his father as the person to be notified in case of emergency. He also stated that English and dramatics were his courses of greatest interest in high school.

Uris's departure from the immense Reading Terminal station in Philadelphia was as memorable as it was tearful. Hundreds of other new recruits were there with their families as loudspeakers called the recruits to assemble on the platform for their first roll call. At the end came the command to enter the railcars. The opening scene in *Battle Cry*, Uris's first novel, though set in Baltimore rather than Philadelphia, is similar. The excitement, sadness, elation, and despair of families separating from their sons dominate the action. Uris's father recalled the dramatic event: "the long train slowly moved away, [and] hundreds of hands waved good bye" (AUTO, 139). The news from the European fronts was bad, and there were already rumors of thousands of Jews having been killed by the Nazis.

An undated letter from San Diego, where Uris began his Marine Corps basic training in 1942 and written on Marine Corps stationery, reveals Uris's awareness not only of the anxiety he caused by enlisting but also of his transformation from a young man to a marine: "I'm glad I joined the Marines now even though it was against the will of everyone. I'm sure they agree with my feelings that it was the best thing. I'll admit that for the first few weeks I wanted to run home to Mama but now that I've gone through the worse. . . . I feel that I can call myself a man for the first time in my life."[34]

Such a feeling would stay with him throughout his life.

EAGLE, GLOBE, AND ANCHOR

For his 19th birthday, he [Leon] urged me to send him a handgun.
—WILLIAM URIS, IN HIS AUTOBIOGRAPHY

T HE WELL-KNOWN INSIGNIA of the U.S. Marine Corps—an American eagle astride the globe with a fouled anchor behind—symbolizes the three-pronged reach of the corps: on land and sea and air. *Semper Fidelis,* "always faithful," adopted as the Marine Corps motto in 1883, is an equally commanding expression of the core value of brotherhood. Originally the title of a march composed by John Philip Sousa, then conductor of the Marine Corps Band (he appears briefly in Uris's *O'Hara's Choice*), the phrase is the lynchpin of the marines, representing fidelity at any cost. Such camaraderie sustained Uris in battle and beyond.

Uris was not slated to fight when he signed up in January 1942. Written clearly at the bottom of his service-record card is "not to be assigned to combat duty," likely because of his age. He would not turn eighteen until 3 August 1942. This exemption was not to last, however. His outstanding performance at radio operator's school and his rating as a sharpshooter led to his being assigned to the Second Battalion of the Sixth Marine Regiment, which was sent to the Pacific. Action at Guadalcanal and Tarawa would result in Uris's promotion to private first class. But the road to such achievements, detailed in a series of vivid letters to his half sister Essie and his mother, tell of a young man's trials, loneliness, and danger in preparing for battle.

On 23 January 1942, four days after enlisting in Philadelphia for the duration of the national emergency (rather than for a specific number of years), the five-nine, 150-pound Leon Marcus Uris, serial number 359195, arrived as a member of the Twelfth Recruit Battalion at the recruit depot in San Diego, California, with the rank of private.[1] His recruit train had crossed the United States, stopping in Buffalo, Chicago, Texas, and California. He had enlisted as a reserve, which meant that after the conflict, he would serve an additional six months but receive a $100 bonus. On 22 February, he transferred to Casual Company at the recruit depot, and on 2 March joined the First Recruit Battalion, then transferred to the signal detachment of the radio company the following month. On that date (1 April 1942), he received his military assessment: a 3.5 out of 5 for military efficiency, a 3.5 for neatness and military bearing, a 4 in intelligence, and 5s for obedience and sobriety.

But the record does not reveal the mixture of anxiety and pride he felt as a young recruit. As he wrote to Essie, he initially believed he was leaving "with bad feelings towards almost everyone, a thing which I don't want. The fact is I was so run down from worry I was *sworn in* with over 101 fever and I had to go right to bed."[2] In the same letter, he reveals that he will be training in San Diego, but he does not want his mother to know this until he reaches the West Coast. After he arrived at the recruit depot, he told Essie "it is what I wanted and I love this sort of life and I'm happy, so I guess that's the most important thing."[3] But three weeks later, he asked why she hasn't written: "If you are sore at me please write and say so because the suspense of not hearing any word from your family is enough to make a guy sick."[4]

A week later, he detailed with pride his hour-by-hour activities in boot camp and included a picture of his platoon, asking that she excuse "how we look as we were all sick from a heavy needle a few hours before."[5] Active days began with reveille at four, followed by cleaning and mopping the barracks, drill, chow, clean up, and more drill. Every other night there were training films, which tended to be about warfare, venereal diseases, or how to clean equipment. Sometimes there were boxing matches, and Uris would both box and manage a boxer during his enlistment. Many of these details appear in the early chapters of *Battle Cry*. Drill, he explained, included plain and fancy marching, rifle exercises, inspection, field combat, obstacle courses, landing parties, bayoneting, and establishing beach-heads. For inspection, the men and their weapons had to be spotless. "Boy! Have I learned to take orders," he told Essie in February, but he was happy to endure the physical punishment because it proved to himself that he was "man enough to take it."[6] The only thing he couldn't get used to was getting up in the middle of the night. What he wanted most were letters from home.

Uris switched platoons because he spent a few days in the hospital, moving from the 143rd, his old unit, to a new one, the 236th. But his admiration for the 143rd, the best graduating platoon at the base, remained so high that he made it the recruit platoon of his first novel, *Battle Cry*. Uris continued to do well in boot camp, reporting on 16 March that he had earned three medals, "one for Expert Bayonetman, one for high completion of Basic Training and the last for Marks-manship with a small bore (.22 cal) rifle. On the latter I shot 211, only four points below Sharpshooter."[7] On record day, however, heavy rain and 24 mph crosswinds interfered with everyone's shooting score. He managed to make marksman, but when fifteen "invisible points" were added, he rose to sharpshooter, although he would not receive extra pay or an official rating. He also began to write about his buddies and the importance of comradeship.[8]

Following his test on the rifle range, Uris took exams to become a radio operator. Three hundred took the tests, trying for one of twenty-five spots. He didn't think he had much of a chance but ended up with an average in the high 90s, "including (get this) 95 in spelling which was my second worse mark."[9] Uris recognized his poor spelling early, a characteristic of his writing throughout his life.

Various leaves allowed him to scout out San Diego, which he did not like, since servicemen were "soaked double" and "a decent female is as scarce as men from Mars. But I always manage to have a good time with my buddies." And "I will say that the Marines are more respected by the civilians here than the Army or Navy. Drunk or sober, he is always neat and walks down the street with snap."[10] Wearing the patch of the Second Marine Division, a shield with five stars and a torch held aloft and bearing the motto "Silent Second, Second to None," was for Uris an honor.[11]

Uris's pride in the marines spilled over into lectures to his family. A remark by his father about Russian soldiers being better than the marines resulted in a seventeen-page letter filled with facts and clippings. Essie would also be getting one, he added, because she had compared Uris to a dogface (soldier), especially to a draftee: "In our opinion, they are the lowest form of military life that exists."[12] He then went on to document the Marine Corps's emphasis on spotlessness and the importance of a clean rifle, which was inspected every day "by a major who wears white gloves and you lose liberty for a week if he has a speck on them." A marine was proud of his rifle, and Uris knew "1000 parts of it and the function of each part," facts highlighted in *Battle Cry*. But, he stressed, "don't ever compare me with a Dogface (I get madder as I go on). More than one fight has started that way."

In the same letter, he reasserts his pride as proof that his decision to join the marines would do the family proud. To Essie's husband, Harry Kofsky, he claimed, "I'm awfully proud of the uniform I wear. When I left home I was determined to be a good Marine so my family would change their mind about their worthless brother."[13]

Uris's ten weeks of training to become a radio operator began in late April 1942, and he enjoyed it at once, especially the secret codes. He also saw it as providing him with future employment "anywhere in the world, even the Soviet Union with high pay." He did well, his 97 percent average earning him the title "hot spark," first in his group. "A 'hot spark,'" he told his sister, is "supposed to be a natural at sending and receiving. I can take 12 words and send 20 which the rest of the class is 6 and 12. . . . I'm shooting at the Gold Seal of Honor on my diploma."[14] By 11 July, he had transferred from the radio company of the signal battalion, pleased with his marks and accomplishments, to the headquarters company of the Second Battalion, Sixth Marines. His signal school rating was 73.20 out of 100, and his official duty was listed as "Radio Operator, 776."

In another letter, typed on a special typewriter at his radio school—in all capital letters, a style duplicated in his later prose, notably in *QB VII*—he noted that he could say nothing about what he was learning; it was to be "kept in strictest confidence so please don't ask any questions about what I am doing in classes."[15] In a rare sentimental moment, he admitted, "You know Mom, since I've been away, I appreciate a lot of things that I took for granted when I was back home. And I am ashamed to say that it took the Marines to show me what a swell mother I have." He confidently added that "you can be sure when I come back you'll have a son to be proud of."

On a form that asked for "Duty Desired," Uris wrote "Public Relations." He also took nine and a half hours of training in chemical warfare, and in October 1942, he was promoted to private first class.

Of course, none of these details indicate the excitement or anxiety brought about by his training, or the overall importance of the Marine Corps for Uris. Only his letters to Essie and his father—and the fictionalized account in *Battle Cry*—tell of how marine life and combat reinforced his ideas of justice, patriotism, courage, and the urge to write. Further, his novels are marked by research, preparation, and detail, three elements that describe the readiness of marines for combat. As he later explained, "The Marine Corps pushed me into finding strengths I never knew I had. Perhaps I would have never known. I owe them my becoming a man, and the ordeals I underwent laid a foundation of stamina I had to have later as a novelist."[16]

BOOKS AND WOMEN

At radio school, Uris also read, notably an unusual novel by William Blake titled *The Copperheads*. He received the book, he told Essie, "from the Front Line Fighters Fund of the I.W.O. [International Workers Order]. On the bookplate it said 'with sincerest appreciation to your contribution to victory.' Well I sure was proud. My picture is also going to appear in their magazine shortly so look out for it."[17]

What Uris did not know was that William Blake was the pseudonym of William James Blech, a Jewish communist from New York who had lived with the Australian writer Christina Stead in London. They immigrated to the United States, settling in Hollywood, where she became a screenwriter, and mixing in communist circles. During the McCarthy era, they returned to Britain. Blake published *The Copperheads*, a novel of the Civil War, in 1941. Focusing on the manipulative money dealings of several shady New York stockbrokers who were eager to make a quick fortune during the war, the novel appealed to Uris's developing sense of outrage at injustice. Its style and focus may have influenced Uris's later writing. On the dust jacket of the first edition, Uris would have read that Blake "led a baroque existence, hence his predilection for the picturesque and the social in fiction."[18] The comment anticipated Uris's own life and career.

According to the jacket flap, the Civil War was "fought on the battlefields of Bull Run and Gettysburg but it was first lost and then won in the money marts of NY's Wall Street . . . *The Copperheads* [is] the story of the first organized fifth column in America . . . The facts, extraordinary as they may at first appear, are absolutely authentic." Again, the blend of politics and history fascinated Uris.

The colorful writing appealed to him, and he would later imitate its style. The first sentence reads, "My heart leaped as high as the gulp in my throat when I read the telegraphic news item 'South Carolina has seceded from the Union.'" This is followed by a swift move in time—"five days later"—a technique Uris would employ. In fact, the opening of *Mila 18* is parallel, beginning with a journal entry, a date, and a character expressing anxiety about the impending invasion of Poland by Germany (*M18*, 3). But the active prose is what perhaps made the greatest impression on Uris. Several paragraphs later is this sentence: "The rookery at 10 Wall Street buzzed with excitement as the clatter drowned the locust clicks of telegraph keys" (9).

During his training in San Diego, Uris also accelerated his pursuit of women, which was relentless throughout his military service (1942–1945). First, there was Pearl, the girl "back home." Uris wrote to Essie that he broke off their relationship before he left "because I told her I wanted no obligations from her," but it didn't work.[19] She got his address from his father, and their letters became serious, "even though I keep telling her she doesn't have to be faithful. She won't accept it. I only thought I was doing what was fair, things being as they are, so uncertain." He thought they would marry when he came back, but Pearl was threatening to come to California to marry him.

A marine chaplain supported the idea of Uris marrying before he went overseas, but he was hesitant because of his age. His toughness as a marine and his role as a radio operator reinforced his independence and courage: "This is no kid's game and I don't think you've realized the change in me. I've learned to love a fight. When I come back I'll be a man who can support myself, a good provider, and will be able to look anyone square in the eyes. And I can see I did it all myself."[20] This resolve and determination would characterize not only much of Uris's later life but also the characters he created.

Two weeks later, things changed (as they always did between Uris and women). He told Essie that he had a girl in Los Angeles who was in her early twenties "and just about as gorgeous as they come. 5'2"—106 lbs and she doesn't claim to be a goody goody."[21] She wanted to pay his way up for a weekend at Capistrano beach; "as I said, I hope I'm not cheating [on Pearl] but I wasn't born brainless." Pearl wrote everyday, and things still looked the same, but, he told Essie, "I like this girl in L.A. very much." "You might think I'm an unsettled kid," but "this is the first time I've gone out with a woman (she is 22) and, well, frankly, I like it very much this way."

In June, he revealed to Essie that he actually had two women, one in Los Angeles and one in Mission Beach, just outside San Diego, with whom he had been involved for two months. Both girls were in such a relationship "for the first time and both of them think I'm going to marry them. Well I should be sweating blood but [am] not even worried frankly. In six weeks I'll get my transfer and I'll be safe (I hope)."[22] He tried to justify his cavalier attitude: "I've gotten some pretty rugged treatment in the last few months [and] I don't know how long I'll be able to enjoy it so I'm making it while it's good." As for Pearl, he called it off. She wrote threatening letters for weeks. He responded by saying he loved her very much but "figures that she can do a lot better for herself." Three days later, he wrote to Essie that he and Hannah, the woman from Los Angeles, were also drifting apart, although he admitted that "she is the best I've ever had."[23]

To impress women, Uris added two years to his age, mentioned his young career as an actor, and highlighted his loneliness. His special come-on? "Dying doesn't frighten me as much as the thought of never seeing you again—(that always does the trick). I know I'm crazy to think I have a chance with you but I just had to tell you—I couldn't keep in any longer."[24]

What makes his monologue remarkable is the tone and fictional authenticity. It sounds right, and Uris displays here, and in other letters, the style and narrative energy that will characterize his later writing. He was one month shy of his eighteenth birthday, but didn't hesitate to offer advice to fellow marines on how to romance young women: go easy on the first date. Let them believe they are morale builders, "then comes the big climax—you have to pick them untouched because a girl who has been out with too many Marines knows the lines like a book."[25] And yet, at the end of this display, Uris could still say that he loved Pearl—"maybe because I never wanted to pull any of that stuff on her. And she is about the only girl I never tried to get a screw out of. Sometimes I think I'll go nuts thinking about her."

Two and a half weeks later, Pearl was back in the picture. They talked formally about an engagement, although her mother was taken by surprise and wanted to know their plans. He asked his sister for help in acquiring a ring, but before matters got too far along, his transfer overseas came through. His attitude toward marriage quickly changed: "I'm not going to get married for a hell of a long time . . . They are much sweeter when you can leave 'em."[26]

Six months later in New Zealand, he offered this reflection, while in the midst of several relationships: "As for liberty—I still hang around from gal to gal. I just can't get situated—they either try to get serious or I tire of them. I gave up Mary as hopeless—I can't stand the ritz she tried to sling. I prefer just a plain old home spun Wave to her. Right now my interest is in Barbara Ferguson, a red head (something new)."[27] In summing up his attitude, he told his mother, with bravado, that he would still play the field, although this ignored his deep, ongoing relationship with Betty Cogswell, a New Zealander.[28] In *Battle Cry*, the relationships between several marines and New Zealand women are central to the story.

Uris's first overseas stop was Wellington, New Zealand, where he remained from 9 November until 26 December 1942. His unit then set off for their first combat, on Guadalcanal, arriving on 4 January 1943 and fighting, with brief breaks, until 19 February 1943. He departed on the 20th, returning to Wellington on 25 February 1943 to begin a long period of rest and recovery, which was marked by new romance and the chance for him to follow another, early love: theatre. He would not go back into combat for some nine months (1 November 1943).

Uris turned nineteen during this time, and for his birthday, he asked his father for a handgun. His optimistic letters, his father writes, were cheerful but tinged with a sense of foreboding about the war. But he definitely wanted a gun: "He specified the size, the caliber and the quality. Anna and I had a problem to find one, then obtain a permit from the Police department, and permission from the military command to send it to him. After a few days of intensive search, I finally bought one, secured the necessary permits, and mailed it to him" (AUTO, 143).

During this period, Uris told Essie that he had been reading *See Here, Private Hargrove*, an amusing set of columns stitched into a book by Marion Hargrove. The comic tales retold the author's humorous adjustment to army basic training at Fort Bragg, South Carolina, and how his hapless behavior led to constant missteps and confusions. Yet it also recorded how the green recruits became soldiers who were proud of their accomplishments, despite the looming war. The book became a number one best seller in 1942. Most importantly, perhaps, it was a record of a young soldier writing about his experiences in the service, which may have planted the idea for Uris to someday write up his own adventures. The novel went through twelve hardcover printings in 1942, selling 410,000 copies; in paperback, it sold 2.2 million copies, figures that Uris would himself attain with *Battle Cry* and exceed with *Exodus* and *Trinity*. In 1944, *See Here, Private Hargrove* became a popular movie starring Robert Walker, Donna Reed, and Robert Benchley.

Another title that would impress Uris was *Yama (The Pit)* by the Russian author Aleksandr Kuprin. "Read it," he wrote to his mother in May 1943, "it's light
and will leave you thinking. I really enjoyed it."[29] The novel is anything but light.
In the tradition of Abbé Prévost's *Manon Lescaut* or Emile Zola's *Nana*, the book
is a vivid account of life in a brothel, in this case in a region of Odessa known as
Yamskaya Sloboda, or Yama. The work describes the prostitutes and their clients
in a style that mixes realism and romance. Kuprin, called by his translator the
enfant terrible of Russian literature, wrote in the tradition of Russian critical realism. Anton Chekhov, Leo Tolstoy, and Maxim Gorky admired his work. Kuprin's
first popular success was *Poyedinok (The Duel;* 1905), an indictment of military life
(he was a former officer). Publication of the first part of *Yama* created a sensation
in 1909, as did parts two and three (1914, 1915). An English translation appeared
in 1922. In the author's postscript, Kuprin notes that some two million copies of
his work circulated worldwide.

The sensationalism of Kuprin's topic appealed to the young Uris, the style even
more so. Kuprin used informal speech and often created neologisms or outland-
ish words: "Not only does he resort to colloquialisms and slang, but to dialect,
cant, and even actual argot. Therein is his glory—and perhaps his weakness."[30]
The nonliterary writing and the emphasis on experience and detail appealed to
Uris, whose own style would reflect this method.

Kuprin also wrote against injustice, much the way Uris would. Furthermore,
his characters analyze why they act the way they do, showing Uris that ideas
have a place in fiction's treatment of social history. The philosophical Yarchenko,
for example, acknowledges that prostitution is "one of the greatest calamities of
humanity," but clarifies "that in this evil not the women are guilty, but the men,
because the demand gives birth to the offer."[31] This leads to an indictment of a
deep-seated Russian immorality regarding not only prostitution but also government, the military, and personal behavior. Kuprin also believed that authors
had to experience what they wrote about; only in that way could they establish
authenticity for their readers. To Essie, Uris said of *Yama*, "It's a killer—read it.
The thing only leaves the 'whore' house twice in 400 pages but of course it was
[for] educational purposes I sought it. I've also knocked off a few more books—
what's coming over me?"[32]

GUADALCANAL

In his letters home, Uris reported very little about his combat experiences, partly
because of censorship and partly because of fear of creating worry. Only indefinite
references to hardships—something was a "grind" or there was illness—pepper

his letters. On the day his unit arrived on Guadalcanal, however, he wrote this mysterious paragraph to Essie, foretelling what would emerge as the finished novel *Battle Cry*: "There is a story—I can't tell it to you now but someday all your mystery will end. I doubt if you'll believe what I tell you. Orson Welles wouldn't dare write it, but someday you'll know."[33] Only once in his correspondence does he refer to the loss of life, the death of a platoon member on Guadalcanal, and only occasionally does he mention the wounded.[34] His pal Red Garvis was hit with shrapnel in his leg and had to be flown to the States, but there were no further details. To find out more about the fighting, one must turn to its accurate portrayal in *Battle Cry* (originally titled *The Beachhead*); chapters 6–10 of part three describe the physical horrors of battle in special detail.

Guadalcanal was as brutal as its depiction in James Jones's *The Thin Red Line* (1962). The novel re-creates the shock and struggle of a group of raw infantry recruits battling for the island. Uris's battalion, however, did not see action on Guadalcanal until the end of the six-month conflict. More specifically, Uris and his headquarters company arrived on Guadalcanal on 4 January 1943, after the marines had established a foothold and an airfield. But the Japanese were equally determined to retake the island, sending numerous naval expeditions to bombard it, at one time in late October 1942 ordering two battleships to shell the airfield. By 4 January 1943, Uris's group was part of a reinforcement-and-replacement plan for making a final push to eliminate any Japanese still dug in. The entire marine contingent, including the Second Battalion, totaled 16,351 men.[35] A major offensive by the marines on 10 January initiated a six-week final effort.

The fighting in this last drive up the coast was fierce, compounded by malaria as well as other jungle diseases such as dysentery and dengue fever. As early as October 1942, malaria was claiming as many U.S. casualties as Japanese artillery, bombs, and naval gunfire. But reinforcements made the difference, which culminated in the pincer movement that ended successfully on 9 February.

When *Battle Cry* narrates the arrival of the Sixth Marine Regiment on Guadalcanal, Uris switches to a diary style to convey both urgency and chronology. But he underscores the irony of their activities: at first they do not fight but carry supplies. They miss the chance for a battle landing (as would happen at Tarawa) and have to wade ashore with equipment. As the narrator of the novel (Mac) reports, they had been in the mud for six days, helping with the drive forward but not fighting. The company was more effective at transporting supplies from the beach to the command post, two miles inland over ridges.

The next diary entry in the novel, for 22 January 1943, depicts several violent encounters Uris witnessed, notably marines using flamethrowers to destroy the Japanese hiding in caves. This was the first time those weapons were employed in the war (BC, 255–256). The writing here becomes vivid and violent. When the marines are attacked the next day, Danny Forrester shoots and then bayonets a Japanese soldier—but when he can't pull his bayonet out of the soldier's chest, he fires off another round, "which splattered him with blood and insides of the Jap"; then, because the dead man's eyes were still open, Forrester smashes the face in with his rifle butt (BC, 260). Brutality takes control as violence becomes endemic. Further scenes reveal Japanese tactics, including imitating injured marines and engaging in hand-to-hand combat (BC, 266). And in an assault scene, Uris adopts a famous marine line as an officer, pointing to a gully they must take, shouts to his men, "Come on, you Whores—you'll never get a Purple Heart up here. Follow me!" (BC, 270).

Uris saw action and likely faced several dangers, not least of which was "jungle rot," a skin infection caused by the damp, insects, and bacteria. Ten days after Guadalcanal was secured, Uris and his debilitated unit left. The capture of the island was a turning point in the war, marking not only the first Allied land offensive in the Pacific but also the end of Japanese advances beyond the Pacific positions they held at that time.[36] But the cost was high: 1,752 soldiers and marines were killed or missing in action. The Sixth Marine Division, which was formed on Guadalcanal, suffered 1,200 casualties.[37]

In a letter to Essie, Uris wrote nothing about the fighting, only that he had a cute beard, was very black from the sun, and had "a swell collection of souvenirs and a bunch of fantastic stories to tell."[38] Eight days later, he reported that he had been in the hospital for four days and back on the line again, but was now upset because he learned that Red Garvis had a shrapnel wound in the right knee. But "I can announce," he claimed with bravado, "that I and the rest of us weren't as afraid as we thought we'd be. We only got madder than hell. When the going gets hot we stand up and yell 'f——— Tojo' and let 'em have it." "The 6th Marines," he added, "are [the] calmest deadliest and fightingest gang of men in this war. We are the pride of [the] Marines and we have the best and most competent officers in the world."[39]

NEW ZEALAND INTERLUDE

Uris returned from Guadalcanal ill: he weighed only 118 pounds and suffered from rheumatism, malaria, and blood poisoning. "On top of that," he told his sister, "all of us were mentally sick. Yes honey, I picked up a lot of grey hair."[40] He was not alone: according to one account, 95 percent of the surviving troops of the Second Battalion, Sixth Marines had some form of tropical disease, principally malaria.[41]

On his return from the "Canal," 25 February 1943, Uris began a lengthy stay in New Zealand that mixed recovery with recreation. Frequent furloughs and adventures meant a remarkable change from the deprivation and devastation of Guadalcanal. Many of these adventures found their way into *Battle Cry*, including the rescue of fellow marines being "rolled" by pimps and whores, and the separation of one of his important romances into two stories: that of the marine Andy Hookans, who falls in love with and marries a New Zealand widow, Pat Rogers, and that of Lamont Jones, known as L. Q., who befriends a married woman (*BC*, 299–308). Uris based this adventure on his own experience, but with a significant difference. In the novel, L. Q. does not have an affair with the wife, Grace, nor anything serious with Gale Bond, a woman with whom he is fixed up at a tennis club. Uris, however, did.

Like L. Q., Uris met a well-meaning New Zealander on a train who immediately invited him home to meet his wife and nine-year-old son. This was in April 1943 in the midst of Uris's nine-month recovery in New Zealand after Guadalcanal. John and Betty Cogswell instantly welcomed Uris, and he was often their guest, although they lived some distance from Wellington, where he was stationed. To his half sister, he admitted that he fell in love with Betty, who was playful, caring, and clearly enamored of the young American, who was charming, entertaining, and a trifle vain.[42] Physical contact was at first good natured, but he implied it quickly became more serious, and he enclosed a letter from Betty to Essie in order to illustrate her fondness for him. Earlier that month, he had ironically written to Essie that he was instituting a new policy of not getting too serious with women: "Freedom is too damn swell. I've seen too many guys get that letter from the most precious girl in the world—who just forgot about them as soon as another pair of pants came into view. Boy I almost made the fatal mistake once—it was a close call."[43]

Food, rest, the races, movies, and dancing were among his activities with Betty; Vera and Grace, Betty's two sisters who lived in Wellington, were equally kind hosts. He became accustomed to visiting them three or four times a week. The domestic scene appealed to him greatly: it was order, comfort, and pleasure: "These are real people who just through simple homespun 'dinkness' make a guy feel like he is a human being again."[44]

On several occasions, Betty Cogswell came to visit her sisters, although her trips were in reality excuses to see Uris, who always entertained. In a letter to Uris ("Dear Fideles"), she expressed how much she missed him and how upset she was at not being able to see him off on the train back to Wellington: "I did want to say goodbye and weep on your shoulder; they wouldn't keep you in the Elite Corps after I had finished mussing you up. But as you say, perhaps it was just as well."[45] The letter ends with her writing "we miss you a whole lot, most of all, because my foot has nothing to kick beneath the table, and so *au revoir*."

In May 1943, Uris told his mother that New Zealand might seem to be a bed of roses, "with good living conditions—good food—the show and most of all Betty and her family, [but] I still feel restless and want only one thing and you know what that is. No matter how wonderful things may be I can never really be happy until I can return."[46] By 9 November 1943, some three weeks before he would ship out to Tarawa, Uris told Essie that he might not come back to the States. He loved New Zealand, and his and Betty's affair had become intense.[47] He did not tell Essie that Betty was married. Ironically, when Uris did finally marry for the first time, his wife's name was Betty.

In the same letter to Essie, Uris added that he thought his father "spread it a bit thick about the Battle flag. I didn't like it." Uris was referring to a bloodstained Japanese flag that he sent his father from Guadalcanal. A story in the *Philadelphia Record* (2 October 1943) reported that a "back-the-attack" show and dance with film star Victor Mature had had as its centerpiece a "blood-stained and tattered Japanese battle flag," which drew the attention of 50,000 at town hall. The flag had been received, the paper went on to say, by "William Uris of 4130 Parkside Ave. yesterday from his son, Private First Class Leon M. Uris of the Marines." A letter from William to Essie included a photo of him holding up the flag; the picture had been published along with an article in Yiddish in the *Morning Freiheit* (17 October 1943).[48]

In his letter to Essie, William asked whether he should send the clipping to his son; he had already sent an account in English, adding that his picture had also been taken for the *Philadelphia Inquirer*. Ending the letter is reference to his son's "ambition to continue writing" and his own promise to help in any way to get Leon's "writing published. Leon loved and still loves to write." This is one of the earliest statements confirming Uris's ambition.

When not training for beach landings, enjoying a furlough, or chasing women, Uris learned how to play the harmonica and managed a Native American boxer named Johnny Gates, a former middleweight amateur champion. On 9 April 1943, Uris reported that his boxer had won the regimental light heavyweight title "in a breeze and is now in training for the Division Championship."[49] His interest in this sport derived in part from his own experience. While in San Diego in late June 1942, Uris had stepped into the ring and boxed twenty two-minute rounds in the company gym: "Had a date to box this Sunday from a week ago and the next thing I knew it was a grudge fight. So I warmed up 5 rounds and the guy didn't show up so I warmed up another 5 slow rounds and then he shows up." In the ensuing match, the smaller Uris was knocked down six times in the first four rounds, but then "I got mad and it took 6 more rounds before I tagged him but he finally quit."[50] Boxing appears in *Battle Cry*, and in 1954 one of Uris's unproduced screenplays was *Ringside*, the story of a boxer's rise and fall.

Other than Betty, the big event in New Zealand was the production of Uris's play *Fourragere Follies*, named for the *fourragère*, the shoulder braid worn by the Sixth Marines to honor their valor in France in the First World War. To his mother, he wrote that he was "back in my old racket again. P. G. Smith, Johnny Etheridge (two buddies) and I are writing a show which will be put on shortly in a big theatre in town. All three of us have had big roles to slaughter and that grease paint will sure feel good again."[51] The theatre was the Wellington Opera House, and the enthusiasm was so great that the division recreation officer reported that the general and his staff would have a box, "so it's really a big thing. As it stands now, we will have a smash hit on our hands—I hope."

The revue was a group effort between Uris, Etheridge, and Smith. Uris wrote the finale, in which he stressed the solidarity between the marines and their New Zealand compatriots as they joined to defeat the Japanese. The finale, he told his mother, featured a set that represented the barracks at night, as well as crosscut dialogue from soldiers from all over America, each voice with a different accent. Uris took the part of a Brooklynite representing "the City." Relying on idiomatic language, the final speech was a ringing endorsement of the united effort to defeat the Japanese. Creating a tapestry in sound for the revue encouraged Uris in his use of different narrators and shifting points of view to distinguish the marines in *Battle Cry*.

A performance at the St. James Theater received this headline in the *New Zealand Free Lance* (2 June 1943): "American Marines Entertain with Hot Numbers and Riotous Fun." Photos of the cast in performance exhibit exuberance and professionalism, one caption praising the "1 hr. and 15 minutes of high pressure entertainment." An earlier headline had read: "Marines Put it Over Excellently, Unrehearsed Frolics on Wellington Stage" (*New Zealand Free Lance*, 31 May 1943).

The show was a hit despite only three weeks of partial rehearsals and no complete run-through until the first night.[52] To Essie, Uris wrote that the show was a "thunderbolt and is being acclaimed. For two hours . . . they split their sides on the comedy, cheered the music and were deathly silent in the serious scenes and it was a thrilling experience."[53] The show was to be repeated, but Uris gave up his part to "remain a writer, as well as director and . . . business manger." But there was also a down side. Working hard meant the return of malaria for many, including Uris. But recovery was quick.

The show was an indisputable sensation. Uris's excitement over its triumph renewed his enthusiasm for the theatre, which he decided to pursue upon his return to the States—not only in a new revue, *Situation Out of Hand*, but also in his efforts to mount a touring production of *Fourragere Follies* with veterans of the show. He would also attempt to get the text published.

While in New Zealand, he rapidly impressed an acting family and their daughter. After their first formal meeting, he turned on his charm, and "they listened up and I had things going my way before long. Mary [their daughter] is a sweet gal but I'm afraid they try to be too high hat. I cut them down a few notches but I like to go somewhere where I can take off my shoes and unbutton my collar."[54] Later, he wrote: "I still see Mary on occasion but I expressed my view of her before (too high brow). Every time we get together, I give her hell and she loves it. Strange, there is very little sex interest. Just a nice and intelligent friendship . . . But as I said, it's best not to see any one girl too often. I enjoy her company and she got out of the habit of putting on airs on me—I call her Maggie—but I don't want to get to like her too much."[55] The next month he was back with Betty.

In mid-October 1943, he reported that he and Betty were getting serious, adding "I can't say that I'm sorry . . . It was hard to keep fighting against it. Now we are trying to make plans and believe me it's mighty hard too. But, nevertheless, we are both taking it slow and easy and wisely. Right now she is making me sane—and we aren't doing badly either."[56] Yet within three weeks, he told Essie that at last he was "coming to my sense about Betty—Boy was that close—another month or so there and I might have married."[57]

TARAWA

By the end of October 1943, the New Zealand idyll was coming to an end. Uris and the Second Marine Division shipped out for one of the bloodiest and most difficult battles of the war, Tarawa. The three-day battle for this small atoll, part of the Gilbert Islands, was a near massacre, a story of confusion and bloodshed. Uris departed on 1 November 1943 and would remain in the Gilberts until 28 November 1943, when he was sent to Hawaii to recuperate from malaria and dengue fever.

Tarawa was the first test of the U.S. amphibious doctrine of assaulting a heavily defended beach in daylight; it also marked the Pacific debut of the Sherman tank, although few of them survived the intense, seventy-six-hour battle. Tremendous tactical problems, which created congestion on the beach, death in the water, and confusion at sea during the 20–23 November landing, resulted in heavy casualties. On the morning of the landing, it was not clear whether the tides would be high enough to get the heavy landing craft over a dangerous barrier reef and deposit the men on the beach. The assault plan unraveled when many marines had to wade ashore some hundreds of yards from behind the reef, making them easy targets for the dug-in Japanese gunners. Entire platoons were lost as Japanese heavy guns targeted navy landing craft, making it impossible for the tanks they carried to get ashore. Betio Island, the key island in the Tarawa atoll, seemed impregnable.

The battle for Tarawa continued for three and a half bloody days at an immense cost: 1,115 marines and sailors killed or missing, and 2,292 wounded. All told, some 6,000 Japanese and Americans died in the space of three hundred acres. Nearly ninety hospital corpsmen for the Second Marine Division alone suffered casualties (out of a total casualty count of 3,097 for the division), a mark of the severity of the fighting. At one point, a blackened, derelict landing vehicle tracked (LVT) drifted ashore, filled with dead marines. When the battle was finally over, burial parties could not dig a grave without exposing another body.[58]

Tarawa was also where Uris, who had come under fire before, had what he referred to as his most dangerous wartime experience. During a break in the midst of the mop-up operation, he was sleeping on the beach and was nearly run over by an amtrack (amphibious tracked vehicle) that failed to see him—the "closest I came to being killed."[59]

Of his time on Tarawa, Uris was candid—forty-four years after the battle. Speaking at the dedication of the Tarawa Monument at Long Beach, California, he said that on 20 November 1943, while with a marine task force just off Tarawa, "I was neither hero or coward, I was able to do what was expected of me."[60] After the battle for Betio, "my memories of Tarawa were rather romantic. . . . As the last reserve battalion, we had drawn few casualties at the main battle site." He was in the last reserve battalion assigned to chase the remnants of the Japanese garrison across a couple of dozen linked islands that made up the rest of the atoll. Forty-five miles and three days later, they trapped them and "fought our own intimate little war. We remained on Tarawa for several weeks to garrison and defend against a possible counter-attack from the Marshals."

After an unfit Uris returned to the United States, his "buddies, the 2nd Battalion of the Sixth Marines, were cut to pieces on Red Beach on Saipan. I was filled with guilt and remorse for not having been there."[61] Years later, he met Colonel Ray Murray, of his former battalion, in Marin Country. To Uris's shock, Murray turned to him said, "Oh, hello Uris. Did you ever get around to writing that book?" Uris then explained:

> I realized that my commitment to the corps could not be fulfilled until I had earned their respect at the typewriter. And believe me, the typewriter is the worst weapon ever created against the soul of man. I am proud to be here because so many of the writers out of the second world war wrote bitter novels, damning their branch of the service, damning America, and damning the officers and men they fought with.

Well, I hated war as much as any of these authors, but I love my fellow Marines as brothers and I respected and trusted my officers.[62]

In three days at Tarawa, the Second Marine Division took more casualties than U.S. troops had incurred at Belleau Wood (during the First World War in 1918) in three weeks: "At Tarawa, we had almost as many casualties as we had taken in six months on Guadalcanal. [But] just as the battle of Belleau Wood stopped the great German onslaught on Paris in WWI, so did the bravery at Tarawa shatter Japanese illusions."[63] Uris ended his speech with a gung ho tribute: "On that terrible day in November of 1943, what kept them coming through chest high water when their only armor was the thickness of their dungarees? Faith in the Corps, faith in each other and love of their country. Each man said to himself, silently, 'I am a Marine.' and they were Marines, every one of them. They were the finest ever seen."

One of the more important aspects of the marines, which Uris underplayed, was anti-Semitism. But when asked directly about that sort of prejudice, he was evasive: "I had no real Jewish Background and half the guys knew I was Jewish and half didn't. It bothered me because I didn't want my friends turning on me. So I just kept quiet about it. I didn't go to Catholic services and I didn't go to Protestant services and I didn't even know if there was a Jewish service. That's what I meant by denying."[64]

STATESIDE

Ill with malaria, dengue fever, and a recurrence of asthma, Pfc. Leon Uris shipped out from Tarawa on the USS *Prince Georges* on 8 January 1944, arriving in Hilo, Hawaii, on the 20th. He transferred to Pearl Harbor, where he left on the MS *Bloemfontein* on 12 March 1944 for San Francisco, arriving six days later. He recuperated at the Oak Knoll Naval Hospital in Oakland, California, his combat days over.[65]

Uris officially remained with the Sixth Marines until he received a transfer on 2 March 1944 to the V Amphibious Corps, which transported him back to San Francisco. He remained at Oak Knoll until 12 August. When fully recovered, he joined the supply depot in San Francisco for two months; he then transferred to the Second Separation Company on Mare Island and was honorably discharged on 27 October 1945. He had continued his enlistment until 1945 partly to meet requirements for disability pay.

Uris's return to the States was bittersweet. In a letter to his mother, he told her of the joy as well as the pain of first sighting land: "I don't guess I can even be really happy until all my buddies are back too."[66] He didn't know what the future held or how long he would spend recovering. He was eating and sleeping well, and there were a "bunch of Waves around here too—living right on the compound[.] They are OK in the Army and Navy but the name 'Lady Marine' makes me very sick in the stomach. I fear I'm narrow minded."

The Oak Knoll Naval Hospital was a large facility accustomed to treating tropical diseases. Uris made a quick recovery, reassuring his family that he was rapidly improving. One measure of his regained energy was his renewed pursuit of women. He reported to his mother that he was dating a colonel's daughter who went to an exclusive school here: "She's an awful nice kid and I enjoy her company. We are going to see 'The Student Prince' next week."[67] He added: "I'm now a member of the Veterans of Foreign Wars. . . . If I might, Darling, I'd like to give you a citation for bravery. You've conducted yourself in the best tradition of Mothers. I know the burdens you've carried for the past two years."

Most importantly, his hospitalization encouraged him to renew his principal literary pursuit at the time, playwriting. Two and a half months after his return, Uris organized a revue that he wrote and codirected with R. D. Mayfield, and that was to be performed at Oak Knoll on 29 May 1944. An article in the base paper, the *Oak Leaf* (27 May 1944), previewed what would be the first original play at the new central auditorium: "'Situation Out of Hand' [is] a real side-splitter. It's what happens when two daughters of an Army Colonel are in love, one with a marine and the other with a sailor."[68] The plot of the two-act comedy, however, is slightly more complicated. One of the two daughters is secretly married to a sailor, but the colonel favors another suitor, an army lieutenant. To add to the complications, the other daughter is in love with a marine—played by Uris—suspected of being a spy. What happens behind the colonel's back forms the action, which was all the more interesting because Uris was involved with a colonel's daughter at the time.

In one of his many scrapbooks, Uris included a black-and-white photo from the play and scribbled beneath it "172 laughs in 55 minutes." Coverage of the revue appeared in the Oakland, San Francisco, and Baltimore papers. An article in the *Chevron*, a marine paper on the West Coast, headlined its feature with "Second Play in Year produced by Marine." It described Uris as recovering after eighteen months of overseas duty and noted that he wrote his first play, "Fourragere Follies . . . in his off hours while he was stationed in New Zealand. It played with great success before Marine audiences there." A story with Uris's photo in the arms of an actor, Pat Connel, appeared in the *Leatherneck* (the official marine magazine), with the welcome headline "Marine Playwright."[69]

Earlier, in July 1944, while working on *Situation Out of Hand*, Uris also drafted a new play to enter into a national serviceman's contest. He called it *The Parent*

Spark; no copy of it appears to have survived. At that time, he and his girlfriend Marilyn had reached a stalemate, but he handled it with characteristic panache: "Well—her misfortune. Women around here are plentiful and they all make nice salaries and know how much I make so I'm not too unhappy."[70]

Uris was also developing another skill: writing radio scripts for the War Bond Office. Preparations for these publicity broadcasts included scripting all the interview material. One of them, dated 20 November 1944, opened the sixth war-loan drive and noted that the date was the first anniversary of the Battle of Tarawa. Uris wrote the introductions plus the interviews, beginning with a talk by Mr. W. W. Crocker, the chairman of the drive, who told listeners that the war was not over. There was a need for more cargo planes, cargo vessels, superfortresses, and amphibious equipment for the beachheads that had to be taken. He urged listeners to buy at least one extra hundred-dollar bond during the drive. The dramatic tone foreshadowed some of Uris's later, urgent prose.

MARRIAGE AND POLITICS

As his relationship with the colonel's daughter waned, Uris began to court a twenty-two-year-old marine staff sergeant at supply depot headquarters: Betty Beck from Iowa. A December 1944 letter to his mother provided the details in his best battlefield style:

> First, and I think you know your sonny boy, she is a very attractive girl, has a beautiful figure and the best pair of legs in Frisco. Lovely hair, a beautiful set of white teeth and light complexion and dark blond hair. She . . . comes from the town of Waterloo, Iowa, from a middle class family. Both of her parents are from Denmark and her father is a successful builder. . . . Betty is very quiet except in her own circle of friends but has lots of good stuff on the inside and lots of common sense. And a very wonderful sense of devotion. Mostly, she has lots of faith in me and my work.[71]

What the letter didn't outline was Betty Beck's love of books or her enlistment in the marines at age twenty after two years of college (and never having left Iowa). She was in the first company of female marines, and because of her college experience, she was made sergeant and sent to San Francisco to work at the supply depot headquarters, where she would meet Uris. Three months after meeting this eastern-bred young man of Russian-Polish origin, she married him.

Betty's family, who thought less of Uris's plans, raised objections. Candidly, he wrote that her family was really blowing the roof off the house. Her father says that if she marries me she never need to come home again and they want to send her Mother out here to stop us. For my own part, I'd like to tell them all where to go, but there is Betty to consider. No matter what I think of them, they are still her parents and she loves them. I just have to take her feelings into it. But I'm not going to give her up—nor am I going to let them rule and ruin her life. She is taking it very hard and it's a trying period but things will work out for the best I'm sure. As soon as things cool down a little I'll have Betty write to you.[72]

The situation troubled Uris, but they married while they were both still in the service, her commanding officer warning her that he won't go far. She responded by declaring he would be a great writer.[73]

Uris enjoyed married life, which unexpectedly became entangled with marine politics. On the night of 27 February 1945, Uris was one of several marines who led a protest at the offices of William Randolph Hearst's *San Francisco Examiner* for its printing of an editorial that day that praised General Douglas MacArthur as a strategist and hero. The article criticized the marines for the high loss of life at the Battle of Iwo Jima, drawing comparisons to the deaths at Tarawa and Saipan. Heavy assaults against fortified beach positions seem foolhardy, especially when compared with how MacArthur won back the Philippines without the "decimation or exhaustion of American forces." MacArthur, the paper declared, is "our BEST strategist. He also SAVES THE LIVES OF HIS OWN MEN . . . why do we not USE him more . . . why do we not give him the supreme command of the Pacific war?" The marines took offense: the editorial implied that they did not know how to fight, protect their men, or win battles.

Uris and a group of marines confronted the managing editor in his office. He tried to stall them when they demanded space for a response: no one but Hearst could grant that. They demanded to speak to him. At that moment, the shore patrol and the police riot squad arrived. Uris and the other seventy-five marines refused to budge. A committee of three, including Uris, then met in the managing editor's office and pressured him to call Hearst. Through his secretary, Hearst guaranteed space for a response, and the next day Uris, Betty (a marine sergeant), and three others returned with their own editorial, which clarified the marines' actions and corrected the sinister implications that the marines acted carelessly. One sentence expressed the tone of the whole: "To hint that the Marines die fast and move slowly on Iwo Jima because Marine and Naval leadership in that assault was incompetent is an attempt at a damnable swindle of the American people." That day, 28 February 1945, a version of it appeared in the paper.

Uris made sure the incident was well covered, providing an account to the Associated Press and *Time* magazine. The opening sentence dramatically conveyed the action and foreshadowed the style he would apply in his own fiction: "Police and Navy Shore Patrol answered a riot call to William Randolph Hearst's *Examiner* tonight when a group of 60–70 U.S. Marines—identified as Pacific veterans—crowded into the editorial rooms, protesting an editorial which said the Marine Corps is paying 'perhaps too heavily' in lives for Iwo Jima."[74]

Most of the San Francisco dailies suppressed the story, however. Only the "courageous little Daily Peoples' World" gave the event any attention, declaring that the marines had "roared" into the office to demand a retraction. On Thursday, 1 March 1945, the *San Francisco Examiner* printed a letter to the editor signed by the marines, but not a retraction. The edited letter rationally showed that Mac-Arthur often landed at unopposed beaches and islands, while the marines faced heavily dug-in defenders relying on small but effective forces. The original letter also criticized MacArthur for his self-serving actions. The incident passed, and the Hearst papers continued to demand that MacArthur be given full command of U.S. forces in the Pacific. Nevertheless, the event demonstrated Uris's activism when faced with injustice, especially against his beloved marines.

In an April 1945 letter to his mother, Uris continued his account of political life. He and Betty lived at 909 Franklin Street, only three blocks from the peace conference, and "since the death of Roosevelt, we have all felt the urgency of this meeting succeeding."[75] But he urged his mother not to count on their coming east "till the war is over," although they hoped then "to able to get a nice car and travel across the country in our own good time." Most importantly, "we are undecided what to do after the war but you can be assured that we will go into business for ourselves, whatever it is."

In an earlier letter, he noted that they had participated in San Francisco culture by seeing a production of *Othello* with Paul Robeson and attending concerts. "Married life," he continued, "is sure wonderful and we are both very happy and contented."[76] The apartment looked great, and "Betty is a wonderful, loveable girl and I consider myself damn lucky." Life also had a regularity to it that he appreciated: "We both put in a big day's work and usually eat and go to sleep or go out someplace—I've fallen so far behind in all my writing that everyone is sore at me but I'll honestly try to do better in the future."

Uris later reported that he was given a column in a new base paper that was scheduled to start in a month or so: "So now I'm launching a career on newspaper work. Anyhow, it seems like a lot of fun. Also, I've put in a request to start a dramatic group."[77] He also told his mother that he was preparing an article titled "Blood on the Beaches" for a new magazine, *Opportunities on Parade*, which would have a circulation of a hundred thousand.[78] The magazine published its first issue in May 1946, although Uris's piece was not in it. The article is an early draft of several scenes in *Battle Cry*.

But with the war over, Uris began to think of moving with Betty to larger quarters and to considers different careers, including that of producer-dramatist for the Veterans Drama League. The pressing issue was housing. He noted that Henry Kaiser was putting up houses that came equipped with refrigerators, stoves, landscaping, health benefits, dishwashers, and "everything."[79] They were very cheap, and the financing terms were "swell." He wrote to inquire and perhaps "grab one off and get established. Well, I've been married over four months now and find my wife sweeter and more lovable every day."

To further himself, he signed up for several English courses through a correspondence school. He and Betty improved their lot by ordering a new car, which they would pay for with war bonds. And although they had no income for the few months after Uris's discharge, he nonetheless offered to help his mother with expenses for Uncle Eddie's illness as soon as he was able.[80] In a postscript, he added that there would be "no grandchildren for a while."

During this time, he also tried to get a play produced. A rejection letter from Laura Wilck in Hollywood reads: "Sorry but SITUATION OUT OF HAND by Leon Uris won't do. I appreciate your thinking of me but the script is too amateurish."[81] A rejection letter from the New York story department of Twentieth Century–Fox explained that the work didn't qualify as filmable material.[82] Exhibiting his early reaction to critics, Uris wrote in ink across the bottom of the letter: "This guy is nuts."

The year 1945 did see the publication of Uris's first work, however: five letters in *Jewish Youth at War: Letters from American Soldiers*, a volume published in New York by Marstin Press, which had been started by Israel London, a Yiddish publisher, printer, and journalist.[83] Edited by the Yiddish poet and critic Isaac E. Rontch, *Jewish Youth at War* contains excerpts from ninety-three Jewish men and women who served during the Second World War. Almost all the letters are by the children of Jewish immigrants whose parents "came to America by choice" and for whom there was no confusion of identity: "The American Jewish soldier fights as an American and as a Jew," Rontch asserts.[84] It is likely that William Uris sent Rontch letters from his son; Rontch had printed Yiddish poetry in *Freiheit* and may have published a request for material there.

Introducing "This Is My War—Personally," the title of Uris's three-page contribution, is a biographical note, which incorrectly states he was wounded at Tarawa. A thumbnail photo shows a grainy but youthful Uris in uniform. The dates of the letters, all to his father, are from March 1943 to May 1944 and begin with a summary of conditions on Guadalcanal: "bugs, mud to your waist, and sun so hot you nearly burned. Then there were snipers, planes, machine guns and artillery. . . . But we'd do it again and again until we can come home" (*Jewish Youth at War*, 223). Patriotism mixed with bravery is underscored in his letter of 6 July 1943, in which he tells his father he will soon send him a Japanese battle flag. Uris proudly states that "the Jap it was taken from won't be around to claim it—I saw to that" (223). He suggests that the flag be used for fund-raising. In November of that year, he announces that he wants to stay in the Pacific until the job is done: "This is my war—personally and I am glad to be in it. Not only for my grandmother but for Joe and Sam Stone who died in Spain—for Red who is now a cripple for life from the leg wound on Guadalcanal" (224). Proud of his contribution, he reminds his father that two cousins have also joined up.

A May 1943 letter, however, reveals that he is homesick and unhappy partly because his play *Fourragere Follies* will not be seen by his family. He stresses its theme: the Yanks are as sentimental and home loving as those they are fighting with, the New Zealanders, against the Japanese. He then quotes his overly romantic speech in the finale, beginning with "It's the little things in life that we will fight and die for" and then moving on to even larger sentimentalities (224–225).

The final letter, dated 14 May 1944, is from the Oak Knoll Naval Hospital. For the first time he mentions suffering nightmares from the Tarawa landing: only six in his landing craft reached the beach. He also suffers from knowing that his buddies are still out there fighting while he is recovering in the hospital. He ends with a ringing endorsement of American democracy and the marines, for whom it is not the religion but the man that counts. The paragraph, summarizing his view of the fighting, is a valuable summary of his war and identity:

> America, my country, is my love. I've fought beside Catholics, Protestants and Mormons, Indians, Irish, Italians, Poles. They liked me because I was a good man and a regular fellow. And I've seen 750 out of 900 of us who left the States die or be shot up at Guadalcanal and Tarawa. There was a Jewish boy in my platoon—who was well hated. He was a coward, a general no good. We made his life miserable, not because he was a Jew, but because he was a rat. And another Jew, Captain Bill Scherewin—I worked for him. He has won three Navy Crosses. He led a glorious assault which I was in. We loved him and would follow him to hell. (225)

In this paragraph are the themes Uris will develop in *Battle Cry*, the behavior and testing of a mixed group of young men sent to war. And in the tone of this letter is the sincerity and conviction that would stand behind his constant efforts to oppose injustice and discrimination.

A review of *Jewish Youth at War* in *Commentary* magazine singles out only one writer for comment. The reviewer, critical of the pious and sanctimonious tone of the letters and the awkward, juvenile style of the writing, nonetheless highlights one account for its honestly felt experience of the most frightening event of any war: death. He then quotes the letter about nightmares, the Tarawa landing, and the changes it brought about. The unidentified author was Leon Uris.[85]

For six months after leaving the service, Uris organized and was president of the U.S. Marines Veterans' Association of the Pacific Coast. In August 1945, he assisted in the production of a Guadalcanal memorial show performed at the Civic Auditorium in San Francisco. Uris wrote and directed the blackout sketches and was master of ceremonies for that segment. The Tommy Tucker band played. He also took on the editorship of *Pacific Veteran*, the association's newsletter. There was also an effort to remount *Situation Out of Hand* for a five-day run.

The slightly altered play (the plot involved the daughters of a college professor rather than a colonel) would be sponsored by the War Finance Committee, which would tour the play for the fifth war-loan drive with Steve Courtleigh of the New York stage playing the lead. At the last minute, however, a protest from army public relations canceled the production: "Fun was poked between the services in the script and at that time, Army and Marine Relations were strained over an incident on Saipan."[86] Nevertheless, the play was a success in a San Francisco production.

Many ads and several short articles about the performance appeared in the San Francisco papers. An advertisement in the *San Francisco Chronicle* (18 March 1946) described the work as an "An Original Farce in 3 Acts" with this blurb: "Only fault with play is it has too many laffs—if such a thing is possible.—J. Shelley." Listed as a performer on the handbill for a March 22 production was "Lee M. Uris."[87]

Herb Caen, "the [Walter] Winchell of San Francisco," plugged the show in his 19 March 1946 column, which was headed "It's news to me." "Try to catch 'Situation out of Hand' staged by Vets Drama League," he wrote. "The league was formed by Leon Uris, a Tarawa campaigner[,] and all the gents in the cast have miles of campaign ribbons battle stars, etc."[88]

But the failure to tour the play and declining support for the Veterans Drama League meant Uris had to turn to other employment. After several attempts, he landed a job at the *San Francisco Call-Bulletin* as a district sales manager, first in San Francisco and then in Marin County. A new stage in his life began. He and Betty would soon move to a small house across the bay in Larkspur, await the arrival of their first child, and a few months later adjust to the nightly sounds of Uris typing in the attic as he began to draft and redraft his first novel.

BATTLE CRY AT LARKSPUR

3

Sure, it's got guts . . . sure, it's got gore . . . but what it's got most of is GLORY!"
—BATTLE CRY, DUST JACKET (1953)

ESPITE ITS APPEARANCE after *The Naked and the Dead, Guard of Honor, From Here to Eternity,* and *The Caine Mutiny, Battle Cry* stood alone.[1] Among these original novels of the Second World War, Uris's was the only one to express a positive, supportive view of the military despite the carnage, confusions, and loss of life inherent in war. Patriotism not nihilism, heroism not cowardice, defined its themes, which were welcomed by the marines and the public. The writing and publication of the book were more of a challenge, however. And even though he wrote some six or seven years after the fighting in the Pacific, Uris was still able to re-create the intensity and danger faced by marines in battle, as well as their lives at home.

Uris and Betty moved to 62 Piedmont Road in Larkspur, California, in 1947, a step up made possible by his first full-time job, at the *San Francisco Call-Bulletin,* and made necessary by the birth of their daughter, Karen, earlier that year. As a district circulation manager (formal title: division manager) responsible for some twenty-six paperboys, he earned seventy-five dollars a week, plus a car and expenses. But if he were approved as a union member (which he later was), his salary would go up. Competing with the *San Francisco News,* the afternoon *Call-Bulletin* had a large circulation, although the rivalry was cutthroat. Working in the city, Uris had to, first, increase circulation in a black neighborhood, then in a "hoodlum" district, and finally in the Sunset District, "where all the middle classed peasants dwell."[2] To his delivery boys, he was both "a father confessor and boss," but he always found time to play ball and entertain them.[3] In the same letter, he suggests that he might attend school next fall, "perhaps law." A touch of asthma, however, possibly related to his malaria, slowed him down, but the flare-up, plus the need for more room, accelerated his search for brighter and larger quarters across the bay in Marin County.

Larkspur, a small town fifteen miles north of San Francisco across the Golden Gate Bridge, just west of Corte Madera and south of San Rafael, was their choice. Magnolia Avenue, the single main street, contained a three-block commercial area, with a mission-style city hall and fire station at one end and the popular art deco Lark Theatre at the other. One mile south of town and up secluded Piedmont Road, redwoods surrounded the two-story Uris home with its modest front porch, lawn, and garden. Mount Tamalpais loomed behind, and Madrona Canyon, with even greater stands of redwoods, was nearby.[4] The pastoral location and drier weather made Uris's frequent trips to San Francisco to oversee deliveries, subscriptions, and routes bearable.

Uris was now earning ninety dollars a week, and Betty was completing a "6 month hitch at the Warden's Office at San Quentin Prison" not far away.[5] He soon started gardening and took great pride in his roses and home repairs: "Kid, this is it! I don't know if you can picture an old slum bred alley rat like me puttering in the garden, but that's just what I do on my days off." Betty remained a delight: "She is all anyone could ever dream of as a wife, mother and companion and one of these grand days I hope to pay off the way I feel in minks, diamonds, maids and Buicks." He had never been happier, he says, and was "writing immortal classics destined for the waste basket," noting that he had completed approximately one-third of a book. He was also pleased to learn that he would be transferred from San Francisco to county circulation in Marin, so he wouldn't have to commute.

But Uris was having problems with his mother: "My Doctor tells me I have hidden complexes concerning her." He felt sorry for her and called her "pathetic," although any regrets he had were "hidden someplace in back of my mind . . . but I do not regret my choice in making my break and finding a new life away from that former gruel." Uris's estrangement from his mother may have been related to her withholding of love, persistent creation of guilt, and inability to respond emotionally to her son. His marrying a non-Jewish woman and remaining on the West Coast may have also been factors. He told Essie that while he loved his mother a great deal, "every time I wrote to her she came back with attacks and sob stories I just couldn't stomach. Maybe when she sees Karen [his daughter] we can patch up and try again."[6]

Admitting that Betty's parents were, "to put it bluntly, Jew haters before we married," he reported that after they met him, they grew quite fond of him and vice versa.[7] He added: "Betty is quite proud of the Jewish people and me." As for himself: "I've worked out problems that I guess only time and experience would conquer—and I can understand my place now as a Jew and what it means. You can bet your bottom dollar if I weren't married, I'd be over there shooting A-rabs."

Uris wrote this in 1949, the year after Israel's declaration of independence, and it illustrates how his Jewish identity was taking on a more activist character. Unlike his indifference or avoidance of his Jewishness in the marines, he was now prepared to acknowledge, defend, and celebrate it.

THE BEGINNINGS OF *BATTLE CRY*

While working for the paper and watching his family grow—Karen was born in 1946, Mark in 1950, and Michael in 1953—Uris started to work consistently on his first book. He had begun writing what would become *Battle Cry* shortly after his marriage; during the war, he had written down some slang expressions but lost the notes.[8] In the summer of 1946, before and after his move to Larkspur, he began to shape the work originally called *The Beachhead*, which originated in prose accounts of selected war experiences.

A letter dated 23 September 1946 summarizes his early efforts with the manuscript, and an undated letter (ca. 1953) provides additional information on the book's progress. He also stresses Betty's important role. It is a lengthy but helpful summary. After noting that the work in progress is titled *The Beachhead*, and emphasizing the support of literary agent, he reports:

> I've completed five hundred pages and have three hundred more to go of rough copy and then translate the whole works. I get home from work at eight thirty at night and generally go up to the garret about nine thirty and with my beret, wine and bread work past mid-night, depending on what section I'm tackling. At current rate I do about four thousand words a night; on my two days off, I knock over eight or nine thousand. The completed book will run over two hundred thousand words—or roughly six hundred pages in print. Some fun huh! Betty is wonderful—besides keeping the house, the kids and the garden . . . she cooperates a hundred percent in keeping everything clear for me to work. And she works right along side of me on the editing etc. She reads as many as six books a week and is invaluable in aiding of working out various problems.[9]

Uris committed himself to such labor because he saw success ahead: "Frankly, I sometimes wonder if I'm off my rocker—but I keep seeing $$$$$$$$ and fans and all the junk that goes with it—(Why lie about it—that is what I want among other things)."

Betty constantly encouraged him. She was his first reader and was especially helpful with grammar, something he never mastered. Indeed, his later research assistants spent a great deal of time correcting his typescripts. When writing,

Uris's intensity and imagination allowed little time for editing. He had a story to tell, and he told it quickly. But Betty was more than a grammarian. She also shaped the content, at one point telling Uris, after he announced that he was going to kill the character Andy Hookans, the lumberjack who falls in love with a New Zealand war widow, that if he did, she would never sleep with him again. Uris restored marital harmony by having the character lose only a leg in battle.

In an April 1953 article about Uris, a reporter wrote that if "Mrs. Uris hadn't been a Marine Sergeant herself, I don't think she could have stood it—caring for kids, Leon, enduring his moods, his exultations."[10] The day before yesterday, the reporter wrote, Uris took some of his advance and bought a new car and gave the keys to Betty, "a small down payment on her sacrifices."

While drafting early portions of the novel, Uris sporadically sought to break into print. He finally succeeded in late 1950 with an intemperate article on the selection process for the all-American football teams. He sent off his short essay to *Esquire*. To his amazement, it was accepted:

9 June 1950

It was certainly refreshing to hear Gus F. Fan blow his top—and do it with such eloquent conviction as you did in ALL AMERICAN RAZZ MATAZZ. Instead of having the office boy or night watchman initial the rejection slip, as you suggested, we thought that you would be even more pleased if we bought this article for an early publication. How does a price of $300.00 strike you?

As soon as I receive an okay on the price from you I will air mail you our check.

Cordially,
Donald Cormack[11]

Uris was stunned.

The article appeared in the January 1951 issue, with a long paragraph on Uris (and his photo) in the "Backstage with Esquire" section, which emphasized his outspokenness. It additionally noted that the twenty-six-year-old had spent four years with the marines and that he had been with the *Call-Bulletin* since 1947. There was no mention of future literary work. In the article itself, Uris opposed the unsystematic method of selecting all-Americans, which he found unrepresentative. It falsely imposed regional balance, to the detriment of a section of the country that might have a surfeit of talent. Concern for the overall failure to acknowledge first-rate football players from secondary schools, plus the duplication of all-American team selections, resulted in his indictment of "NON AMERICA teams."[12] He offered his own solution of a single selection board for the country. The detail and research Uris exhibited in his article, expressed through the confident tone of reform, suggest the style of writing that would characterize his fiction.

The acceptance of his article, along with the payment for it, convinced Uris that he could write, and he began to type his novel enthusiastically, working nightly in a small alcove—an enclosed second-story porch—in the house. Betty was again crucial to his work: "She never forced me to write, [but] neither did she discourage me against it and she always harbored the faith that I would do it. . . . The entire thing was stored up in my head and just came out when I sat at the typewriter."[13] Betty remained his editor telling him to rewrite and rewrite some more. And she recalled her words to the marine commanding officer who told her not to marry Leon Uris because he was a lazy, no-good fellow: "I know someday he's going to be a great writer."[14] Uris dedicated *Battle Cry* to her.

It took Uris nearly three years of after-work and weekend writing to complete the book—and he was frank "in crediting the union's contract with the pay and conditions that gave him the time and freedom from financial burden to complete it."[15]

REJECTION AND PUBLICATION

Uris wrote the ending of *Battle Cry* at the *Call-Bulletin* during a press run. "Someone had left a free typewriter," and while he waited for the paper to come off the presses, he completed the manuscript on the vacant machine.[16] He explained: "If I write too much one day, I can't write the next. Don't ask me why but my best hours seem to be between 5–8pm. I wrote *Battle Cry* by working from 9–12pm every night and 16–18 hours on my day off." The massive final manuscript was replete with repetitions, awkward sentences, structural problems, and incorrect punctuation. A steady stream of rejections arrived at his home, one letter arriving the day Uris and Betty received word that Karen had contracted polio.[17] The illness and the news devastated him.

In a 1966 interview, Uris admitted that this was the low point of his life, the convergence of the *Battle Cry* rejections and Karen's battle with polio. He vowed to God that if she were not crippled, he would never ask for anything again. But he didn't entirely keep his promise: as she recovered, he admitted that he continued his search for fame and fortune.[18] A scene in *Mitla Pass* replays the moment, although in the novel his daughter has had an accident rather than polio. In a hospital chapel, the writer-hero, Gideon Zadok, pleads with God to let his daughter live. In turn, he declares: "I'll work at that fucking newspaper the rest of my life and I won't complain, okay? I swear I'll never complain about not becoming a writer . . . man, that's all I can give you. Please don't take my baby" (*MP*, 65).

Betty was again the rock. She continued to encourage him, tend to their small son Mark, and take the bus into San Francisco to visit the hospitalized Karen—all while pregnant with her third child, Michael. After Karen came home, she would exercise her daughter's atrophied muscles daily on the kitchen table and take her to the hospital three times a week for physiotherapy. She did what needed to be done.

Uris did not give up his faith in Karen's recovery or in his book, not even when he carried the manuscript to Howard S. Cady, the West Coast editor of Doubleday: "I took it to him—2200 pages in a suitcase—and he told me—'Cut this down to 3 lbs.'"[19] Uris did, and Cady thought there were possibilities. The novel was then known as "Blood My Battle Cry" and had made a powerful impression on Cady in spite of its obvious need for tightening and cutting. Cady had already started Uris on revisions when Doubleday New York notified him, however, that with *The Caine Mutiny* a steady best seller for them, they would not acquire Uris's book.

Cady, however, would not relent; he believed in the talent of the young novelist who had written his war novel some ten years after the events, allowing him to process and reevaluate what happened. Unlike Norman Mailer, who wrote *The Naked and the Dead* soon after returning from the war, Uris took time to digest his military experience, although, as he said, it was always present as "a slow burn."[20] He mentally started the novel many times while in the corps, but "because of the flops I had after the war—a veteran's newspaper, magazine—I developed a fixation about writing and went out of my way to avoid it. All the time though, it was doing a slow burn inside me."[21]

The novel was a kind of delayed response to his war experiences, as he made clear in an interview: "I'd been feeling my way along in writing since I was a kid, long before I joined the Marines."[22] Because of the time that elapsed between his combat experience and the writing of the book, "the heat of battle was gone and I probably was not so impassioned about it, less confused than if I had begun it earlier." He added that his best buddy in the marines was Carlisle J. Mendez, of New Orleans, who was killed on Saipan. He based a character in the book on him. Uris also wanted "to decipher Marines as individuals, to explain this strange hold the Corps has on them or why retreat is worse than [fighting]." He hoped it would be a "factual biography" of the corps, with the "Corps itself as the composite hero," that would focus on a "normal group of enlisted officers . . . telling their romances, personal problems and their feelings on being welded into a fighting unit."

In an unusual sign of literary cooperation, after Doubleday turned down the manuscript, Cady wrote to Ted Purdy, Putnam's editor in chief, describing the work. Purdy wired Uris, asking to see the manuscript. Purdy liked it and gave it to his associate, Virginia Carrick, to read. She, in turn, told her husband, Lynn Carrick of Lippincott about it, and he, having been an officer in the marines, contributed advice on some points of marine lore. Editors of three publishing companies "thus had a hand in preparation of the story."[23]

A telegram from New York dated 15 September 1952 reported the good news: Putnam would publish the book.

A contract arrived three weeks later, and he signed it on 10 October 1952. It called for delivery of a 200,000-word manuscript not later than 15 December 1952. He would receive a $500 advance on signing and another $500 on delivery and acceptance of the completed and revised manuscript. On the first 7,500 copies, Uris would receive a royalty of 10 percent of the retail price, 12.5 percent on the next 2,500 copies with 15 percent thereafter.[24] The contract also contained an option for Uris's next novel, and he later reportedly signed a contract for a second work, a newspaper story set in San Francisco, although it was never written.

A book contract, however, did not guarantee control over the manuscript, especially for a new novelist. When Uris received the first galleys of his novel, he immediately noted a change. The first-person narrator, Mac, who begins the book and then introduces four of the six parts, had disappeared. Without consultation, Putnam had removed him from the novel. Incensed, Uris wanted the narrative returned to its original form. A journalist friend at the *Call-Bulletin* who had once been a novelist told him he was at a crossroads: if he rejected the change, the book might be cancelled. If he accepted it, he would be compromised.

His friend then confided that in a similar situation, he had remained silent and accepted his publisher's suggestions, admitting to Uris he had been a fool, "because a man can never go back once he compromises his personal integrity."[25] Uris then made up his mind: "I sucked in a deep breath and after several days of agonizing, I told the publisher the deal was off unless he returned my galleys in the original version. One day after the deadline, the publisher gave in. The trench warfare and gut-wrenching decisions never end, and you must learn to hang tough early."[26] He retells the story in *Mitla Pass* (*MP*, 67–69).

Cady had been critical to the publication of *Battle Cry*, and Uris never forgot him. He acknowledged his role by naming his third child Michael Cady Uris, born in 1953, the year the novel came out. Uris further acknowledged Cady's help by naming the writer accused of libel in *QB VII* Abraham Cady.

With the narrative question settled, the book went into production, and excerpts and galleys received advance praise. Banking on the success of previous war novels like *The Caine Mutiny* and *From Here to Eternity*, and on an early endorsement from the Marine Corps, which allowed the use of its insignia on the dust jacket, Putnam authorized a print run of 25,000 copies. Within the first two weeks of publication, it received 5,000 reorders and gambled on printing another

10,000 copies. Initial sales were higher outside New York, probably because out-of-town papers gave it better reviews. Within six weeks of publication, *Battle Cry* was number two in the nation and had gone through seven printings, eventually appearing in fourteen languages. In August 1953, the Sunday editions of the *San Francisco Examiner* printed a complete serialization of the novel.

Putnam thought so highly of the novel that it prepared an unusual incentive for readers: a money-back guarantee if readers were not satisfied, the first, it claimed, in modern American book publishing. But shortly after publication, Putnam received a testy letter from a reader named Noel Siru, who told the publisher the book was nothing but "rotten tripe"—and demanded replacement with *From Here to Eternity* by James Jones, published by Scribner's. The letter, however, was a hoax. Reversing the letters of the author's name revealed the writer's true identity: Leon Uris, who was echoing a comment from one early editor that the novel was the "worst piece of tripe written in the English language."[27] His sense of humor, confidence, and even arrogance were on display.

One question raised by Uris's novel, however, was its purported accuracy: was it fact or fiction? Anticipating the question, Uris included a disclaimer that addressed what would become a feature of his work: the fictional use of historical fact. At issue was whether to fictionalize the names of "units, ships, battles and places." He could not, of course, fictionalize the entire Pacific war, so he concluded that "to do justice to a story of the Marine Corps . . . a sound historic basis would be the only fair avenue of approach." However, he admitted that "there are many instances where events have been fictionalized for the sake of story continuity and dramatic effect" (BC, 1). Importantly, "story continuity and dramatic effect" were concepts borrowed from screenwriting. History remained the basis of his novel, but it was adjusted to fit the demands of his narrative. Uris repeatedly explained his fictional use of fact, telling one interviewer that "the book is historically true as far as the maneuvers of the troops are concerned but the plot is fiction based upon my own experiences."[28]

In his prefatory statement, Uris identifies his actual unit, the Second Marine Division and, more specifically, the Sixth Regiment, Second Battalion, Fox Company. However, he wants to be clear that the officers in these units did not resemble the "imaginary characters in the book," whose personal habits and outlooks derive from his imagination alone (BC, 1). With this set out, his story begins.[29]

BATTLE CRY

The novel pits inexperience against experience. Framed by the personal narrative of Mac, a grizzled sergeant with thirty years in the marines, the story outlines how a group of recruits are changed from green young men into a fighting unit that was tested by Guadalcanal, Tarawa, and Saipan. They are led by the almost superhuman Major Huxley, nicknamed Highpockets, who thinks nothing of leading a grueling, sixty-mile march with heavy packs in order to best another unit and prove his men the fittest (BC, 358–372). They succeed, but then he insists that they march back in record-setting time as well.

The traditional plot of shaping the untested into effective marines begins at boot camp in San Diego, which Uris presents with vivid empathy. Drawing on his own training and experiences, he spends the first two parts of the novel concentrating on the physical and mental education of the men and their escapades, since women figure importantly in the story.

Drinking and fighting are the main predeployment activities, and Uris provides the details, and when necessary, the sentiment. This is evident when the former high school football star Danny calls his girl back in Baltimore just before Fox Company ships out and each member gets on the phone, drunk and happy (BC, 189–191).

Wellington, New Zealand, becomes the focus of part three as the marines prepare for battle and unhappily leave normal life. Romances begin and end; Uris fictionalized several of his own encounters through the character of Andy Hookans and the widow Pat Rogers. Marion Hodgkiss, another member of the squad, was a short-story writer who timidly brought books and language to the company. His drunken encounter with Major Huxley, however, is one of the more comic episodes in the novel (BC, 221–223). The competition among the diverse set of men, set against preparations for battle, provides tension until they ship out. Botched practice landings at New Caledonia foreshadow their landings at Guadalcanal.

Uris describes battles well, especially their grimness, danger, and triumph. Meeting no resistance at first, the squad is nervously excited to be at last at war, but fear and panic soon take over. Displaying independence and determination, Huxley stands up to General Pritchard of the army by requesting that his men undertake a beachhead assault rather than land after the fighting (BC, 246). Denying Huxley's request but aware of the antagonism between the army and the marines, the general privately admits to his aide that if he were on the lines "fighting for my life," he would call for a couple of marines: "I suppose they're like women . . . you can't live with 'em and God knows you can't live without 'em" (BC, 246).

Uris then shifts to a diary form to tell part of the story, opening on 19 January 1943 as the fighting on Guadalcanal unglamorously begins. Strafed by Kawasaki Ki-108s, the marines are forced to find additional cover. Malaria and jungle rot then begin to ravage the men. When a Japanese soldier tries to infiltrate the marine line, Danny shoots him and then goes out to bayonet the wounded soldier. Uris's writing is disturbingly vivid: "The Jap's hand made a last feeble gesture. Danny plunged the Steel into the Jap's belly. A moan, a violent twitch of his body. . . . It seemed to Danny that his belly closed tight around the bayonet. Danny tugged at his rifle, it was stuck. He squeezed off a shot, which splattered him with blood and insides of the Jap. *The eyes were still open.* He lifted the gory weapon and with its butt bashed madly again and again until there were no eyes or face or head" (BC, 260). Horror and action mix in this passage, equaled by later passages describing Marion's desperate hand-to-hand combat when surprised by a Japanese soldier (BC, 266–267).

An interlude in the battle opens part four, but the men have been changed by the jungle fighting. Despite their exhaustion, Huxley restores full discipline, forcing them at one point to march seventeen miles in the sun. Their return to New Zealand following Guadalcanal allows for romance as well as self-renewal, and Uris interjects opera (Georges Bizet's *Pearl Fishers*), as well as literature (*War and Peace*; BC, 324). Uris's own experience with Betty Cogswell forms part of the story as L. Q. Jones, on a ten-day leave, unexpectedly meets a family and is invited to their home. New characters enter, notably a draftee named Jake Levin, a Jew who must prove himself to his new outfit by accepting every menial task and yet perform them well. When they discover he was once a Golden Gloves boxer, however, he suddenly gains respect. His heroic death while directing a landing craft at the battle of Tarawa is an act that unites him with his comrades (BC, 422–424).

But the return to war soon becomes the focus as another new character appears, Captain Max Shapiro, who is also Jewish; though he has an erratic but courageous record, he shortly proves himself to be a brilliant and brave strategist. A troublemaker and a legend, he is, nonetheless, useful for Uris's revision of the stereotype of Jews as weak and easy victims. Shapiro is brave and tested by battle. Uris at this point also begins to include real names in his fiction: two islands in the atoll the men are about to attack are named "Betty" and "Karen," after his wife and daughter (BC, 388).

The men of the Sixth Marines want to fight, but they are prevented from doing so by the military command. Instead, they back up the assault teams. But as the fierce battle for Tarawa is about to begin, setbacks and confusions dog the landing teams, catastrophic errors that Uris dramatically retells. Many soon die near the island's pier and beach as "Huxley's Whores" finally go in to fight (BC, 399–400, 404ff.). Uris repeats the vivid style he used earlier in the novel, and the Tarawa sections are gripping in their violence. Danny again finds himself alone with a wounded Japanese soldier, although this time he does not bayonet him (BC, 407). Huxley, however, is embarrassed that his men were not in the first assault but the cleanup. Yet stunning images of death and destruction still dominate the scenes, like the description of the radio operator, killed while in position, frozen "erect, his earphones on and his hand on the key of the smashed radio" (BC, 433). Once the battle is over, heat and monotony lead to demoralization and illness.

Part six of the novel opens with "Huxley's Whores" still "bringing up the rear," as Mac complains (BC, 473). Huxley, now a lieutenant colonel, confronts his superior to request a beachhead assault in the next campaign. General Snipes at first refuses but, recognizing Huxley's grit, reluctantly agrees (BC, 448–479). The chance to fight in a new battle lifts the men's spirits. Red Beach One on Saipan is their target, and the remainder of the novel focuses on the landing and violent fighting there: "The blood ran deep under a murderous staccato of careening bomb bursts and geysers of hot metal mixed with spurting sand and flesh" (BC, 488). Death is everywhere. Huxley is wounded after his orderly dies when he throws himself on a live grenade to protect his commander. Huxley loses a leg, but he still tries to command, ordering Mac to return to the command post when the sergeant tries to help the seriously injured Huxley (BC, 491). A final scene at the medical tent reinforces the carnage, which a coda contrasts: Mac, returned to the States, surveys a group of new recruits enthusiastically boarding a train in Baltimore and heading out to war.

Throughout the novel, the dramatic voice of the experienced Mac vies with lapses into sentimentality. Mac's account of the battle of Guadalcanal shows the former. A letter from Huxley's wife and the reunion of Danny with his sweetheart, Kathy, illustrate the latter tendency. But Uris also tricks the reader: early on in the fighting, we conclude that the badly injured Danny dies after being carried to the medical tent on Saipan. Surprise! He is alive. The alternation between irony and sentiment can disorient a reader, creating both alienation and involvement with the characters. Uris's style is often taut, dramatic, and off-color when he is writing about battle, but mawkish and maudlin when writing about romance. And cliché always verges close to overstatement, as this sentence illustrates: "The tingling anticipation of pending action dampened my palms as I plodded on toward the channel which would bring our journey to a close" (BC, 435). Uris strives for transparency, but rhetoric distracts him. In the novel, Uris shows two related worlds, one of hope and romance, the other of reality and death.

Uris is uncritical of the marines and their bureaucracy. In fact, his aim is to present them in a positive light even when the issue is anti-Semitism. Uris shows very little of this prejudice in the novel other than a few comments made to Levin, who will die a hero. His opposite, the legendary Captain Max Shapiro, also dies heroically, showing that Jews are as brave as anyone else in war. Both figures are prototypes of the "tough Jews" who will soon populate *Exodus, Mila 18*, and *Mitla Pass*.[30]

A bloody encounter at Saipan is the climax of the novel, although Uris never fought there. He was sent home to the States because of malaria and dengue fever but felt guilt over the loss of many of his buddies in the fighting. The Saipan section honors the bravery of these men while addressing his remorse for not having been part of the battle. The novel ends with a newspaper account of the American victory on Iwo Jima and the photo of the marines planting the U.S. flag on Mount Suribachi.

A HUGE SUCCESS

Uris's first fan letter, mounted in one of his scrapbooks, indicates early reaction to the book.

> Congratulations, buddy on an authentic novel about the Marines. Sorry it couldn't have been written about the best outfit like the 4th Raider Battalion or the 4th Marines; but you did the best you could with the outfit you know.
>
> Seriously, you have done a first rate job, and I'm telling the reader of the Chattanooga "Times" that you have. I think I know what I'm talking about in a literary way. I know damned well what I'm talking about in a Marine Corps way.
>
> Very truly yours,
> John McCormick
> Roosevelt's Raiders
> 4th Marine Regiment
> 32 months in the Pacific
> 2 Purple Hearts[31]

For Uris, this was exactly the kind of praise he sought. Lieutenant Colonel C. S. Nichols, of the Historical Section of the U.S. Marine Corps, praised the novel in *Military Affairs*, adding that "the dialogue is hard-lipped and an authentic record of Marine jargon of the period, cleaned up just enough to remove it from the realm of smut—not enough to render it unrealistic."[32]

Other reviews were equally positive. The poet, physician, and wartime editor of *Yank*, Merle Miller, claimed in the *Saturday Review of Literature* that Uris may have started "a whole new and healthy trend in American war literature."[33] There was clearly a difference, Miller writes, between novels of the First and Second World Wars. The former expressed hatred for war but not the men and officers who fought in them. The latter seemed to despise both war and warriors. Uris wrote a very different kind of war novel because he was "not angry or bitter or brooding. He obviously loves the Marine Corps, even its officers." This established a new pattern that could influence later writers.

The marines honored Uris for his writing with a medal and a citation at the February 1954 Marine Corps Combat Correspondents Association meeting at the Gramercy Park Hotel in New York. The award was for the person who had contributed the most in 1953 to "public appreciation of the spirit and ideas of the US Marine Corps."[34] Uris was just thirty.

Battle Cry was second in coast-to-coast balloting by book critics for the best novel of 1953, losing to Alan Paton's *Too Late the Phalarope* but coming in ahead of Saul Bellow's *The Adventures of Augie March*. A readers' poll in the *Saturday Review of Literature* likewise named *Battle Cry* one of the best American books of 1953, and it remained on best-seller lists for fifty-two weeks.[35] As proof of its popularity, Bantam Books released 600,000 copies of the paperback in October 1954. *Battle Cry* quickly became the fastest-selling paperback of the year.

FROM THE PAGE TO THE SCREEN

Hollywood, also, did not waste any time. Seeing the immediate appeal of the novel, Warner Bros. bought the film option only a few months after the book appeared. The studio had built its reputation on a series of gritty successes like *The Maltese Falcon* (1941), *Casablanca* (1941), *The Big Sleep* (1946), and *A Streetcar Named Desire* (1951), and now wanted to capture the audiences that were flocking to *From Here to Eternity*. Rumors then started to fly, Louella Parsons writing that Jack Warner wanted John Wayne for *Battle Cry* (in the event, Lex Barker and Guy Madison would test for roles).

Uris, alert to the possibility of new creative challenges and a larger income, negotiated a contract for film rights that saw him hired as the screenwriter, a task entirely new to him. Warner Bros. purchased the rights to the novel in July 1953 for $25,000, a tiny sum by Hollywood standards. But Uris negotiated the right to do the screenplay, which was worth more in prestige, experience, and future dollars. This was also a Hollywood first: the first time a first-time novelist had managed to gain script rights, although the inexperienced Uris would not find the transfer of the book to the screen easy.

Uris began work at the studio on 15 August 1953, moving his family from Lark-spur to 5174 Woodley Avenue in Encino, in the San Fernando Valley, not far from the 110-acre Warner Bros. lot in Burbank. He needed to be close to the studio, and at the same time he was gambling on future Hollywood employment and a possible career as a screenwriter. He was contracted to work on the screenplay for a minimum of four weeks at a salary of $750 a week.

Uris had an office on the lot; in fact, writers were required to work on the lot, and had to report at a certain time and stay until the day was over. This discipline reinforced Uris's own sense of writing as a daily assigned task. As a former marine, he took to the discipline with ease. But on his first or second day, he had a surprise when his secretary casually mentioned that there had been another screenplay with the same title done about ten years earlier. "What? Where is it?" he asked. She retrieved it a day later, and he was doubly shocked when he saw the writer's name on the blue cover page: William Faulkner.

Faulkner had been hired by Warner Bros. in 1942 after working in Hollywood on and off since the 1930s. Money, not art, kept him coming back. Warner Bros. hired him at a salary of $300 a week, which was shamefully low for someone of his stature. But fiction writing did not pay, and he needed money, telling Bennett Cerf a month earlier that he had only sixty cents in his pocket. He had just sent in a new short story, but he worried that it might not sell, and his creditors were getting anxious. Furthermore, options in his contract obligated him to Warner Bros. for the next seven years.[36]

Faulkner authored, first, an original screenplay based on the career of Charles de Gaulle and the Free French movement; it was never produced. His next assignment was "The Life and Death of a Bomber," which was to portray civilian involvement in the building of American bombers. It went nowhere, and for two months Faulkner did little until Howard Hawks chose him for his next war movie, to be called "Battle Cry."

This big-budget film—reported to cost three and half million dollars—was to be an epic with separate sections depicting American, British, French, Russian, Chinese, and Greek resistance to the Axis powers.[37] The film originated with Hawks and his agent, Charles Feldman, who tried to meld five separate properties they owned.[38] A single script would be unique in that it would be an original work rather than an adaptation.

Initially, Faulkner worked alone with Hawks on an outline, which was at one point summarized as the "Defense of Liberty all over the world."[39] The first 140-page treatment was scrapped, however, and a new one started, which eventually extended to 232 pages. But Hawks now felt another writer had to be brought in. Twenty-six-year-old Steve Fisher, who wrote *Destination Tokyo*, joined Faulkner, but at a salary of $800 a week. Fisher did the Russian sequence, Faulkner the Chinese. Faulkner also had the principal role of pulling the separate threads of the story together.[40] Unexpectedly but happily, Faulkner's option was picked up by the studio for another year at $400 a week. He continued to work on the script, writing the French section, and by July a revised 117-page version existed.

The experimental arrangement of the separate episodes in the initial treatment of "Battle Cry" suggests the complicated plot intersections of *The Sound and the*

Fury or *Light in August*.[41] In the midst of revisions and memos, Steve Bacher, an assistant to Hawks, defined the title for him, emphasizing that it is "the sound that wells up out of the human spirit when you attempt to take away from man all those things with which he lived."[42] When such things are threatened, free men will resound with "a defiance, an affirmation and a challenge against which lust and ruthlessness shall not stand," words incorporated into the voice-over that opens the film.

As Faulkner continued to revise with Fisher's assistance, Hawks began the production process; Lauren Bacall screen-tested for one of the roles. But by August 1943, escalating costs had sunk the project. With no production underway, Hawks was about to miss some important deadlines. Faulkner's credited time on the film ended 13 August, but the four-month project had stimulated him to write hundreds of pages. No other studio project before or after would generate so much enthusiasm from Faulkner. But he responded badly to its cancellation, returning to heavy drinking and brooding over his being rejected for a military commission because of his age and lack of education.[43]

Uris must have been startled to discover Faulkner's script, although it differed widely from his own proposed treatment. To find that a writer of Faulkner's reputation (he had won the Nobel Prize for Literature in 1949) had preceded him was a challenge that made him determined to avoid embarrassment. In *Mitla Pass*, Uris praises Faulkner, at that point identifying with the shabby treatment he had received in Hollywood (*MP*, 89–91).

Early publicity for Uris's movie, before he got down to drafting any pages, mistakenly drew from the outline of Faulkner's film, emphasizing the absence of story continuity: *Battle Cry* would be a series of episodes connected by the common thread of the causes that impelled "the united nations of the world in the fight for freedom."[44] This likely resulted from confusion in the publicity department over which film was being prepared.

Uris thought that by adapting his own novel, he would be able to sharpen his skill at storytelling, visualization, and dialogue. He worked assiduously on the project, having frequent meetings with the producer, Henry Blanke, and the director, Raoul Walsh. But his first efforts were not a success, as an unsigned seven-page Warner Bros. memo makes clear. The first problem was length: although it was 167 pages long, it lacked the necessary scene or shot-for-shot breaks of speech, which, when added, would undoubtedly increase its size. "The first urgent need is for cutting," writes the reader, although he finds no ready remedy: "The various episodes seem too meshed and interwoven to give a quick clue to this kind of trimming."[45] This sort of tight construction was a holdover from a novelist's, not screenwriter's, approach. The only effective cutting would be "a dogged, ruthless snipping, page by page, eliminating the scores of small dissolves with their overly-documented facts and dispensing with all the repetitious scenes and situations, of which there are many."

The problem was clear: "The author actually has attempted to transfer bodily from one page to another almost the entire contents of the book." The "sprawling nature" of the story is unsuited for film, which requires a discipline of shape. Actions that could not be dramatized were "still being carried along in exposition," creating tedium and lack of interest.[46] Other points made by the reader: conflicts lack development; there is a great deal of excess emotionalism; the early training scenes could be eliminated because of the familiarity of similar sequences in many other films; Mac's narrative should be reduced and his diction made consistent (he quickly goes from sententiousness to barroom belligerence); figures completely slip out of character at convenient moments; and the general theme of presenting an authentic history of the Sixth Marine Division is obscured. An extensive rewrite was the advice.

Uris renewed his efforts, adjusting the script to the criticism, making the necessary scene changes, and altering the dramatic pacing and dialogue. Yet the studio wanted the script to be like the book and so discouraged any deviation. There was one departure, however, done more to mollify the marines than the studio. In the novel, Danny Forrester has an affair with a navy officer's wife. In the movie, the naval officer was changed to a dollar-a-year man. It was OK to philander on the screen but not above one's rank, commented one critic.[47] In *From Here to Eternity*, however, it seemed acceptable: there, Burt Lancaster had an affair with his commander's wife, Deborah Kerr.

THE ANGRY HILLS

While Uris was revising the *Battle Cry* script, he decided to write a second novel, more or less to see whether he could still do it. He also had fresh material that extended his interest in the Second World War and fighting: an autobiography by his uncle Aaron Yerushalmi, which arrived at Uris's San Francisco apartment in early 1947, secretly smuggled out of British-controlled Palestine. He immediately thought it could be published on its own. Acting as his uncle's literary agent, Uris attempted to place the work. No one was interested.

The 219-page penciled manuscript on onionskin paper was difficult to read: his uncle had filled every bit of every page with text in his small, cramped handwriting. Uris found it a challenge to prepare a synopsis of the material. He later told his Putnam editor, Ted Purdy, that he had been unsuccessful in placing it, but, he added, "I know you'll agree that this is one of the most amazing accounts you have ever laid eyes on and for many years I've begged my uncle to let me retain possession of the MS to use as the basis for a future novel. Right now I feel several years and a couple of books from trying a job the proportion of this."[48]

Uris let the work sit from roughly 1947 to 1953, but still asked Purdy for some advice: "Would the book have any value *as is*? I could write it up straight and do a clean job in six or eight months. Would it have a decent sale?"[49] Impatient, he decided to act: while working on the screenplay for *Battle Cry*, he wrote a first draft of what was originally called "Hellenic Interlude." And he wrote it in six weeks. Why? As he told another editor at Putnam, "First, to prove to myself I could still write and second, against a deadline. I admit it is very sloppy and agree that the final drafting must be done with a great deal of care to tighten up the story."[50]

The result was uneven at best. Drawing only partially from the autobiography—his statement at the beginning of *The Angry Hills* (the published version) suggests a more thorough dependence on that work—he fashioned an espionage novel that essentially focuses on capture and escape. He also concentrates the action in Greece, neglecting the autobiography's account of a German prisoner-of-war camp followed by a move to Germany, another internment camp, and a final transfer and escape by Aaron Yerushalmi in Yugoslavia.

Bob Amussen at Putnam was unenthusiastic about Uris's first draft, explaining that much of the plot was implausible.[51] Why was Michael Morrison, a doctor from San Francisco with no espionage training, given the job of getting a microfilm out of Nazi-occupied Greece? Second, at the point in the war during which the novel is set, the Nazis had not made any progress in the development of the atomic bomb, so would have had no interest in the secrets he was removing; perhaps the plans could involve radar or sonar. An episode involving amnesia was also not believable. Amussen also suggested changing the ending.

Uris's literary agent, Willis Wing, was also skeptical about the story, suggesting the material Morrison retrieves in Greece should not deal with nuclear fission, but neither should it be radar or sonar.[52] He also objected to Morrison's fanciful, even comic, method of secreting the microfilm capsule by shooting himself in the buttock, placing the capsule in the wound, and then cauterizing it with a heated nail. Could this be done, he asked? Uris answered that that he went over it with several doctors, although he admitted to not ever having tried it. "From the look of the two reports," Uris quipped to Amussen, "I write a hell of a lot better in Greek than in English."[53]

While Putnam's editorial group had reservations about the manuscript, the publicity department did not. The fall 1954 catalogue advertised *Hellenic Interlude* as a forthcoming title, stating, "The material for *HI* is authentic. It is drawn from the diaries and notes of Uris's uncle who was in Greece during WWII and was captured by the Germans and had many of the experiences attributed to the hero of the book."[54] Catalogue copy also noted that Uris had recently put the finishing touches on his screenplay for *Battle Cry*.

Uris borrowed the title "Hellenic Interlude" from his uncle's autobiography, in which it ironically conveys disillusionment with British military power. The autobiography documents the deprivation, malnutrition, disease, and danger the British army faced in Greece in 1941. Essentially an account of the Palestinian Brigade, Palestinian Jews who joined the British army to fight in the Second World War and were sent to Greece, the autobiography explores the tension between nature and war, beauty and destruction. After a preface that questions the value of war, it opens with this sentence that sets the register for the work: "From the day we arrived [in] Greece (on 13 April 1941), until we were gallantly taken prisoners of war, only sixteen days elapsed."[55] The work inverts ideas of heroism and action, as Uris had done in *Battle Cry*.

The other register is a lyrical appreciation of the natural beauty of the country, which the autobiographer cannot easily integrate with the brutality of the attacking Stukas, the machine-gunning of innocent people, and the destruction of villages far from the major conflicts. Descriptions of horrible conditions in cells, trucks, trains, and camps alternate with the quiet pastoral beauty of the countryside. Uris reproduced this aspect in *The Angry Hills*, which similarly alternates between brutality and beauty. The cruelty portrayed in Europe oddly balances what he described in the Pacific in *Battle Cry* and prepared him for what he vividly narrates in *Exodus*. The autobiography also contains a great deal of material about life as a prisoner of war, since the uncle was captured several times.

The role of Jews as soldiers is another crucial topic in the autobiography, and it would be instrumental in shaping Uris's own sense of the Jewish hero, a man of action unafraid to risk his life for the right cause. In the autobiography, Jews are fighters, courageous and willing to do battle. But the fighters present a dilemma for the Germans: are they Jews or soldiers, and would the Geneva Conventions apply to them? The answer was not clear.

In the first draft of the novel, there is a great deal of brutality and violence involving Yichiel and his wife, provoking this remark from an editor: "Overdone, even for Belsen—and I don't think US public is much interested now (even if they should be)."[56] Uris, in the early draft, went on to write that by the ninth day of interrogation, Yichiel had spoken "no more than two words since he's been here. There is a constant fire burning in his eyes. I don't think that even death can quench it. Yichiel is a Jew and through his silence I think I've learned more about the Jews than any words or any books. His spirit is beyond defeat."[57] Such determination and intensity will appear more strongly in the Jewish heroes of *Exodus*.

The Angry Hills extends Uris's presentation of Jews, which began with Levin and Shapiro, the two marines in *Battle Cry*. In "Hellenic Interlude," the presence of Yichiel and his doomed wife Elpis, two persecuted Palestinian Jews, anticipates the death and danger experienced by numerous Jews in *Exodus, Mila 18*, and *Mitla Pass*, but also prepares readers for the reverse: the politicized "tough Jews" who became the hallmark of Uris's later writing. Since Uris wrote the novel while he worked on revisions to the script of *Battle Cry*, the two experiences played off each other: the techniques of screenwriting influenced the writing style of *The Angry Hills*, and the subject matter of the novel (Jewish fighters) influenced Uris's approach to his next work: *Exodus*.

Uris acknowledged the importance of the autobiography as a source and imported numerous events from it into the novel: a train ride, an escape, a haunting dead horse in a village square, the massing of soldiers on a beach for an aborted rescue, the indiscriminate bombing of civilians, and the destruction of villages. But he dropped the ironic tone and the POW experience, which were essential to the first half of his uncle's account. Uris translated the singular survival of Aaron, however, into the adventure of Michael Morrison, now an American journalist who spends the entire novel escaping from German agents. Also, Uris did not visit Greece before writing the book, although his later practice was to tour extensively the countries where his novels were to be set.

One of the most significant changes involved the object given to Morrison to smuggle out of the country. In "Hellenic Interlude," it is a capsule of microfilm listing possible troop displacements and scientific data. In the published novel, it is a list ("the Stergiou list"; AH, 88) of Greek double agents working for the Germans. In the novel, the threatened Morrison memorizes the list and rips up the remains. In the first draft, as mentioned earlier, Uris was more ingenious and unwittingly comic.

Oscar Dystel, the president of Bantam Books and soon to become a close friend of Uris, warned him not to publish the novel, believing it inferior to *Battle Cry*. Putnam offered the same advice and turned the book down. Uris did not listen, although at the last moment he questioned the value of its appearance to his new publisher, Bennett Cerf of Random House.

On 22 September 1955, days before publication and on stationery from Hal Wallis's production company—by then he was working on *Gunfight at the O.K. Corral*—Uris sent a night letter to Cerf. With a mixture of cynicism and irony, it read:

ON THE EVE OF THIS INCONSPICUOUS EVENT THE PUBLICA-
TION OF "THE ANGRY HILLS" LET ME OFFER MY SINCERE CON-
DOLENCES ON A DATE THAT WILL LIVE IN LITERARY INFAMY.[58]

Cerf replied a few days later:

YOUR CONDOLENCES ARE MISPLACED. WE LOVE OUR BABY. THINK HE'S BEAUTIFUL AND HOPE HE WILL HAVE A LOT OF LITTLE SISTERS AND BROTHERS IN THE YEARS TO COME. BEST. BENNETT

Uris was the more accurate of the two: the reviews were devastating, as *Harper's Magazine* made clear: "As one who had not read his best-selling *Battle Cry*, I approached this novel with anticipation and excitement. I put it down with astonishment and disappointment. There is a plot here and quick narrative but no writing at all." There were no transitions between events and no "literary quality."[59] A Virginia paper neatly summed up the problem: "Uris now divides his time between writing novels and writing for film. He did not divide it sharply enough here. It is simply the time-worn fable of a native American being caught in the web of international intrigue."[60]

Uris responded to these negative views by continuing with his screenwriting career and with his script of *Battle Cry*. He would soon tackle a project in a genre that would strongly influence his fiction writing: *Gunfight at the O.K. Corral*, a western. And then, through his new agent, Ingo Preminger, Otto Preminger's brother, he would sell a new script to MGM before he even wrote a word of what would become, in revised form, his third novel, *Exodus*.

HOLLYWOOD

4

Every novelist should go to Hollywood. . . . Sure
it's a rat race. Life is like that anywhere.
—LEON URIS, 1955

A LL BALTIMORE SEEMED to turn out for the world premiere of *Battle Cry* on 1 February 1955. The 2,800-seat Stanley Theatre was sold out. The mayor, the marines, city dignitaries, movie stars, and the screenwriter, the Baltimore-born author of the novel, arrived to much fanfare on Howard Street, where excited crowds were blocked off by the police. Inside, the evening began with a marine reserve band rising from the orchestra pit to play the national anthem. Al Ross, a disk jockey, then introduced the mayor, who introduced Uris to great acclaim and a standing ovation, presenting him with a scroll proclaiming him "an honored and outstanding" citizen of the city. Posters plastered downtown had, in fact, announced the premiere of "Battle Cry by our own Baltimorian Leon Uris." Many in the audience were old school mates from City College, his Baltimore high school.

The film star Dorothy Malone, whose mother was from Baltimore, appeared next, and then "the high point in the evening, Tab Hunter . . . who sent several hundred teenagers into a state of delirium. His remarks were punctuated with perpetual small squeals from the audience"; the applause for Raoul Walsh, the director of the movie, was "pale in comparison," wrote a reporter.[1] After more flashbulbs, the guests, including Tab Hunter, left, and so, too, did the teenagers. At eight thirty the next morning, Hunter appeared at the Paramount Theatre in New York, handing out nylons to the first one hundred women who attended the first showing of the film.

The filming of *Battle Cry* had begun once the script and cast were approved. Van Heflin (Major Huxley), Aldo Ray (Andy Hookans), Mona Freeman (Kathy), James Whitmore (Mac), Dorothy Malone (Elaine Yarborough), Raymond Massey (General Snipes), Anne Francis (Rae), and Tab Hunter (Danny Forrester) were among the stars. James Dean screen-tested for the role of Danny, but was turned down.[2]

The director, Raoul Walsh, was a Warner Bros. favorite. He had done *High Sierra* (1941) with Humphrey Bogart, *White Heat* (1949) with James Cagney, and a controversial war movie, *Objective, Burma!* (1945). Its sweeping action scenes showed how a group of American paratroopers, sent as an advance unit into Japanese occupied Burma, reclaimed the country singlehandedly. However, the British resented the film because it suggested they had had no role, and the lord chancellor banned the film after its first showing.

Shooting *Battle Cry* began on Vieques Island, Puerto Rico, in February–March 1954. From the beginning, Walsh decided to treat his actors like marines in boot camp: they slept in tents, were up at five thirty for inspection and drill, and ate with actual marines who were allegedly on maneuvers on the island, offering to "instruct" the actors. The Guadalcanal and Saipan scenes were filmed there over a four-week period. The Marine Corps, which understood the propaganda potential of the film, allowed Warner Bros. use of actual documentary footage, which worked for portions of the Guadalcanal battle, but because the movie was to be shot and shown in wide-angle CinemaScope and the marines had not used anamorphic lenses to record the fighting on Saipan, that battle had to be restaged.

Actual marines filled out the ranks of extras. Huxley's attempt to land and hold the exposed left flank on Red Beach One at Saipan was a major scene. But there were technical difficulties, especially with rifles. As a marine general, acting as a technical adviser, pointed out, carbines were not available for the attack on Guadalcanal, but they were used at Saipan. Studio supply had to fly them in from California before filming of the Saipan segment could begin. Some scenes took three days to prepare, and the twenty special-effects men went through all twelve tons of their explosives within three weeks. Another five were shipped from San Juan. Throughout the filming, Walsh paraded about in his director's garb: cowboy boots, riding breeches, tweed sports coat, and eye patch, lending a rakish air of glamour as well as drama.

The company then moved on to California: Camp Pendleton, Simi Valley, the Warner ranch at Calabasas, and then the large Warner sound stages in Burbank, which were used for the romantic scenes, filmed last. After three months, the rough cut was done, but there was a constant battle with the Breen Office, the office charged with assuring the public that every Hollywood film met the standards of the Production Code. One example from February 1954 concerned language in the script: "They gave in on letting us use the word 'tramp.' They won't budge on having a bed in the Dragon den room where the B girl is rolling Ski.

... Unfortunately, the expression 'hold on to your hats' or any variation thereof is expressly forbidden by the code."[3]

Advertising for *Battle Cry* soon preoccupied the studio and Uris. The initial debate centered on the value of using a suggestive image, perhaps one recalling the memorable shot used to promote *From Here to Eternity*: Deborah Kerr in the arms of Burt Lancaster on a beach, both of them half buried in water. The *Battle Cry* illustration showed a partially dressed Tab Hunter embracing the long-legged Dorothy Malone, who leans back against a table, wearing only a bathing suit. Hunter's arms are tightly wrapped around her shoulders (in the film, Malone, playing Mrs. Elaine Yarborough, suggests the two go for a swim after she invites Hunter back to her apartment). The studio argued that the suggestive picture would shift attention away from the battle scenes. According to the publicity, the film was more about "boys and their babes than it is about battles."[4]

To guarantee public interest in the film, ten weeks before its release in February 1955, Bantam Books went to press three times and printed 900,000 copies. When a fourth printing soon became necessary, *Battle Cry* became the fastest-selling paperback of 1954–1955. A photograph of the socialite Barbara Hutton confirmed the popular impact of the novel. In a newspaper shot marking her return to New York, she prominently clutched a copy of *Battle Cry*. The headline read: "Don't call me Mrs. Rubirosa," referring to her marriage to Porfirio Rubirosa, a Dominican diplomat, polo player, race-car driver, and international playboy. Their marriage lasted fifty-three days. Another publicity photo showed a dancer from *The Ed Sullivan Show* engrossed in the book while backstage.

A *Battle Cry*–themed float in the Tournament of Roses Parade in Pasadena, California, on New Year's Day 1954 provided further exposure. The televised parade—with its "famous books" theme—was seen by millions, and Warner Bros. gained unprecedented publicity. The Marine Corps supplied the personnel for the thirty-foot float, which included an outsized copy of the book made of red and white chrysanthemums. In the front were a seahorse of white chrysanthemums and a landing craft of green galex leaves. The sea effect was constructed of candytuft and blue delphiniums, with a beach made of tan chrysanthemums. Dominating all was the Marine Corps emblem in a wave of gold chrysanthemums. Marines who had seen combat in Korea were positioned coming out of the landing craft, dressed for battle, while two dress marines sat in the back alongside a large replica of the opened book with "Battle Cry" written across its pages. The float cost three thousand dollars to construct.[5]

As production of the film neared completion, Uris discovered a magazine called *Battle Cry*, which promised "Action Packed Tales of Real Combat." Angrily, he asked the studio whether "there [is] anything that can be done legally to put these sons of bitches out of business?"[6] The legal department tried to stop the publication from using the name, but with little effect, especially after learning that the magazine had probably been in print before Uris published his novel in April 1953 (the studio had purchased the rights to the book in August of that year).

Previews began as the final cut was being made; the first took place at the Fox Beverly Theatre on 25 September 1954. Among the invited guests were studio head Jack Warner, Uris, Raoul Walsh, the head of publicity, plus others. Several months later, on 9 December 1954, a press preview was held at the Pantages Theatre in Hollywood.

The Marine Corps commandant, General Lemuel Shepherd, had previewed the movie just days before. On the day of the press preview, he wrote that it was a "tremendous film: recruit camp, wartime field training and the impact of actual combat all achieved a degree of realism which I have never before seen in a motion picture made for entertainment."[7] Nevertheless, he had to withdraw his earlier offer of official Marine Corps participation in promoting the picture. The unstated reason was the moral behavior (or misbehavior) of the marines in the film. In other words, sex.

Columnists were quick to seize on the reasons for the Marine Corps' refusal to support the film, one columnist agreeing that it was overly focused on the salacious: "If all you ever saw of the Marine Corps is *Battle Cry*, you would carry around the impression that womanizing was the first duty of the outfit. You never saw such a lupine bunch. . . . This picture could just as honestly have been called wolf call. Most of the technical advice could have been given by Mae West."[8]

But if the marines and some reporters had doubts, the Navajo Nation did not. The Navajo tribal committee of Arizona officially thanked Warner Bros. for "depicting the heroism and intelligence of the Navajo during WWII in *Battle Cry*."[9]

A month before the general release of the film, in an interview with the *San Francisco Call-Bulletin*, Uris praised his Hollywood experience. Only a few years later his outlook would change.

At the Baltimore premiere, Uris stayed to watch the movie with Betty and members of his extended family, who came from Philadelphia, Norfolk, and, of course, Baltimore. The next day, elated by the adulation and praise, he enthusiastically began a nine-city tour to promote the film, flying first to New Orleans. His father was so thrilled with the event that while stopping overnight during the trip home to Philadelphia in a snowstorm, he couldn't resist signing his son's name to a copy of the book and presenting it to a honeymooning couple that had attended the premiere. As William Uris put it in his autobiography: "Leon! please forgive me for 'forging your signature' which I autographed on their book 'Battle Cry'" (AUTO, 195). The night before, the couple had met both Dorothy Malone and Leon Uris. When told they were his parents, the couple was overwhelmed.

A telegram from Baltimore to Mort Blumenstock, the head of publicity at Warner Bros., gives a sense of the excitement:

> 1 Feb. 1955. Baltimore
> Witnessed greatest movie premiere opening ever Battle Cry Stanley Theatre emphatically stated by Mayor Thomas D'Alesandro, George Crouch, others. Theatre complete sell out twenty four hours advance with turn away crowds in tumultuous crush. . . . [Tab] Hunter overwhelmingly top young star today. Bobbysoxers literally mobbed Tab all appearances.[10]

A controversy soon followed, however. The mayor of Baltimore, who wrote to the president of Warner Bros. requesting the premiere, designated February 1955 as "Battle Cry Month in Baltimore." He, of course, attended the opening, and earlier that day in a ceremony at City Hall had given Uris the key to the city. But nine months later, Uris returned the key because the mayor put his book and 499 others on a list of objectionable literature for juveniles. Other titles included *Mr. Roberts*, *From Here to Eternity*, *The Blackboard Jungle*, and works by Hemingway and Faulkner. The mayor apparently handed out the list to booksellers from the National Organization for Decent Literature.[11]

Battle Cry premiered in Los Angeles on 2 February 1955; the mayor and city council adopted a resolution declaring the date "Battle Cry Day." The film opened in two theatres: the Paramount downtown and the Egyptian in Hollywood. Attendance figures for the Paramount, which showed *Battle Cry* and *On the Waterfront* that day, were close for both films, the seven o'clock showing recording 2,165 for *Battle Cry* and 1,825 for *Waterfront*. Earlier shows that day had closer numbers—and larger crowds because of the Miss Battle Cry contest for women age eighteen to twenty-five. The finalists were selected on the movie's opening day in the theatre lobby. Additional, though less glamorous, promotion was provided by the nine-city tour in which Uris accompanied the film.[12] At the Allen Theatre in Cleveland, for example, Uris sat in a sandbagged foxhole in front of the theatre with two dress-blue marines. It was supposed to represent a radio outpost with Uris dramatically speaking on a radio handset. Other photos show Uris wearing a tie and holding a pipe while autographing copies.

THE HOLLYWOOD LIFE

Uris clearly loved the movies—the attention, publicity, and celebrities as well as the knowledge that thousands, even millions, might see his work. Uris also loved Hollywood; its writing practices set a pattern for his entire career as a novelist, not only in establishing financial standards he felt his work deserved, but also in presenting him with writing habits (set hours, discipline, a separate office, a secretary) and techniques he would employ in all his later work.

Understandably, Uris liked the money, the apparent respect, and the treatment of writers by the studios. He also felt that writing was more disciplined and more professional in Hollywood. Everyone worked hard, as Nathanael West humorously noted: "There's no fooling around here. All the writers sit in cells and the minute a typewriter stops someone pokes his head in the door to see if you are thinking."[13]

In answer to those who criticized writers for selling their work to the movies, Uris replied that he had written *Battle Cry* in an attic, working until two every night after spending the day as a circulation manager for a San Francisco paper. By contrast, he wrote the movie version in an air-conditioned office with a secretary and at a salary of nearly $1,000 a week. Which, he rhetorically asked, was better?[14]

The public, he went on to say, had to realize that "film rights are simply a part of the way the writer makes a living for his family . . . The fact is that few novelists understand the film medium or [are] able to adapt to it."[15] But Hollywood has not always been fun: "I started over a dozen films and completed two. Sometimes I walked out, other times I was asked, not politely, if I would kindly leave the studio . . . Despite the series of failures, I still believe in films. I believe a film can capture the heart of a novel."[16]

The trick to good screenwriting? Giving up control of one's work and realizing that "words are not precious or immortal. I had to take a 505 page, quarter of a million word book and boil it down to 130 typewritten pages of screenplay using dialogue, description and camera directions. In so doing I had to be a ruthless editor of my own baby, deciding largely what would go and what would stay."[17]

Earlier, he had unequivocally—though naïvely—declared that "every novelist should go to Hollywood. It's a great experience. Sure it's a rat race. Life is like that anywhere [but] I believe a writer can keep his dignity there."[18] And soon Uris began to look and dress like a screenwriter-producer. He was trim, athletic, and prematurely gray, and for an interview he "wore a bright red polo shirt, Levis and white leather slippers as he settled behind a five egg omelet and the first of four big glasses of orange juice in his hotel suite."[19]

Uris enjoyed Hollywood, especially the glamour and the openings. In late May 1954, for example, he and Betty attended the premiere of *The High and the Mighty*. Betty Uris's blue lace dress and velvet coat stood out against the floodlights, while Uris's tuxedo, given to him by a writer at Warner Bros. and altered by the studio, fit him perfectly. They had driven their Singer slowly past a barrier, their police pass prominent in the window, and stopped across from packed bleachers and six floodlights illuminating the Hollywood sky. The crowd cheered the unknown couple as John Wayne greeted them and the three had their picture taken. Then Uris and his wife walked down a roped-off carpet to the entrance of the Egyptian Theatre. In the lobby, a smiling Uris autographed a large promotional poster propped up for the stars to sign. Phil Harris, Jane Wyman, Fred MacMurray, Robert Stack, Virginia Mayo, Joan Bennett, and Victor McLaughlin were there. Uris met Ronald Reagan in the men's room.[20]

At this moment, the twenty-nine-year-old high school dropout, ex-marine, and author of the recently published novel *Battle Cry* was poised at the edge of renown. A trailer before *The High and the Mighty* showed a few scenes from the unfinished *Battle Cry*. The evening at the Egyptian represented the world Uris eagerly wanted to join and anticipated the one he would achieve. Within four years, with the publication of *Exodus* and *Mila 18*, he would become one of the best-known and most successful novelists in America and beyond, honored by governments, sued by collaborators, and acknowledged to be one of the most important storytellers of his generation. He was a writer who chose history as his subject, research as his method, and narrative as his technique. But in the spring of 1954, Uris was still finding his way, capitalizing on his war experiences, building a career as a screenwriter, and attending to his wife and three children. It was an exciting time, one that confirmed his determination and anticipated his forthcoming fame and financial success.

The script of *Battle Cry* exhibits his best early effort with the form. He truncated the novel so that the multiple stories of the individual men and their women became the focus—there isn't even a hint of fighting until eighty-four minutes into the film. The voice-over narration of Mac throughout differs from his voice in the novel, which was essentially limited to the prologue of each of the six parts. Additional changes were made to meet the Production Code guidelines and to streamline the story line. And yet for all of these changes—the Saipan battle is the only extended fighting, and that comes in the last fifteen minutes or so of the film—there are some passages taken verbatim from the novel. Most notable is the exchange between Lieutenant Colonel Huxley and General Snipes. As Huxley recklessly stands up for his men and their determination to take a beachhead rather than be kept in reserve to mop up, as at Guadalcanal and Tarawa, some of the dialogue comes from the novel, including the final exchange in which Snipes, at last, reveals some humanity.

Several other scenes are visually stronger than their counterparts in the novel, notably the sixty-mile march. The snaking line of marines marching in formation to and from Foxton, brutally suffering on the return but determined to either outpace the driven Huxley or show up the First Battalion, which chose to return to Camp McKay on trucks, is dramatic. The battle scenes on Saipan are similarly vivid, not so much in the individual details, which are strong in the book, but in the larger scenes of the marines following the armored personnel carriers across the fields while being attacked by hidden Japanese machine-gun positions. The injury to Huxley occurs behind a cloud of smoke as he crosses a swamp, and his chest wound and Andy's effort to help are powerfully rendered (in the novel, Huxley's leg is blown off and it is Mac who tries to help him [BC, 491]). But when Huxley manages to pull out his .45 pistol and order Andy to leave him and return to the command post, it seems more like a moment in a western than in a Second World War drama set in the Pacific.

Other adjustments were made to language. Whereas Uris's novel is direct and conversant with marine lingo and idiom, the film seems cleaned up. "Huxley's Whores" in the novel become "Huxley's Harlots" in the film. And where insult, anger, and anti-Semitism have a role in the novel, they disappear or were sanitized for the movie. Much is made of the code-speaking Navajos in the film; one scene shows the Japanese tapping into marine radio lines but being unable to decipher the language of the two Indians conveying important military information. Sentiment also colors a great deal of the romance in the movie, especially the love between Marion and Rae, which flourishes until he discovers she is a hooker (although he is conveniently killed off in the novel and film, ending any chance of marrying her).

Reviews of the movie alternated between temperate and enthusiastic. The *New York Times* complained that it was another patriotic and eager tribute to the military, this time the marines, whose prowess as lovers exceeded that as fighters. Yet the critic noted also that there is a kind of Rover Boy innocence to the film, which is tied to melodrama.[21] When Huxley's body is carried back to camp on Saipan, his men, after a moment of grief, silently pull out their long bayonets, attach them to their rifles, and charge off into the jungle to avenge his death. A pattern of rectitude pervades the film, the critic suggested, occasionally leavened by limited humor, as when the radio operators are caught sending coded, off-color limericks. This is cited twice in the film but not once in the novel.

The success of *Battle Cry* meant more work for Uris. The studio assigned him to director Nicholas Ray, who had a new project titled *Rebel Without a Cause*, a study of juvenile delinquency. Uris was enthusiastic about the project, which got underway in the late summer and early fall of 1954, and he spent ten days as an apprentice social worker in juvenile hall to learn about the problems of juvenile offenders. He also rode with police officers to see how they handled challenges on the street. For Uris, this was crucial research—much as being a marine had been for the writing of *Battle Cry*. An unsigned 7 October 1954 memo to the producer expressed enthusiasm for Uris's interest, noting that he was once in charge of forty boys for the *San Francisco Call-Bulletin*.[22] Uris threw himself into the research, as did Ray. However, when Ray saw Uris's first efforts at a script, he was unhappy.

Dated 13 October 1954, the five-page sketch, headed "Rayfield," stressed the placid middle-class town and world of the parents, not at all what Ray wanted. He sought something dealing with attitudes and behavior of the unruly young. A week later, Uris prepared a twenty-four-page treatment that was better balanced between the middle-class parents and the rebellious adolescents but written with too much tedious detail and too many descriptions of faults, petty interests, and parental bickering. The view was too small-town, and not universal enough. Uris also blamed the teenagers' delinquency on the fact that they lived in a housing project, an angle that Ray definitely opposed. Ray wanted Uris to drop the intellectual approach and tell the story directly. Uris needed to get into the heads of the teenagers.

By November, Uris had prepared a second draft with more focus on the kids, not the families, but Ray was still unhappy and wanted another writer. Uris was taken off the film for reasons that seem similar to the early critique of the *Battle Cry* script: too detailed, not enough drama, and too little expression of the characters' psychology.

Although Uris did not write the screenplay, an image from Uris's treatment of *Rebel* remained in the movie: a scene in which Jimmy covers the sleeping Plato with a jacket. Uris also boldly suggested how Amy (to become Judy and be played by Natalie Wood in the film) sought, and was starved for, her father's affection. Ray suggested something of this, along with the motif of possible incest.

THE DEVELOPMENT OF A STYLE

Uris's scriptwriting taught him the value of the visual. Not surprisingly, he began to conceive of events cinematically, with the visual dominating his writing: he saw history and conveyed that experience to the reader. Details as well as encounters are visual. Dress, movement, background, and action are all seen with the eye. From film—and later, photography—he learned to create images that matched his narrative skill. He read histories, reference books, memoirs, and letters as much for their images as for information. The need to balance images and narrative in films taught him where and how to begin a scene, often with action that introduces a character and then follows events guided or plotted by history. Uris learned to write, or at least refine, his style while working on scripts for the studios.

Uris had a modest narrative talent when he started, one shaped more by urgency than structure. But by completing the final manuscript of *Battle Cry* and then working immediately on the screenplay, he refined his writing skills. He combined politics, history, and action into a strong narrative with a visual foundation, often dangerous but always romantic. Some writers see a conflict between being a novelist and being a screenwriter, but Uris linked the two, bringing the techniques of screenwriting—a crisp presentation of character supported by sequence and scene, plus narrative and continuity—to his fiction. He also understood the importance of audiences and the reach of films, whose viewers far exceeded the readers of novels. So why not try to write for them? That was his goal and the explanation for his approach and appeal: to gain an audience. Throughout his career, he often wrote adaptations of his own work: *Battle Cry*, *The Angry Hills*, *Exodus*, *Topaz*, and *Trinity* (unproduced).

Uris's style was not literary but reportorial: direct, colloquial, understandable. It was unsophisticated, but, like him, it was immediate, popular, and clear. A hit with readers but not critics, he sought audiences not awards. Writers with causes were his models: Steinbeck, not Fitzgerald. He rarely challenged history. Rather, he adapted it. Fact was always mixed with fiction, even when the story was drawn from his own life, as in *QB VII*. This novel, based on his 1964 trial for libel in England, became a dramatic fictionalization of the characters' lives and a reliving of the horrors of the Holocaust. His construction of the final courtroom scenes, however, differs from the details recorded in the trial transcript, a work he prized and kept on display in his New York apartment. Yet readers loved the novel and turned it into another best seller.

Again, it was by visualizing his story that Uris could help his readers imagine the past intensely. For example, the preface to the third part of *QB VII* is a history of the Royal Courts of Justice and a portrait of British legal practice (*QBVII*, 203–209). The following section, on the formal opening of the legal year, which begins with the lord chancellor and his procession, is worthy in its detail of Cecil B. DeMille (*QBVII*, 209–212), although after the panorama, Uris zooms in on a single conversation between the lord chancellor and a prospective court nominee, Anthony Gilray. Throughout Uris's fiction, passages display cinematic properties, including multiple camera angles, fully blocked scenes, and pointed dialogue, thereby offering a corollary to Walter Benjamin's remark that "history does not break down into stories but into images."[23]

Uris understood the strength of images. Not surprisingly, he took pictures while researching his novels, later referring to them for context, detail, and setting. Boxes of slides and photos from research for *Exodus*, *Mila 18*, and *Trinity* form an archive of thousands of images. His third wife, Jill Peabody, was, and remains, a photographer, and they produced two photo books together (*Jerusalem: Song of Songs* and *Ireland: A Terrible Beauty*). He also published *Exodus Revisited* with a Greek photographer.

Uris took pride in his screenwriting. In 1961, a critic noted that he was the first novelist he knew to number his screenwriting credits along with his novels in his list of works. And since all his novels at that point had been made into movies, "he must indeed think of himself as a writer for the screen."[24]

Screenwriting was, in short, critical for Uris's development as a novelist. Whether writing the screenplay for *Battle Cry*, or a fight film alternately titled "The Fighter" or "Ringside," or drafts of *Rebel Without A Cause*, or adaptations of *Exodus*, *Topaz* and *Trinity*, Uris improved the craft of his storytelling through film writing. Scene, sequence, and structure became a resilient formula for him—but sometimes with difficulty. After struggling with the fight story for the producer Milton Sperling, Uris was given a shot at "The Billy Mitchell Story." That also failed, but such setbacks did not deter him from spending many evenings seeing movies, including *The Cruel Sea*, *The Caine Mutiny*, and *On the Waterfront*.[25] Such viewing was not just for pleasure.

Uris learned to write screenplays by studying them. In his early days at Warner Bros., he asked to see several classic films and made notes on the use of certain shots for emphasis, the role of camera angles to heighten dialogue, and the importance of editing in moving from scene to scene. *Mitla Pass* describes the use of this study method during a screening of *High Noon* (MP, 83). The result of this effort would be Uris's most important film effort, the original screenplay for *Gunfight at the O.K. Corral* (1957).

Flashbacks, close-ups, long shots, zooms, inserts, dissolves, fade-ins, pans, and establishing shots, as well as cuts, intercuts, foreshadowing, and tracking shots appear in Uris's fiction. Often, his novels seem storyboarded, as if the plot had been rendered in a series of sketches with a line or two under each drawing expressing the main action. Uris, who worked with large charts of characters, time lines, and maps of the action, seemed to have absorbed the process of filmmaking as well as of screenwriting. He structured many of his novels on a vivid sequence of scenes that develop the narrative line of action. His novels often seem to be constructed like scripts, as if he began with the ending, moved to the beginning, and then carefully placed the plot points. Dramatic construction, determined by history and the constant need to move forward, shapes his stories, which rely on the common screenwriting practice of eight sequences within a three-act frame or three-part structure.[26] Production values always seem to be on his mind, reflected in his use of exotic locales, detailed settings, and often-remarkable dress.

Uris's research assistants—he used them repeatedly—were like script supervisors, who make sure shots and action match while ensuring continuity from scene to scene. They also keep details of the daily shooting sequences for themselves and the film editor. One of Uris's research assistants when he was writing *Trinity* detailed her daily habits: gathering the previous day's pages for proofing, copyediting, and retyping, then following up on notes (queries regarding details or information, or requests for additional research materials) he left on four-by-six-inch slips of paper.[27] One example from October 1974 is a request to a Mr. Colin Robertson: "I would like to know," Uris begins, "what the standard British Army light weaponry consisted of during the Boer War (1899–1902). That should include a rather detailed description of the infantry rife. Was this a bolt-operated clip containing several bullets or a single shot weapon?"[28] He also wanted particulars on the officers' pistols as well as on the kind of dynamite used by sappers at that time.

In the afternoon, Uris and his assistant would spend several hours reviewing the progress of the story, research projects related to the manuscript, or outline new topics. She also reminded him not to get lost in the historical aspect of his project, posting a large sign that read "THIS IS A NOVEL" over his typewriter. Research subjects could include the weather in a certain area of Ireland, the type of bullets used in a particular gun, or the quickest route through the backstreets of Ulster. And because she was a poet, Uris asked her to compose poems that the characters might write at certain points in the story.

Steinbeck, Uris's favorite novelist, also employed cinematic and dramatic techniques, although it was not until his fourth novel, *Tortilla Flat*, that he made a sale to Hollywood. But after the 1936 sale, he developed a strong interest in the mass audience of the movies and what could be done to attract them. Certain scenes in *In Dubious Battle* (this can be said of Uris as well) seem written for the camera. Action and dialogue, not internal revelations of character, describe the work of both writers. The opening sentence of *The Red Pony*, which Steinbeck adapted for the movies, is typical: "At daybreak Billy Buck emerged from the bunkhouse and stood for a moment on the porch looking up at the sky."[29] Uris's *Mila 18* opens with "drops of late summer rain splattered against the high window which ran from the floor to the ceiling" (*M18*, 2). Pictorial narration was common to both writers.

Any number of Uris's novels extend the techniques of film. *Exodus*, for example, opens with an establishing shot: a plane landing, with the words "WELCOME TO CYPRUS" by William Shakespeare (from *Othello*, act 4) immediately visible, and then a quick close-up of Mark Parker, followed by a cut to the distant hills of the northern coastal range. A medium close-up of Parker standing in the aisle precedes his encounter, also in medium close-up, with the Cypriot customs inspector, which occurs before he learns that Kitty Fremont is unable to meet him. A wait for a taxi after being interrupted by a fellow traveler comes next. A flashback to the lives of Kitty and her now-deceased husband accompany him in the cab, interspersed with comments on the history of Cyprus, generated by his arrival in Nicosia. Flashbacks to Mark's own life balance those of Kitty and her husband, Tom. In six pages of text, Uris generates a montage effect as the overlapping images and narratives continue until Mark arrives at Kyrenia and the Dome Hotel.

Techniques from screenwriting and film are used throughout the novel: the use of dates to introduce each episode echoes the title boards used in silent films to mark the passage of time, horrific close-ups show Dov Landau working in the gas chambers of Auschwitz (EX, 148), and the figurative use of tracking and crane shots dramatize the escape from the Acre prison, one of the highlights in Otto Preminger's film of the novel (EX, 438–448).

Other moments in Uris's fiction that incorporate similarly cinematic features include the dramatic encounters between German officers and Jewish officials of the Warsaw Ghetto in *Mila 18*, which are often backlit and posed. In the meeting between the leader of the Polish Home Army commander, Roman, and the Jewish soldier Andrei Androfski, the latter pleads for guns and support while "Roman leaned against the window sill and bit on the ivory holder with the studied gestures of one who knows he is on stage" (M18, 364). In *QB VII*, a wide-angle, panoramic shot captures the Canadian and British attack on Dieppe while the hero of the novel, Abraham Cady, flies overhead with a squadron of American Eagles; this shot is followed by a zoom-in on his battle with three Messerschmitts, during which his plane is hit and dramatically limps to a British airbase. The scene alternates between close-ups of his attempts to fly and medium shots of his disabled Spitfire eventually landing (QBVII, 103–106).

Trinity, Uris's epic account of Ireland from 1845 to 1916, unites many of these techniques in a novel structured as a sequence of large scenes supported by the interaction of characters. Whether it is the discussion between Caroline Hubble and Conor Larkin of the provenance of the great Jean Tijou iron screen at Hubble Manor (TR, 355–361) or the brutal military tribunal that passes a fifty-year sentence on Larkin for his attempted arms smuggling (TR, 618–620), Uris employs cinematic elements to convey the drama. Perhaps no episode is more effective in combining cinema and fiction than the dramatic Londonderry shirt-factory fire, which takes place in Chapter 14 of part four. A series of crosscuts show the sixteen-year-old Terry Devlin emptying the ashes and cinders from the stoves needed to heat the irons to press the shirts (cinders he spills begin the fire), two girls who join others on the roof of the building to enjoy seventeen minutes of sunlight and fresh air on their break, Lord Roger staring in disbelief at the growing fire from the distance of his office, and finally the attempted rescue of the nearly seventy women on the roof, more than half of whom leap to their deaths. Uris provides an effective alternating rhythm of distance and detail, danger, and destruction that is entirely cinematic (TR, 385–392).

GUNFIGHT AT THE O.K. CORRAL AND THE IMPORTANCE OF THE WESTERN

Showcasing the techniques Uris learned while writing the *Battle Cry* screenplay and the piecemeal work that followed was an original screenplay he wrote in 1955–1956, *Gunfight at the O.K. Corral* (1957). Written for Hal Wallis and directed by John Sturges, this western showcased what Uris had learned from his Hollywood assignments: how to blend camera angles, dialogue, and action through such techniques as fade-ins, continuity, panorama shots, and the three-act, establish-develop-conclude structure.[30] He began work on *Gunfight*, based on the magazine story "The Killer" by George Scullin, in June 1955 (Paramount took him off the unproduced "Night Man" for this project), and he finished the "final white" copy in March 1956. *Gunfight* displayed his new métier best, and he, in turn, transferred what he had learned from writing movies into the construction, narrative, and characterization of his later books.

Uris had from the outset a clear idea of the character of Wyatt Earp in the film, which differed from the portrayal in other treatments. Essentially, he saw Earp as "a man with problems," not a legend or a hero.[31] An early biography emphasized Earp's nobility, and a more recent television series stressed his violent and possibly unsavory past, including the chance he was an accomplice in a stagecoach robbery. Uris diverged from both views, preferring to see a psychological figure, "a lonely, unhappy man haunted by the death of his young wife and also by his own reputation as a fearless gunfighter." To Uris, the story of Earp was "not of a hero but of a human being, a man frozen within himself." Consequently, Earp fights off every human element in his life. When he meets Doc Holliday, his opposite, they unexpectedly become friends, Holliday recognizing him as his alter ego.

Uris's work on the script showed his willingness, at least at the outset of his career, to accommodate and work with others, notably the producer, Hal Wallis. As a neophyte screenwriter, Uris listened to Wallis, who made it clear, for example, that there was a problem with continuity as well as with the simplistic presentation of the Wyatt Earp–Doc Holliday friendship. Holliday was a killer, and Earp perhaps the most outstanding lawman in the West, yet Uris had to show how they grew to respect each other. Uris solved this problem, as he would solve later ones when editors he respected (such as Howard Cady and then Ken McCormick) objected to plot devices, poor characterizations, or excessive detail. Screenwriting was Uris's writing workshop.

Gunfight at the O.K. Corral opens with three figures appearing in the distance and riding against a deep blue sky toward the camera, with appropriately dramatic music by Dimitri Tiomkin establishing tension. Uris would repeat such openings in his fiction, beginning with *Exodus*, which opens with a plane swooping down on the island of Cyprus, prefiguring an entrance into a world of anxiety and danger. *Mila 18* begins with a similar sense of anxiety: a diary entry stresses German intentions and the writer's fear. Most directly imitating the *Gunfight* opening is the beginning of *QB VII*: an indistinct figure runs toward a guard hut in a field near Monza, Italy, in November 1945. The lone figures that cross the landscape in *Gunfight* repeat themselves in the opening of *Topaz* when three CIA officials head to the White House to brief the president on the Soviet missile buildup in Cuba. Even his last novel, the posthumously published *O'Hara's Choice*, opens with a lone figure riding a horse from Quantico to the post road in Virginia, across the Potomac from Washington. Such establishing shots of a lone figure or group set against a vast landscape, emphasizing isolation and potential danger, were common in westerns and irresistible to Uris.

But *Gunfight* offered Uris more than the chance to improve his technique; it dramatized a series of themes that he would elaborate in his own work: brotherhood, heroism, the sacrifice of women to a greater cause, male stoicism masking anger, and an ability, increasingly restrained in his later work, to portray complex relationships governed by an ironic respect for opposing figures. The relationship between Wyatt Earp (Burt Lancaster) and Doc Holliday (Kirk Douglas) seems oppositional at first: Earp represents the law and virtue, Holliday, killing and immorality, but Uris structures his script to show the common bond of the two interwoven figures.

Uris relied extensively on the conventions of the western for this screenplay and his later fiction: the traditional opposition between law and violence, the conflict between social and legal borders. *Gunfight* elevates and refines the separation between the city, where social custom and right behavior reign, and the country, where the landscape is unbordered and lawless. Appropriately and ironically, the final, climactic gunfight occurs in a corral (a bordered physical space) at the edge of the town, yet one large enough to allow for acrobatic self-defense involving a bridge, a gully, a covered wagon, and several sheds while also offering an escape route to the country. The corral is a metaphor for the value and necessity of separating law from disorder. Importantly, the film is about containment and the need to restore and maintain borders.

In his later novels, Uris sought to reinvigorate the myth of the frontier, transporting it to other countries and thereby altering Frederick Jackson Turner's view that it had become exhausted and involuted. Making a nation, in fact, is the theme of Uris's largest novels, *Exodus* and *Trinity*; sustaining a belief in nation building defines his next two most important works, *Mila 18* and *QB VII*. Uris coupled the continuation of the frontier myth with the western and with European history to reinforce resistance to a host of historical and political forces that threatened to dismantle or overrun minority groups or outsiders like the Jews or Irish.

Borders enforce and maintain the separation between order and disorder. Uris would express this view through the maintenance of divisions between Palestine and its Arab neighbors; or between the Warsaw Ghetto and the invading Nazi troops; between the vestiges of a cultured Europe and the anarchy of Auschwitz; between a besieged, airlift-dependent Berlin and Soviet expansion; or between Ireland and the invading British. The frontier, for Uris, was an essential means of dividing order from chaos, justice from crime. So the western was the pre-eminent genre for Uris because it codified and reinforced essential separations between culture and anarchy while offering a parable of the American Dream. But equally important was the notion that the frontier is a concept not bound by time or place.

The western supplied archetypes that Uris found useful throughout his writing: heroes and antiheroes, strong men of virtue and weak men of evil. *Battle Cry* might be thought of in these terms: it is no accident that Captain Max Shapiro dies with his two pistols blazing at the attacking Japanese during the battle of Saipan, falling to his knees as his guns empty and he is shot (BC, 498). Uris also drew on the western's inherent structural element of conflict, which is necessary to create drama. A sympathetic character put in danger increases tension and involves the viewer or reader emotionally. Also, the visual, external focus of a director challenged to portray character in film affected Uris's style of portraying characters in fiction. He rarely if ever reveals the inner life of his subjects because he follows the cinematic principle of showing rather than telling, using action rather than thought. Inner conflict or doubt rarely has a place in Uris's fiction or the American western.

Uris could transpose the western to other lands and overlay its romanticism with socially engaged, crisis history. Israel, Poland, Ireland, or Cuba could be the site. "You can write westerns in any part of the world," he affirmed in 1976.[32] The genre possesses that flexibility, as numerous critics have emphasized. Additionally, by employing the western, Uris was able to elaborate a kind of pioneer individualism that marries the mythical to the historical. In a sense, Uris did not accept the passing of the frontier; he simply found it in other places and times. This takes on a comic form in the costume Gideon Zadok wears to a Jerusalem party in *Mitla Pass*. He goes as a cowboy, and is called that by the smoldering Natasha Solomon, the Hungarian survivor he meets and has an affair with (MP, 309–315). Later in the novel, the image becomes conflated into a composite figure when Natasha tells him, "I love mean little five-foot-eight, Jew, cowboy, writers" (MP, 421). Uris even titles one section of the novel "High Noon," an homage to the classic western film (MP, 398). Earlier, at the end of *Topaz*, a Parisian cabdriver congratulates the protagonist, Michael Nordstrom, after hearing that the Russians have removed their missiles from Cuba: "You are tough guys, like cowboys." "Sometimes" is the reply (*TO*, 341).

The western genre had yet a further dimension that appealed to Uris: an undisputed moral clarity. Good and bad were self-evident. Rarely could there be a mix-up; indeed, they might even at times be united, as Doc Holliday realizes when he tells Wyatt Earp that they are essentially the same. They prove this when they later fight together to dismantle the Clanton gang. In *Exodus*, Uris shows the importance of underground organizations like the Haganah, a Jewish paramilitary organization, in justifying the moral right of Israel to exist, even if its tactics meant bloodshed. Illegal immigration was the only way for Israel to establish itself; in *Trinity*, the Irish Republican effort was the only way to oppose British exploitation of the country.

Another feature of the western is violence expressed through battle, often at the cost of justice. Wyatt Earp's bringing of order to Dodge City and later to Tombstone, where he goes to aid his brother, is not unlike the earlier struggle of the marines to overcome the melee and violence they face on Guadalcanal and Tarawa in *Battle Cry*. A series of later fighters also battle to establish justice, order, or morality. Ari Ben Canaan stands out in *Exodus* but so do Andrei Androfski in *Mila 18*, Abraham Cady in *QB VII*, and Conor Larkin in *Trinity*. "There's no better plan than a bullet," says the cowboy Roy Rogers in *Young Bill Hickok* (1940), summarizing the attitude and action of many of Uris's characters. And it is no accident that one of Ari Ben Canaan's weapons is a bullwhip, a characteristic tool in a cowboy's arsenal.

Not surprisingly, violence permeates Uris's work. From *Battle Cry* to *O'Hara's Choice*, it dominates. It might be the slaughter at Tarawa in *Battle Cry* or the Arab attacks in *Exodus* or the flogging of Conor Larkin in *Trinity*, but Uris's work expands a tradition of violence that has defined not only the western but also much American writing.[33] For Uris, violence became a way of solving problems. Interested in boxing from a young age, in the marines he fought, and managed a fighter, and later wrote a screenplay titled "Ringside." He understood the power of violence and did not shy away from it. History, of course, confirmed this behavior, whether it was the Jewish resistance fighters in the Warsaw Ghetto, represented in *Mila 18*, or the description of the medical experiments at Auschwitz, retold in *QB VII*.

Heroes, especially male, were an additional feature of the western that appealed to Uris. Hard, masculine, brave, isolated, and unwavering, they fulfilled Uris's need to create figures who showed no fear, no emotions, and no doubt. They seemed to act beyond reason. "I don't just do something. I stand there,"

Clint Eastwood uttered in 1992, summarizing the posture of moral and physical courage expressed in the western.[34] Uris rejected ambivalence; hence, his characters act rather than think, fight rather than talk. The awkward or wooden dialogue in Uris's work reflects the western's tradition of minimal speech.

But *Gunfight at the O.K. Corral* also departs from the western genre in several ways: in the creation of a sophisticated female gambler of uncommon beauty who likely unites—or so we think—with Wyatt Earp at the end, in the fashioning of a dandified antihero fated to die because of his tubercular cough (Doc Holliday), and in the establishment of a complex relationship between the male protagonists, who seem at first to be antagonists, unexpectedly coming to depend on each other (this is reminiscent of a number of the relationships in *Battle Cry*). Uris also created a moderately ambiguous ending: following the violence of the shootout, Earp renounces the law, throws down his badge, and heads to California, perhaps to be with his love, Laura. Earlier, although intending to marry her, he had left her to help his brothers in Tombstone fight the Clanton gang. His commitment to uphold justice remained unwavering, as acknowledged by Holliday's benediction as Earp leaves: "So long preacher," he mutters, referring to Lancaster's virtuous, uncorrupted behavior.

Holliday, by contrast, displays savoir faire. Sitting down at the end to gamble yet again, he offhandedly remarks, "Gentlemen, what's the name of the game?" He, too, has given up a woman: the not-always-righteous Kate, with whom he had a love-hate relationship. Such separations of the hero from the heroine anticipate what will happen with Dov Landau and Karen in *Exodus*, or Conor Larkin and Atty in *Trinity*. The union at last between Ari Ben Canaan and Kitty Fremont in *Exodus*, or between Sean O'Sullivan and Ernestine Falkenstein in *Armageddon*, follows from a romantic formula Uris had difficulty resisting rather than from complex characters' demands for union. History—or genre—prevented such psychological connections. The western and the romance, the two overarching genres for Uris's work, alternately contrast and intersect throughout his novels. His heroes and heroines often define their love through resistance or opposition—much like characters in a western, who often start from opposite sides of political, emotional, and even cultural fences.

A final point about *Gunfight*: Uris replaced historical accuracy with imagined structures and altered events to meet the needs of his narrative drama. The shoot-out depicted in the film, for example, is entirely fabricated. In the film, Jimmy Earp is made the youngest brother and is killed before the showdown; in actuality, James Earp was the oldest brother. And none of the Earps were killed before the shoot-out. Furthermore, Ike Clanton did not die in the shoot-out at the corral, and the Earps, though lawmen, had competing cattle interests with the Clantons. Some historians even suggest that the Earps and the Clantons had warrants for the others' arrests.[35] Such historical displacement in favor of story would characterize Uris's later work.

In 1970, Uris explained his technique as writing "within a framework of basic truth and credibility."[36] Less mythological than John Ford's account of the same gunfight in *My Darling Clementine* (1946) but less realistic than John Sturges's *Hour of the Gun* (1967), another version of the shoot-out, *Gunfight* and its success—its total U.S. gross at the box office was $11,750,000, bumped up with $4.7 million in rentals—validated Uris's method. Often, however, he would sacrifice genuine historical complexity for the sake of an epic-sized image.

For Uris, the western and its mythology offered a conceptual structure loaded with devices for defining differences and identifying codes between classes, cultures, and races. Uris also expanded the genre's use of pseudohistorical narrative in his historically driven fictions while showing that human heroism, whether in the Warsaw Ghetto or during the Berlin airlift or in Tombstone, Arizona, could shape the course of future events. He even experimented with the genre in a script called "The Gringo." In the way that he generously borrowed features of the western and applied them to moments of European crisis or Middle Eastern history, he seemed to be suggestively following Chico Marx's comic dictum: "I'd like the West better if it were in the East" (*Go West*, 1940).

The western gave him a style not just for his language but for his dress: cowboy hats and jeans were often his preferred form of attire, as the author's photo on *The Haj* (1984) illustrates: a smiling Uris wears a large cowboy hat and a western-style winter coat. The décor of his Aspen, Colorado, home, where he lived for some eighteen years, was an eclectic blend of the Southwest and the Middle East.

DISILLUSIONMENT WITH TINSELTOWN

Hollywood, the origin of Uris's writing practice, also became his greatest burden. His later work with Otto Preminger and Alfred Hitchcock would further his skill, although not his success as a screenwriter (they each fired him from their projects).[37] Hollywood also taught him how to finance his work. By selling the options for books not yet written, he was able to obtain the funds necessary for his travel and research. This was his technique for *Exodus*, *Mila 18*, and *Armageddon*. Only later did he shift to a new form of financing his writing: the three- or four-book deal, which resulted in a large sum that was payable in increments over several years.

But at the outset of his career, the movies financed Uris's travel and research. MGM, for example, footed the bill for his prospective Israel novel (originally to be a movie script), while Mirisch Productions paid the expenses for research "behind the Iron Curtain," as the papers phrased it, purchasing the option for the film rights of what would become *Mila 18*. In 1959, following the success of *Exodus*, he signed with Columbia Pictures for what was believed to be the first multiple book-film deal in the movie industry.[38] Uris also tried to produce the films made from four of his novels. And years later in *Armageddon*'s "Note of Thanks," Uris acknowledged "Columbia Film Studios, which sponsored my research" (AR, n.p.).

Uris later turned against Hollywood, believing that the writer was no more than "the court jester": "He's probably the only one with any brains, but he's the only person you can change over ten times."[39] Like many writers, Uris became disillusioned with Hollywood because it refused to listen to what he wanted to say and certainly did not give him any artistic control. He was fired from a production of his second novel, *The Angry Hills*, starring Robert Mitchum, because the producer felt he did not understand his own characters. Otto Preminger fired him from *Exodus* because he believed Uris would not satisfy how he, as director, thought the novel should be transposed to film. And Alfred Hitchcock fired him from *Topaz* because he felt Uris wanted too much control over the work.

Uris then sought to produce his own work, holding on in particular to the rights to *Mila 18* and *Trinity*. But various possibilities never coalesced, and he was unable to assert the artistic or financial authority he sought. But he remained completely fascinated by the movies and never lost his self-confidence or his desire to make in it the movies. Screenwriting continued to fascinate him: in August 1964, for example, as soon as he had finished a story treatment of a projected western for Paramount, "The Gringo," he immediately began the screenplay of *Armageddon*. And up to his death, he worked and reworked a screenplay of *Trinity*.

Mitla Pass (1988) interestingly summarizes his negative view of Hollywood. After success with his first movie, called *Of Men in Battle* in the novel, the hero becomes a successful script doctor and impresses a studio head, who offers him a three-year deal, producer credit, and a hefty salary. He rejects it, declaring that the freedom of a novelist is worth more than the money he might earn. "The town is stacked against writers," he tells his wife, who is eager for the stability and income he is turning down (MP, 84). He even invokes Faulkner and his unhappy time in Hollywood, but this does not satisfy his wife, who urges him to accept the deal. The best he can do is to pursue the chance to write an original western, which in reality becomes *Gunfight at the O.K. Corral*. The fictional Gideon Zadok, modeled on Uris, displays a negativism toward Hollywood that Uris himself tried to temper, because even as an independent producer, he knew he had to work with the studios.

Uris learned quickly the difference between the movies and publishing:

the studios had cash, which they were willing to advance, while publishers had good intentions but small bank accounts. However, he would soon finesse the "generosity" of the studios into lucrative book contracts.

The early filmmaker D. W. Griffith once said, "People don't go to the movies to read."[40] It might be said that people don't pick up a Uris novel for the style. They read his work for a story told in vivid scenes that he makes immediate and real. The movies made Uris's novels possible; Hollywood taught him a method of writing while underwriting his projects. In a letter from the fifties, in fact, he suggests to a friend that he might want to become a producer, although the pull of literature was greater.[41] Authors, he thought, might be remembered, while producers could only become rich.

EXODUS, OR "THE BOOK"

In all directions we are surrounded by history.
—LEON URIS, *EXODUS*

I
T MAY HAVE ARRIVED when an American tourist handed a copy to a Jew while standing on a train platform in Lithuania. Or when the son of the Israeli consul general in Leningrad passed it on to a group of dissidents. Or when a German copy, secretly sent to refuseniks in Riga, began to appear in a Russian translation, which took an hour a page to type and nearly a year to complete. No matter how it got there or what form it took, *Exodus* in its samizdat (self-published) version became an underground Russian classic of the seventies that led, in the words of one refusenik, to "the national rebirth of Jewish youth in the Soviet Union."[1]

The story of Leonid Feldman from Moldova, then part of the Soviet Union, highlights the danger.[2] He was astonished when he heard that his sister's boyfriend had been arrested for reading a book. Although unsure of the title, he decided to read the book himself. Three years later, he waited one night at eleven in a dark corner of a park. He was handed a heavy briefcase. "Take a taxi and go home, but you must return with the manuscript to this spot by seven a.m., finished or not," said the courier. "No one must know what you've done." No one told him that reading it was dangerous. No one told him the title; it was known only as "the book." "Have you seen 'the book'?" "Who's got 'the book'?" many would quietly ask.

Feldman, a former chess champion, was then a twenty-one-year-old high school physics teacher. "The book," however, changed his life: he could explain the principles of relativity but not Abraham and Isaac. He had never heard of the Torah and didn't know Jews had been around for 4,000 years. From "the book" he learned of the Holocaust and that Hitler had hated Jews and Russians. Angry when he ended his reading because his government had lied to him and taught him to hate himself, he became a different man.

"When I finished that book, I was another Leonid Feldman," he declared in 1988. The book led to an application for immigration, a refusal, a confrontation with the KGB, prison, a hunger strike, and finally freedom. Travel to Israel and America followed, as well as study at the Jewish Theological Seminary and ordination as the first Conservative rabbi from the Soviet Union. He credited Uris for "making me a free and a happy man."

Persecution was not limited to the 1970s. In 1985, Leonid Volvovsky was convicted of slander for distributing anti-Soviet literature, namely, *Exodus*. Several months earlier, a Hebrew teacher in Odessa had received a similar sentence. For Soviet Jewish activists, *Exodus* was more meaningful than the Bible, read not as literature but as history. To honor the work, Russian Jews titled one of their earliest underground samizdat typewritten publications *Ishkod*, the Russian word for "exodus."[3]

The translations, of course, varied, since each translator's knowledge of English or German could range from the rudimentary to the sophisticated. Many translations were inaccurate and incomplete. One version by ideological Zionists entirely dropped the love affair between Kitty and Ari because they could not accept a Jew having a romance with a non-Jew. The samizdat editions were also remarkably uneven in their appearances: sections were typed on different kinds of paper and in different typefaces, because different typewriters had to be used to avoid detection (all typewriters were registered with officials; owning an unregistered private typewriter was then illegal in the Soviet Union). Private citizens could not own duplicating machines either, so carbon paper, difficult to obtain, was used, but burned each night after a page or two had been translated. Bindings were often simple, and translations frequently lacked a title page. It was considered reckless as well as dangerous to be circulating a censored book— hence, its designation as "the book."[4]

An Israeli who served in the embassy in Moscow from 1959 to 1962 reported that he and other members of the staff gave away many copies of the paperback version of the novel after it appeared in 1959.[5] Copies arrived through diplomatic pouches as part of a Mossad operation. This important edition included a statement by Uris on the novel (the statement was dropped from later reprints). Emphasizing the miracle of the rebirth of a nation, Uris celebrates the heroic restoration of a people and a land in colorful prose. *Exodus*, he writes, "tells the story of the Jews coming back after centuries of abuse, indignities, torture and murder to carve an oasis in the sand with guts and blood." *Exodus*, he emphasizes, is "about fighting people, people who do not apologize either for being born Jews or the right to live in human dignity."[6] No one opening the book could overlook this declaration, which preceded the title page.

Surprisingly, *Exodus* did not begin with Uris but with a vice president of

MGM, Dore Schary. A former screenwriter who had won an Academy Award for the 1938 hit *Boys Town*, Schary was a politically active Jew who had lectured on anti-Semitism to soldiers during the Second World War. In the early forties, he rose through the ranks at MGM, but quit when the studio rejected his attempt to make a parable about Hitler and Mussolini in the form of a western. Schary was a religious Jew at a time when most Jewish studio executives hid their faith; he also strongly supported Jewish organizations.[7]

By the mid-1950s, some seven years after he returned to MGM, now as vice president of production, he thought it was time for someone to write the story of the new state of Israel—which he, of course, would then film. At the time—1955—Uris's agent Malcolm Stuart of the Preminger-Stuart agency (Otto Preminger's brother Ingo was a partner) was visiting studios to seek funding for a Uris film project loosely related to the new country. Stuart had proposed the idea of writing on Israel to Uris one day at lunch. Ingo Preminger then suggested that Uris go to Israel to conduct research.[8] Schary knew Uris was a novelist who was making a name for himself as a screenwriter, or, as he preferred to be called, "Hollywood writer." It was a match.

Uris had sensed the dramatic possibilities of the story of Israel from his writing about the Palestine Brigade—Jewish fighters for the British—in *The Angry Hills*. However, he at first thought the topic too complex and vast. He also lacked a formal Jewish education, did not read or speak Hebrew, and was not even a bar mitzvah. But he wanted "to find the anatomy of a miracle," the rebirth of Israel, and when Schary offered him $7,500 as an option for the as yet unwritten narrative, tentatively titled "The Big Dream," Uris felt confident enough to undertake the project—with implicit support from Random House for a possible book on the topic.[9] He signed a contract with MGM in January 1956—although in the round-robin of studio politics, Schary was fired from the studio nine months later, partly because he was a politically active "egghead."[10] When informed of his firing by the new head of Loews, which then owned MGM, Schary offered another reason for letting him go: he was studying conversational Hebrew.[11]

Uris had initially put off writing the story of Israel because of the amount of preparation and information needed to do the job. But he began to learn more about the country, starting with a meeting with Netanel Lorch, the Israeli consul general in Los Angeles and later author of *Edge of the Sword: Israel's War of Independence, 1947–1949* (1961). He also began to amass a large reference library and soon felt he could do the work with proper support and preparation. *Battle Cry* had grown out of his immediate experience, and *The Angry Hills* from his uncle's autobiography; *Exodus* would emerge initially from study, reading, and travel. He spent three and a half months reading nearly 300 books, immersing himself in the history and politics of the region. He also gave up smoking and undertook a new, though modest, regime of physical training: daily tennis with an instructor.[12]

At the start of his work, Uris was still unsure whether he should continue with the well-paying career of a screenwriter or seek the more lasting (but less lucrative) career of a novelist. He decided to finesse both by accepting the movie option for a screenplay-book yet to be written. This way he could have his Hollywood income precede his royalty advance and then use it to fund his trip, while also ensuring the existence of a film whether or not the book was a success. He also recognized that whereas a reputation as a screenwriter would be inadequate for his ego, being known as a writer might ensure some longer-term popularity. He also felt he needed to resurrect a faltering career as a novelist after the dismal reception of *The Angry Hills*. A novel about Israel might be the answer.

Uris also had a personal motive for writing the book: the reexamination of his own Jewishness. Until then, he had never identified strongly with Judaism or religion. The history of the Jews meant something to him culturally, but not spiritually and certainly not personally. But the image of the "soft" Jew angered him, and he was determined to replace it with one of strength. He undertook to recast Jews as tough and resilient heroes rather than submissive victims. This was a projection of his own self-image as a battle-tested marine, independent character, and outspoken defender of justice. And if necessary, he would never turn away from a fight. As his father commented in an interview shortly after *Exodus* appeared, "He was a strange boy. I have never known such will power."[13]

The narrative Uris constructed of the Israeli past—the resistance of the Israelis to British and Arab aggression (Uris always linked the two)—confirmed his belief in Jewish strength. He undertook to do no less than remake the image of the Jew in the post-Holocaust world. But he also realized that to succeed, he had to create a dramatic and universal story that would appeal to a non-Jewish world, especially in America.

But the story would be his, in both its passion and its identity. The image of the freedom fighter on the book jacket of *Exodus* expressed Uris's own tough and aggressive self-image. This took emblematic form when he later had the wrought-iron gate to his Aspen, Colorado, home shaped into the figure, bordered by two Stars of David. In a not so subtle way, Uris signaled to visitors that he, too, was cast in this manner. The Saul Bass logo for the film *Exodus*—four arms reaching up in the air with a fifth holding a rifle—would be equally powerful.

In an early letter to his mother, Uris tells her that he has learned how to fight, something that Israel, a country of fighters, mirrored.[14] Ever since joining the marines, he had seen himself in this way. "I was tough. I used everything to my advantage. I could be ruthless. I hurt a lot of people on the way up," Uris boldly told an Associated Press interviewer some years later.[15] He was also inspired to write the novel because he was "thrilled by the Israeli army. Jews in the field kicking hell out of somebody. They'd stopped apologizing for being Jews. I wanted to stop apologizing too. I wanted to write an affirmative and aggressive book about the Jewish People."[16]

From the outset, Uris was clear about his audience as well as purpose: "I am not writing this book for the Jews or the Zionists. I am writing this book for the American people in hopes I can present it in such a way that Israel gets what she needs badly . . . understanding."[17] Once committed to the project, Uris read histories, memoirs, government reports, autobiographies, and the complete transcript of the Nuremberg war-crime trials. He also spent time making contacts, initially through the Israeli Foreign Ministry. Uris saturated himself with accounts of Judaism and the history of Israel before he left, reading stories of the Irgun (a militant Zionist group that operated in British Palestine) as well as the efforts to establish the Israeli army.

Exodus was not, of course, the first novel to deal with the establishment of the state or the history of the Jews.[18] Earlier novels had presented the refugee problem, the life of the early settlers, Zionism, and the fight with the Arabs. Arthur Koestler's *Thieves in the Night* (1946) and Zelda Popkin's *Quiet Street* (1951) are two of the earliest, although Meyer Levin's *Yehuda* (1931) was the first fictional account of life on a kibbutz in modern Palestine. Koestler's work, subtitled *Chronicle of an Experiment*, focused on Arab and Jewish tensions before the British withdrawal and partially builds on the years 1926–1929, when Koestler lived in Palestine, first as a farm laborer and then as a correspondent. Uris was aware of the book, citing it as one of the few that deeply engages with the problems of the region.

Exodus differs from these earlier efforts in a number of ways: Uris prepared extensively before he departed for Israel; he had Israeli support during his visit; he was determined to set the rebirth of Israel within the larger context of Jewish history and immigration; and, perhaps most importantly, he wrote for non-Jewish readers and against the stereotype of the victimized Jew. Uris also worked hard to publish the novel on the tenth anniversary of the state, thereby gaining immediate publicity and sales for his work (he missed the date by only three months). But it appeared at a time—September 1958—when Jewish writers were being embraced by the mainstream American readers.

URIS IN ISRAEL

In May 1956, just after he arrived in Israel—Uris landed on 13 April 1956 via Copenhagen and Rome—he outlined his approach to the story to his father. He sought to correct romantic visions of the country and its heroes: "I must caution you again. I am writing a book for Americans . . . Gentiles . . . not for the Jews. . . . I must show her as a human place and not an ultra-glorious utopia. . . . The real Israel . . . is a nation of young Marines . . . The fighter knows Israel was won by a gun and it will be saved by a gun. . . . The spirit of Israel is the strength of her fighters."[19]

Israel welcomed Uris as a minor celebrity. He was known to the public as the author of *Battle Cry*, and his standing was enhanced when a special showing of the film took place in Jerusalem two weeks after he landed. Uris attended and donated a number of autographed copies of the novel. In the advertisements for the event, he was identified as "Leon Uris-Yerushalmy," a reversion to his father's original name. An invitation from the U.S. ambassador to Israel to attend a Fourth of July celebration was typical of the reception he received. But sometimes his prominence worked against him. At a gathering of some five hundred at the Edison Cinema in Jerusalem, for years a site of secular European and Zionist culture and one of the largest movie houses in the city, the audience questioned him about his work and that of other leading twentieth-century novelists. He admitted he hadn't read them. "Uris was no intellectual," Ilan Hartuv, his Israeli guide, who was present at the evening, recalled.[20]

A former mayor of Kiryat Shmona, Hartuv came from a family of first pioneers. However, a quarrel with Golda Meir, then labor minister, led to his resignation as mayor, but he did join the Labour Ministry itself and then the Ministry of the Interior. Soon he was transferred to a junior post in the Foreign Ministry, where he was assigned to assist Uris in his research and travel. During the eight months they spent together, Hartuv acted as translator, secretary, and facilitator. He was not, however, a driver. Uris preferred to do that himself.

Uris was eager to meet military commanders and see battlefields. Hartuv suggested that he also meet Arabs and Druze (members of an Islamic sect, mainly in Israel, Lebanon, and Syria). Hartuv also introduced him to Moshe Pearlman, himself a widely published author (*The Army of Israel* [1950] among other titles) and for a short while the army spokesman. At the time, Pearlman was working for Teddy Kollek, who was soon to become executive director of the prime minister's office. Uris even had a late-night meeting with Yigdal Allon, a former Palmach commander (the Palmach was the strike force of the Haganah, the precursor to the Israel Defense Forces).

Hartuv facilitated Uris's meeting a number of important fighters and leaders of the country, beginning with Joseph (Yosefle) Tabenkin, a former Palmach commander of the Harel Brigade who was instrumental in securing a route to Jerusalem in 1948, which allowed supplies to be brought to the city under siege. Yigael Yadin, the second chief of staff of the Israel Defense Forces, was another source, as was Moshe Dayan, the defense minister, although Uris's four-hour meeting with Dayan became no more than a long critique of the prime minister, Moshe Sharett. (Sharett was not interested in meeting Uris.) Uris and Hartuv learned more about Dayan from meetings with his sister and parents.

Uris also spent time with Shumel Tamir, a lawyer. Tamir had had a prominent role in the Irgun, taking part in operations against many British targets, notably the February 1944 attack on the income tax offices in Jerusalem. In 1946, he was deputy commander of the Jerusalem district and in charge of the Irgun intelligence unit in Jerusalem. Uris also briefly met Golda Meir. At all of these interviews, Uris took notes, using a tape recorder only to record his own personal impressions of events.[21]

Hartuv taught Uris about Israeli history but could not get him to correct his intentional errors. The attack on the prison at Acre, which led to the rescue of Akiva and Dov Landau in the novel, was the most egregious (EX, 438–448). ETZEL (the Irgun) led the actual attack, but in the novel, Uris blends the group into the Maccabees, led by the Haganah commander Ari Ben Canaan. This would never have happened. Uris knew it was incorrect but insisted on attributing the action to his hero: he needed to show him in command. After the release of the film, Hartuv had to meet with Menachem Begin, the former commander of the Irgun, to calm both him and a delegation. He explained that although the actual group that did the deed was obscured, "you come out quite well" in the movie and book.[22]

Hartuv took Uris to Cyprus, where they met a Cypriot merchant in Farmagusta, Prodromos Papavassiliou, who had helped Jews escape from British deportation camps and reach Israel (he is Mandria in the novel). "Papa," as he was known, offered assistance to the more than 52,384 Jewish refugees interned in the camps between 1946 and 1949.[23] Hartuv later returned to Cyprus with Otto Preminger for the filming of *Exodus*, and subsequently worked with Uris on *Mila 18* and *Exodus Revisited*.[24]

Uris drove, walked, and even flew for his research. One of his most exciting trips was a secret flight to bring out refugees from Yemen, which he makes the focus of Chapter One of Book 5 of *Exodus*. To his father, he wrote that they flew into Iran and returned: "The big moment was when the plane sighted Israel. Whooping, applause and crying... quite touching. These people were from deep in the hills and very backward."[25]

By June 1956, Uris had finished most of his travels, although he still had to go to the Negev, which proved to be one of his most memorable adventures. The first American to be taken on a patrol of the desert (where the temperature hit 120 degrees), he joined a squad of sixteen Israeli paratroopers. The route was through ravines and wadis, over slate fields and mountains, crisscrossing the path of Moses and the Twelve Tribes along the Egyptian and Jordanian borders toward Eilat. The journey was so memorable that he later recounted it in *Mitla Pass*. But there was also plenty of danger during Uris's visit: a bomb went off outside his hotel window in Nicosia, he was shot at by Arabs in Jerusalem, and he was only seven miles from a major battle on Israel's border with Jordan.[26]

With his research almost complete, Uris set himself up in a third-floor studio overlooking the Mediterranean at the Accadia Grand Hotel in Herzlia. The hotel, proud to have the writer, donated the room, which he transformed into an office. Its balcony overlooked the sea, and it was there he began to sift through his notes, taped interviews, and slides. Uris had photographed wherever he went, and he used these images to refresh his eye when writing about episodes and landscape. After his return to the States, he would often show friends slides of his travels around Israel. In total, he would cite (allowing for some exaggeration) twelve thousand miles traveled, almost two thousand interviews, two miles of recording tape, 1,500 photographs and more than six hundred pages of notes, all from Israeli sources.[27]

But in midsummer 1956, there were still further interviews and research to conduct and people to see, although he hoped to be home, he told his father, by mid-July.[28] However, he soon realized he needed more time in Israel and decided that he wanted to write the story there. Staying in Israel was important for Uris because he could continue his research and write with the conviction and authenticity he needed in order to complete the novel. He asked Betty to fly over with their three children and their dog, Duffy.

He also grew more confident about his story and approach: "I believe it will be like a breath of spring air for the American people to meet Mr. Avi [*sic*] Ben Canaan, the fighting Jew who won't take shit from nobody . . . who fears nobody. He will be a departure from the Mailer . . . Morningstar apologetics."[29] The work of Jerome Weidman (*Enemy Camp*) and Meyer Levin was also an anathema to Uris, who wanted to underscore the aggressive Jew, the strong Jew. Levin's *The Old Bunch* (1937) and more recently *Compulsion* (1956), about the Leopold and Loeb murder case, contradicted Uris's perception of Jews as active and forceful.[30]

The arrival of Betty, with Karen (age ten), Mark (six) and Michael (four), on 2 August 1956 meant a new phase of life for Uris, who had located a home for the family on the edge of the Sharon Valley near Tel Aviv but close to the Accadia Hotel. Surprisingly, Betty and the children adjusted easily, and she also took up home teaching duties, instructing Karen and Mark. Most of their neighbors were South Africans, and the husbands were away in the army. The situation seemed ideal—with the Mediterranean behind them, the Sharon Valley in front, and green surrounding their home—at least for three months.

But Betty was indifferent to her husband. The likely cause was her suspicion that he had a girlfriend. In fact, he had several; the first and longest affair was with an

Israeli who worked as a flight attendant for a Czech airline. Uris met this woman through a taxi driver–tour guide named Hans and carried on with her for several months, spending long hours with her at his hotel and seeing her at every opportunity. He wanted her to move to America, and eventually arranged for her to immigrate to Chicago. She went, although she had little more to do with Uris.[31]

Uris's behavior in Israel occasionally led to controversy. During a trip to Eilat, he met a woman in a restaurant and soon took her back to his hotel room. When Hartuv returned later to the hotel, the management anxiously greeted him outside. "Something terrible has happened," they told him. "Uris has a *woman* in his room!" Histadrut, the Israeli national labor union, which owned the hotel, did not condone such behavior. The manager insisted Hartuv act. What could he do? He rang Uris and explained the situation. Uris promised that the girl would be gone in a few minutes. Nearly an hour later, she left.[32]

Uris's only unsuccessful conquest was his attempt to seduce the head of a bureau in the Defense Department. The woman wouldn't hear of Uris's propositions, because she was most likely involved with Moshe Dayan, who was known for such pursuits. On another occasion, a woman Uris admired asked for a room adjacent to his at the Accadia. It was eagerly arranged, but to his disappointment, she simply wanted a water view to enjoy a weekend with her husband.[33]

In September 1956, Uris wrote a full description of his progress to his editor: it was time to let him know "what the hell is going on with the Kosher *Battle Cry* (as Dore Schary has dubbed it)."[34] He described his family situation and his free room at the Hotel Accadia, which was furnished "to my working tastes. I have a balcony overlooking the sea. . . . I am hoping to take one or two breaks during the writing of the book to kick over a few quick money magazine articles." In the lengthy and detailed summary that followed, he expressed confidence in the quality of his work.

At ten o'clock on a Monday night in late October, he heard a radio bulletin: "Israeli paratroopers have landed near the Suez Canal." At first, he and Betty felt no direct danger and decided to take things day by day. But by the following afternoon, events were moving swiftly, and as fighting raged in the Sinai Peninsula, the American government warned its nationals to leave.

Fighting continued until 7 November, when Prime Minister Ben-Gurion gave a victory speech in the Knesset, although pressure on Israel by the United Nations, the Soviet Union, and the United States not to hold the occupied land led to a partial withdrawal, which was announced the next day. In March, Israel left the occupied land, replaced by UN forces, although passage through the Straits of Tiran had been established with Eilat becoming an open port, significant for its allowing the development of the Negev and the building of an oil pipeline between Eilat and Beersheva.

Uris, of course, had no idea of the big picture. On Monday, November 5, he went to Tel Aviv to investigate a possible escape but all outbound airlines were booked for weeks and commercial flights were discouraged because of the danger of Egyptian bombing. Fear of his family being trapped made him anxious, and late in the afternoon he went to visit Sholem Asch, the distinguished eighty-year-old Yiddish writer then living at Bat Yam. "I did not bargain for putting my family in danger and losing two years' worth of work," he told him. Asch replied, "The book will be written if you are the kind of writer I think you are." "Will you leave?" Uris asked. "This is where I belong. I am a Jew and a writer," Asch answered.[35]

But Uris had to get his family out: if there was any chance of danger to the children, they and Betty had to leave. He would stay behind and try and report on developments. Uris then contacted the U.S. embassy, and was told by his friend Colonel David Peterson, an air attaché, that he should depart. For the rest of the day, Uris and Betty debated whether to go or stay, but on Monday night, tension increased as Israeli troops tore across the Sinai. Tuesday morning, the embassy advised all Americans to depart, and he drove to Tel Aviv to book a flight out, but there was no space. At three he was in Colonel Peterson's office, where he was given a memo authorizing him to get the family on a U.S. rescue flight. It tersely read: "Please assist Mr. Leon Uris to complete arrangements for the evacuation of Mrs. Uris and her three children." But before Betty Uris and the children could go, she had to sign a statement saying she accepted transportation provided by the United States government "on a reimbursable and space available basis."[36]

Overnight, Israel went from peace to war with "terrifying efficiency," as Uris wrote in a dispatch to the *Philadelphia Inquirer* (written on Accadia Hotel stationery) during the fighting.[37] Men quickly departed to designated assembly areas and moved silently to the borders as cars and buses came off the roads to clear the way for military transports. Colonel Peterson had told Uris that four Globemaster cargo planes were expected from Germany that night and that he and the children should get to Lydda Airport immediately for evacuation.[38] This time there was little hesitation. By candlelight, the family rapidly packed what they could into their marine seabags and in a blackout drove toward the airport, Karen having painted out the headlights on their car. Before they left, Uris wrote out a series of cables for Betty to send when they arrived safely. In less than an hour, they loaded their Austin and headed to Lydda, which was difficult to locate even in daylight.

They arrived to join hundreds of others in the dimly lit terminal, where suitcases and people were piled high. There seemed to be little hope during the six or seven hours of waiting. Karen and Mike dozed, but Mark, age six, began to cry. Uris took him aside and explained to him how wonderful it was to be an American and "so important that they would send a real army airplane all the way from Germany just for him." When his son said he wanted his father to come, Uris gently explained "that a writer had to stay on the job always."[39]

While they were waiting, the news broke that Britain and France had issued an ultimatum that they be allowed to occupy the canal and mediate between Israel and Egypt. Betty, who had been so courageous, broke down, asking to be taken home. The thought that the fighting might end, added to her fear of being separated from Uris, convinced her to postpone their departure. Uris said no, the danger was still too high. At two in the morning—after they had been at the airport seven hours—there was a report of the planes approaching, and by three the mammoth aircraft had landed. When he saw the crew of "cocky clean cut American lads emerge. . . . I knew at that moment [that] my taxes . . . were well spent and my wife and kids were safe."[40] They moved through customs, fed the children Dramamine, and said a scared and heartbroken good-bye. At four he walked with them to the giant Globemasters, flying boxcars, and the long ramp that led into its cavernous cabin. Embassy personnel in a panic raced ahead of them. But everyone got on swiftly in the rush to get airborne before daylight and possible attack from the Egyptian air force.

As others boarded, they handed Uris their loose change, but in the haste, a woman in the crowd slipped and broke her leg, a memory that remained with young Mark.[41] Uris ran into the plane and kissed them all good-bye, and then with a friend, Bob Zion, stood on the runway and watched the belly close and "gobble up our families."[42] The plane roared down the runway into the stars. "Soon it was silent." He then slipped his hand into his pocket and felt a piece of paper: the list of things Betty had left for him to do. He smiled when he read the first item: "Cancel my appointment with Boris the hairdresser."

On 4 November, he received a telegram: "ARMY TRANSFER ROME BEAU-TIFUL WAIT INSTRUCTIONS UNTIL WEDNESDAY CARE AMERICAN EMBASSY LOVE/BETTY."[43] The planes had flown first to Athens and then on to Rome, where the family was safe.

Uris then began what he would call the shortest career of any war journalist, filing three dispatches, the first being a dramatic account of his family's departure. His second details a trip to the border settlement of Nahal Oz, which straddled the Gaza Strip, to report on the murder of a young farmer-soldier. Uris attended the funeral and witnessed the determination of the settlement to continue: "There were no tears on that sun baked mound, no hatred . . . everyone knew his job and repeated a silent vow never to quit." Moshe Dayan, the Israeli chief of staff, had come for a wedding, but now he spoke a eulogy that reinforced the courage of such settlements.[44]

In his third "battle report," Uris summarized a trip into the Sinai, but before he could get anywhere to cover a story, the fighting ended. "Even in these days of souped up warfare, the Israeli cyclone must have set some sort of record," he writes in his dispatch.[45] Unable to get his family back into Israel because of an American "blockade" and unable to earn any money by selling a series of stories about the Sinai campaign to the Hearst chain, Uris decided to pack up. Reluctantly, he left Israel on 29 November on KLM flight 286 from Tel Aviv to Rome with five pieces of luggage, including Duffy (the dog), but not before issuing a public statement on his departure. In a short letter of gratitude, he wrote: "I return to America with but only one thought. To write a book worthy of our people."[46] His reunion at the Hotel Regina Carlton with Betty, who was under the weather from the ordeal, and the children was joyous.

WRITING *EXODUS*, HOLLYWOOD DISTRACTIONS

Back in America, Uris understood the difficult job that awaited him, which he described as "the decision of what to use and what to omit, and how to use the facts fictionally." The goal remained not to tell the story of Israel for a partisan audience "but for the average American who shares a tremendous moral heritage with the Jews of Israel."[47]

In New York, Uris spent time with his East Coast agent, Willis Wing, and his publisher. He thought Random House would publish the book, and a tentative contract was drawn up, but he realized that it did not provide what he believed would be enough money for him to devote himself exclusively to the project. He and Wing decided to explore other possibilities, and they went to Doubleday, where years later Uris's editor Ken McCormick recalled the scene and Uris's enthusiasm: "I'll never forget the time you came in to talk to Brad and myself about EXODUS. You paced up and down the office and before you were through, the room was full of that novel."[48]

With Doubleday, Uris and Wing shortly negotiated a three-book contract dated 25 February 1957. The first work was to be an untitled novel on Israel; the second, an untitled novel on boxing (likely based on his unproduced 1954 screenplay "Ringside"); the third would be an unspecified novel (which would become *Mila 18*). Uris received a lucrative advance of $25,000, including $7,500 on signing, making it possible for him to devote the coming year to writing what would become *Exodus*. Uris and the family returned to 5174 Woodley Avenue in Encino, where he would begin work in earnest.

The actual writing of *Exodus* was a labor and not always of love. Some weeks it moved swiftly, others slowly. Uris admitted that it was often hard to sleep after spending "eight or ten hours describing Auschwitz or Treblinka."[49] He was also ironing out minor contract details with Doubleday; a formal announcement was to be made in ten days. He and Betty were also thinking about moving, partly because of freeway construction near their home: something more rural with, perhaps, a pool and tennis court he told his father.[50] He also mentioned the changing title of his book: originally "The Big Dream," it became "The Land is Mine," then "Awake in Glory," and then "Exodus." Another alternative was "Beyond the Jordan," but Uris objected to it. *Exodus* was picked and dropped fifteen times before it became the final choice.[51] He also reported that his former mentor, Howard Cady, has just taken over at Putnam and that Ted Purdy, his former editor, has become president of Cowan-McCann.

In the midst of writing the work, Uris offered opinions about his contemporaries, dismissing James Jones and vilifying Norman Mailer, especially for *The Deer Park*. Both writers, he felt, should be forgotten because their work was driven by "hatred and confusion and distrust of human beings."[52] Herman Wouk was overrated but not Hemingway, Steinbeck, or Fitzgerald. Arthur Miller and Eugene O'Neill were also high on his list.[53] He admired John Hersey, claiming that *The Wall*, about the Warsaw Ghetto, is "the finest novel I ever read." It's hard to believe, he continues, that this former anti-Semite could write so sympathetically about the Jews: unquestionably, "he is our most underrated novelist."[54] Social conditions motivate all the big books of literature, according to Uris. They are the history of the times and deal with injustice. The problem was how to channel the vast, sprawling material of the past into a work of fiction.

In March, he reported on his progress to his father, saying he had completed about one-quarter of the manuscript.[55] But length and structure were creating problems. The book was moving slowly, although the stumbling block of the title was out of the way. He also reminded Doubleday that Israel's tenth anniversary was coming: "It's a great target. Otherwise, I'll be happy to have Moshe Dayan stage another war for us on pub date."[56] Just before sending the first part of the novel to them, 350 typed pages, he asked for criticism, but no major discussions until "the entire work is finished. I am afraid of becoming derailed by going back."[57]

While sharing his progress with his father, he assured him that he shouldn't worry about Doubleday cutting up the manuscript: "I'm a pretty mean man inside a story conference and usually get my own way."[58] However, he would later recount how he had to cut down his nearly one million words to a quarter of a million. His productivity also increased after he bought his first electric typewriter.

Uris originally conceived of the novel as comprising five short novels, each named after a book in the Bible and tied together by the common subject. Flashbacks to 1890 would balance the main story set between 1946 and 1949. To his editor, he explained that he would rather send in each book of the novel as he completed it, asking that Doubleday save its criticisms until he is done; that way he wouldn't be distracted from the whole.[59] He did admit, however, that the introduction of journalist Mark Parker at the beginning was a flaw. He did nothing with him except forget him at the end of the novel. He was used, he admitted, "as a deception to lure the non-Jewish reader into the book."[60]

In the midst of his writing, Uris worked for eight weeks on *The Big Country* for Gregory Peck and Billy Wyler. A recommendation from Hal Wallis in May 1957, after Peck and Wyler had a private screening of *Gunfight at the O.K. Corral* in advance of its general release, made them want Uris. Peck and Wyler needed revisions for the script of *The Big Country*, which had been drafted by Jessamyn West, who had also written the novel that was the basis for Wyler's previous hit, *Friendly Persuasion*. They offered Uris $1,000 a week; he turned them down because he was in the middle of working on *Exodus*. The British producer of *The Angry Hills* also contacted him, offering $25,000 for six weeks' work on the screenplay of that novel and making this unintentionally comic remark: "We have to get Uris because no one on earth knows Greece like he does"![61]

On 8 May 1957, Uris accepted a revised offer from Peck and Wyler offer. At $2,000 a week, the money was too good to refuse. He would also receive a percentage of the gross, only the second time a writer had been granted that concession (the first was James Jones with *From Here to Eternity*). Eight weeks' work on *The Big Country* would also be a rest from Israel, which had occupied him since late 1955.[62] He saw *Gunfight* at a press showing and thought it looked better the second time. Its general release a week or so later brought strong reviews; his editors at this time also loved the portions of *Exodus* they saw, and Oscar Dystel, the president of Bantam Books, told Uris he had ordered another 100,000 copies of *Battle Cry* on the anticipated interest in *Exodus*.

Peck and Wyler, however, soon proved to be difficult. Peck was nice, he wrote, but a worrier; Wyler was "a real tough one. . . . I'm [also] a hard man to work for but the box office figures on *Battle Cry* and *OK Corral* keep him [Wyler] listening. Boy! Do we battle."[63] By June, things were falling apart: disagreements with the script plus personality clashes meant trouble. The connection would end when the contract is up, he noted, but "I made a lot of money and didn't waste much time and did get a rest from *Exodus*."[64] Within a month, he was liberated from Peck and Wyler.[65] The film project had no sooner ended than Raymond Stross, the British producer of *The Angry Hills*, arrived. He wanted Uris to do the screenplay: it was difficult to land a star without a script, and impossible to get a director without a star. Even though he had financing, Uris put him off.

The future looked bright. Not only did the family plan to move—"I'm not tied to a studio and have no reason for not finding a more suitable . . . out of the way . . . peaceful place"—but his agent, Malcolm Stuart, and business manager, Herb Schlosberg, also hoped that after *Exodus*, he wouldn't have to take any more outside assignments. Instead, "I'll stay at home and do my own screenplays on my own time and after they're finished, I'll make my deals with the studios. I'm afraid I'll always have personality clashes otherwise. I can't stand idiocy."[66] The future for Uris at this stage seemed to be in film rather than fiction, but the immense success of *Exodus* would sway him to continue with his special formula for turning out best sellers: Jewish history edged with romance and buttressed with fact. While all this was going on, he and Betty took their first weekly Hebrew lesson. He hoped to be able to speak a little Hebrew when he returned to Israel in about six months.

Doubleday pressured him to get on with the novel and suggested a firm deadline. He resisted. In his letter of response, Uris tells Doubleday he will not "cool off" (that is, lose interest) while writing the novel, because he began planning the book "before I wrote *Battle Cry*"—an exaggeration.[67] He then explains in almost cinematic terms why he starts the story in the middle and on Cyprus: to get the action going with his major characters already in a drama. The remainder of the letter outlines the novel in detail and includes this assurance: "There won't be a dull or slow page in the whole works." He adds that his time away from the book has recharged his batteries: "Eighteen months solid concentration along with the misadventures of the Uris family had me at a low ebb." What he does not mention is that work on the *Big Country* screenplay spilled over into his construction of scene and character in his novel.

His father, however, continued to be an irritant, causing Uris to write several strong replies, one containing an important statement about the purpose and style of the book: "This book is not written for a few people who indulge in high level thought planes but for the masses to understand. The intricacies of Judaism and Israel MUST be simplified for the average reader."[68] He had earlier clarified his intention: "My job is to simplify all the complex dealings and fit it in with the characters I have created. This is the most difficult type of novel to write."[69]

Uris circulated the finished manuscript in the spring of 1958 to allow several interested parties to comment on it. One of the most important responses came from Moshe Pearlman, writing from the prime minister of Israel's office.[70] Pearlman had read the typescript copy sent to Uris's uncle for possible publication in Israel, as had Ilan Hartuv.

Pearlman focused on details: change the medal a hero receives from the Victoria Cross to the Military Cross—the former was too elite an honor and would constantly call attention to the hero. Clarify that Eichmann was not a Jew, although he did visit Palestine in 1937 to discuss large-scale Jewish immigration. The most important suggestion had to do with the term "Palmach rather than Hagana in the first part of the novel." According to Pearlman, many readers would have heard about Haganah but not Palmach. To repeat the term would be to suggest that "Palmach was a dissident organization rather like Etzel. Palmachniks

were members of Hagana and the Palmach was an integral unit of Hagana . . .
Don't you think it might be a good idea to substitute a few 'Haganas' for a few
'Palmachs' in the first part of the book?" Uris did not comment.

EXODUS PUBLISHED

Two months before the publication of *Exodus*, Uris's name resurfaced in the press.
The *New York Times* crossword puzzle of 8 July 1958 asked, "Author of *Battle Cry*?"
"Uris," of course, was the answer. The appearance was not coincidental. This was
one of several prepublication steps taken to increase publicity for his new novel
and a sign of his growing presence in popular culture.[71]

On 4 August, Doubleday announced in *Publishers Weekly* that "a major motion picture production of EXODUS is planned by Otto Preminger." The novel
would appear the following month and become the third film to be made from
his fiction.

Published on 23 September 1958, the book had a distinctive blue cover with
"EXODUS" in type that evoked Hebrew lettering. A freedom fighter stretched
the complete length of the book jacket, his rifle barrel casually pointing upward
to the author's name. Maps are used for the endpapers and to introduce each of
the five books of the novel (an intentional parallel with the five books of Moses
that make up the Torah). A biblical quotation accompanies each of the maps
that introduce an individual section. Additionally, a map of the Middle East
emphasizing the minuscule region of Israel appears inside the front cover. The
rear map is a close-up of the country, the verso the northern part of the land, the
recto the southern. Uris clearly felt the need to situate the reader geographically
throughout his 626 pages.

Opposite the title page Uris lists his two screenplays as well as the titles of his
two previous novels, in an attempt to draw as much attention to his film writing
as to his fiction. There is also a statement on the fictional elements of the novel.
It notes that "many of the scenes were created around historical incidents for
the purpose of fiction" and that all the characters, except public figures "such as
Churchill, Truman, Pearson," are fictitious. In the 1959 paperback, a statement by
Uris preceding the title page reiterates his commitment to the Jew as fighter and
hero and ends with yet another movie reference: after criticizing those who show
the Jew as self-pitying or as riding "the psychoanalysis coach," he says such attitudes "have been left where they rightfully belong, on the cutting-room floor."

The back jacket of *Exodus* contains an iconic image: Uris standing in army
fatigues in the desert, alongside a military jeep with his hand on a MG 34 machine
gun that is pointing skyward. The caption reads: "With a patrol in the Negev

Desert." "This appears romantic," he said of the photo, "but the fact is it was 127 degrees in the shade and if I were not holding on, I would have collapsed."[72] Nevertheless, Uris felt this was the most dramatic adventure of his entire stay in Israel and one that he repeatedly mentioned as demonstrating macho prowess and cowboy heroics. He dedicates the book to his three children and his wife, Betty. The hardcover edition cost $4.50.

Sales were initially slow: a modest but respectable 32,000 copies were sold within the first five weeks, despite moderately strong reviews. By the end of January 1959, however, the number had more than tripled. According to *Publishers Weekly*, the number of copies sold grew to 94,000, and afterward showed rapid growth. By the end of February, it was selling approximately 2,500 copies a day. On 30 March, Doubleday reported 165,000 copies sold, although *Publishers Weekly* added 10,000 copies to that figure. It became number one on the *New York Times* best-seller list on 17 May 1959, some nine months after it first appeared. By 1 June 1959, 261,891 copies had been sold, and by late September, a year after it first appeared, nearly 390,000 copies had been purchased. Bantam prepared to release the paperback (priced at seventy-five cents) in October, increasing its print run from an initial 1.5 million to 2.9 million because of demand from outlets that had never before sold books. According to *Publishers Weekly*, by 13 November 1959, sales registered 399,384 for the hardback and 1,675,000 for the paperback.

And soon Uris was offering commentary on his novel. In one article, "He Went for Broke," Uris says he followed George Bernard Shaw's advice: "Begin at the end." "I had a deep feeling about telling a story of Israel," he explained, "I had ideas about it but before I started to write anything I figured out my climax and then made all preceding material support it directly."[73] This was a simplification; his actual method was to review his research, double-check details, construct a plot, and then write, working long hours daily. The experience of writing regularly for a movie studio came in handy.

While hardcover sales of *Exodus* were going strong, Uris went public with his motives for writing the novel and set his fiction against those of his contemporaries, expressing impatience with introspective Jewish writing. In a *New York Post* interview, he challenged those Jewish American writers who wrote confessionally. They were apologists: "They spend their time damning their fathers, hating their mothers, wringing their hands and wondering why they were born. This isn't art or literature. It's psychiatry. . . . Their work is obnoxious and makes me sick to my stomach." He had a different motive for writing *Exodus*: "I was just sick of apologizing—or feeling that it was necessary to apologize. . . . We Jews are not what we have been portrayed to be. In truth, we have been fighters."[74] To remake the image of the Jew and Judaism was his goal.

Uris treated history liberally, taking liberties with events, facts, time lines, and character; *Exodus* aimed at impact rather than strict accuracy. The novel opens dramatically with a date, "November 1946," followed by a quotation from *Othello*. Mark Parker, a journalist, arrives on Cyprus to meet his friend Kitty Fremont, a widowed American. The story quickly shifts to Jewish refugees held in British camps on the island, after flashbacks about the lives of Kitty and Mark. A second reunion opens Chapter 2, that of David Ben Ami and, swimming out of the sea, Ari Ben Canaan (EX, 13). The adventure and intersection of these characters is about to begin, set against the menace of British control, imprisonment, and abuse of refugees.

Uris moves the narrative swiftly forward and backward. The refugees held in Caraolos, Cyprus, in British detention camps become the focal point of the first book of the novel. These forces intersect as Uris jump-cuts his story line to introduce the Greek Cypriot who will help Ben Canaan secure a ship to illegally transport children to Palestine. Uris will use intercutting throughout the novel: later, he shifts from David Ben Ami taking Kitty to Mea Shearim in Jerusalem during Sabbath preparations to, on the next page, Ari Ben Canaan getting into a taxi, being blindfolded, and then being driven to a secret location to meet his uncle Akiva, the head of the Maccabees (EX, 343–344).

Lengthy flashbacks supplement the proposed escape of the children on the ship. The first is of Karen, the object of Kitty's unacknowledged affection, since she lost a child similar in looks, and is dated Cologne, Germany, 1938. For forty pages, Uris recounts her life, telling the story of German Jews trapped in the country and how some were able to send a single child out to safe haven in Denmark. A second flashback tells the story of Dov Landau, beginning in Warsaw in 1939. It is the story of Dov and his role in the ghetto uprising of January 1943. He miraculously survives, only to be sent to Auschwitz at age thirteen, allowing Uris to write chillingly about the camps. Dov's skill as a forger saves his life.

Book 1 ends with the desperate, guilt-ridden British undersecretary in the Foreign Office cabling Cyprus to let the ship the *Exodus* go. Book 2 describes the arrival of the *Exodus* in Palestine, followed by a lengthy flashback about Ari Ben Canaan's family and their origins. It starts in Russia in 1884, permitting Uris to outline life in the Jewish Pale of Settlement. The writing becomes palpitant: "As Russia came to power, the flaming sword of Islam came up from the south" (EX, 204).

Uris condenses much political history of both Russia and the Middle East, from Turkish rule to the Balfour Declaration of 1917, the organization of the Haganah, the army of self-defense, the aggressive Irgun, and the increasing indifference of the British concerning the fate of the Jews. Ari Ben Canaan places an increasingly vital role as a Haganah commander but suffers the tragic murder of his early love, Dafna (EX, 292–293). The loss explains his stony silence and unemotional behavior when we meet him at the opening of the novel. He turns to work for Aliyah Bet, the illegal immigration of Jews into the country. This long flashback ends only with the bombing of the British headquarters at the King David Hotel on 22 July 1946 (EX, 317).

The lives of the new arrivals and the slow romance between Kitty and Ari take up most of Book 3. Violence defines the action, however, with the Maccabees (in actuality the Irgun) in conflict with the Haganah. Two stories soon merge, however, with the settling of Gan Dafna (the Garden of Dafna), the children's settlement where Dov and Karen live, and the continual battle with the British and now the Arabs.

Kitty meets Harriet Saltzman, the elderly director of the Youth Aliyah program, who offers this explanation of an Israeli's intensity and purpose: "A person wakes up every morning in doubt and tension—not knowing if all he has slaved for will be taken from him. Their country is with them twenty-four hours a day. It is the focal point of their lives" (EX, 341). The statement is key to understanding the ethos of the novel and Kitty's grasp of Israel.

As Uris shifts to the late spring of 1947 and the United Nations vote on a Palestine mandate, the novel take on an even broader scope. There are personal and political distractions, including Ari's finally admitting his longing for Kitty, as well as British reprisals for the murder of the vindictive Major Caldwell. The bombing of the Zion Settlement Building and the attempt on the Yishuv Central building unites the Haganah (with its strike arm, the Palmach) and the Maccabees. Battles take place, including a skillfully planned escape of Dov and Akiva, a Maccabee leader, from the supposedly impregnable Acre prison. And before the end of Book 3, Kitty realizes that she indeed belongs in Palestine and at Gan Dafna.

Uris next takes up the UN vote, concentrating on the international drama of the vote for partition by offering a day-by-day account of the politicking. The next major scene—and Uris largely structures the book from one major scene to another—is the declaration of the State of Israel on 14 May 1948, re-creating Kol Yisrael's (the Voice of Israel) radio account of the declaration, allowing him to present reaction from around the country and the world (EX, 539–541). But in a dramatic, foreboding tone, he notes that while the crowds danced the hora in the streets of Tel Aviv, Egyptian bombers took off to bomb the city and Arab armies crossed the borders. He again divides his story by regions, as if a camera were panning across the country and swooping in for close-ups before moving on to the next scene, in order to create a sense of simultaneity.

He begins the final book with rescue flights to neighboring countries to retrieve Jews, focusing on a group of Yemenites rescued in Aden. Then, a sudden leap to 1956 and Nassar's blockade of the Suez Canal and the Straits of Tiran, while fedayeen marauder gangs burn fields and attack settlements. Karen places herself in jeopardy by going to live at a new frontier settlement, and when Kitty visits her, she explains that she must stay and fight: "We have outlived everyone who has tried to destroy us. Can't you see it, Kitty? . . . Israel [is] the bridge between darkness and light" (EX, 614–615). The final chapter occurs on the eve of the first seder of Passover. The principals, except Karen, are there, but all is overturned when Ari brings news of her murder. This devastates all, and Ari finally breaks down in Kitty's arms, declaring his love and need for her, while Dov, Karen's lover, rededicates himself to fight for Israel. The novel ends with Dov beginning to read from the Haggadah, the story of the Jews' escape from Egypt.

Uris changes facts to suit the novel and allows story to control history. He justifies this because his work is fiction not history; he strives for effect rather than accuracy. Character, drama, action, and suspense control events, allowing for the adjustment of fact. Events find new placement, documents become rewritten, and characters take on an air of unreality. Sabras (native-born Israelis) hide their emotions, to the chagrin of Israeli readers, while he inverts the arrogance, recklessness, overconfidence, and stubbornness of the people to represent strengths, not weaknesses.[75]

Readers loved it, as the 24 June 1959 best-seller list in the *Los Angeles Times* confirmed: *Exodus* was number one, followed by *Doctor Zhivago*, *The Ugly American*, *Lady Chatterley's Lover*, *Dear and Glorious Physician*, and *Lolita*. When the paperback appeared, marketing went into high gear, creating the fastest-selling work ever published by Bantam. New mass-marketing campaigns were undertaken to get the title out, although the public was skeptical that the paperback was complete. Even after almost 3.5 million copies were in print, Bantam received letters from readers saying that "many do not believe that this small book can actually contain all the material in the original edition." This prompted Bantam to include a "Publisher's Note," which appeared at the end of Uris's introductory statement and assured readers that "*all* Bantam editions of EXODUS . . . are complete and unabridged—the original book, word for word."

Included in Bantam's promotion were twenty-one-inch-high freestanding cutout figures of a freedom fighter and a sabra woman. The publisher distributed 2,500 of these "stands," which carried the tagline "Today's bestselling novel of Heroism and Desire." Bantam also sponsored an *Exodus* window-display contest, similar to one that had occurred for *Battle Cry*. Large truck banners depicted the cover along with the announcement "Now in Paperback, The bestselling novel." Additionally, all standard Bantam titles published in September, October, and November 1959 had an *Exodus* ad on their back covers: this amounted to more than six million notices on forty different titles, including Luke Short's *Saddle by Starlight*, Dorothy Worley's *Dr. Jon's Decision*, and the reprint of *Battle Cry*.[76]

Reviews of the novel certainly helped. Or rather, some reviews. The *Saturday Review of Literature* praised the work, as did the *New York Times Book Review*, the critic calling *Exodus* a "passionate summary of the inhuman treatment of the Jewish people in Europe ... and of the triumphant founding of the new Israel."[77] History was both its advantage and disadvantage: "Unlike most historical novels in which the events of a period merely provide décor, *Exodus* offers history as its hero," but the characters are something of an intrusion. According to another reviewer: "It's a story that calls for a simple minded rhetoric of an unmodulated mind. For Jewish readers it offers the glorification of courage in Jews. It's David and Goliath or Shane turning on his tormentors and winning."[78] In essence, the novel succeeds as portable, romanticized history.

Others were not so laudatory. "The best way I can describe *Exodus* is to say it is the *Three Musketeers* of the Israeli wars. It is a grand mixture of adventure and truth," Herman Wouk pronounced, with more charity than enthusiasm. The *San Francisco Examiner* referred to it as a "rambling compilation of past and present history [with] alternately good and bad writing," while the *Nation* cited its typecast characters and adolescent eroticism. The reviewer essentially read the book as a great adventure that taught some history and presented Israel and its heroes as Americans and Jews, which is how Americans would like to imagine them.[79]

Vigorous response to the book continued throughout the year; one of the most vocal critics was Menachem Begin, who spoke at Carnegie Hall on 20 November 1960. The poster advertising the event read: "The most authorized person in the world to tell the truth of EXODUS / the Israeli Leader / Menachem Begin / Ex commander-in-chief of the Irgun (the Jewish Underground Organization) / on / EXODUS—FACTS AND FICTION / at / CARNEGIE HALL / SUNDAY, NOVEMBER 20, AT 8:30 PM."[80] "Fact—Greater than Fiction" was the way one paper summarized the talk.[81] Begin, who was the head of the Freedom (Herut) Party in Israel and the supposed inspiration for Akiva in *Exodus*, criticized Uris for failing to mention the Irgun directly in the novel. Before a jam-packed New York crowd, he also declared that he was not Akiva and objected to the irrational and psychologically disturbed portrayal of the Maccabees. Yet he defended the actions of the Irgun, claiming that the Palestinian problem had come to the attention of the UN because of their actions. Begin also recounted the Irgun attack on Acre, on 4 May 1947, and said that the UN had not acted out of the blue, which is the impression given in *Exodus*. The Irgun operation against Goldschmidt House in Jerusalem in March 1947 was an important event that had initiated a debate in the British

House of Commons, resulting in a British outcry for a UN special session on the Palestine question.[82]

The identification of errors and corrections in the novel began to appear in the press, including criticism of Uris's demonizing of the Arabs. Various reviewers documented that the Arabs in Palestine at the time of the novel's setting were not at all like the stereotypes Uris portrayed, barbaric, unclean, cowardly, and ignorant.[83]

Philip Roth challenged the picture of the Jew as fighter, pointing out that to take pride in such behavior was nothing to be proud of. For Roth, Uris corrupted the morality and integrity of Judaism by promoting the violence necessary for its survival. Robert Alter noted how a "double sentimental myth" had developed: the Jew in this type of fiction is an "imaginary creature embodying both what Americans would like to think about Jews and what American Jewish intellectuals would like to think about themselves."[84] Uris's overdetermined milieu prevented his characters from claiming their own independence.

One of the strongest criticisms came from an Arab source: a thirty-four-page pamphlet by Aziz S. Sahwell. Countering what he saw as propaganda with fact, the author challenged the accuracy of the work and the treatment of Arabs. Uris's three goals, says the author, were "to justify the violent establishment of a Jewish state on Arab soil, to glorify Israel's military 'valor' in accomplishing its unlawful purpose and to slander and discredit all Arab people."[85] The critic comments on each book of the novel, pointing out what he claims to be distortions. Uris did not respond, although he kept a copy of the document in his archive.

There was more generous praise, however, from critics who assessed the book's importance to the Zionist movement in America and its role in maintaining public memory of the Holocaust. Uris anticipated a "virtual tidal wave of American anti-Zionist sentiment" but decided to acknowledge it through his American protagonist, Kitty, permitting her to remain skeptical, distant, and unsympathetic toward the plight of the Jews.[86] Only through the heroism of Ari and young, displaced Karen, who was Jewish but had been reared by Danish Christians during the Second World War, does Kitty reluctantly come to accept the moral right of the Jews to reclaim and defend their land. Through his heroic sabras, Uris established a definite connection and feeling of responsibility for Israel among American Jews, who suddenly wanted to become Zionists. But Israelis were, themselves, critical. No group of Jews anywhere was as perfect as those shown in the book, one Israeli said. "We thought we had about convinced the world we were just normal people until *Exodus* came along," said another.[87] Readers worldwide, of course, disagreed.

What reviewers or commentators could not deny was the impact of the book on the cultural consciousness of Americans. It is difficult to recall the indifference or discomfort America and American Jews had toward Israel at the time. The United States had voted for partition, but then withdrew its support of the country, preferring to take a neutral position. American Jews, while sympathetic to the plight of the young country and in a state of disbelief that Israel had been able to hold off Arab armies in the war of independence, were still hesitant to support the country. Zionism seemed ideologically one-sided, and Zionists seemed aggressive, strident, and threatening to Jewish American assimilation. American Jews were also upset or confused by the Suez crisis of 1956, even though it led to the opening of the Straits of Tiran.

Exodus changed all that. In Uris's presentation of heroic figures who could not only repulse but conqueror an enemy, a new identity for Israel emerged. Israel, linked to Holocaust survival, now meant triumph, with Zionism the key. "Tough Jews" suddenly became admired, although they were not always noble, as some critics pointed out.[88] But the impact of *Exodus* on the psyche of Americans, Jew and non-Jew alike, was incalculable. Not only did travel and contributions to Israel increase, but the perception of the country, and by extension the perception of Jews, changed. They were no longer victims but heroes. The sheer number of copies sold meant that many experienced Jewish history and heroism dramatically and romantically. Jewish activism made Israelis, and by extension all Jews, admirable, their willingness to fight and determination to win overpowering, even ennobling. The impact on Soviet Jewry a decade later was similarly intense. Such responses transcended quibbles about literary failings. The novel was a success for other reasons, culturally reinscribing a gallant, daring view of Jewish history and identity. In a 2001 critique of American policy toward the Middle East, the critic Edward Said commented that "the main narrative model that dominates American thinking still seems to be Leon Uris's 1958 novel *Exodus*."[89]

Popular culture soon reconstructed public memory as the value of the Holocaust and Zionism altered from despair to triumph. *Exodus* foregrounded these topics for Americans, not just Jews, partly as a result of Uris's literary strategy not to include an American Jew in the story. It was also the result of showing, in the tradition of the western, the triumph of law over crime, morality over immorality, and the ability to establish and maintain a homeland. America approved. *Exodus* showed that the Holocaust and Jewish identity, even in the Diaspora, were inextricably linked.

Uris pairs the Jewish catastrophe of the Holocaust with the Jewish triumph of Israel. They became the two pillars of Jewish American identity: "out of the ashes of Auschwitz, the birth of Israel."[90] This became part of the mythic American consciousness *Exodus* promotes. New Israel replaced old Europe, which the American Jew welcomed, encouraged by the American English dialogue in the book. Ari is both the new Israeli and the American Jew as Uris wanted him to be portrayed, originating as the hero of a western. Myth shaped history. But while Jewish-Gentile differences could be bridged, Jewish-Arab ones could not. Arabs remain violent, uncivilized, and unlawful, making personal relations impossible (Ari will never permit his sister Jordana to marry his friend Taha).

The Americanization of *Exodus* depicts Israel as the culmination and redemption of the Shoah (Holocaust) while it puts Jews at the center of fantasies of American heroism. The destruction of the old Jew in the Shoah, from one perspective, represented the end of Jewish impotence. The birth of Israel and the virile Israeli showed a new Jew to America, one distinct from the self-conscious, sexually awakened, materially oriented American Jew seen in works like Philip Roth's *Goodbye, Columbus*, which was published the following year. Bullets, not chopped liver, become the new ammunition.[91] Being Jewish now had a cachet, and the success of *Exodus* reconfirmed for the American reading public the acceptance of Bellow, Roth, Malamud, and other Jewish writers who gained immense popularity in the sixties.

Uris employed the Hollywood tradition of personalizing history and reducing politics to a family romance (brother versus brother, for example, as in the strife between Akiva and Barak ben Canaan). And he was not shy about it. Whether out of egotism, self-confidence, or chutzpah, he believed he could tell the story of the state and the history of its people through fragmented stories of individual lives.

Unlike Bernard Malamud, who defensively said, "I'd rather write about Israel if I knew the country. I don't, so I leave it to the Israeli writers," Uris challenged this attitude by educating himself about Judaism, Zionism, and Palestine, and spending eight months researching the people and the land.[92]

Prime Minister David Ben-Gurion summed up best the popular reaction to *Exodus*. Asked what he thought of the novel, he replied that he usually didn't read fiction, but he had read *Exodus*. What did he think of it? Smiling, he answered, "As a literary work it isn't much. But as a piece of propaganda, it's the greatest thing ever written about Israel."[93] A newspaper article from the same time reported that members of the United Nations delegation stationed at Government House in Jerusalem regularly received copies of the book for study.[94]

THE MOVIE VERSION

Ben-Gurion was right: not only did Zionism find greater support in America than before, but suddenly everyone wanted to be Jewish also—or at least visit Israel. National pride increased, as did donations to the Jewish National Fund. Tourism took off. The unprecedented wave of visitors frankly puzzled Israelis, as did the tourists' expectations that they would be meeting characters from the book.[95]

The man partly responsible for this reaction was the autocratic, Viennese-born Hollywood producer-director Otto Preminger, who declared, after he read an advance copy of the novel, "I couldn't put the book down. Immediately I knew I had to make the picture."[96] A United Artists publicity statement went on to describe Preminger as a man of fastidious taste: "Wave a good book or excellent play script in front of him, and he'll want it for the movies." His previous successes had included *Porgy and Bess* (1959), *Bonjour Tristesse* (1958), *The Moon Is Blue* (1953), and *Anatomy of a Murder* (1959).

In his autobiography, Preminger recalled the day in the early fall of 1958 at his brother Ingo's home in Los Angeles when he spied a few boxes filled with a manuscript.[97] Curious, Otto asked, and was told, that it was a novel about Israel, the property of MGM. Nevertheless, he began to read it and supposedly couldn't stop, knowing immediately that he, an Austrian-born Jew who was a success in America, had to make the film. Ingo told him the Uris-MGM contract was for an outright purchase of the rights for $75,000, which included partial payment for Uris's services. In New York, Preminger went to the president of MGM, Joseph Vogel, telling him he wanted the book. It wasn't for sale, Vogel said. Preminger then explained that if MGM made it, the Arab countries would likely close all MGM theatres and ban all MGM films. Preminger added that Vogel, a studio president, could not afford an Arab boycott, but as an independent producer, Preminger could. There was still no deal, although mention of the possible boycott at an MGM board meeting raised doubts. A week later, Preminger had the rights—but he still needed money.[98]

Preminger went next to Arthur Krim of United Artists for funds for production costs, knowing Krim was partial to Israel. Shortly after, he had an initial budget of $1.75 million, exclusive of stars' salaries. The amount was later raised to $3 million.[99] Preminger then began to work on the script with Uris. A publicity photo from this period masks the difficulties between these two uncompromising figures. Uris stands with his arm around Preminger, who is reading a copy of the early script pages. The caption, as supplied by United Artists publicity, reads: "The Script Looks Good. Hollywood producer Otto Preminger (left) reads approvingly first pages of the screenplay by Leon Uris (right) adapted from Uris' 640 page novel, *Exodus* which Preminger will film." The words and image are ironic, given the men's impending disagreement and subsequent feud.[100]

At first, Preminger and Uris labored through a third of the script, but "it was hopeless"; Preminger claimed that Uris couldn't write a screenplay, although Uris's side of the story emphasizes contrasting approaches.[101] Preminger believed that part of the problem was dialogue. Uris made his characters in the script sound as if they were in the novel, not the movie. Dialogue meant to be heard is very different from dialogue meant to be read. They disagreed, and by mid-January

1959, Uris was off the picture (although he received a $20,000 severance payment, on top of the $20,000 he had already been paid).[102] There is disagreement about whether Uris ever completed a version of the script. Preminger claimed he did; Uris said he did not and in fact did not write so much as a single word of dialogue for the director. With hindsight, Uris said, "I sensed trouble the moment I met Otto, a man hated by everybody."[103]

Never one to overlook a conflict, Uris publicized the break with Preminger, who accused him of being incapable of writing dialogue. Uris, in turn, repeatedly refused to see or comment on the movie. Preminger added that when Uris tells a story, he "is too much of a partisan." The novel has a "pox against all the enemies of the Jews in it, and that is difficult to defend."[104] Years later, an interviewer asked Uris about problems working with Preminger: "I've heard you had trouble with screenplays." Uris answered: "I don't have trouble with screenplays. I write very good screenplays. Otto Preminger has trouble reading screenplays."[105]

But Uris never forgot an insult, and being fired from the film of his most popular work rankled. Ten years later, when Preminger and Uris turned up at a White House reception given by President Johnson for the prime minister of New Zealand, Preminger went up to Uris to greet him. The writer turned away and refused to speak. The conflict between the two egos continued, exacerbated by Preminger's view of what he had been able to do for Uris's novel: "I, as usual, . . . tried to make the characters, beyond the novel, very real. I tried to get the motivations right."[106] As Uris tells it, Preminger dropped him from *Exodus* because Preminger was dismissive of the book; the movie took precedence. In turn, Preminger supposedly told Uris, "No matter how bad the book is, I'm going to make a great picture of it."[107]

First to replace Uris was Albert Maltz, a blacklisted member of the Hollywood Ten, then living in Mexico. Maltz worked diligently on the script and visited Israel for research. But his draft was excessive: four hundred pages long, more an epic than a film. Needing someone else, Preminger turned to another blacklisted writer, Dalton Trumbo, in December 1959. This, too, caused a scandal because of his status. The director was in a bind, however. Actors had been signed, and shooting was to begin in April, but a "shootable" script was still missing. Uris's draft was too stiff, full of unusable dialogue, and emphatic about the anti-British, anti-Arab conflicts, which Preminger wanted to downplay. Maltz's script was too long.

Uris's mistake with the script was that he (and Maltz) tried to adapt the entire novel to the screen. Trumbo realized this would not work: there were simply too many stories in the book. When he met with Preminger, Trumbo asked a crucial question: "Which story did he want to tell?" Preminger answered immediately, "The birth of Israel."[108] Later notes on the script by Trumbo to Preminger confirm that he solved the structural problem with Uris's novel, which splintered the historical story into three parts (the *Exodus* ship, the Haganah-Irgun rivalry, and the conflict between Arabs and Jews). Trumbo's solution was to concentrate throughout the film on the UN vote on partition as the principal interest of all the main characters.[109] He also removed references to Jewish claims of a divine right to Palestine.

Objecting to the anti-British and anti-Arab themes in the novel, Preminger had Trumbo show that the Israelis were sympathetic toward the British. "Through a few changes from the book," he believed his version came closer "to the truth and to the historic facts" while avoiding propaganda: "'It's an American picture after all, that tries to tell the story, giving both sides a chance to plead their side.'"[110] Uris was, of course, incensed by this alteration.

Other changes from the novel to the screen: concentrating the action into a three-month period (September–November 1947), ending just after the UN vote for partition; making some of the passengers on the *Exodus* adults; and shifting the theme from nationalistic Zionism to peace and brotherhood. Trumbo also introduced comedy, notably the scene in which Major Caldwell (Peter Lawford) peers into the eyes of Ari (Paul Newman) while declaring he can spot a Jew anywhere, though he fails to recognize Ari as one. The elimination of Kitty's anti-Semitism, present at the beginning of the novel, and making her husband a photojournalist who was killed in Palestine during a Haganah operation, rather than a marine killed on Guadalcanal, are additional modifications. Ironically, Kitty falls in love with a member of the organization responsible for her husband's death.

The film also presents a more optimistic view of Arab-Jewish relations. For example, Taha remains a friend of Ari and the Jews, even when pressed to fight. In the novel, he breaks off that friendship when Ari refuses to allow him to marry his sister, Jordana. The film also suggests that ex-Nazis, one of whom appears as a character, incited the Arabs against the Jews. No such cause occurs in the book. Additionally, the novel ends with bittersweet optimism at the Passover seder, which celebrates both the original Exodus and Israelis' implicit arrival in the promised land, although darkened by the news of Karen's murder. The film ends with Ari standing over the shared grave of Taha and Karen and offering qualified hope that Jews and Arabs will some day live together; the Palmach then pile into trucks with the air of deputies charging off to capture a gang of bandits in a western, eager to defend the country from further attacks.

Exodus was the first major American film shot entirely on location in Israel, with Preminger converting part of Galilee into a huge movie set. The shooting schedule ran from 24 March to 1 June 1960 in Israel and then from 5 June to 3 July 1960 in Cyprus. Preminger visited the country from London (his base was the Dorchester Hotel) several times in 1959 to scout locations, network with politicians, and finalize details. Publicity accompanied each of his trips. Moshe Dayan attended a dinner party for Preminger at Rehovot during one these visits. On these trips, Preminger held court at the Dan Hotel in Tel Aviv, and after six months of preparation, he was ready to bring the technical crew, generators, costumes, extras, and actors to Israel. The Hotel Zion in Haifa became the production company's headquarters.

Filming in Israel presented challenges, logistically and cinematographically. One reporter joked that "to film it [the movie], the producer took a bigger army to Israel than the Israelis used to fight the Arabs."[111] He employed a cast of five hundred and dozens of crew members; brought technicians from London, Rome, and the United States; hired two destroyers; shifted fifteen thousand props around the desert; and had the courage left to call his twenty thousand extras "the best behaved crowd I have ever seen."[112] But Preminger warred with his stars. Paul Newman, who enjoyed discussing character motivation with his directors, found that Preminger wanted his actors to do only what they were told. Newman arrived in Israel with five pages of notes for Preminger. The director scanned them, admitted they were interesting, but announced, "If you were directing the picture, you would use them. . . . As I am directing the picture, I shan't use them."[113] Preminger ruled decisively: when United Artists later begged him to cut the lengthy, 212-minute film, he adamantly refused.

He could even move ships. When a modern ocean liner, the SS *Jerusalem*, regally sailed into Haifa and into the frame of his complicated setup for the arrival of Jewish refugees on the *Exodus*, Preminger immediately had his executive assistant call the Israeli minister of trade and industry to get the ship out of the way. The minister was on the phone in minutes, listening to Preminger outline the cost of resetting the scene and shutting down production for a day. Money would be lost. A compromise was reached on the spot: the passengers would disembark, but the ship would leave immediately, returning hours later to offload luggage—but only after Preminger had finished his shooting.[114]

There were other problems: 250 extras had been hired to play escaping prisoners in the Acre prison-break scene, but 253 people were counted as fleeing. Three inmates from a nearby mental ward had joined the "escapees."

Preminger hired as adviser to the film Major-General Francis Rome, who had commanded British troops in the Haifa area at the time of the 1947 attack on the Acre prison. The Israelis loaned him Colonel Gershon Rivlin, one of the former leaders of the Haganah. The two got on surprisingly well, swapping stories of "past rivalries." General Rome advised on matters of the British army in the film, and Colonel Rivlin gave advice on how to blow up British installations and smuggle arms into the country.[115]

One of the largest challenges was how to get sufficient people into the Russian Compound for the important concluding scene, the announcement of the UN vote on partition. Upward of at least twenty thousand unpaid actors had to be there. The solution? Ilan Hartuv had the answer: hold a lottery (quite popular in Israel at the time) and issue thousands of free tickets. In addition to monetary prizes, there would be six grand prizes announced at the climax of the big scene: six round-trip tickets to the opening of the film in New York. Response to the raffle was astonishing, and some forty thousand people from all over the country appeared. As the raffle results were announced, a tremendous cheer erupted— equal to the excitement that broke out when Preminger announced to the throng that Adolf Eichmann had just been caught and brought to Israel (Ben-Gurion made the public announcement on 23 May 1960).[116] Moviegoers assumed, of course, that the crowd was reacting to the news about partition.[117]

Criticism of the film began the moment casting was announced. In the novel, Ari Ben Canaan is dark and has a large build. Paul Newman was slight and had a fair complexion. And although Ben Canaan is a Middle Eastern Jew, Newman speaks with an American accent in the film. Dov Landau is blond in the novel, making it possible for him to pass from the Warsaw Ghetto into the city. Sal Mineo, who played him in the movie, was dark. Additionally, in the novel Dov only observes the young boys and girls selected for sexual service by the Nazis at Auschwitz; in the film, he reveals he was a participant, during a tension-filled scene in which he proves why he is worthy to become a member of the Maccabees. In the film, he transforms himself from a powerless and degraded victim into a proud fighter.[118]

Exodus premiered at the Warner Theatre in New York on 15 December 1960, followed by showings in Chicago and Beverly Hills. It was a hit, with sold-out shows throughout January 1961. The New York opening drew Preminger, Adlai Stevenson, Leonard Bernstein, Billy Rose, Paddy Chayefsky, Myrna Loy, and Maria Schell. Reviewing for the *New York Times*, Bosley Crowther thought the film too long, at three hours thirty-two minutes, and too episodic: as a result, it was not dramatically compelling, the fault of Preminger and Trumbo. They also temporized the presentation of the tensions between the Arabs, Jews, and British. There was more tension between the Haganah and Irgun than between the Jews and the British and the Arabs, he wrote.[119] Nonetheless, *Exodus* was tops at the Christmas box office, beating out *Spartacus*.

Criticism of the length, however, continued, and many agreed with the comedian Mort Sahl when he stood up at a premiere and announced to the audience and Preminger, "Otto, let my people go."[120] A cartoon bookmark was also symptomatic: two goats are in a field, and one, while eating the film of *Exodus*, turns to the other and says, "I enjoyed the book better."[121] Nevertheless, reviews of the film were sympathetic, acknowledging the difficulty of transferring Uris's "corpulent" novel, with its multiple stories, to the screen. Analyses of the film have interpreted it as a model text for the heroic-nationalist genre in Israeli films. The promotion of Zionism as liberation of the land became a myth that influenced Israeli cinema for nearly two decades.[122]

Exodus quickly set box-office records around the country, and was nominated for three Academy Awards: best supporting actor (Sal Mineo), best color cinematography, and best score, the only award it won. Ernest Gold wrote the music, which Ferrante and Teicher recorded, and the title song became a pop hit. One personal consequence of the film was Sal Mineo's romantic involvement with Jill Haworth, the fourteen-year-old actor who played Karen, which continued for many months. The movie earned more than $8 million in domestic rentals; in 1962, Preminger sold his interest in the film to the production company for $1 million.[123]

At thirty-four, Uris had achieved international fame, although he still thought of himself as a screenwriter as much as a novelist.[124] But it was his identity as the author of *Exodus* that stuck over the next decade and beyond. The novel—aided by the film—would continue to record vast sales and affect millions. Sales of *Exodus* far exceeded expectations as it found a worldwide reading public despite its lack of literary merit.[125] Summarizing the paradox is the comment of a *Washington Post* reviewer concerning another popular novel: "It's a lousy book. So I stayed up to until 3 a.m. to finish it."[126]

HISTORY AND RESISTANCE

Everybody killed the Jews.
—ADOLF EICHMANN, TRIAL TESTIMONY IN JERUSALEM, 1961

WHAT TO DO NEXT? That was the question Uris faced after the acclaim, attention, and money generated by *Exodus*. He was a rich, recognized writer. But what would follow? In part, the question answered itself. Writing the Warsaw Ghetto section of *Exodus* (Book 1, Chapters 22 and 23) had troubled him, as had the interviews he conducted in Israel with ghetto survivors. He wanted to memorialize their courage in a work that would continue his theme of the fighting Jew. He wanted to show that in even defeat they had triumphed, and in death they had survived. He also wanted to return to Israel to acknowledge his role as its literary spokesperson and, at the same time, to use the trip to fashion another book about the country, this time in photographs. To help him, he enlisted the Greek photographer, Dimitrios Harissiadis.

But first, there were appearances to make. On 19 September 1959, Uris was onstage with Golda Meir and Levi Eshkol at the Sherman Hotel in Chicago.[1] His status as a voice of North America Jewry was immense, and the National Economic Conference for Israel was not going to pass up the chance to have him on the dais with the leading Israeli political figures. Uris, a willing supporter, became a frequent speaker at Jewish organizations throughout the continent, and many awards followed.[2]

Next month he was back at high school, receiving John Bartram High's Outstanding Alumnus award (26 October 1959). This was ironic, since he had left school before graduating in order to join the marines in January 1942. The report in the Bartram High paper did note that he received a war diploma from the high school, but failed to record that it was more honorary than authentic. Nevertheless, he impressed the students with his oft-repeated quip that, fortunately, "English and writing have absolutely nothing in common."[3]

In response to the immense popularity of *Exodus*, other writers came forward with stories, no doubt trying to gain attention: Yitzhak Perlov, for example, a Yiddish writer from Tel Aviv, claimed that he had published a novel in 1949 in Argentina called *Exodus 1947*. He was one of the 4,500 passengers on the *Exodus* that had to return to Germany. His novel is about the journey. Others tried to capitalize on a certain type of notoriety. A passport clerk in the offices of El Al claimed he was being taken for a forger and regarded with contempt because his name was Dov Landau. He requested an injunction against the local distribution of *Exodus* because he had been mistaken for the book's character of the same name. His request for the injunction was denied, and he was ordered to pay costs, but he also filed a separate $4,400 libel suit against the publisher and distributor of the book.[4]

While doing research for *Exodus*, Uris had visited the Warsaw Ghetto Fighters Kibbutz. A number of survivors of the Warsaw Ghetto uprising, known as the "Ghetto Fighters," went on to found Kibbutz Lohamey ha-Geta'ot (literally: "Ghetto Fighters Kibbutz"), north of Acre. The founding members included Yitzhak Zuckerman, ŻOB (Żydowska Organizacja Bojowa (Jewish Fighting Organization) deputy commander, and his wife, Ziviah Lubetkin, who also commanded a fighting unit. In 1984, the members of the kibbutz published *Dapei Edut* (Testimonies of Survival), four volumes of personal testimonies from ninety-six kibbutz members. The settlement also features a museum and archives dedicated to remembering the Holocaust.

Although the Warsaw Ghetto revolt failed, it nonetheless exhibited the courage of Jews in resisting oppression. Uris felt a novel on the subject was justified and would be an extension of his theme of the Jew as hero. Uris then sought to duplicate his arrangement with Dore Schary, although this time with Mirisch Films. In the spring of 1959, he arranged to go to Israel and Poland, a trip made possible by a new deal to sell motion-picture rights to a new book on the ghetto as well as to write the screenplay. The independent movie unit would finance Uris in his research. The deal fell through before he got started, but he and his agents (Ingo Preminger and Malcolm Stuart) penned a new, precedent-setting agreement that had Hollywood talking. A four-picture arrangement with Columbia, it was seen as representing the "rising prestige of the writer in Hollywood."[5] The contract was believed to be the first multiple-book deal in the movie industry (recall that with *Battle Cry*, Uris had become the first first-time author signed to do his own screenplay). Uris would also produce the movies from the four unwritten novels. Remarkably, Columbia signed without seeing any outlines or manuscripts. The head of the Screen Writers Guild claimed that the contract between the writer and studio was unprecedented.[6] Doubleday was to publish the novels.[7]

Before Warsaw was Israel, where Uris returned to conduct research for his proposed novel, tour the country with his Greek photographer for *Exodus Revisited*, and participate in the shooting of a documentary starring Edward G. Robinson. Uris left Los Angeles on 8 March 1959 and arrived in Tel Aviv on the 19th after a week in London. He would stay until April 30. He would be in Copenhagen for just more than a week before flying on to Warsaw, where he would spend five days, arriving on 9 May. By the 16th, he would be back in Los Angeles.

Uris's arrival in Israel was news. The Foreign Ministry invited him to lunch, and various organizations feted him. But his first job was a film: Uris wrote the script for a fund-raising documentary for Israel bonds narrated by Edward G. Robinson. Titled "Israel," the forty-minute Technicolor film depicted dramatic sites from biblical and contemporary times. Elmer Bernstein composed the music, which was played by the Israeli Philharmonic. Entirely filmed on location, it included footage of Ben-Gurion at home in the Negev desert as well as various social and economic projects.

Exodus Revisited was in some ways a parallel work, a pictorial record of modern Israel. A photo sequel to his novel, the book vividly shows the past and present of the country. Uris even reread *Exodus* and picked individual sentences to reproduce in the new book in addition to supplying captions and commentaries to Harissiadis's photos.

The narrative, however, is erratic, veering sharply between terse, factual commentary and effusive prose separated by evocative black-and-white photos. The writing alternates between the simple and the overwritten: "The Jewish people gave to a groping mankind its first great bridge from darkness to light" (EXR, 350) is one example, an echo of a line from *Exodus* in which Karen tells Kitty the value of Israel (EX, 614–615).

A prophetic tone dominates the book, whether in the story of the revolutionary Simon Bar Kochba, who nearly defeated the Romans, or in the account of the 286 defenders of Masada, who held off Roman legions for three years, only to die when they were betrayed (EXR, 38–39). Throughout the narrative, Uris intersperses facts: Armageddon is at the end of Wadi Ara; Jaffa is the oldest port in the world; eucalyptus trees were imported from Australia "to help drink up the malarial swamps" (EXR, 56). He also summarizes the three aliyahs (immigrations) to Israel and individual heroes in the struggle for Palestine, such as Sarah Aronsohn, who was painfully tortured by Turkish police in her home before she was able to commit suicide (EXR, 58–59).[8]

Dedicated to David Ben-Gurion, *Exodus Revisited* offers a truncated history of Israel with short prose transitions made up of one- or two-sentence paragraphs.

Christian, Muslim, and Jewish religious landmarks are captured in the black-and-white images of Book One, which has a minimal amount of text. Uris used a different method in his later nonfiction book *Jerusalem: Song of Songs* (1981; photographs by Jill Uris), which contains a lengthy outline of the political and religious history of Jerusalem.

In many ways, *Exodus Revisited* acts as a guide, even a set of footnotes, to Uris's novel. For example, not only does he detail the defenses of such isolated kibbutzim as Dagania, Ein Gev, and Ayelet Ha Shahar—a northern kibbutz that was able to down a Syrian fighter jet with a single rifle shot (every man in the kibbutz modestly took credit for firing the shot), an event that was amalgamated in the story of Gan Dafna—but he gives the sources of some of the most dramatic scenes in the novel. One of the most notable was the night hike with the children from Gan Dafna as the kibbutz faced attack. This had occurred at the mountaintop Kibbutz Manara in the Huleh Valley, where the children were dangerously transported down the mountain between enemy lines to relative safety on the valley floor (*EXR*, 103). The siege of Safed receives equal treatment, and the book includes a photo of the handmade postage stamps used on smuggled letters (*EXR*, 108).

Exodus Revisited concludes with a recounting of the adventures of Antek (Yitzhak Zuckerman, a leader of the resistance) in the Warsaw Ghetto, which provided a critical source for Uris in writing *Mila 18*. The graphic paragraph summarizing the resistance ends with "we hung on for forty-two days. . . . Not bad when you consider that the entire country of Poland held for only twenty-six" (*EXR*, 257). Uris spent a week interviewing residents of the Ghetto Fighters Kibbutz and recording details of their struggle, especially the story of Ziviah Lubetkin, a heroine of the ghetto fighting, who survived by crawling through sewers in fetid water.

The book includes several photographs of Ben-Gurion, the most telling being a shot of him conducting a Passover seder inside a tent with paratroopers in the Negev; the image recalls the concluding seder of *Exodus* and anticipates the late scene in the bunker of Mila 18 of another seder. The final picture is of the sea, captioned by the statement, borrowed from *Exodus*, that Israel is "a bridge from the world of darkness to the world of light" (*EXR*, 279).

THE WARSAW GHETTO

After his time in Israel and a stop in Denmark, Uris went to Poland, his arrival headlined in the *Hollywood Reporter* as "Hollywood scripter slides back of Iron Curtain." According to the paper, Uris became the first Hollywood writer "ever to slide back of the Iron Curtain to research a pic he'll pilot."[9] In communist Poland, the period of Stalinization had ended in 1953 with Stalin's death, and the 1956 Poznan worker riots had led to the selection of Wladyslaw Gomulka as the reformist leader of the Polish Communist Party. But Uris still had difficulty obtaining permission to see the remains of the ghetto and Jewish memorials.

His trip was short. The Hotel Bristol in Warsaw served as his base, and Uris would make the hotel the home of the sophisticated Nazi Horst von Epp in the novel. For a week, Uris was subjected to bureaucratic runaround, and received cooperation from the government only after he had shouted at an official for almost half an hour. "Life in Poland is detestable," he said: "They speak of new freedom [but] the word freedom there doesn't mean the same thing it does here. They have no real freedom."[10]

Uris later described his visit to a human stockyard near Lublin and the failure of the community to prevent the obvious march to slaughter: "Standing on a hill above Lublin I got the full impact of it. The great tragedy was that when the victims would be brought in cattle cars to the Lublin siding to be marched in open view to Maidanek—not a voice in all the city would be raised."[11]

Warsaw was something of a return for Uris, reversing the movement of his father, who, in his memoir, wrote often of his travels through the city, especially at the start of his trip to Palestine. Uris had a strange experience there: "I'm a bad sleeper. I have insomnia, but when I got to that Warsaw hotel room, I lay down on that bed and slept for 20 hours like a baby. I had come home. I had come to Warsaw and I was doing something that was obviously pressing very hard to get out. And I had periods like that during this book."[12]

The ghetto itself was 1,000 acres, or 100 city blocks. At its height, it held 37 percent of Warsaw's population on 4 percent of its land. In the Warsaw of 1959, a modern housing complex stood over the destroyed rubble. Nearly three years into the war, after nearly 90 percent of the ghetto's inmates had been sent to the camps, the resistance took place. The battle began on Passover Eve, 19 April 1943, and ended in May with the fiery destruction of the ghetto.

Before the outbreak of the Second World War, Warsaw was the largest center of Jewish life in Eastern Europe: approximately 375,000 Jews lived there, nearly 30 percent of the total population of the Polish capital. Jewish newspapers, theatre groups, sports clubs, and political parties flourished as the population absorbed émigrés from eastern Poland and parts of the Soviet Union and Lithuania. Isaac Bashevis Singer, who, with his brother, would later flee Warsaw, writes vividly about the culture of Warsaw in *The Family Moskat* (1950), emphasizing the secular as well as religious aspects of its Jewish culture. Many neighborhoods were entirely Jewish, especially in the northern sectors of the city, with assimilationists living next to the Orthodox.

The invasion of Poland on 1 September 1939, however, and the fall of Warsaw on 28 September, brought a quick end to that life. Jews had to wear the Star of David, while property, including radios, was confiscated. Jews were forbidden to change their place of residence and forbidden to use the railways without special permission. They were soon barred from certain professions and excluded from entering restaurants, bars, and public parks. They had to use special carriages on public trams. Following the confiscation of their personal property was the confiscation of monetary assets, all bank accounts being forfeited to the Nazis. Jewish response to these decrees, however, was muted, even if life became unbearable. Those who were on certain "wanted lists," including Menachem Begin, escaped if they could.

Repression of the Jews increased with the construction of the actual Warsaw Ghetto, beginning in March 1940 when signposts that read "Infected Area" were erected at the entrance of streets densely populated by Jews. That same month, the *Judenrat* (governing body) received a map of the area, and was told to build a wall around it.[13] Adam Czerniakow, a former union leader and chairman of the *Judenrat*, tried to convince the authorities to cancel the orders. He was ignored, and in late August 1940, work on the ghetto began, turning the existing Jewish quarter into a bordered area. On Yom Kippur, 12 October 1940, loudspeakers in the city notified the Jews that a ghetto was being formed and that free movement in and out of the area would continue only to the end of October. Significantly, the Germans carefully avoided the word "ghetto," preferring to describe it as the "Jewish Residential Quarter of Warsaw," a phrase also employed without choice by the *Judenrat*.[14]

When the ghetto was sealed on 16 November (unlike medieval Jewish ghettos, which were closed only at night), more than 375,000 people found themselves crowded into an area of one and a half square miles. The German governor of Warsaw, Ludwig Fischer, in a report of September 1941, calculated that roughly 108,000 Jews lived in one square kilometer (0.39 square miles) of the ghetto, in comparison with 38,000 per square kilometer in residential Warsaw.[15]

The ghetto was irregularly shaped: at one point, the houses and sidewalks of Chlodna Street were included in the ghetto, but not the road, which was considered "Aryan." The wall around the ghetto was a little more than eight feet high and topped with barbed wire; it had twenty-two gates, reduced in time to thirteen and at the end to only four. German, Polish, and Jewish police guarded the entrances. Approximately 26,000 Jews lived on Pawia Street, and 20,000 on Mila Street. Black marketeering and begging coexisted, and the dead lay exposed everywhere. Photographs from the ghetto show the crowded and destitute conditions; no shot is more haunting than that of a six-year-old boy and his mother, hands raised high and marching before a German soldier who is pointing a gun at him. Uris alludes to this scene in *Mila 18* (*M18*, 509).[16]

The Nazi explanation for the ghetto was simple. Officially, it was to stop the spread of typhus; unofficially, to contain and then destroy the Jews.[17] The Germans' eradication of the quarter in mid-May 1943 confirmed their original plan. Memories of it survived through journals and fiction, individuals and art, marking its mythic power, which was confirmed by the news in January 2006 that a Jewish history museum will be built where the ghetto used to stand.[18]

Despite the hardships, life in the Warsaw Ghetto included educational and cultural activities conducted by underground organizations. Hospitals, public soup kitchens, orphanages, refugee centers, recreation facilities, and a school system were formed. Some schools were illegal and operated under the guise of soup kitchens. There were secret libraries, classes for children, and even a symphony orchestra.[19]

Rampant disease and starvation, as well as random murders, killed more than 100,000 even before the Nazis began mass deportations from the ghetto's *umschlagplatz* (collection point) to the Treblinka extermination camp, sixty-two miles to the northeast, during Operation Reinhardt. Between 22 July and 21 September 1942, approximately 265,000 ghetto residents were sent to Treblinka. In 1942, Polish resistance fighter Jan Karski reported to Western governments on conditions in the ghetto and on the extermination camps. They paid no attention. But by the end of 1942, it had become clear that the deportations meant death; many of the remaining Jews decided to fight.[20]

On 18 January 1943, the first instance of armed resistance occurred, when the Germans started the expulsion of the remaining Jews. The Jewish fighters had some success: the expulsion stopped after four days, and the ŻOB and ŻZW (Żydowski Zwiazek Wojskowy; Jewish Military Union) resistance organizations took control of the ghetto, building shelters and fighting posts, and began to operate against Jewish collaborators. During the next three months, all inhabitants of the ghetto prepared for what they realized would be a final struggle.[21]

The last battle started on Passover Eve, 19 April 1943, when a large Nazi force entered the ghetto. After initial setbacks, the Germans, under the field command of Jürgen Stroop, systematically burned and blew up the ghetto block by block, rounding up or killing any Jews they could capture. Significant resistance ended on 23 April 1943, and the German operation officially concluded in mid-May, symbolically culminating with the demolition of the Great Synagogue of Warsaw on 16 May 1943. According to the official report, at least 56,000 people were killed on the spot or deported to Nazi concentration and death camps, mostly to Treblinka.

What resources did Uris have to tell his story? Initially, only the accounts of survivors whom he interviewed in Israel, Warsaw, and London. His 1959 visit to the Ghetto Fighters Kibbutz in western Galilee had a tremendous impact; there he heard firsthand the stories of Antek and Ziviah Lubetkin, hero and heroine of the Warsaw uprising. Antek had led the forty-two-day ghetto revolt; Ziviah had commanded the women's brigade and kept a diary of what happened. His week at the kibbutz imprinted on him the human dimension of the suffering but also courage of the Jews, who fought with little but survived through determination. As Ziviah Lubetkin recalled their escape from the ghetto: "For twelve hours we moved inch by inch in the canals in pitch blackness holding hands in a chain," waiting for thirty-six hours beneath a manhole cover until help arrived.[22] Uris dedicated *Mila 18* to the Lubetkins and to Dr. Israel Blumenfeld, a scholar and Warsaw Ghetto fighter.[23]

The stories and the survivors at the kibbutz moved Uris so profoundly that he later became national chairman of the Ghetto Fighters' House and Museum, heading a fund-raising drive. He also donated a portion of the manuscript of *Exodus* for display in the museum. In April 1960, he and Ziviah Lubetkin spoke at Hollywood's Temple Beth El as part of an observance of the ghetto uprising. This was a heroic time in America. In July 1960, the Democrats nominated John F. Kennedy for president. Uris attended the Los Angeles convention as a delegate and Kennedy supporter.

Besides firsthand accounts, Uris had texts and testimonies retrieved from Yad Vashem (the Holocaust memorial and archive center in Jerusalem), notably Emanuel Ringelblum's *Notes from the Warsaw Ghetto*, published in 1958, although Yiddish excerpts had begun appearing in Warsaw between 1948 and 1952. The existence of this archive, one of the most immediate records of ghetto life, is itself remarkable.

Ringelblum was a historian, high school teacher, activist, and social worker. As German repression increased and the ghetto was sealed in November 1940, he realized the importance of keeping an account of what happened, initially to document German oppression and later to record atrocities. He organized a clandestine group of "historians," who called themselves Oneg Shabbat (Joy of the Shabbat) because they met on Shabbat. Through them, he began to encourage the residents of the ghetto to tell their stories via journals, letters, circulars, diaries, and essays—any form of documentation. The group gave classroom assignments to schoolchildren and later incorporated their reports into the archive. They began to collect records, decrees, drawings, eyewitness accounts, newspapers, even ration cards. Of course, the accumulation of such material was illegal, so Ringelblum recorded events in letters to relatives, which were never sent. Rabbi Huberband, a colleague, wrote his account in the margins of religious books. And everyone contributed—smugglers, students, professors, and policemen—the purpose expressed by nineteen-year-old Dawid Grober, who wrote in August 1942: "What we were unable to cry and shriek out to the world we buried in the ground."[24]

As material accumulated and the uprising was about to begin, action was taken to preserve the archive. On three occasions, part of the archive was buried in one of ten metal boxes or three large milk cans. The first cache was buried on 3 August 1942, the second in February 1943, and the third in April 1943. Three of the ten metal boxes were discovered in September 1946, and two of the milk cans in December 1950. The remaining seven boxes and the other milk can have not been located. Nonetheless, more than 25,000 pages of documents have survived, including a 1943 ghetto poster: "He who fights for life has a chance of being saved: he who rules out resistance from the start is already lost, doomed to a degrading death in the suffocation machine of Treblinka . . . We, too, are deserving of life! You merely must know how to fight for it!" Oneg Shabbat managed, as well, to smuggle out three reports detailing ghetto conditions to the Polish government in exile in London.[25]

Uris used the diary form of Ringelblum's *Notes* as part of his structure for *Mila 18*, as had John Hersey for his novel *The Wall* (1950), which cited a fictitious Levinson archive, supposedly written in Yiddish and discovered in the ghetto. Uris had read Hersey's novel before he went to Hollywood in 1954 but did not reread it while working on *Mila 18*. He was critical of it because it put the Jews in a position of slavery, which he abhorred.[26] Uris used the diary form to document the increasing violence of the German attack on the ghetto rather than to focus on the fate of individual characters. Preservation of the archive became the crucial goal of the Jewish fighters, while destruction of the archive became the aim of the Nazis who had heard that such a record existed. In the novel, the importance of the escape of the Swiss-employed American journalist, Christopher de Monti, lies not only in the preservation of his life but also in his knowledge of the location of the archive, which, at the end of the novel, he vows to reclaim. His December 1943 entry, which ends the book, also marks the end of the narrative journal.

Ringelblum's *Notes from the Warsaw Ghetto* sets the tone and even the theme of Uris's novel. Late in his account, for example, he describes the *morituri* (Latin for "those who are about to die"), the bitter pessimism that defines the mood of the beleaguered Jews. However, he then writes: "Most of the populace is set on resistance. It seems to me that people will no longer go to the slaughter like lambs. They want the enemy to pay dearly for their lives. They'll fling themselves at them with knives, staves, coal, gas . . . They want to die at home, not in a strange place . . . They calculate now that going to the slaughter peaceably has not diminished the misfortune, but increased it."[27]

Many of the particulars in *Mila 18* reflect details from the diary, beginning with the Good Fellowship Club, which is Ringelblum's Oneg Shabbat group. Ringelblum is the model for Alexander Brandel, an amateur historian. In the novel, the smuggled report on the extermination camps is loosely based on one of the three similar reports compiled by Oneg Shabbat.

Of course, Ringelblum's was not the only surviving journal of life in the ghetto. The journals of Chaim Aaron Kaplan, a teacher, and Stanslaw Adler, an officer of the Jewish police in the ghetto, are equally important. Mary Berg, the daughter of an American citizen repatriated in 1943, kept a diary from October 1939 to July 1942.[28] Dr. Janusz Korczak, a noted physician, educator, and director of the orphanages in the ghetto, also kept a diary. His selfless act of accompanying two hundred children deported from Warsaw to Treblinka in the summer of 1942 remains one of the noblest acts of the war. He would not leave the orphans, choosing instead to go with them on the trains, holding the hands of two of his youngest pupils.[29]

MILA 18

Because it narrates a single cataclysmic event, *Mila 18* is a more successful narrative than *Exodus*. In this work, Uris does not attempt to tell the entire history of the Jews; rather, it is the history of the Jews of a particular time and place, narrated with vivid details and action. Four parts organize the novel: the defeat of Poland by the Nazis; the organization of the ghetto by the Nazis and the awakening of the Jews to the Nazi reality; the slaughter of the Jews and the resistance; and finally, the epic forty-two-day battle. He also shows how communists, fascists, Zionists, collaborationists, and assimilationists in the Warsaw community could (sometimes) work together.

But Uris could not resist romance, an integral part of his formula for popular fiction. Here, it is the story of the journalist Christopher de Monti and the married Deborah Bronski, which competes with the graphic account of Jewish resistance. Foregrounding the story is Andrei Androfski, a Polish cavalry officer who knows that the only hope for the Jews is to strike back at the Nazis. His love is Gabriela Rak, an American Catholic who chooses to remain in Warsaw rather than escape. Again, Uris favors a Jewish hero with a non-Jewish lover (like Ari and Kitty in *Exodus*). He reverses this in the secondary romance: the non-Jewish de Monti and the married Jewish woman Bronski. To offset the partisan actions of Androfski is Alexander Brandel, a scholar, historian, and pacifist determined to save the Jews by not resisting the Nazis.

The novel, like Uris's other books, is plot-driven, and action shapes character.

Flashbacks are minimal, their absence creating a narrative momentum that drives the reader and the story forward. But Uris exposes the weaknesses as well as the strengths of his characters through their choices, which become moral statements. He relies again on a journalist to frame the story: here, Christopher de Monti takes the role played by Michael Morrison in *The Angry Hills* and Mark Parker in *Exodus*. De Monti, however, has a much more important role than his predecessors, alternating between apparent complicity with the Germans, especially with the propaganda specialist Horst von Epp, and commitment to his love for Deborah, sister of the heroic Androfski, but married to the sickly and morally paralyzed Dr. Paul Bronski. Androfksi is the Ari Ben Canaan of the novel, a Polish Jewish fighter extraordinaire.

De Monti's recognition of his own moral complicity with the Germans leads to his heroic efforts to get a secret report on German concentration camps out of Poland and to escape so that he can return to Warsaw after the war and recover the secret archive stored throughout the ghetto. But he must give up his beloved Deborah, leaving her to her fate in the ghetto in order to convey to the world the history of the German atrocities, recorded and stored in boxes, milk cans, and other containers throughout the ghetto. He sacrifices personal happiness for history.

Of greatest importance to Uris was the theme of fighting Jews, first outlined in *Exodus*. His program was to liberate the Jews from the image of victim, coward, or willing prisoner. Uris expands his treatment of tough-Jew characters, finding in the ŻOB a turning point in Jewish history. David Ben-Gurion recognized this in mid-February 1943. On the day he and others honored the defenders of Tel Hai, a settlement in Galilee that fought to the last man rather than surrender, Ben-Gurion acknowledged the news of the defeat of the ghetto uprising but celebrated the Poles' resistance and courage as a new example for all Jews of "heroic death."[30] The stereotype of the passive Jew of the Diaspora was erased, the uprising of the Warsaw Ghetto proof of Jewish valor.

The actions of the ŻOB confirmed Uris's view expressed in an interview shortly after the publication of *Exodus*: "We Jews are not what we have been portrayed to be. In truth, we have been fighters."[31] For Uris, Jews were no longer ambivalent; history wouldn't let them be. The Holocaust and the creation of Israel consolidated those tough Jews of the past, like the Maccabees. Warriors not rabbis became the new heroes, a transformation underscored by successes like the Six-Day War in June 1967 and the raid on Entebbe in 1976. Ariel Sharon replaced Gimpel the Fool. Masculinity, strength, and, if necessary, violence defined the new Jew. Passivity and weakness were gone, replaced by Jewish power. Uris knew the answer to the question posed by the character Jakov in Isaac Bashevis Singer's novel *The Slave*: "Must a man agree to his own destruction?"[32] For Uris, the answer was an unequivocal no.

In *Mila 18*, Uris takes up the theme of resistance with determination, although to his credit, he represents the controversy surrounding the decision to fight. When Alexander Brandel seeks Rabbi Solomon's support in the novel, there is a lengthy discussion whether doing nothing or taking action is better for Jewish survival (*M18*, 136–138). Faith is not enough of a defense, Brandel tells the rabbi, and suffering is not salvation, as the novel proves. Androfksi and others attempt to convince the ghetto leaders that to resist is to regain dignity and infuse new meaning into being a Jew. They must fight to survive and to oppose the deportations. They translate into resistance the aged Rabbi Solomon's view that God's will is to oppose tyranny. This offers them the moral foundation for the violent defense of their world, despite facing overwhelming odds.

Uris's writing also does battle, this time with history and sentiment. Too often he resorts to flourishes that compound cliché with excess. "Death spewed from the skies" is a simple example (*M18*, 89). Another: "Jewish guns vomited into their midst, spewing three years of pent-up rage" (*M18*, 476). His enthusiasm for action leads him to substitute rhetoric for style. A good deal of the novel also concerns the secret movement of individuals in and out of the ghetto, each crossing, of course, creating immense danger and the threat of immediate execution. Suspense is paramount, and when action occurs, it is presented dramatically and convincingly.

To maintain the narrative and prevent it from losing credibility amid all the impossible adventures and strained loves, Uris includes passages from a journal kept by Alexander Brandel, which was modeled on the work of Ringelblum (see *M18*, 114 or 277–281 for example). Balancing Brandel's historical accounts of the slow destruction of Warsaw are the subjective experiences of those trying to survive in the ghetto. Military communiqués full of dates, locations, and military details also add to the objectivity of the narrative while forwarding the plot. The text even reproduces a telegram from Hitler authorizing the invasion of Poland, as well as various deportation orders (*M18*, 79, 312–313). Adolf Eichmann appears several times. The variety of narrative entries and historical figures keep the reader engaged despite the suffering and tragic nature of the overall situation.

Uris does not avoid the deprivation and pain of living in the ghetto. In fact, it is one of the most powerful and affecting features of the book. He writes vividly of starvation, interrogations, and battles. He even shows children being killed at whim, at one point a girl of three (*M18*, 359). But he also shows how the clever Jew can outwit the obtuse Nazis, as when the young Wolf Brandel is caught and questioned by the Nazi Gunther Sauer—and exhibits steely determination even when the beaten Rebecca Eisen, his contact, is thrown into his interrogation room and collapses (*M18*, 240–246).

Politics is also not forgotten. For the resistance to work, competing groups must cooperate. But unlike *Exodus*, in which Uris combined radical factions into a single group, *Mila 18* maintains the independence of the differing units. But Androfksi, the leader, acknowledges the importance of cooperation if they are to succeed (*M18*, 269).

Despite the sensational aspects of the story, Uris resists showing the final destruction of the last fighters and the death of Androfksi or Wolf, the two final leaders. He does, however, provide plenty of violence, especially as the battle to destroy the ghetto continues, which creates such frustration for the Germans that at one point Oberführer Funk shoots one of his own officers in a rage (*M18*, 501). The German assault on the final bunkers of the resistance is dramatic (*M18*, 515–516). Deborah, who has devoted herself to protecting the orphaned children of the ghetto, dies in her brother's arms. But Uris ends the story with the dramatic escape of de Monti and others through the sewer tunnels as characters romantically fight for their liberty: "Gabriela took a short barreled shotgun from inside her trench coat" (*M18*, 537). They must survive to reveal to the world the history of life in the ghetto, hidden in boxes and milk cans.

Mila 18 appeared while Eichmann was being tried in Jerusalem (June 1961), Uris capitalizing, again, on worldwide interest in the fate of the Jews. But unlike the tragic testimony and recounting of painful loss in the courtroom, Uris's novel celebrates the courage of resistance fighters who, knowing they were in a hopeless battle against superior Nazi forces, did not give up or surrender. The battle against the Germans takes on almost mythic proportions. Mila 18, the address of the house that served as the command post for the fighters, assumes symbolic as well as historic importance.

Reception of the novel was strong among readers, weak among critics. Again, Uris was deemed melodramatic, accused of transforming a tragic story into an overheated account that favored emotion over fact. The *New York Times*, however, favorably compared the novel to John Hersey's *The Wall*, claiming that *Mila 18* was "authentic as history" as well as "convincing as fiction."[33] The *Guardian* took a different view, calling the book "nothing but a long sickening scream of anger and horror and racial pride."[34] The theatricality of Uris's presentation undercut the suffering the novel should have dignified, while the dialogue approached only that of a B movie. There were also errors: Uris claims that the Jesuits led pogroms against the Jews in the Middle Ages, years before the order was formed; he places a Ferrari automobile in pre–First World War Italy, decades before the car company was formed (1947); he credits John Steinbeck with having written a section of John Milton's *Paradise Lost*. There are also many grammatical errors and sections of sloppy writing. As one critic wrote: it is a failure as a novel, but a success as a manifesto of Jewish heroism.[35]

Mila 18 became a Book-of-the-Month Club selection and was so popular that the young writer Joseph Heller had to retitle his first novel *Catch-22* instead of *Catch-18*.[36] Uris's name was becoming a brand, and his work was marketed as "Leon Uris's new novel." Titles almost became secondary to the promotion of the author, who could be relied on for historical detail, action, and, of course, romance. The novel spent thirty-one weeks on best-seller lists, and for Uris, its importance was clear: "If Israel was Exodus, Warsaw was Genesis—it was the first time Jewish people fought under the Star of David since the fall of the temple."[37]

ARMAGEDDON

Uris, however, did not rest on the success of *Mila 18*. In May 1961, he began research on what would become his next novel, which would feature a military hero embroiled in postwar politics and the Cold War. For this work, to be called *Armageddon*, he traveled to Berlin, East Germany, and the Soviet Union. A set of slides from the trip records him flying into Moscow and includes photos of the Kremlin, a rally in East Berlin, and the Olympic Stadium in Berlin. Earlier, in 1958, he had had a photo taken of himself proudly crossing over into East Berlin and posing with a guard.[38]

The setting is again Europe, and the action takes the reader from the end of the Second World War through the first years of the American occupation of Germany and the Berlin airlift. The novel displays American courage, know-how, and determination, its patriotic author making it clear that America knew how to rebuild as well as fight. His unrepentant view of American power and expertise, despite communist threats and latent German hostility, persists throughout the book. In a later interview, he declared: "I really feel there would be no world without America."[39] In chronicling the career of Captain Sean O'Sullivan as a military administrator and an assistant to Brigadier General Andrew Jackson Hansen in the restoration of German cities, Uris blends historical detail with romance and politics while confronting the larger issue of redefining crime and punishment. The novel covers the transitional postwar period, when the Americans dealt with the remnants of the Nazis and guilt at their own actions while responding to the new threat of communism.

The Berlin airlift is the central event of the book, and in characteristic style, Uris undertook plenty of research. From the beginning of the project, he worked closely with the U.S. Air Force (USAF), which made archives available to him from its records center in Wiesbaden. Uris began by conducting on-site research. He had been to Berlin as early as 1958, when he went to meet the director assigned to film his second novel, *The Angry Hills*. Out of deference to the victims of the Holocaust, Uris had previously refused to travel to Germany but reversed his stand, treating his visit as a personal challenge. During a visit in 1961, he confronted communism when he crossed into East Berlin. But the East Germans were uncooperative and made it difficult for him to travel about and conduct his research.

The novel also gave him trouble partly because it was his most factually based work; the book stayed tied most closely to its sources. In seeking to re-create the postwar era, he seemed unable to release himself from his research. The consequence was a set of clichéd characters and staged events.

Uris's access to USAF documents, some of which had been released only a few years earlier, hindered rather than helped the novel. His heavily marked copy of the two-volume *USAFE and the Berlin Airlift, 1949: Supply and Operational Aspects* indicates his attention to detail, much of which he incorporated into his story.[40] This official history of the airlift supplied him with precise information on the number and type of aircraft, flight patterns, load factors, landing details, and estimates of needed supplies. It was invaluable.

The stopping of all passenger trains on 1 June 1948 between the western zones and Berlin was precisely the type of detail Uris loved, as well as the blockade of five coal trains bound for Berlin on 10 June 1948. He also underscored information on the removal of certain radio equipment from the cargo planes in order to increase their load capacities. Facts, figures, and charts added to the information. Of particular interest to him was the addition of a fourth squadron of thirteen C-54 Skymasters from the Seventh Air Force in Hawaii, which was ordered to Germany to bring European Command operations and spare crews up to full force. They joined aircraft from Alaska and the Caribbean.

Details on Lieutenant General Curtis LeMay, commanding general of the USAF in Europe, also fascinated him, especially the entry that on 29 June 1948, LeMay himself flew one of the C-47 cargo planes into Tempelhof airport and, while awaiting the unloading of his aircraft, held a conference with the theatre commander, General Lucius D. Clay. Uris loved specifics, such as the way coal from various German dealers was packed in U.S. Army duffel bags, each weighing approximately 50 kilograms, or about 110 pounds. Or the 9 July 1948 communiqué from the Soviets that their air force would undertake an indefinite period of instrument training in specified areas within the Frankfurt-Berlin corridor without filing any flight plans. The purpose, of course, was to harass the U.S. Air Force.

An overload of this type of information, along with nationalistic outbursts ("We have to love America the way our parents did," shouts General Hansen [AR, 12]) interferes with the development of the novel, which opens almost a year before the end of the war. Plans for the rebuilding of Europe are underway, and O'Sullivan, promoted to major, develops a pilot project for a German city, the fictitious Rombaden. Uris then introduces an epic poem, *The Legend of Rom-*

baden, to partly explain the appeal to the Germans of establishing a master race and Nazism (some readers believed this to be an actual text; Uris made it up). It also contains the seeds of what O'Sullivan believes to be German anti-Semitism. Complicating matters is his natural hatred of the Germans because they killed two of his brothers in the war. Although he hates all Germans, he not only has to work with them but also falls in love with a beautiful German woman whose father was apparently involved with the Nazis.

A fictitious concentration camp named Schwabenwald introduces readers to the horrors of the camps. Determined not to let the Germans forget, O'Sullivan orders the residents of Rombaden to tour the camp before they are issued ration cards, as was done after the war at Dachau and other camps in Germany and Poland. Almost all the inhabitants of Rombaden deny knowledge of the camp. The anti-Nazi rebel Ulrich Falkenstein, recently liberated from the camp, challenges O'Sullivan's attitude of Allied help, declaring, "I am a German and my first duty is not to Allied victory but to the redemption of the people" (AR, 94). The nobleman and Nazi sympathizer Ludwig von Romstein is his counterpart.

The novel focuses on a new threat, the Russians, which allows Uris to provide a good deal of Russian history in order to contextualize their presence. When O'Sullivan finally goes to Berlin, he understands clearly the new danger. Part II of the novel returns readers to April 1945, when the Soviets enter Berlin. Characteristically, Uris focuses on a few characters to represent history, in this case Bruno Falkenstein, the brother of Ulrich. The family's story, a mixed account of sympathy with and distrust of the Allies, becomes a brutal retelling of Soviet atrocities and neglect. Uris then provides biographical notes on the new Soviet leaders, turning the novel briefly into a political textbook. The final third of the book pits the Americans against the Soviets in a battle for Berlin. The Soviets use various tactics and obstacles to prevent the American entry and redevelopment. Uris demonizes the Soviets and almost satirizes the Americans, especially in their belief that German self-determination will be strong enough to stop the Soviets, who turn to coercion and terror to maintain control.

Uris then turns to a journalist (again), Nelson Bradbury, to document the Soviet threat. If Berlin were to fall, all of Europe could come under communist control. As General Hansen states in a presentation to the Joint Chiefs of Staff in Washington, Berlin will be "our Armageddon" (AR, 460). Part 4 of the novel dramatizes the Berlin airlift, focusing on General "Crusty" Stonebreaker, who was modeled on General LeMay (General Lucius Clay was likely the prototype for USAF commander Barney Root). The crisis plays out against O'Sullivan's love for Ernestine Falkenstein in overwrought prose: "Ernestine tried to touch him as he sweated and knotted with the pain of his dreams" (AR, 623). By June 1949, the airlift had succeeded, but O'Sullivan discovers that Ernestine's father is a war criminal (AR, 604–605). Ernestine insists that O'Sullivan prosecute her father, although that means the end of their love. Again, as at the end of *Mila 18*, noble action supersedes personal happiness. In his grief, O'Sullivan realizes that he "cannot make peace with the Germans. . . . No real peace can ever be made until we pass on and the new generation of Americans and Germans make it" (AR, 625).

Structurally, the multiple stories and the quantity of political information distort *Armageddon* so strongly that its focus becomes unclear. Too many official reports entered as text further distract the reader. Some of the writing is visceral, as when a Russian general beats a Russian officer, but the sentimentality, which is strongest when Uris writes about relationships, undercuts the intensity of the action.

Doubleday did not concern itself with such matters, preferring to promote the book as superior to anything else Uris had written. Borrowing from earlier reviews, the ads trumpeted:

> More "crammed with action" than BATTLE CRY
> More "poignant human drama" than MILA 18
> More of "a magnificent epic" than EXODUS
> THE NEW URIS BESTSELLER TOPS THEM ALL!
> ARMAGEDDON
> A NOVEL OF BERLIN BY LEON URIS[41]

Within five weeks of its publication in June 1964, *Armageddon* had moved to third place on the best-seller lists. Its acknowledgments included support not only from various USAF officers but also from Columbia Pictures, which had funded his travel for a possible screenplay (the usual Uris scheme). And ironically, despite the impending breakdown of his own marriage, Uris provides a useful comment on love in the novel. The Soviet adviser Igor tells O'Sullivan, from whom he requests safe passage to West Berlin for his girlfriend, that love is "to know the faults and the wrongs of that which you love . . . and go on loving just the same" (AR, 610).

Uris proudly told his father that portions of *Armageddon* had been bought by the *Saturday Evening Post* after he had written only one-fifth of the book. He expected big things from its publication, and it did become a Literary Guild selection. But it is probably the least recognized of his books—"perhaps it was politically at the wrong time in the wrong place," he admitted in an interview.[42]

Armageddon received unusually harsh reviews. William Barrett in the *Atlantic* dismissed it as "not serious literature but journalism. . . . His characters are flat and one-dimensional, as if already prefabricated to the Hollywood movie in which they are bound to appear."[43] Herbert Mitgang in the *New York Times* began his review with this sentence: "Leon Uris, one of the leading cliché-mongers of mass-cult, has constructed another of his non-fiction novels."[44] He then warns readers not spend the seven dollars for the book: "Mr. Uris's latest epic is laughable as either fiction or nonfiction." Furthermore, Uris was again following John Hersey, whose novel *A Bell for Adano* dealt more effectively with the American occupation of Europe. The *Denver Post*, however, saw the book as "a testimonial to the determination of the free world to prevail where oppression exists."[45] The rhetoric reflects the jingoistic tone and presentation of America in the novel, which the *Chicago Tribune* upheld: "Drama so intense, significance so great that the reader's interest is caught at once and held to the end."[46]

The novel sold more than 380,000 copies in hardcover, in itself a sort of answer to *Time* magazine's scathing review, which started, "Hmm. Bank balance down. Time to do another Big Novel" and ended by noting that *Armageddon* "reads as if it were not written at all but dictated, Napoleon style, at top speed."[47] "Thank goodness I write for the masses and not for *Time!*" Uris responded. "They were wrong about *Exodus* too."[48] In the same interview, he remarks that he would soon be moving to Aspen, not because of the smog in Los Angeles but because he loved skiing.

Despite the negative views, the novel was an immediate best seller. Doubleday printed 85,000 copies to start and had 60,000 presold (mostly to the Literary Guild, its own book club). By November 1964, more than 310,000 copies were in print, the same month it was banned in South Africa because it mentions communism. Excerpts in the *Saturday Evening Post* generated interest also. Soon, it settled as number four on the best-seller list, after John le Carré's *The Spy Who Came in from the Cold*, *Candy* by Terry Southern, and *Herzog* by Saul Bellow. Plans to film the novel, however, ran into delays and then postponement, as one paper explained: "His last novel, *Armageddon* was bought by MGM but it's temporarily on the shelf because of anticipated production difficulties involved in re-enacting the Berlin airlift."[49]

Uris capitalized on his appeal, however. In the mid-1960s, he negotiated a precedent-setting contract with Harper and Row, which gave him 100 percent (instead of the usual 50 percent) of all payments for paperback and book-club rights for his next novel. This would be for what would eventually become *Topaz*, a novel with as much intrigue in its origin as its plot.

Uris and Jacqueline Susann promoting each other's best sellers, ca. 1966.

*Uris's Russian family, including his father, William Wolf Uris (center,
standing), his grandmother (seated), and two uncles, Aaron (wearing a hat)
and Ari (wearing a white shirt). Photo courtesy of Karen Uris.*

Uris in a studio shot at age four, 1928. Photo courtesy of Karen Uris.

Uris at age ten, January 1934. Photo courtesy of Karen Uris.

Uris (second from right) in Situation Out of Hand, *performed at the Oak Knoll Naval Hospital, Oakland, California, 1944.*

Uris in a marine trench coat, December 1944. The photo was sent to the parents of his fiancée, Betty Beck, with this caption: "He's squinting dreadfully here—has blue eyes and nice eyebrows." Photo courtesy of Karen Uris.

Uris and Betty Beck in their Marine Corps uniforms, January 1945. Photo courtesy of Karen Uris.

Uris and Betty in Clear Lake, California, December 1945 or January 1946. Photo courtesy of Karen Uris.

Uris standing in front of a car belonging to the San Francisco Call-Bulletin *during his career as regional circulation manager, ca. 1952.*

Uris signing copy of Battle Cry *for a female admirer, 1953.*

Uris in a Pittsburgh storefront with his arms around two marines, 1953.

Showgirl reading Battle Cry *on the set of* The Ed Sullivan Show, *New York City, 1953.*

Uris and Raoul Walsh examining the script of Battle Cry, *1954.*

Uris with the cast of Battle Cry at the world premiere in Baltimore, 1 February 1955.
Left to right: *Uris, Dorothy Malone, Tab Hunter, Mona Freeman, and Raoul Walsh.*

Uris and his children Mark and Karen with Burt Lancaster
on the set of Gunfight at the O.K. Corral, *Hollywood, 1956.*

*Uris on the veranda of his home on Amestoy Avenue, Encino, California,
during the writing of* Exodus, *ca. 1957. Uris is in his favorite writing outfit,
including loafers without socks. Photo courtesy of Karen Uris.*

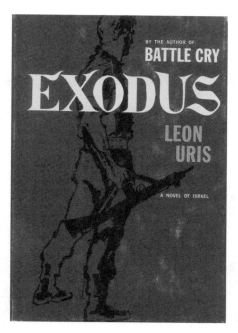

Exodus *cover, design by Sydney Butchkes,*
drawing by Harlan Krakowitz, 1958.

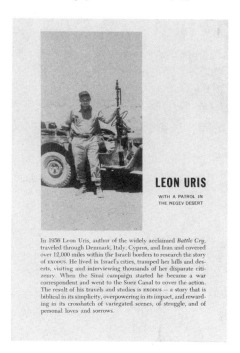

LEON URIS

WITH A PATROL IN
THE NEGEV DESERT

In 1956 Leon Uris, author of the widely acclaimed *Battle Cry*,
traveled through Denmark, Italy, Cyprus, and Iran and covered
over 12,000 miles within the Israeli borders to research the story
of EXODUS. He lived in Israel's cities, tramped her hills and des-
erts, visiting and interviewing thousands of her disparate citi-
zenry. When the Sinai campaign started he became a war
correspondent and went to the Suez Canal to cover the action.
The result of his travels and studies is EXODUS — a story that is
biblical in its simplicity, overpowering in its impact, and reward-
ing in its crosshatch of variegated scenes, of struggle, and of
personal loves and sorrows.

Exodus *back jacket, showing a 1956 photo of Uris*
with a machine gun in the Negev.

Uris and Otto Preminger examining the screenplay of Exodus, *Hollywood, 1958.*

Uris at the Mandelbaum Gate, Jerusalem, 1960.

*Uris in London during the 1964 libel trial that would become
the basis of* QB VII. *Photo courtesy of Karen Uris.*

Uris and Betty at dinner in Hamburg, 1965. Photo courtesy of Karen Uris.

Uris skiing, Aspen, 1966. Photo courtesy of Karen Uris.

Uris on the porch of his Aspen home while writing Topaz, *1966.*

Uris and Margery Edwards, Aspen, 1968.

The stained-glass window in Uris's library in his Aspen home, 1971. Photo by Jill Uris.

Uris in his Aspen study, 1972. Photo by Jill Uris.

Uris and Jill in Aspen.

Uris and Jill, Portland, Oregon, October 1981. Photo by Geoff Parks.

LEON
MARCUS
URIS
PFC
US MARINE CORPS
WORLD WAR II
AUG 3 1924
JUN 21 2003
AMERICAN MARINE
JEWISH WRITER

Gravestone of Leon Uris, U.S. Military Cemetery, Quantico, Virginia. Photo by I. B. Nadel.

LOVE AND LITIGATION

I like my Jews mean and fighting.
—URIS, 22 DECEMBER 1964

JUST BEFORE THE PUBLICATION of *Armageddon* in the spring of 1964, Uris
needed a safe haven. Not because of the novel, but because of the publicity and pressure of a London libel trial instituted by a Polish-born British
citizen who claimed that Uris had defamed him in a passage from *Exodus*.
The trial generated international headlines, which Uris sought to escape. Mexico
was the answer.

Settling in Acapulco to write a screenplay for Paramount in February 1964,
Uris joined a cadre of other writers who found the locale conducive to a relaxed
style of work: Tennessee Williams, Budd Schulberg, Robert Roark, and Ernest
Gann all enjoyed the sun and sea. By June 1964, after his victory in London, he
told his father that he had more or less settled in Acapulco after a long motor trip
through the country with Betty, and was now sitting down to write a screenplay to
be titled "The Gringo," set in Mexico during the Porfirio Díaz era.[1] The screenplay
of *Armageddon* would follow, which he would coproduce. He was also trying to
make a deal for the film rights to *Mila 18*.

Acapulco was a respite from the tensions of publishing, and he told his father that there was "every possibility" that he would "build a part-time home in
Acapulco: my health is wonderful. I water ski every day and find life on the sea
generally very healthy."[2] Betty came and went, going first to Aspen to assist with
plans for a new house—Uris had bought a parcel of land on Red Mountain in
February for seven thousand dollars—before coming down to the Las Brisas
Hilton in Acapulco. She then went back to Malibu for Karen's high school graduation, which Uris missed. She and the family returned to Mexico in July after
closing up their Malibu beach house in anticipation of the move to Aspen.

London was a battle, however. A libel action for damages caused by defamation
had been brought against him by a sixty-one-year-old surgeon, Dr. Wladislaw

Dering. Dr. Dering had been a prison doctor in Auschwitz from August 1940 to January 1944. The cause of the action was a single sentence in *Exodus* referring to a "Dr. Dehring," who performs medical experiments dealing with human sterilization (*EX*, 146). Dr. Dering of London claimed it was libelous. It led to an eighteen-day jury trial beginning 1 April 1964 in Queen's Bench VII at the Royal Courts of Justice in the Strand. Conducted in Greek, Polish, Hebrew, English, German, French, and Ladino, the trial became a sensation, receiving coverage around the world.

The issues went beyond one man's reputation. The case addressed morality and ethical behavior in the face of human horror. Twenty-two witnesses from Auschwitz representing some 130 prisoners subjected to medical experiments gave testimony, in many ways echoing the momentous testimony at the Eichmann trial in Jerusalem, which had taken place only three years earlier.

Uris, with the backing of his English publisher William Kimber, knew he had to fight the case. The year before the trial, the printer Purnell & Sons Ltd. had published a public retraction and apology for handling the book and had negotiated an out-of-court settlement of £500 with Dr. Dering. Uris, of course, with his pugnacious nature, relished the chance to challenge Dr. Dering in court and eagerly pushed his publisher to do the same. Pretrial briefs debated the value of the case, known as *Dering v. Uris and Others*, but it went ahead. Leading Uris's defense team was Lord Gerald Gardiner, later lord chancellor of England. Seven witnesses spoke on behalf of the plaintiff, Dr. Dering, twenty-two on behalf of the defendants, both sides bringing forward Holocaust survivors. The most important speakers, however, were silent: the names in a registry of surgical operations written partly in Dr. Dering's hand from the camp's prison hospital.[3]

Twenty-three days after the trial began, and after eighteen days of testimony, the jury returned a verdict on 6 May 1964. The jury of ten men and two women found in favor of Dr. Dering, awarding him one halfpenny (the smallest coin of the realm) in damages. But the plaintiff also had to bear court costs, and the judge ordered Dr. Dering to pay the expenses of Uris and his publisher as well. The victory was clearly Pyrrhic, as a telegram from Uris to his father stated. It simply read: "THE VICTORY IS OURS LOVE BETTY AND LEON."[4] Dr. Dering died a year after the trial, and Uris and his publisher decided not to press his widow for the outstanding court costs. Yet he remained proud of his triumph, displaying a three-volume leather-bound transcript of the case in his Aspen home and later in his New York apartment.

Betty was with Uris in London that spring, and supportive throughout the ordeal, although they were having difficulties. Uris's abrasive manner—he was always battling producers and agents and in this instance his publisher, which had been reluctant to support him, as well as the plaintiff—spilled over into his personal life. He could be demanding, preferring to command rather than cooperate. He also took things personally, especially slights and insults, the more so if they occurred within the family. Willful and aggressive behavior, partly learned from standing up to his father and his intrusive manner, made him insistent (others said unreasonable) and difficult. His relationships were governed by a double standard: he could challenge anyone, but could never himself be challenged. Life with Betty became fractious as well as fragile. In June 1966, he would refer to their relationship as "a life of continuous warfare."[5]

In June 1964, he and Betty were back in Acapulco, having taken a 3,000-mile road trip across the northern part of Mexico, part of his research for a film but also, and more importantly, a chance to reconnect. He was expecting to finish the screenplay by September and then to immediately begin a screenplay of *Armageddon*, which had been sold to MGM, a project he would coproduce with Marty Racking, of Los Angeles. There was also talk of a film of *Mila 18*. Betty suggested a property in Mexico for them to buy, all part of a possible reconciliation. Sales of *Armageddon* were not large, but Uris expected it would "have a sales pattern like *Exodus* that is, make its big move after Christmas."[6]

In early July 1964, the entire family joined him in Mexico, first at the Las Brisas Hilton in Acapulco and then at a small villa. The country increasingly appealed to him: "I need a few years of peace before renewing serous writing," he told his father, who continued to disagree with or dismiss him.[7] The publication of *Armageddon* did not bring Uris the fatherly approval he sought: "It has been another painful experience for me not to have received a single word from you about *Armageddon*," he wrote from Acapulco in July 1964, adding, "Literary critics I have enough of . . . I only have one father and when his only son spends several years of soul searching and at hard labor in the creation of a book it seems that a few kind words concerning the effort would be in order."[8]

In August, his daughter Karen made plans to go to Colorado State University at Fort Collins, majoring in Spanish and international relations. He had also just been elected to the Jewish Academy of Arts and Science, the first academic honor he received. Israel struck an *Exodus* medal "in honor of the first blockade runner 30 years go" and presented him with the first one.[9] He had finished the story outline of the Mexican film for Paramount and was eager to begin the screenplay for *Armageddon*, which was beginning to bring in money, receiving the largest paperback-reprint guarantee in publishing history. In October 1964, Paramount Pictures and the Yugoslavian government signed a joint venture for the filming of *Mila 18*. Betty, meanwhile, left for Aspen, and he purchased a small parcel of land in Acapulco.

But as his reputation grew, his relationship with his family, especially with his wife, began to disintegrate. Throughout the early sixties, Uris, as one family member explained it, increasingly believed that the world revolved around him and that he was entitled to lecture others on politics, the economy, or society, a habit inherited from his father.[10] He also began to demean those who were close to him, displaying little empathy for or understanding of their problems. He sought control and felt he could exert it if he exposed others' weaknesses. According to his children, his behavior was often contradictory: generous in giving time to causes and fund-raising, but niggardly with both time and money for his family. On one hand, Uris could proudly tell his father about his honors but, on the other, castigate his father for neglecting his work. He would alternately praise and blame his children. His behavior could be friendly one moment but cruel the next; years later, he would not talk to his children for long periods or else kick them out of the house, only to welcome them back later. Consequently, those closest to him never really got to know him; he didn't allow it. If he trusted you, you were in the inner circle; if not, you were out.

His sociability at this time also seemed to alter. Formerly gregarious with friends, both in Larkspur and Encino, he increasingly withdrew from them, an act Betty at one point attributed to his decision to quit smoking.[11] He also fought with his celebrity status as his fame began to create conflicts: one moment he wanted people to pay attention to him, but the next he would be upset if they paid too much. He would welcome recognition from the maitre d' of a restaurant but be upset if the chef ran out of the kitchen to greet him and prepare something special.[12] In the midst of these contradictions came the move to Aspen, a world different from any he had known.

ASPEN

Aspen in the 1960s had its share of free-loving, drug-using hippies and would soon attract figures like Hunter S. Thompson and even serial killer Ted Bundy. Long a magnet for ski bums, rebels, and others who found the extraordinary natural surroundings, purified air, and dry, powder-like snow irresistible, Aspen was an unlikely place for a popular writer to settle, but at the same time it was absolutely right. Removed from Hollywood and New York but accessible to both coasts, Aspen provided Uris with a retreat from the demands of public life and allowed him to indulge his passion for the outdoors. Skiing and tennis became his focuses, and when he wasn't holed up in his writing studio, part of the striking double A-frame house he constructed on Red Mountain, he was on the slopes or the courts.

Aspen tolerated fame and privacy, outlandishness and extravagance. When Uris arrived, he had already achieved immense acclaim for *Exodus*, which he would regain with *Trinity*. But in between, his profile and income shifted, although he continued to write with discipline and dedication.[13] Aspen provided him with the proper balance between social recognition and distance, although he would often write to friends that he was not a monument to be visited and so refused to meet the many friends of friends who felt, for one reason or another, entitled to visit the valley's most prominent writer. Nevertheless, he always viewed Aspen positively, telling his father that "the atmosphere is conducive to good writing and longer living. . . . I personally have always desired this type of life and I think it will work out fine."[14]

But Aspen was not just snow and ideas. It had a dark side marked by scandal, murder, suicide, and drugs. In 1976, for example, the glamorous French actress Claudine Longet accidentally shot and killed her lover, the ski champion Vladimir "Spider" Sabich. Her story was that Sabich was showing her the proper use of a gun when it went off and wounded him in the stomach. The prosecutor argued that the two were having difficulties and that, in the midst of a fight, she shot him. The charge was murder. Andy Williams, her ex-husband, flew to Aspen to be with her. The jury found her guilty of "reckless endangerment." She could have been sent to prison for two years but, instead, served only thirty days in jail. Aspen was outraged, even more so when she served her time only after returning from a Latin American vacation. She then married her defense attorney.[15]

Aspen came to define celebrity culture, becoming a celebrity itself. Other writers in residence included Clifford Irving, best known for his forged "autobiography" of Howard Hughes, and the elegant prose stylist James Salter. This was a world where porcini-dusted elk or Jack Daniel's–marinated caribou became de rigueur, or at least common fare. The intrigue, money, and undercurrent of a louche counterculture offsetting the jet-setting crowd were irresistible. One reason Aspen appealed to the star crowd was that it never made a fuss over them. The social code meant never asking for an autograph and never looking impressed. "Be blasé, don't notice" was the mantra.

Aspen also meant available young women, although sometimes there was a price to pay, as one experienced Aspen rogue admitted, noting that there were only three types of women in the town: "tourists, married and coke whores. You're lucky if you can find one who's not one of those."[16] But the young women kept coming, and in this environment, Uris found the track of his personal life derailed. This was what Hunter Thompson meant when he called Uris "Aspen's leading stag movie fan . . . who writes books."[17]

For a writer like Uris, the glitz was both good and bad. The lifestyle was attractive, but he intentionally avoided it. He did have his favorite haunts, including restaurants like The Steak Pit and The Tippler, where his friend Walt Smith, a musician, restaurateur, and bon vivant, often played. The dark but western-style

J Bar at the Hotel Jerome was another favorite spot. As he settled in, his friends were locals rather than celebrities: Freddy Fisher, an incomparable Aspen fix-it man and personality; Francis Whitaker, one of the few blacksmiths still in Aspen and a source for details about blacksmithing (used in the early pages of *Trinity*); Martie and Ken Sterling, the owners of the Heatherbed Lodge; Dr. Harold Whitcomb; and Dr. Robert O'Hare.[18]

It is likely Uris knew little of the Aspen culture when he first appeared at the door of the Heatherbed Lodge in December 1960. The lodge sits at the base of Aspen Highlands Mountain, which is 463 feet higher than Aspen Mountain and offers numerous expert trails as well as the longest vertical drop of any ski resort in the state. Aspen Highlands was where Uris would become a certified ski instructor under the guidance of the Swiss skier Fred Iselin.[19]

Ken and Martie Sterling operated the Heatherbed, which became the subject of Martie's comic memoir *Days of Stein and Roses*. Uris loved the informality and atmosphere of the place, which was several miles out of town toward the famous Blue Bells, two startling mountain peaks. The Heatherbed was also the subject of one of his few published essays. Appearing in *Ski Magazine*, "Heatherbedlam" narrates misadventures at the Heatherbed.[20]

Uris loved the outdoors and the thrill of skiing, which he would share with all three of his wives. And he made sure his children knew how to ski expertly, his son Michael becoming a racer. One of Uris's happiest periods some years later was when he received his ski instructor's badge. In his *Ski* article, he noted that he was writing the film script of *Armageddon* in one of the Heatherbed's rooms until the ski season began and that every morning he got on his Honda (trail bike) and buzzed out to the Heatherbed to write in splendid isolation.

Uris returned to the Heatherbed Lodge often, preferring its semi-isolation and quiet to the activities at home, at one point using it for several months as his office while working on a film script. He had a room at the south end of the building, and the owners built a separate outdoor staircase that allowed him to enter and exit unnoticed. He would arrive each morning on his motorcycle, actually a dirt bike, ahead of his secretary, Sheila DeVore. Together, they would go through his mail, and then he would write for hours until he needed a break, usually running downstairs to split firewood for the lodge in order to clear his head before going back to work. Physical activity was his antidote to typing, according to Martie Sterling.[21] The Heatherbed was also gaining in reputation: it was visited by Alex Haley and the British drama critic Kenneth Tynan, thereby continuing the literary tradition of Aspen, which was also the birthplace of famed *New Yorker* editor Harold Ross.

Uris enjoyed Aspen so much that he decided to move there, first renting a house and then, in February 1964, buying a lot on Red Mountain on which he thought he would build a small winter home. Not everyone celebrated the idea, however, notably his children. They found the constant relocations difficult: as soon as they had settled in and made new friends, they were uprooted. From Larkspur to Encino to Malibu and then to Mexico, the family was constantly moving. Picking up and leaving repeatedly felt much like a military life, his son Mark felt.[22] Aspen was another major change, but one that had the potential for being permanent.

Uris rented a house in town after buying the lot. The seller was Fritz Benedict, an architect who had first seen Aspen when he trained there with the Tenth Mountain Division of the U.S. Army. As soon as the war was over, Benedict had returned to the States and bought the 600-acre Red Mountain Ranch for twenty dollars an acre. He put in housing developments, designing many of the homes himself. Construction on Uris's new house was to begin in the spring of 1965 at 5 Wrights Road. In December 1965, Uris and his family moved into to a semipermanent residence in Aspen, finally moving into their own home on 2 May 1966.

The house, a unique double A-frame design, was, at the time, thought to be one of the largest A-frame homes in the West. By the time of its sale in 1989, it had grown to six bedrooms and five and a half baths, plus a nanny suite, for a total of some 8,000 square feet. A large detached garage with a caretaker's suite and a separate office-cabana building overlooking a hot tub and pool added to the home's distinction. Located midway up Red Mountain, it had a fabulous view across the valley to town and two magnificent mountains: Aspen and Shadow. Uris would occasionally move his typewriter out to one of several decks and work while facing the magnificent view. The living room was on the second floor, set there to obtain the finest views of the valley.[23]

A marvelous, though anomalous, Gothic-style library was a few steps off the dining room, adjacent to a massive white fireplace in the living room. The library would later display a stained-glass window at one end, outlined with the traceries of pointed Gothic arches. Standing before the large south library window was a handsome nineteenth-century-style desk flanked by two massive candlesticks. Bookshelves lined both sides of the room (reference works that had not made their way to his office were often found here); in the center was a refectory table surrounded by tall, red-upholstered wooden chairs with a large U carved on the back of each. Hanging from the tops of the bookshelves would be an increasing number of academic "collars," which were part of the robes worn by Uris when he and his later wife, Jill, received honorary degrees. The library also held Uris's collection of hats.

Off the library in a small, eave-like space was the paperback library, the location of the numerous paperback editions of his work in various languages.[24] The actual library was largely for show—and a favorite setting for photographs—[25]

though it was sometimes used as a second dining room. Uris worked and wrote in an office that was connected to the main house by a walkway and adjacent to the pool. Below this office was one for his research assistant, whose work ranged from correcting pages (spelling, punctuation, grammar, mechanics) to pursuing research questions and overseeing the progress of the current novel. At some point each afternoon, Uris and his assistant would meet to review new material or new assignments.

The doors to the house were unique. Rather than evoking something of the rustic ski environment of Aspen, they reflected past grandeur: they were two massive, oversized steel doors with inset copper plating rescued from the original Denver customhouse by Uris's close friend Charles Goldberg (a junk and metal dealer) and trucked to Red Mountain. Visitors needed two hands to open them. At the center of the wrought-iron gate that led up to the house—Uris's office was just past the gate and to the left—was the image of the freedom fighter from *Exodus*, seeming both out of place and yet at home in the rustic vernacular architecture that defined Aspen. Francis Whitaker, an Aspen blacksmith, manufactured the gate.

Uris enjoyed visiting Goldberg's junkyard and later brought to Aspen twelve stained-glass windows that would go into his library, a brass chandelier that was half gas and half electric, and old Corinthian columns to be used at the entrance. They were from the International Trust Company of Denver. He also had a large oak panel with an intricate carving of an owl, which had surmounted the courtroom doors in the old customhouse. Another highlight was a large stained-glass window that had once been in the Mining Exchange Building. Goldberg remarked: "I think he's going to start his own yard up in Aspen he's bought so much."[26]

Ironically, while Uris was constructing his house, a young, seventeen-year-old skier from Massachusetts was looking across the valley from Aspen Mountain and asking her ski instructor about that red gash on the mountainside. Leon Uris's new home, she was told. Some five years later, Jill Peabody would be Jill Uris and find herself living there.[27]

Completion of the house did not mean, however, peace. Uris promptly filed a lawsuit against his architect, displaying his usual aggressive, argumentative nature. He complained that situating the house over a creek bed had weakened its structure. A leaky roof needed to be redone. He also thought the house was too close to the road that circled above it in the rear, a fear confirmed in 1970 when a large yellow dump truck overturned and landed in the narrow backyard, a wheel spinning just outside the kitchen window. Uris insisted that the truck remain there for some weeks while he pursued another lawsuit against the builder-architect. And even after he sold the house in 1989 to the media baron Mort Zuckerman, he launched a lawsuit against the businessman concerning promises unfulfilled.

In his mountain studio, with its view across the valley to Aspen Mountain and Aspen Highlands with Mount Hayden's sharp peaks separating the two in the distance, Uris could feel both above and yet a part of nature. The city below meant observation and perspective, which he metaphorically brought to history and its major players. His location seemed to represent the novelist as observer and participant in the past. Uris wrote at a U-shaped desk surrounded by cork walls on which were pinned maps, charts, historical details, plot points, and character features. Reference books, catalogues, and history texts stood stacked up on the floor and on bookshelves around him. His office also featured a leather couch and chair, a 1,000-year-old Star of David, letters from Harry Truman and John Steinbeck, and an invitation to John F. Kennedy's inauguration.

Uris wrote on an IBM Selectric, often from late morning to early evening, although he called himself a "twilight writer," working best between four and seven.[28] Aspen appealed to Uris because he could be both an outsider and an insider. He could be forgotten and recognized, leaving and returning without a fuss. His home, however, was a symbolic statement to Aspen: its scale and location were signs that here was a writer at home in the past and the present, a man of action who understood and defended both justice and history. And no matter what challenges his personal life presented, his work and ideals were defined for all to see.

Uris preferred to keep his work separate from his home, perhaps a holdover from his studio days, when writers went to bungalows on studio lots to write. The practice also lent an air of professionalism to his work. In a brief profile of Uris, Ken McCormick, his editor at Doubleday, emphasized that Uris was a restless man but intense about his writing.[29] A cast of characters from his current project was often pinned to the wall of his office. He usually wrote for three to five hours a day, producing from six hundred to a thousand words, unless he was moved to explosive action, when he would turn out three thousand to four thousand words. A secretary ensured his privacy during working hours. After work he would ski or walk his two Alaskan dogs, taking them in his Jeep to a nearby national park.

THE END OF A MARRIAGE

But while Aspen provided Uris with the mental and physical space to write, Betty found herself more and more unhappy. Marital problems escalated as she became increasingly upset by Uris's constant traveling and his troubling behavior with other women, which was likely an extension of his insecurity and need to impress. She also found that life in Aspen was isolating. She did not enjoy the outdoors, and although she could ski, she disliked it. And while she tolerated life in town, she felt that the move to the then-remote mountain resort only confirmed the dislocation in their lives. Domestic stability was in jeopardy.

Uris and Betty had separated three times over the past decade, once while he was writing in Mexico. Fights and arguments began to be regular features; as early as February 1954, she had written in a diary that "Lee decides again that maybe he likes me—had another long talk on all my faults. I can't dwell on my loved one's faults like he can."[30] He was often in a "moody rampage," she wrote, caused as much by problems with the filming of *Battle Cry* as by his personal outlook. He had formally finished his screenplay and left Warner Bros. in March 1954, and in May he had an offer from MGM, but in July he was back at Warner Bros., working on a boxing film. In September, she recorded another fight: "Lee still mad but made up finally."[31] Battles with the studio also continued, especially with the producer Milton Sperling, who shifted Uris from a fight movie to the Billy Mitchell story. But by the early sixties, there was little rapport between the couple. Life, Uris told his father, had narrowed "down to a continuous brawl."[32]

Uris dominated his business relationships as firmly as his personal ones. He was often hard on his lawyer–business manager Herb Schlosberg, "almost downright mean at times," said his son Mark Uris.[33] He could also be that way with his children and friends: "he wanted things done his way," and if others objected, he either turned on them or shunned them.

By the spring of 1966, Uris wanted a divorce; Betty reluctantly agreed. They were both young enough to be able to enjoy some future happiness with others, he reasoned.[34] Betty took the two boys with her to her family in Iowa; Karen visited them later. Uris went off to Florida, where he continued working on his current novel, which would become *Topaz* (1967). On his return to Aspen, he stopped in Iowa to get the children and take them with him for the summer.

So far, everyone had been civilized, but it hadn't been easy: the marriage had been "declining badly for some four or five years," and "all hope" was "completely gone" of his living with Betty.[35] In a note to his father six months later, he was less polite, reporting that Betty was asking for too much money in the divorce: he told her she was "going to have to fight it out in court," and he cut off all direct communication between them.[36] Nonetheless, his morale was high as he looked forward to "what is probably going to be the first freedom in my life." Betty agreed to a property settlement and planned to relocate to Santa Monica; Uris would remain in Aspen, overseeing final construction of the house. A month later, in August 1966, Herb Schlosberg, his business manager, visited, and about forty friends dropped by to celebrate Uris's forty-second birthday, arriving in a large cattle truck to the sound of shotguns being fired into the air. At this time, his enthusiasm for his new novel, ten chapters of which were written, was also extremely high.

Betty was less upbeat. While he could adjust to living alone, she seemed to be confused over the developments and incapable of making any decisions. He, by contrast, spent time getting his new house in order, writing, and getting his life organized: "Of course, I went through a series of enormous low points, but did not wake up in the morning thinking about it all day."[37] Betty, in the meantime, went to court over the settlement she had originally accepted.

In the meantime, Karen had dropped out of college, planning to marry a young man from Philadelphia—although by September, to Uris's relief, she had called it off. A truce with Betty was also arranged, at least through the fall of 1966. She also told Uris that she wanted to take instruction in Judaism. By September, however, the truce had collapsed, and he decided to go forward with the divorce. Karen would be with him through the winter, working in Aspen. The events distracted him from his writing, but that had "always been the case with us in one way or another."[38]

In November 1966, Uris noted the presence of a new friend, Marge (Margery Edwards), and that the focus of his new novel, titled *Topaz*, would deal with "the decline and fall of the French-American relations in the past few years."[39] In court, he won a motion for temporary alimony, although Betty was going to fight it. Uris, who had opened two modest bookstores in Southern California (one in Sherman Oaks), offered them to Betty for a dollar as part of a settlement. She refused. He decided that she just wanted to live off the alimony, calling her "lazy."[40] Five weeks later, he was still struggling with the case as the other side tried to wear him down, but they didn't "realize what a pair of tough guys Herb and I are and they will have to fight it out in court and then they will get a fair and just settlement."[41] A belligerent Uris stepped forward, ready for the challenge; he wanted little to do with Betty now. A week later, he felt better: "From the top of the mountain the troubles seem much smaller. I've begun skiing again." Margery Edwards had also become a good friend, and although there was "nothing at all serious" between them, Uris did "enjoy her companionship."[42] The comment was, of course, misleading.

Before year's end, he provided an update on the divorce, reassuring his father that he and Herb had "been in and out of litigation for over a decade" and were not the "type to get sick or squeamish about it."[43] Having a father who had argued with him for years had also prepared him for battle. But three projects were distracting him from the conflict and the anticipation of seeing *Topaz* in print: the motion picture "The Gringo," which he wrote in Mexico two years ago; a film of *Mila 18* in development with the Yugoslavian government; and a musical of *Exodus*, for which he wrote the script and lyrics, although challenges remained before it could be produced.

Uris's outspokenness, of course, could be harmful—to his family as well as to others. An insomniac, Uris always took sleeping pills. And after as many as three vodka martinis a night, he could become intolerant and, at his worse, emotionally abusive. When a little marijuana or cocaine was available, his behavior could become even worse. In later years, marijuana brownies would regularly be served, sometimes unknowingly, to dinner guests. He could be hard on people, always testing their friendship as his emotions became exaggerated and he challenged others.

For a year he did not speak to his daughter Karen, and when his youngest daughter, Rachel, went to boarding school in Connecticut, even though he was by then living on Shelter Island, New York, he did not visit her once.[44] On another occasion years earlier, when his son Mike had left records strewn about on the floor of his room, Uris angrily took them and threw them out the window. When he discovered this, Mike reacted indifferently. Several days later, more records lay on the floor, and Uris again angrily flung them out onto the hillside, where they broke. But he acted too quickly: Mike had thrown his father's records about, and Uris became the victim of his own behavior. By the time he left Aspen, in 1988, he had alienated almost everyone.

TOPAZ

One of those he alienated was Philippe de Vosjoli, who provided much of the material for *Topaz*, which was written in Aspen. Uris met Vosjoli, a "retired" member of the French secret service, in Acapulco in the late spring of 1964. The general manager of the Las Brisas Hilton introduced the two: "I was separated at the time, and we were both living [with] difficulties and we became very close friends and there was an introduction of some papers regarding his memoirs and so forth," Uris stated.[45] Through Vosjoli, Uris then heard of shady dealings and communist infiltration of the French intelligence corps.

Vosjoli had been the Washington liaison between the CIA and the French secret service. Anatoli Golitsin, a Soviet spy who defected to the West in Helsinki, claimed that there were moles in the French secret service (le Deuxième Bureau) and that a group of Soviet agents—who may have included the French deputy prime minister—were working at the cabinet level, close to Charles de Gaulle. However, there was not enough evidence to take any action. Nonetheless, Golitsin insisted that at least six French intelligence officers, including two colonels, were Soviet moles. James Jesus Angleton, the CIA's director of counterintelligence, informed Vosjoli of these developments.[46]

Did the KGB control French Intelligence? Vosjoli thought so. When he was ordered to set French agents to spy on American nuclear-missile sites, he protested: France had no interest in spying on the United States. When his orders were not changed, he resigned, but was told in November 1963 that he would be assassinated if he returned to France.[47] Vosjoli had also gathered information about Soviet missiles in Cuba for the CIA. He refused to identify his sources to French intelligence, fearing that Soviet spies in France would pass the information to Moscow. One of his sources was Castro's sister, Juanita, who in *Topaz* is Juanita de Cordoba, the secret mistress of the hero, Devereaux. When Uris met him in Mexico, Vosjoli had drafted an autobiography, *Le Réseau Topaz* (The Topaz Network), which recounted these adventures.

Uris was suspicious at first, but after long discussions with Vosjoli, he began to believe the story and offered to help the former agent publish his autobiography. But literary agents and publishers were not interested, and there was some concern over the security of the manuscript, which Vosjoli took to Uris, then in Los Angeles, for safekeeping. Uris accepted it in sealed envelopes, which he turned over to Schlosberg for protection. In the spring of 1965, Uris met with his publisher and editor from Bantam in Denver to discuss the possibility of writing a new work on Nazi war criminals still at large. Uris felt that the war-criminal topic was too vast, but he remembered Vosjoli's story. A conversation with Vosjoli followed, and soon Uris looked at the documents and saw their potential. He and Vosjoli then met in New York, and the two came to a working agreement concerning payment and royalties, a fifty-fifty split.[48]

After receiving assurances from Vosjoli that he would have full rights to the material, Uris went to Bantam with a proposal for a novel. By going to Bantam first, Uris was trying a new arrangement. He knew that for his novels, the value of the paperback edition was greater than that of the hardback. Instead of negotiating for a hardback first and then entertaining bids for a paperback, he tried to do the reverse. Bantam agreed, even though Uris wanted to be paid 100 percent of the paperback royalties and not to split them with a hardback publisher, the standard practice. In late May 1965 at the Algonquin Hotel in New York, with Schlosberg present, Vosjoli signed a memorandum in which he agreed to Uris's control over the material for the purpose of the Bantam deal. The memo would lead to a later disagreement.[49] The document, dated 27 May 1965, guaranteed Vosjoli an equal share of royalties and film profits from the book to be written by Uris.[50]

Uris then invited Vosjoli to join him in Aspen in late June 1965 and act as researcher and "technical advisor" for the book; his main job would be to check the accuracy of the intelligence details and covert practices.[51] To distract curious parties, Uris and Vosjoli set up a dummy project: a book on Nazi war criminals. Did Uris believe there was a Soviet espionage ring operating within the French government? Possibly, but it was a novel he was writing, so its truth did not have to be proved. Uris even formally denied having much interaction with Vosjoli, although this was easily disproved.

When Vosjoli arrived in Aspen with his companion Monique, Uris found a new concern: fear that French intelligence would come to get Vosjoli. Uris's worry prompted him to purchase several handguns. After a few months, Vosjoli went to Florida, although during this period the FBI had visited Uris as part of an investigation into Vosjoli. The visit was intimidating, Mark Uris recalled.[52]

Uris began to draft the novel, the second time he had used someone else's material (the first was his uncle's autobiography, the source of *The Angry Hills*). Not only did he develop the anti-American attitude of the French and the possible infiltration of the French intelligence service by the Soviets, but he also centered the action on the Cuban missile crisis. "Topaz" was the code name for the Soviet spy ring within the French government. By September 1966, Uris had finished a first draft and went to see Vosjoli in Coral Gables to review the text for errors.

With characteristically curt dialogue and flamboyant descriptions, the novel tells a story of espionage, love, and international intrigue in Washington, Havana, and Paris. The five-part story begins with a prologue, the identification of Soviet missiles in Cuba. In a flashback to the late summer of 1961, a CIA agent in Copenhagen responds to a Russian defector, Boris Kuznetov. After confirmation of his identity, he and his family are spirited away to the United States. During an interrogation, he implicates André Devereaux of the French secret service, and the plot picks up speed with the revelation of a spy ring in the upper echelons of the French government. To illustrate Uris's taste for excess, the names of Devereaux's dogs are Robespierre and Picasso (*TP*, 31). Shifting to New York in Part II, the plot reveals the presence of Russian missiles in Cuba, and Devereaux heads to investigate; this allows Uris to give his views of the country and the high price it paid to be under Castro's rule. We meet Juanita de Cordoba, the disillusioned revolutionary who is Devereaux's lover and who is able to confirm the placement of the missiles. Under dangerous conditions, Devereaux leaves with proof.

Intrigue greets Devereaux when he returns to Washington, partly because he has agreed not to inform his own government of what he has done, fearful it will get back to the Soviets via their agents in the French secret service. The need to betray one's government in order to be loyal to one's country is the dilemma Uris presents. This section also reveals that "Columbine" is the name of the top agent in Topaz and that the French president plans to pull France out of NATO. The specter of communism controlling Europe continues the geopolitics Uris first outlined in *Armageddon*. As Devereaux flies to France to deliver a letter from President Kennedy outlining the Topaz scheme, the American blockade of Cuba begins.

A flashback to 1940 introduces the final section of the novel, which is concerned with the Resistance. Uris not only provides a history of the Free French forces but also criticizes America's recognition of the Vichy government rather than that led by de Gaulle, who is mysteriously present in the novel as President La Croix. The conclusion ends the flashback: La Croix reads the letter from President Kennedy as he learns of the American actions in Cuba. A Colonel Brune enters the fray and is thought to be the mole Columbine, but Uris twists the plot until the actual Columbine is discovered at the end.

The publication of the book was as controversial as its writing. Doubleday, the publisher originally contracted for the hardcover, pulled out after questioning the authenticity of Vosjoli's story. Uris and Schlosberg were then able to make a lucrative deal with Harper and Row, which, in return, wanted Uris to flesh out the story with an additional twenty thousand. But after seeing the completed text, it pulled out in March 1967 because of concerns about libel. Little, Brown also rejected the manuscript. Uris, with Herb Schlosberg's guidance, then began another search; McGraw-Hill finally published the book in late 1967, although Uris received approximately $100,000 less than his original figure. While this was going on, Uris also had to attend two divorce hearings as Betty tried to get additional monies based on the lucrative Bantam contract. Oscar Dystel, the president of Bantam, testified at a hearing held in Aspen that the contract was null and void, since Uris at that time did not have a hardback publisher, a prerequisite for paperback publication. Even Vosjoli gave evidence.[53]

To make ends meet, Uris contributed to a fast-tracked book titled *Strike Zion!* This so-called instant book about the Six-Day War was published in July 1967 and was written by William Stevenson for Bantam. Uris contributed a twenty-one-page essay called "The Third Temple."[54] It is a thirteen-part testimonial, with biblical references, to the courage and fighting spirit of the Jews, and to the Israelis in particular. The final page of the paperback is a full-page advertisement for *Exodus*, "THE EXPLOSIVE NOVEL OF HEROISM AND DESIRE."

At the last minute, McGraw-Hill almost refused to release *Topaz*. The publisher wanted a waiver from Bantam that freed it from any liability for libel or misrepresentations. Uris, who was on his way to Israel at the time (July 1967), agreed to sign, but Vosjoli did not. Forty-five thousand copies were in a warehouse, and McGraw-Hill threatened to hold them unless Vosjoli signed. Uris threatened Vosjoli: he had already made representations to the publisher that the book was truthful. He argued that Vosjoli was contractually obligated to sign.[55] The latter refused because he thought the waiver was too restrictive and would prevent him from publishing his own autobiographical account of the espionage. In the end, Schlosberg gave assurances to McGraw-Hill that Uris would take full responsibility for the work and assume any liability. But Uris, clearly believing

Vosjoli to be in breach of their contract, did not show Vosjoli a revised Bantam–McGraw Hill contract.

Adding to the scandal surrounding the book, John Scali, a news correspondent for ABC, prepared to expose what Uris and Vosjoli hoped to reveal. Scali apparently knew a great deal about Vosjoli's actions. At a meeting of all three participants at the Shoreham Hotel in Washington, Vosjoli was evasive and ambiguous, Uris protective. Complications, contractual and public, ensued; Vosjoli retained a lawyer, who made financial demands on Uris. Scali's story never aired, partly because Vosjoli asked for a large fee to appear on the television show. Subsequently, Vosjoli sold part of his story to *Life* magazine, which incensed Uris.

For the paperback version of *Topaz*, Bantam issued a pamphlet that was essentially an interview with Uris. Clearly, the potential spy scandal was international news. In 1966, Uris had signed a deal with Columbia Pictures that was tied to the Doubleday publication, but just before the scheduled spring publication in 1967, when Doubleday sought a release, the picture deal also fell through over libel concerns. In October 1967, as McGraw-Hill readied the hardcover for release, *Look* magazine, breaking with its policy of publishing only nonfiction works, printed a two-part preview of the novel, justifying the decision by saying "although it is fiction, many of the incidents are based upon fact." The fee paid to Uris was $75,000.

After the story appeared in Paris, there was silence: Washington and Paris said little, and French publishers stayed away. The appearance of the novel in October 1967, however, renewed debate. Some thirteen countries bought translation rights, although not France. In April 1968, however, a French satirical magazine reported that Vosjoli was about to publish his memoirs, and the *London Sunday Times* announced it would print excerpts.[56] In an interview, Uris claimed that his source had told the truth.[57] *Life* magazine reprinted Vosjoli's memoirs as a cover story, headlined "French Spy Scandal." Universal Studios then acquired the film rights and hired Alfred Hitchcock as the director. Sales took off. Uris loved the attention.

In his interview for the Bantam pamphlet, Uris clarified that the actual name of the spy ring was "Sapphire" but confirmed that the group had infiltrated the highest reaches of the French government. It had also planted disinformation to confuse the French—for example, by authenticating falsified reports. The novel, he claimed, also anticipated the French withdrawal from NATO and the French attack on the dollar.[58]

This episode in Uris's career raises questions about his writing practice: Is research a proper substitute for originality? Is history an adequate source of character and plot? For Uris, the answers were yes; this perhaps explains why he told his son Mark that his novels seemed to write themselves.[59] The plot is already in place; all you need to do is to order the characters and events into a dramatic form. None of his novels contains an original story, with the possible exception of *A God in Ruins*. All the others are drawn from history or personal experience, combined with his sense of observation, and focus on how personal details and historical events reveal character and provide drama and action. His novels are constructed rather than created. A realist and traditionalist who shunned narrative experimentation and formal innovations, Uris preferred the linear accumulation of events leading to a conclusion.

Reaction to *Topaz* was mixed; critics generally complained that his flat style and polemics kept the story from "being a first-rate suspense yarn."[60] The *Los Angeles Times* thought the story urgent, adding that "if it weren't for the incredible soap opera dialogue of the endless love stuff, the book would rank high in the espionage field."[61] *Life* began its review with this sweeping remark: "Here is Leon Uris, a novelist trying to pass once more as a historian—and just when Cornelius Ryan and Barbara Tuchman have conditioned us in the opposite, to expect history to read like a novel."[62]

Criticism of the banal writing style led to the question who but Uris would select as a spy's recognition signal Irving Wallace's *The Chapman Report*. His knack was for being "simultaneously commonplace and improbable" as he "cheerfully ...proposes disasters [and] zestfully marches to meet them."[63] He was a man who clearly enjoyed writing for himself, prompting one critic to cite an Oscar Wilde quip as a suitable epitaph for *Topaz*: "As one turns over the pages, the suspense of the author becomes almost unbearable."[64] The *London Sunday Times* felt it was an admirable compendium of stock phrases and that the only good personality belonged to the French diplomat's girlfriend, "who seems to be a cousin of Carmen Miranda."[65]

Errors could not be overlooked. The Cuban missile crisis occurred in October 1962. In the novel, it shifts between the autumn and spring of either 1962 or 1963 or both. Additionally, the sketch of Fidel Castro is defamatory, the flashbacks are irrelevant, and the American chauvinism is demeaning. Nevertheless, interest in the book was high, all the more so when it was announced that Alfred Hitchcock wanted to film the work.

THE FILMING OF *TOPAZ*

Uris reacted with surprise when Hitchcock called him to say he intended to do the film and wanted Uris to write the screenplay. He was, of course, aware of the director's reputation but not that it had dimmed, especially after the end of his television series in 1965. Hitchcock now relied on the story department of Universal for properties, and it came up with *Topaz*. He found the story appealing because it seemed to be based on a real-life figure who had gathered information about Russian missiles in Cuba for the CIA but had fallen out of favor with French intelligence for refusing to name his Cuban sources and his belief that Soviet spies were operating in the French government. Working with Lew Wasserman, then the head of Universal, Hitchcock undertook the project. Wasserman told him that they would build Cuba on Universal's back lot but that he could shoot the last third of the film on location in Paris and Copenhagen.

Hitchcock met Uris in January 1968. They began having regular meetings in late April, although Hitchcock was apparently defensive and unhappy. When Peggy Robertson, Hitchcock's assistant, greeted Uris, she made it clear that *Topaz* would dust off Hitchcock's reputation and "bring him out of the museum"; it would be his comeback film.[66] From the first, however, the men did not get along. The prickly Uris did not like Hitchcock's need for control, and when he was shown a small office in a cottage on the Universal lot, Uris objected: he wanted a private office in the studio's executive building. Hitchcock's habit was to befriend his writers, frequently having lunch with them. Uris's habit was to work alone. He disliked the daily encounters in which Hitchcock presided over the menu and conversation. But Uris couldn't say no, even when forced to watch old Hitchcock films with the master. Uris had moved to Beverly Hills for the project, renting a house on San Ysidro Drive.

By June, Hitchcock was sending long notes to Uris about the narrative outline, criticizing the writing. One comment advised Uris that the dialogue should be "a little more oblique in describing traitors in the French government . . . My feeling about this scene is that we should use sophisticated, humorous dialogue, otherwise it is going to be a very dull scene."[67] He also criticized Uris's tendency to resort to melodrama, as when the Russian Kuznetov says that "the Soviets might well unleash a nuclear attack."[68] Discussions and revisions continued throughout the summer, although Hitchcock complained to Wasserman in mid-June about Uris and his interference with the production—namely, a suggestion of how to do the main titles of the film, dissolving from the title to a shape that becomes the Capitol in Washington: "As Last TITLE FADES we HOLD on the Capital [*sic*] Dome for a beat in time. From there we go on with the perforated code tape. Didn't you use something like this? Was it in 'Vertigo?'"[69] Hitchcock's acerbic two-sentence note to Wasserman begins: "I don't usually bother you with my writer problems, but I attach a letter from my current writer merely to indicate the quality of thought I am receiving."[70]

By late August, Uris was gone, having received only a portion of his $125,000 fee. He was not unhappy to go, since he felt Hitchcock did not grasp the political complexities of the story, which had so absorbed Uris.[71] The director was constantly trying to impose his will on the material, which Uris instinctively opposed. Hitchcock, however, having had enough of the project, brought back the unfinished *Frenzy* to Universal executives. He presented test footage, slides, and storyboards to Wasserman and his assistant Ed Henry in July 1968. They declined to go ahead and suggested he return to *Topaz*, now with Sam Taylor as his screenwriter; Taylor had written for Hitchcock before—namely, *Vertigo*.[72] Taylor promptly altered the plot of the novel and de-emphasized the romanticism of the story. At Hitchcock's request, he also turned Rico Parra, a Castro critic, into a more sympathetic character.

Details from a story conference of 27 August 1968 acknowledge the feud between Vosjoli and Uris and the work that still needed to be done, especially the sequencing of the Cuban section. The problem was that they had, until then, faithfully followed the plot of the book, at Uris's urging, but now, for purposes of filming, needed to deviate from it. A comment from the story-conference transcript (it may be Sam Taylor speaking), reads: "We have a saying, at least I have a saying, when devising a picture of this kind, logic is dull."[73] After analyzing the novel, the participants noted that there was something fascinating about *Topaz*, perhaps the fantasy quality of a life: "The fantastic qualities that you find not quite plausible are the things that are easy to do in the book and difficult to do in the movie; they do seem implausible"; another voice adds, "It was a great story, but . . . the technical handling of it was pretty jarring."[74] The shooting schedule meant that some scenes were written just days or even hours before they were filmed, and pages were often being rushed to Copenhagen or Paris when location shooting started.

The film itself received uneven reviews: some scenes, like the opening sequence of the defecting Russian agent, were called dazzling, others not. The plot was criticized as too convoluted, but the surface tensions, absurdities, and odd references were "pure Hitchcock," according to the *New York Times*. The actors, however, were forgettable and entirely subordinate to their roles. Only a few key images stand out, as when the anti-Castro female agent Juanita is shot and collapses onto a marble floor, her body framed by the brilliant purple of her dress. It was "a movie of classic Hitchcock effects" whose star was Hitchcock himself, one critic, Vincent Canby, concluded.[75]

At the box office, the film was a financial flop, costing four million dollars to make but earning less than a million. Hitchcock, however, did not forgo his traditional cameo appearance. Thirty minutes into the film, he is shown getting out of a wheelchair at an airport (could he be trying to leave the production?). The only happy experience during this entire period for Uris was his second marriage.

Uris had gone through a difficult time before his temporary return to Hollywood. His divorce from Betty in January 1968 after twenty-three years of marriage had been finalized at the same time he began to consider his 1964 libel trial as the possible subject for a novel and became more deeply involved with the considerably younger Margery Edwards.

Uris had met attractive, Pennsylvania-born Margery Edwards in Aspen, where she was a model and then a jewelry designer. She had recently worked as a silversmith and was thinking about opening her own gift shop when Uris encountered her during the fading days of his marriage with Betty. Their nineteen-year age difference did not bother Uris; in fact, he was proud to be seen with this five-foot-six-inch beauty who had modeled ski clothes. A graduate of Skidmore College, she had moved to Aspen in 1965 for the outdoor life.[76]

One morning in 1968, William Uris received a phone call in Philadelphia from a woman who introduced herself as Margie Edwards. She had arrived from Aspen and brought personal regards from Leon. William invited her over; she was there in less than an hour. A "young beauty . . . tall, blue soft eyes, a gorgeous figure, dressed very simple but tasteful," she spent the entire day with William and Anna (AUTO, 322). She left Philadelphia by train for Berwin, Pennsylvania, where her parents lived. About ten days later, she returned to Aspen but visited William again before she left. She did not answer the question whether she was engaged to Leon. Several months later, when visiting Aspen, William met her again, and shortly after that, Uris and she were married.

Uris and Margery had lived together for almost two years (while Uris was separated from Betty) before marrying on 8 September 1968. Some sixty guests attended the wedding at Temple Israel in Hollywood, the Reform synagogue celebrated on its stationery as "Filmland's House of Worship"; Margery had converted the month before. The wedding of the forty-four-year-old "lion of the bestseller lists"—to quote *Time* magazine—and the twenty-five-year-old former model was widely covered in the press.[77] Herb Schlosberg was the best man, and they planned to honeymoon in England, which would allow Uris to research what would become *QB VII*. Two weeks after the ceremony, but before they left for England, they held an open house at Uris's Red Mountain home. In early October, they attended a White House reception: President Johnson was honoring the prime minister of New Zealand. Guests included Arthur Ashe, Jr., Secretary of State Dean Rusk, and Martha Graham. Uris told reporters it was his thirtieth wedding anniversary: he had been married just thirty days.[78] Otto Preminger was also at the reception, but Uris refused to talk to him. After the reception, Uris and Margery returned to Aspen before flying to London.

Uris was at first ecstatic to be with such a beautiful woman; he was proud to show her off wherever they went. When they returned to Aspen from their England trip, she decided to team up with Uris's friend Walt Smith to establish a John Robert Powers modeling agency, and plans were being made to get it underway. But soon, friction between the couple erupted, leading to an unexpected tragedy. Late in the evening of 18 February 1969, the twenty-six-year-old Margery Edwards shot herself a hundred yards behind Uris's home. The shock devastated Uris, although it later came out that Margery suffered from depression and had had various quarrels with her new husband, who, according to some reports, remained a domineering perfectionist. Petty domestic details would ignite great flare-ups. To the police, Uris admitted that a string of arguments over the previous three weeks had gotten progressively worse. On the evening of 18 February there had been "a pretty hot one."[79]

The day of the suicide, Uris told Margery he did not want to ski with her and refused to make up with her after another disagreement. He met Walt Smith at Snowmass, and they skied together; Uris told Smith that there was a "damn good chance I was going to ask her for a divorce."[80] He had taken "this" for ten years before, "and he did not want it again." This was after five months or so of marriage. After skiing without her all day, he returned home. She again tried to make up, having bought some gifts for Uris and his son Mike (it was his sixteenth birthday), but he rejected her. Because it was Mike's birthday, Uris took him downtown for a few hours. When he came back, he had decided to ask Marge to leave, and at about six he called his lawyer, Schlosberg, to discuss his options. Marge at first listened in, and Uris had to call back on a private line from his separate office. Schlosberg advised separation.

Except as noted, the following account of what happened on the night of Margery's suicide and on the days leading up to it is taken from "Author Uris Testifies in Death of Wife," a story by Barbara Browne in the *Rocky Mountain News* (8 March 1969). According to his testimony at a coroner's inquest held on 6–7 March 1969, Uris, after talking to Schlosberg, told his wife of his decision and ordered her from their bedroom: "We're through. Go sleep downstairs." She said, "I knew it," adding that she had made other arrangements.[81] Shortly after, Walt Smith arrived with a model from the Powers agency in Denver, a woman who had once worked with Margery. Uris told them to wait downstairs in a sitting room, adding to Smith that he had walked into a bad scene and that in the past Uris had often sent Margery out of the bedroom in the middle of the night. But she always came back. This time, when she came down and confronted Uris in the living room, she repeated, "I've made other plans." This angered Uris because he thought she meant with another man. In testimony, he said: "Her walking out like that . . . She usually obeyed me. It was a test of wills, I guess." At the same time, he stated that he was "absolutely and totally in love with this girl, I was pleased that no one else could turn me on even slightly. It was such a change."

Expressing a different view was Anne Burrows, a friend of Margery Edwards, who testified that she had been uneasy about the relationship. The couple had had several fights while dating, and at one point Margery said she doubted whether she could be happy with him. Burrows added: "I know she tried very hard to do everything and be everything he wanted. . . . I don't think he gave her the feeling of security but rather of insecurity." Uris, in turn, said his wife had "a low boiling point" and a "compulsion toward perfection": "We liked to argue but we recognized the fact we were arguing over nothing." A few days before the shooting, on 13 February, they gave a cocktail party. She wanted to clean up afterward but Uris ordered her to bed. She exploded and started throwing things, "including a knife. She came at me very violently." He grabbed her and "must have pushed her. At any rate, she lay on the floor and kicked and screamed like a child having a tantrum." As a result of their quarrel, he moved his handguns from a safe where Margery kept her jewels and placed them on a high shelf under some hats. She must have known, because one of them was the weapon that killed her.

Before finally going to bed on 13 February, Margery said, "You're not going to throw me out are you? You're not going to get rid of me?" She made this plea most nights after they fought, Uris testified. The next morning, she had a small black eye: "It cost me a pair of ski boots and a parka," he said. She replied, "Maybe you ought to punch me in the other eye." She never showed any fear but could not stop contesting Uris and his rules: "It was almost as if she kept the provocation up until I would finally tell her to get out. Almost like she wanted that spanking." Dr. H. C. Whitcomb, the deputy coroner and a friend of Uris, also gave testimony, saying that in his opinion, Mrs. Uris "was constantly challenging the ultimate rejection—death." He later remarked that she "was a loner and a perfectionist . . . a prime candidate for suicide."[82]

Margery had gone out of the house at about seven after their quarrel, taking one of Uris's pistols. A few moments after she left, Uris saw her pause in the driveway, wearing high black zipper boots and a parka, enter the garage, come out, and then disappear from view, heading down the driveway toward Red Mountain Road. Uris added in his police statement, however, that she turned and "looked up at me, there was a look of anguish on her face & it looked as if she wavered for a minute & like she wanted to say something to me. She turned and then continued down the driveway."[83]

About twenty minutes later, he heard a shot, then two others, all about twenty seconds apart. He assumed she was firing at the house "to show me she was good and mad." He then thought of his guns and found that a .38 revolver was missing from his study. He and Smith immediately began a search, but when they couldn't find her, they got into a Jeep and drove slowly down the winding Red Mountain Road in a snowstorm and continued to look. They then drove to the sheriff's office.

The formal search that began shortly afterward continued until two in the morning; the police at one point thought that she had walked down the road and might have been picked up by someone. She was not found until the next morning when about nine twenty when a young man walking down the road behind and above Uris's house discovered her body lying about a hundred yards from the home near a two-foot-high snow-covered hammock. She had fired three shots: one went into her purse, another into her cheek, and the third through her mouth and into her brain. She had apparently been standing on the frozen, snow-covered hammock and looking down at the house when she fired. A suicide note partly expressed her love for Uris but also the view that "if we had both used our [wits] . . . we would have called an end to this affair long ago . . . We each knew the outcome in our own hearts."

The papers had a field day with the sensational story. The *Los Angeles Times* ran a banner headline that read: "BRIDE OF AUTHOR URIS FOUND DEAD." A beaming wedding photo of Margery and Uris appeared alongside the story. The subhead read: "Apparently Shot Herself, Sheriff Says."[84] A week later, Herb Schlosberg conducted a private memorial service in Aspen. The *Aspen Times* quoted Uris: "On the surface there was no apparent reason why Margery took her life . . . We were deeply in love, with more than everything to live for."[85] Her ashes were scattered on Red Mountain. The papers also followed the coroner's inquest, initially raising the suspicion that Uris might have had a hand in her death. He did not.

The inquest confirmed that the death of the twenty-six-year-old had been a suicide. Attending with Uris was his son Michael (who was in the house at the time of the final quarrel) and his daughter Karen, twenty-two. A photo in the *Rocky Mountain News* showed an upset Uris in a dark suit leaving the witness box in front of the six-person jury. He testified that for the ten days preceding the event there had been a series of quarrels. The police report refers to a "series of uncontrollable arguments with her husband," the implication being that she was the uncontrollable participant.[86] Uris testified that the night of their party, 13 February, five days before her shooting, he removed "five loaded guns out his safe and hid them around the house." Nevertheless, she found a .38-caliber Smith & Wesson pistol he owned. His last words to her: "Marge, I want to know where you're going. If you don't tell me, it's the worst mistake you ever made in your life." He also claimed that although he had called his lawyer in Los Angeles to discuss a divorce and had mentioned a separation earlier in the day to Walt Smith, he "was bluffing. We had been through this before."[87]

After several hours of deliberation, the coroner's jury ruled that Margery Uris had taken her own life. The case was closed, but the effect of the suicide on Uris remained. Lacking any desire to write, he had a great urge to be alone. Only when his editor Ken McCormick of Doubleday visited to console him did Uris begin to understand the therapeutic value of writing again. But as he told a reporter in 1984, "No one comes out of a thing like this whole. No one can describe the pain. Once you decide you are going to survive you don't know how much of you is left and you can't really know until you face a test."[88] His reputation shattered and his willpower blunted, his future was uncertain.

"SHORT TITLES, LONG BOOKS, BIG SALES"

Leon Uris is one of the best commercial storytellers among American writers.
—EXECUTIVE EDITOR, HARPERCOLLINS, 2005

FOLLOWING THE DEATH of Margery Edwards, Uris was lost. He went to Southern California for three weeks after the inquest to recover some balance, and then returned to Aspen. But resuming a writing life was difficult until his editor Ken McCormick flew out to encourage, cajole, and remind him that his readers were expecting a new work. This provided a much-needed focus.

Uris had by now perfected the Uris style, summarized in a *Writer's Digest* article as "short titles, long books, big sales."[1] His novels of vivid prose and strong plots based on historical events became a popular staple. To enhance the drama, he included occasional superstars from the world stage: Charles de Gaulle (as Pierre La Croix in *Topaz*), David Ben-Gurion (*Mitla Pass*), Sir Winston Churchill (*Redemption*), and even Ernest Hemingway (*Mitla Pass*). The characters express themselves in terse, often stagy dialogue. Well-drawn, condensed settings form backdrops for an awkward treatment of romance, which is either sentimentalized or unintentionally caricatural, as when macho posturing replaces honest behavior. Characterization is conventional and undeveloped.

QB VII (1970), which was based on Uris's own 1964 trial for libel in London, illustrates these features clearly. The suit, brought by Dr. Wladislaw Dering, had offended Uris's sense of literary freedom and history, and the resulting novel combined the best aspects of Uris's style. His own experiences provided the plot, while London and its grand history provided the setting:

> Jesus, Solomon, and King Alfred rated status over the front entrance of the Royal Courts of Justice, which fronted five hundred feet where the Strand becomes Fleet Street at Temple Bar. These three were joined by twenty-four lesser bishops and scholars.
>
> Moses brought up the rear entrance on Carey Street, a block away. (*QBVII*, 273)

After supplying more concise details, Uris weighs in with a simile: "The court stands as a giant planet of law with its satellites, the surrounding Inns and Chancery Lane" (QBVII, 274). Before describing the barristers' arrival and preparations for the first day of trial, Uris gives a history of England's first law court, which was located in Westminster Hall.

Uris turned to recapturing the experiences of his libel trial at the same time he became involved with a new woman, whom he met three months after his second wife died. In late April 1969, still reeling from Margery Edwards's suicide, he called an Aspen photography center to find someone to teach his son how to take pictures and use a new movie camera. A short while later, a tall, dark-haired woman stood at his door. He was instantly attracted to her.[2] At the time, she was associate director of Center of the Eye, a photographic institute in Aspen. Her pedigree was impressive: the scion of a Boston Brahmin family, she had attended the Concord Academy, come out as a debutante, attended Colorado College in Colorado Springs, and studied photography at New York University. She went to Aspen in 1965 at age seventeen, partly because of an uncle who worked there. Her name was Jill Peabody.

Ten months after meeting and then courting intensely, Uris and Jill Peabody married at the Algonquin Hotel in New York on 15 February 1970, four days short of the first anniversary of Margery's suicide. Jill was six months younger than Uris's oldest daughter. Rabbi Herbert Friedman presided, and Oscar Dystel was the best man. Jill's parents and three sisters attended. Topping the wedding cake was a pair of skiers. Uris and Walt Smith wrote the wedding march, which was later incorporated into Uris's musical *Ari* (based on *Exodus*). Uris and Jill had arrived in New York earlier in the month so that Uris could review galley pages of *QB VII* and Jill could prepare for the wedding. Beforehand, Uris asked Doubleday to open charge accounts for both of them at Lord & Taylor, Mark Cross, Steuben Glass, Bonwit Teller, Saks Fifth Avenue, and Bergdorf Goodman.

QB VII

After the challenges of publishing *Topaz*—including supposed threats on his life—the reason for his acquiring guns—and a court fight over royalties with his French source, Philippe de Vosjoli—Uris turned to his own life for literary material: the Dering trial and the attendant story of the Holocaust and Jewish suffering. To this, he added autobiographical details, notably similarities between the writer-hero, Abraham Cady, and himself. Each was a Jewish writer who lacked a formal education, wrote as a solitary pursuit, and had a strong appreciation of and need for romance. They also wrote similar types of novels: *Exodus* for Uris, *The Holocaust* for Cady. Uris began to work on *QB VII* in mid-1969 and completed it in April 1970, two months after his marriage to Jill.

Uris's ideas about the writer and his practice are particularly acute in the novel; indeed, it would not be until *Mitla Pass* (1988) that he would again be so candid on how a writer functions. Cady's wife is witness to the process, which is, quite clearly, work: "There was no inspiration that people always look for and imagine in the writer. What there was was a relentless plodding requiring a special kind of stamina that makes the profession so limited" (*QBVII*, 146). But she also became a liability, and at one point Cady angrily exclaimed, "I HAD REMAINED A WRITER DESPITE HER" (*QBVII*, 185).

Later in the novel, he tells his son that a writer is always alone, a prelude to a chauvinistic speech about the Hemingwayesque nature of men who want to be around other men and who prefer locker rooms, bars, fight clubs, and places "where we don't have to listen to female dribble" (*QBVII*, 399). Defensively, Cady explains to his son that women don't deserve to "take the crap of being a writer's wife. I busted your mother. If a woman's got anything to give, I drain her"—a remark that was more accurate than Uris might have realized (*QBVII*, 400). Earlier, Cady had told Lady Sarah Wydman that he wasn't capable of "giving all the love I have to a woman, only my children. And I'm not capable of receiving the kind of love a woman like you has. I can't commit, even in a game" (*QBVII*, 243).

"Basic storytelling was the key most authors never learn," the publisher David Shawcross tells Cady at one point in the novel (*QBVII*, 127). For Uris, this was a guiding principle—along with Shawcross's view that the novelist must know "what his last chapter is going to say" and always work toward that end (*QBVII*, 127). Borrowing the language of the theatre, Uris would call this dictum his "curtain line." In *QB VII*, Uris also incorporates an incident involving his editor Ken McCormick and the writing of *Exodus*. At the end of the novel, in a farewell conversation with his lawyer, Bannister, Cady explains that he accepts the new violence erupting in the Middle East. Cady then says when he was writing *The Holocaust*, his editor would "get into a dither every time a new crisis came up and he'd badger me for the manuscript. I told him, don't worry, whenever I finish the book, the Jews will still be in trouble'" (*QBVII*, 500). Uris said almost the identical thing to McCormick when he was writing *Exodus*.

By mid-February 1970, Uris was sending in large sections of *QB VII* to his publisher, but made it clear he wanted no criticism of the manuscript until the entire novel was finished, an important aspect of his writing practice. Piecemeal editing he called "very annoying."[3] In the same letter, he noted that the heart specialist Dr. Christiaan Barnard had married a nineteen-year-old woman, ironically adding: "I think that is awful. What is the world coming to? I have already been picked up twice as a child molester," humorously referring to the ages of both Margery (twenty-five) when she married him and Jill (twenty-two).

Editorial comment on *QB VII*, however, did not pause for Uris's wedding. A day after the ceremony, Ken McCormick wrote a two-page critique of the manuscript, suggesting that Uris begin the novel by introducing Dr. Kelno (instead of waiting until Chapter 2 to do so) and save the panoply of the English courts until the trial began, later in the book. McCormick added that the current opening (focusing on the courts) might work in a film, but not in a novel: "The thing is to hook the reader almost immediately with a human problem, which is what you're going to do with Kelno."[4] Uris listened and made the change. Other questions dealt with structure and what Uris might do to sustain doubt about Kelno's guilt. An internal memo by McCormick identifies actual people and the characters who represent them in the book, an especially important source for determining the counterparts of the doctors and medical aides in the story.[5] Most interestingly, McCormick notes that Dr. Mark Tesslar was based on Dr. Elena Brewda, who was alive and in London at the time.

He adds that the publisher David Shawcross is William Kimber, Thomas Bannister is Lord Gerald Gardiner, and Jacob Alexander is Uris's close friend Solomon Kaufman, a solicitor. McCormick also points out that the weakest section is the second part of the book: it was hard for Uris to write about himself. He adds that Herb Schlosberg, although not in the book, was at the trial and has the three-volume transcript. McCormick ends by noting that Uris will visit Israel in the spring and then New York, spending the summer working on the musical version of *Exodus*. McCormick hoped that Doubleday could finalize the project with Schlosberg "rather than with Lee [Uris] who tends to be a little explosive on this subject." The original draft also had "a lot of sex stuff that simply doesn't belong."[6]

While McCormick and others worried over the text of *QB VII* during the year leading up to its November publication, Uris spent that spring with Jill at the King David Hotel, Jerusalem, then moved on to the Hilton in Tel Aviv. On 2 May, he wrote to McCormick that it was a wonderful visit, the "first time I've seen the old city relaxed and without deadlines."[7] Part of the purpose of his trip was to research a "Russian novel," but he was disappointed at not finding the kind of information that could raise his story above the level of cliché. Editorial communication included the news that Ernest Gann had recently published a novel on Masada, *The Antagonists*, a development that could have interfered with Uris's plans—at one point he had thought of writing a novel on the Roman siege and the sacrifice of the Jewish defenders. Uris replied that Masada was getting a lot of attention but that one should play it cool for now.

He had a new idea.

In April 1970, he had completed the revision of *QB VII*, dedicating the novel to Jill on her twenty-third birthday and to Charlie Goldberg, his Denver friend. The date was 16 April 1970. By September, the book was being advertised as another blockbuster. Nine weeks after its appearance, in November 1970, it was number one on the *Los Angeles Times* best-seller list, ahead of Erich Segal's *Love Story*, Hemingway's *Islands in the Stream*, and Irwin Shaw's *Rich Man, Poor Man*. By March 1971, it was number one on the *New York Times* list, having sold more than 306,000 copies in hardback, aided by a Literary Guild edition in January 1971. Bantam prepared to print 1.3 million copies of the paperback for January 1972; eight years later, it had gone through twenty-two printings.

Getting the novel published in England, however, was problematic. His UK publisher, William Kimber, required several legal opinions on the matter of libel and the identities of actual justices and lawyers. At one point during the negotiations, Ken McCormick wrote to a lawyer that Kimber's hesitancy gave no credit to their efforts at "cleaning it up" for England.[8] But McCormick added that Uris was "overboard on this business of integrity. The fact remains he will not give an inch [as far as altering the text]. In view of this I have a terrible feeling we can't publish this book in England." At one point, an incensed Uris, angry at proposed changes, threatened to pull the manuscript from Kimber.

QB VII was an opportunity not only to reaffirm Uris's fight against injustice and anti-Semitism, but also to outline, again, his idea of the writer and his role in society, which was, essentially, to stay isolated in order to stay objective (*QBVII*, 399). The work was also a chance for Uris to show his familiarity with areas like legal practice, medicine, British society, and, of course, Holocaust history.

The novel also reiterated Uris's skill in fictionalizing history, a practice with predecessors ranging from medieval romances to Sir Walter Scott, Charles Dickens, George Eliot, Victor Hugo, and Alexandre Dumas. Uris used survivors' memories and recollections to form the tragic core of the book, the center of the story he wanted to tell. By merging autobiography with history in this instance, Uris was able to use the London trial as a background for retelling and remembering horrific concentration-camp experiments.

He divides the novel into four parts: "The Plaintiff," "The Defendants," "Brief to Counsel," and "The Trial." Time shifts occur in each section: the novel opens in November 1945 with the surrender of the Polish doctor Adam Kelno, followed by his story in England. There, he is accused of being a war criminal because of his acts at the Jadwiga concentration camp; he defends himself but spends two years in prison in Brixton. After his release, Kelno departs to practice in Sarawak, in northern Borneo. These events announce Uris's theme that the past cannot be escaped. The first six chapters of *QB VII* foreshadow what is to come: although

Kelno moves to the practice of social medicine in Borneo, the remoteness of the island does not ensure his anonymity.

There emerges a parallel story involving Dr. Mark Tesslar, a former accuser of Kelno's living in Oxford, and the curious figures from the past who will be central to the trial, in the fourth part of the novel. Besides Tesslar, these include Justice Anthony Gilray and a series of camp survivors scattered across Europe and Israel.

Knighted for his activities in Borneo (Dering worked in British Somaliland), Adam Kelno reluctantly returns to England to work for the National Health Service in Southwark. Shortly afterward, he is shown a passage in Abraham Cady's novel *The Holocaust* that libels him, and the court challenge is underway. Kelno stresses his constant persecution by the Jews and even the English (Chapters 17–18). With that, the first part of the novel concludes.

Part Two restarts the novel with the story of Abraham Cady and his life in Norfolk, Virginia, where Uris spent his own youth. Details of Uris's father appear as the story proceeds, and Abraham Cady becomes a romantic figure, a fighter pilot (with a brother who died in the Spanish Civil War) and noted war hero who lost an eye in combat. Cady marries an Englishwoman as he begins his career as a writer. His early writing efforts and a separation from his wife take the plot to the point where the first part of the novel ended.

Uris concentrates on character, not events, to tell his story. His conservative narrative style—other than the simultaneous focus on the development of diverse characters, the structure remains orderly—satisfied readers' demands. Such narrative conventionality—such as the use of flashbacks and realistic settings—is at the core of popular fiction that remains unthreatening in its generic or linguistic method (for a contrast, see John Dos Passos's trilogy *U.S.A.* [1930–1936], which uses impressionistic devices such as those he dubbed "Newsreel" and the "The Camera Eye"). And by concentrating on individual characters, the novel makes it easy to absorb the historical background, a practice Uris used in his earliest novel, *Battle Cry*.

"Brief to Counsel," the third part of the novel, begins with a well-drawn, concentrated history of the Royal Courts of Justice, starting with formation of the Inns of Court. Uris then introduces the legal adversaries who will carry much of the novel until its conclusion. Sir Robert Highsmith, based on Peter Colin Duncan, QC, represents Adam Kelno. Thomas Bannister (Lord Gardiner), who is to represent Cady, is a man of impeccable integrity, a former cabinet minister touted as a possible prime minister. The lines of conflict are drawn against a backdrop of financial threats to Shawcross and his publishing firm. The militant nature of the determined Cady, not cowed by the libel suit but eager to fight it, overshadows any possibility of compromise: "I'M ABRAHAM CADY, WRITING JEW," he declares at one point (*QBVII*, 227).

Lady Sarah Wydman, an ally of Cady's, plays a pivotal role in gaining access to society and providing stature for the Cady camp during the trial. Minidramas—will so-and-so testify, can a key witness be located, will enough evidence emerge?—run throughout the scenes leading up to the fourth and final part of the book, "The Trial."

Uris expertly presents the trial, focusing on taut and dramatic exchanges between the key witnesses and the lawyers. He constructs the scenes with a definite sense of legal strategy and direction. Direct and cross-examinations are re-created professionally and without resorting to description of the characters' internal thoughts or the jury's reactions.

Bannister reveals that Kelno misrepresented the number and method of sterilizations he performed in the camp. Tesslar, who also worked in the camp, had disputed Kelno's claim. The scene climaxes when Bannister asks whether Kelno ever struck a woman on the operating table "and called her a damned Jewess."

"No, it is my word against Tesslar's."

"As a matter of fact," Bannister said, "it has nothing to do with Tesslar's word. It is the word of the woman you struck who is alive and at this moment on her way to London." (QBVII, 331)

At that dramatic point, the chapter ends.

Contrasting the tension of the trial are moments of romance, which are generally contrived and wooden in both action and dialogue. When Cady's remarried former wife visits him in London during the trial, she proposes they make love for old times' sake. He refuses because of her husband, although she dismisses him as too English to be suspicious. Cady still refuses, as sentiment battles morality (QBVII, 306).

Taut with legal and medical drama, the novel succeeds in displaying the best and often the worst of Uris's style. At the end, he can't resist letting the preachy Cady lecture readers and others on man's inhumanity. The best lines and speeches belong to the lawyers. In the structured world and language of the court, they eloquently express the arguments and facts of the world of survivors.

Interspersed with the legal drama are horrific accounts of torture and medical experimentation at Jadwiga, retold by a series of witnesses gathered from Europe and beyond. Uris writes movingly here, basing his characters' remarks on actual stories and details from Holocaust survivors (QBVII, 448–456). Suicides, executions, and madness were common.

The final bit of testimony depends on a silent witness, a surgical registry that survived the war. This document, thoroughly examined and confirmed through testimony, corroborates Kelno's direct involvement in medical experiments and his brutality as a doctor. The summation speeches of the two barristers are not outstandingly dramatic, but how could they be after the testimony of the witnesses? Highsmith tells the jury that Kelno was "not a madman, but an ordinary man in an insane situation" (*QBVII*, 491). By contrast, Bannister cites the immorality and inhumanity of Kelno's actions, asserting that "anti-Semitism is the scourge of the human race" (*QBVII*, 495). Kelno has done nothing, he argues, to receive society's compassion. He should be rewarded with nothing more than "the lowest coin of the realm" (*QBVII*, 495). Justice Gilray addresses the jury, and they leave to deliberate. Within ninety minutes, they return with a verdict in favor of Adam Kelno, but they award him damages of only a halfpenny. The novel ends with a brief follow-up with the characters and an even briefer communiqué reporting that Cady's son has been killed in the Six-Day War of June 1967.

One thing that the novel leaves out of the posttrial events is any parallel to Uris's actions after his own libel trial. Dering won contemptuous damages of a halfpenny, the smallest amount possible, but also had to pay court costs for both sides. A year after the trial, Dering died of stomach cancer. His survivors still had an obligation to pay the court costs, but Uris chose not to burden Dering's widow with the loss of her inheritance and did not press for payment. His victory had been moral, and that was enough. In the novel, there is no indication of a similar act by Cady.

COMMERCIAL SUCCESS, CRITICAL DISAPPOINTMENT

Of Uris's novels to that point, *QB VII* had the second-highest hardback sales, after *Exodus*, despite critical complaints about its predictable plot and cardboard, one-dimensional characters. But storytelling was its virtue, as a *New York Times* review emphasized: "Quicker than you can say Uris you are caught up at once in the unfolding conflict."[9] Others easily catalogued its faults, the largest being the dissolution of character, story, feeling, or idea into cliché. Martha Duffy called Uris's style "illiterate shorthand."[10] The novel was neither social history nor literary art.

Christopher Lehmann-Haupt, also in the *New York Times*, was even less generous. The book, he writes, is very undemanding: "One can read it and simultaneously work out tables of actuarial statistics . . . or iron out the snags in Kant's *Critique of Pure Reason*."[11] How did Uris manage to make so few demands on readers in five hundred pages? The key was to know the ending first, an approach attributed to the publisher David Shawcross in the novel. But doing so keeps Uris's mind off the problems of language. And with his plot so carefully mapped out,

Uris never needed to worry about his characters' taking on independent lives. This careful plotting, however, is what makes popular fiction popular. According to Lehmann-Haupt, deciding on the ending first took the story away from the author, preventing him from letting real conflict emerge naturally: "Mr. Uris is always satisfied with what first came to mind, as well as with what probably never got there at all." The final sentence of the review offers a particularly malicious verdict: "You can do anything you like while reading it. In fact, you needn't even bother to read it at all."

The novelist Larry McMurtry was equally caustic. In a review titled "Prose Isn't the Worst of It," he notes that although Uris was again number one on the best-seller list with *QB VII*, no one need respect his writing, which was "cheap."[12] He quotes passages that he labels crude and easy, but the prose was not the worst thing about the novel. The problem, he believes, was that Uris lost his nerve halfway through. For example, he slips in a Freudian flashback of Kelno witnessing a primal scene and wishing that he could castrate his father. This was not basic storytelling or suspense, but a simple device "to telegraph, crudely, the ending." There was also an absence of memorable characters in the novel.

According to McMurtry, Uris relied on what "might be called the Radio Principle. He gives us names and voices and lets the reader's imagination fill in the figures." So why did the novel reach number one? "In brief, Jewish agony. He has the concentration camps to offer; he is an atrocity monger, the first of the Big Sellers to think of writing about laboratory castration." *QB VII* laid to rest the view that the success of *Love Story* might have heralded a return to romantic conventions in popular fiction. *Love Story* was the convention. Now, instead of emotional masochism, as in *Love Story*, there was real sadism, as in Mickey Spillane. And, crucially, it was real sadism delivered in short paragraphs. McMurtry ends with this assessment: "If the Big Sellers have one thing in common, it is their commitment to the short paragraph, five sentences or under, three sentences whenever possible. . . . Unredeemed suffering is a difficult if not an impossible literary subject. Dostoevsky or Kafka might have brought it off. Uris just splashes the blood around."

Nonetheless, *QB VII* caught the public's attention, especially when it became one of the earliest (possibly the first) television miniseries. The cover of *TV Guide* (27 April–3 May 1974) pictured the courtroom scene from the series. The six-hour movie, then the longest in television history, further increased sales of the novel. The cast included Ben Gazzara, Anthony Hopkins, Leslie Caron, and Lee Remick. The drama ran on two nights, Monday and Tuesday, 29–30 April 1974, three hours each night. The show had an immense viewership, although a speech by Richard Nixon about Watergate (preparatory to handing over transcripts to a congressional committee) on Monday night, 29 April, delayed the broadcast by forty minutes.[13] The show received thirteen Emmy nominations, including ones for best script, best music, and best dramatic special; it won six.[14]

ARI

Uris's life had gradually reassembled itself. He had met and married Jill Peabody; *QB VII* was selling well. And now came a chance to return to his first love, the theatre. At the end of 1969, two young Broadway producers, Ken Gaston and Leonard Goldberg, became interested in *Ari*, Uris's musical version of *Exodus*, and backed the show. Following a belated honeymoon trip to Israel, Cyprus, and Europe, partly to research the production, Uris and Jill returned in June 1970 to New York to attend rehearsals and work on the script. Walt Smith soon joined them.

Uris had always loved the theatre, hoping, from his youth, to be a dramatist. His productions in the marines had furthered that desire. Although his career as a novelist and screenwriter flourished, he still wished for a Broadway success. As he said in a late interview: "The stage is to me the ultimate form of writing ... On the stage, it's from this mouth to that ear, and there's very little room for movement."[15] In a novel, he could "put a million men on a battlefield," but in drama, "it's still the playwright's words, and I find this is a challenge that I can't let go by." *Ari* was his chance to show others he could write for the stage.

Before rehearsals were to begin that August, Uris and Jill vacationed for a few days at Gurney's Inn on Montauk, Long Island, where sand dunes surrounded the resort. But Jill was seriously injured when she was thrown from a beach buggy that overturned. She was rushed to a hospital in Port Jefferson with a fractured skull and required emergency brain surgery. She lay in a coma for several days. Uris moved into a nearby motel to monitor her recovery; he saw this episode as another case in which his singular will would help beat the odds. He had written about this on a historical scale in *Exodus* and *Mila 18*, but he was now experiencing it personally. And after weeks of recovery, Jill held the first copy of *QB VII* in her hospital bed, clasping the author photo to her cheek and saying, "So much love!" (quoted in *ITB*, 284). Within eighteen months, she was fully and vibrantly recovered.

Uris understood their uniqueness: "Jill and I are unusual in that we are two people who literally owe each other our lives," he remarked in 1984.[16] In 1989, he elaborated: "We were two people who were very badly hurt and we saved each other. . . . We're both people who crave affection, and crave giving affection and we caught each other at the right moment."[17] He also angrily sued Gurney's Inn for being at fault in the accident and won a $250,000 settlement.

This near tragedy following on the suicide of his second wife welded the couple together. His first marriage of twenty-three years had had rocky periods and long separations. He later claimed that the trouble had been nobody's fault and that the bitterness had faded, "but when I was just coming up as a writer, I don't know if anybody could have handled me. It was impossible to get through to me, and too traumatic for her [Betty], with too many difficult decisions to make and crazy places to travel to."[18] Jill, however, respected Uris's work ethic: "Photography is my minor, the writer is my major" (*ITB*, 285).

After some six weeks of recovery, a period when Uris was going back and forth to New York, since *Ari* was in rehearsal, Jill was able to join Uris in Philadelphia for tryouts. But the play was running into financial difficulties, and Uris requested and received a $50,000 advance from Doubleday to meet expenses. Early critics were not friendly, the *Philadelphia Inquirer* calling *Ari* "a potboiler of a musical" and noting that "the harder it tries, the less it succeeds."[19] As a writer, Uris did "not let a cliché disturb his serene confidence in the yarn." The *Philadelphia Bulletin* observed that *Ari* had "a still life quality that pins the show to the stage and keeps it from becoming the epic musical it would like to be."[20] Characters spoke in "watered down epigrams, as though hoping for some passing stone mason to whip out his chisel and record every word for posterity." The overall treatment of the romantic and dramatic scenes was more in the style of an operetta, with "snapshot-like action" alternating with "heavy exposition and unclear story line."

A tryout in Washington preceded its New York opening on 15 January 1971, which also received harsh reviews. Clive Barnes in the *New York Times* wrote that it could be "praised more easily for its aspirations than its achievements."[21] The error seemed to be in Uris's writing. He tried to write both the book and the lyrics for the musical, tasks that at this point in his career he was temperamentally unsuited for. A musical demands a clear and direct style, which *Ari* lacked; a novel, with its large canvas, can be diffuse and digressive and yet succeed. The caustic review also noted that there was not a single showstopper tune—which might have been a good thing, for *Ari* "does seem the kind of show that once stopped would have difficulty in getting started again."

Nevertheless, nearly forty of Uris's friends came from Aspen for opening night, ending the evening at the Rainbow Room at Rockefeller Center for a party. But the negative reviews forced *Ari* (directed by Lucia Victor and starring David Cryer as Ari) to close after nineteen performances. Although Uris's dream of theatrical success was shattered, he did not give up his love of the theatre. In later years, he hoped to revive *Ari* and would later attempt to write a stage version of his novel *Trinity*. He still believed that the theatre was "the ultimate form of writing" because it relied more on language and action than narrative.[22]

With *Ari* closed and Jill still fragile, Uris needed new work. His first thought after *QB VII* was a short novel (initially on the theme of the Jewish heroes of Masada), but he revised this into a major effort, first referred to as his "Russian novel." Ken McCormick told Uris's British publisher, William Kimber, that the proposed novel lacked a plot, but Uris was planning an elaborate research trip related to the project.[23] And he wouldn't do so if he didn't know that he had a story line. To his peers at Doubleday in September 1971, McCormick wrote that Uris's Russian novel was taking shape but would not be short: "This growing enthusiasm makes me very optimistic because, as you know, he is not a shoot-from-the hip man when it comes to his own books and tends to down-play his ideas until he is sure of them. He is beginning to be very sure of the Russian book."[24]

Uris, however, needed help. And in a letter to the chief of military history at the Department of Army, he requested source materials dealing with the activities of the U.S. armed forces in the Vienna area in 1945–1946. A reply said that limited staff could conduct only a brief research foray and that only unclassified records would be made available—and only in their office at the Washington National Records Center.[25]

Uris was insulted. He made this clear in a reply, first characterizing the help he had received, "in conjunction with my writing," over the past two decades as unlimited cooperation from all branches of the military.[26] He claimed to have been offered the post of "Marine Corps Historian"—an undocumented assertion. In full dudgeon, he imperiously ordered Colonel Fechtman to "rectify this situation immediately" by assigning him a competent historian or researcher "who will be at my service as I need." If the matter was not attended to promptly—he would be leaving the country on 26 September—"I will take the matter up with a member of the White House Staff, who is a personal advisor to the President and see that this comes to the attention of Mr. Nixon." No action on either side appears to have occurred, despite Uris's characteristically belligerent tone.

Not known for his graciousness, Uris at this time surprised Ken McCormick by writing to thank him for his support in the battle with Kimber to publish *QB VII*.[27] Uris admitted that he felt badly about the "few unkind cuts" he had made at McCormick: "I think you ought to know that next to Jill, you have been the strongest influence on the continuation of my career." He then reported that his current project, the "Russian novel," was giving him a hard time: "It took me a long time to lose my 'youthful' idealism and knowing I can do little any more about the agony of man is dejecting to my spirit." He would try to locate some inner peace, admittedly not his forte, by writing his new book.

Uris and Jill were to begin their research trip with a stop in Sweden: he wanted to see a mining operation north of the Arctic Circle. However, a motorcycle accident in Aspen in September delayed the trip by a week. Even after his leg was out of a cast, he needed some therapy before he could undertake the journey. McCormick told Doubleday's Swedish agent that Uris wanted to stay in the Grand Hotel, the best, and also to see travelogue films depicting folk festivals, summer resorts, and the aurora borealis.[28] After arriving in Sweden, Uris went to the north to visit the mines and to meet with the head of the Jewish refugee society in order to learn details and information about Jewish exiles. He also planned to go to the Soviet Union, Afghanistan, and Pakistan.

Uris's trip involved a great deal of planning, and he was happy to have McCormick make all the arrangements, beginning with a book order for *Nagel's Encyclopedia-Guide: USSR* and Arnold Fletcher's *Afghanistan: Highway of Conquest*. McCormick then wrote to the U.S. ambassadors of the countries Uris planned to visit, asking for support. He also wrote to the Ministry of Information in each country. In his letter to the U.S. embassy in Afghanistan, McCormick explained that Uris "depends heavily on accuracy. When he describes a scene or creates a character you believe in the place or man. . . . One thing that separates Mr. Uris from many other writers is his scrupulous respect for fact and that he never misrepresents."[29]

Covering all his bases, Uris even asked McCormick to write to the Chinese ambassador to Canada (the United States had no formal relations with China at the time) and ask for permission for Uris to travel to China. McCormick explained to the ambassador that "the role of the novelist in America is a strong one, particularly where he is writing with a basis of fact."[30] He continued: "People who otherwise find themselves ideologically uninterested are drawn out and educated by the role of the intelligent novelist," revealing how Uris's editor conceived of his writer's work.

A week before this note, McCormick had recorded a phone conversation with Uris, who talked about the new novel this way: "There is a balance of good and evil in man as there is a balance in *nature*. The main character is good but capable of evil. It is an ecological war waged on a psychological level. When expanded to a nation, it can be catastrophic."[31]

As with his other novels, Uris had to see and experience the world he was to write about, in this case the Soviet-Afghanistan connection, understood as part of his proposed story about exiled Russian Jews. Uris was also not bashful about contacting experts. Harrison Salisbury of the *New York Times*, for example, provided a mass of detail about life in Vienna during the last hundred days of the Second World War.[32] As McCormick explained to Sam Vaughan, another Doubleday editor, "Uris is hot and that's what excites me because this was what was going on when he finally saw where he wanted to go on *QB VII*."[33]

In a prearrival note regarding Uris's stop in Australia, which was also on his itinerary, Paul Feffer, a publisher's exporter, explained to his Australian counterpart that Uris was writing a novel "about a man who flees Sweden and in seeking refugee [status] goes from Scandinavia to Afghanistan to Pakistan, down to Australia and finally settles in New Zealand."[34] Feffer then explained that "for Mr. Uris to feel he has authenticity in what he is writing, he wants to spend some time in each of the countries that the fictional character supposedly traverses." John Sargent, an executive at Doubleday, summarized the plot to Ken McCormick as being "about a character in 1939 who is on the lam from Sweden."[35]

At one point in the planning, Uris thought he would be going through India. McCormick wrote ahead to the consul general of India, explaining that Uris was "always interested in accuracy" and was "a friendly witness" who would "write with an eye to fairly representing what he sees. You can trust him."[36] It is a revealing remark, emphasizing Uris's attributes as a writer.

On 11 November 1971 from Kabul, his stop after Sweden, Uris wrote to McCormick, "This trip is pure gold as far as research and background for the novel is concerned."[37] Before Uris's arrival, the U.S. ambassador to Afghanistan, Robert Neumann, made it clear to McCormick, however, that "Mr. Uris is something of a controversial personality in Afgh. because of strong feelings aroused by his book *Exodus* in this Moslem and quite pro-Arab country. However, that is more than sometime ago and I do not anticipate any great difficulties."[38] In Kabul, where he stayed at the International Hotel, his host was a Professor Kahar from Kabul University, who met him at the airport on 23 October 1971 with a car and driver. Uris loved it.

Pakistan was the next stop. Uris hoped to meet people familiar with the 1939 period, especially regarding the Jewish community of Karachi. He began in Peshawar and then wanted to drive to Karachi. After that, Australia and then New Zealand, where McCormick, writing ahead, told a G. S. Bryant that "Mr. Uris is a man who does not believe writing fiction about things he doesn't know first-hand."[39] Uris was expected to arrive on 14 November.

Meanwhile, Jill was having something of a revelation in Ireland. While Uris was traveling across Asia, Jill visited her sister and brother-in-law in London (Afghanistan and Pakistan were considered too rugged for her still-fragile condition). She then went to Ireland for five days with her stepsister and brother-in-law, visiting Counties Kerry, Galway, and Clare. She stayed on for a couple of extra days by herself, and was quite taken with the country and its photographic possibilities. Her letter to Uris expressing her enthusiasm and suggesting he visit prompted the idea of a possible new subject.[40]

Uris later said he discovered Ireland in Afghanistan. He had been traveling with his son Mike, "who had long hair and a bag of tofu draped around his shoulders, and wore sandals," when he received Jill's letter.[41] Dramatizing only slightly, Uris claimed to be looking over the border between the Soviet Union and Afghanistan for a possible "underground railroad story" when he got her "report." "This is the place," she told him, and "in Kabul is where I discovered Dublin," he claimed.

Reunited with Jill back in Aspen after his adventures in Afghanistan and elsewhere, Uris considered his options for his story. But first was skiing. He had won an apprentice ski instructor's pin from the Fred Iselin Ski School clinic in April 1969. He now took up the sport again with new enthusiasm. He also developed a fervent interest in the Denver Broncos football team, attending many games with his friend Charles Goldberg of Denver. For a time, Uris and Jill owned a condominium in Denver. In Aspen, Uris would often rent a room at the Holiday Inn at the base of Buttermilk Mountain so that he could watch the Broncos on cable television. The jacket photo of Uris for *Mitla Pass* shows him in a Denver Broncos cap.

FIRST TRIPS TO IRELAND

Uris had to get on with a new project for financial reasons as well as to satisfy his psychological need to prove his talent once again. By Easter 1972, an Irish trip had been arranged, sponsored by the Irish government and tourist board. David Hanley, a writer, became Uris and Jill's tour guide. They started in Dublin, staying at the Shelbourne Hotel, and traveled to Galway for an Easter Sunday memorial service in a graveyard that Jill photographed in the rain. The next day was sunny, and they went to Belfast for an Easter Monday Protestant rally. The trip lasted less than a week, Jill photographing as they traveled. On their return, they stopped in New York, where they showed her photos and some notes by Uris to Oscar Dystel of Bantam Books. Jill said she had started out doing photographs for a magazine piece, but when the publisher saw them, he was excited and interested in doing a book—if she could get a decent writer. The writer was present. Uris quickly understood that this was an opportunity to narrate and absorb Irish history as well as to promote Jill's career. He could also then integrate his notes into a novel almost simultaneously. Dystel offered them a contract for a photo book on the spot. It would be her first book; until then, her photos had appeared only in the *Aspen Daily News*. Uris also began to see real possibilities for a novel.[42]

In May 1972, they returned to Ireland, renting an apartment in Rathgar, the Dublin suburb where James Joyce was born, from Kevin and Ray Diffley, who became close friends. The apartment later became the setting for a scene in *Trinity*. Their chief researcher and assistant was Geraldine Kelly, who also organized their travels. She had previously been an archeologist. She scheduled photo shoots, gathered information, and arranged interviews for Uris with Irish Republican Army members. They stayed approximately nine months, until January 1973. On their return to Aspen, Jill printed the black-and-white photos, working closely with Uris on the text. Diane Eagle, Uris's assistant, did most of the research for what would become *Ireland: A Terrible Beauty* and for *Trinity*. Uris worked on both books at the same time, but completed *Ireland: A Terrible Beauty* (dedicated to Oscar Dystel, Ken McCormick, and John Sargent) before the novel. Afghanistan and the "Russian novel" disappeared before the sectarian violence and rich history of Ireland (for details, see *ITB*, 286–286).

Jill had become increasingly more important to Uris. With her, there was a meeting of minds. Her photography and creativity and her willingness to help Uris made it possible for him, through mutual encouragement and curiosity, to pursue new ideas and possibilities. She had aided him in completing *QB VII*, which he dedicated to her; she became his partner on *Ireland: A Terrible Beauty* (1975) and *Jerusalem: Song of Songs* (1981). Working with someone this closely was something new for him. He was proud of her and her beauty (although sometimes chauvinistically so, calling attention to her short skirts or figure) and constantly encouraged her in her projects. His connection to her differed from his union with either Betty or Margery. With the former, he had built a family and a writing career. With the latter, he had had little time to build much of anything except an appreciation for her good looks. With Jill, he built a new identity, resulting in another major triumph, one that brought renewed worldwide attention to his work: *Trinity*.

IRELAND

The Irish are about as fouled up as the Jews and it's going to take me at least one thousand pages to set them straight.
—URIS TO IRVING STONE, 1974

U RIS WAS NOT far off. It took him 751 pages to tell the story of Ireland in
Trinity (1976), a novel that sold more than five million copies and stayed
on the *New York Times* best-seller list for one hundred weeks. Preceding it was *Ireland: A Terrible Beauty*, coauthored with Jill. His interest in Ireland
began in 1968, when he was in England to research *QB VII*. He had taken note of
the Irish Troubles largely because the BBC nightly reported on the destruction
and mayhem caused by sectarian violence.

As mentioned earlier, Uris and Jill stayed in Ireland over a nine-month period
(May 1972–January 1973) so that Uris could conduct research for a new novel.
Their visit coincided with one of the most violent years of the Troubles. Four
hundred seventy-two people died; there were more than 10,500 shootings.
Eighteen hundred bombs were planted, more than 41,000 pounds of explosives
were found, and 531 people were charged with terrorist offences.[1] Of course, the
violence in Northern Ireland began before the Urises arrived. On 30 January
1972, fourteen unarmed men were shot dead by a British paratrooper regiment
in Derry after a large civil rights rally. This became known as Bloody Sunday,
which created a wave of anger throughout the Roman Catholic community (the
protesters were Catholic, the soldiers mostly Protestant). The events of Bloody
Sunday "definitely piqued [Uris's] interest in writing a book," Jill remarked.[2]

Uris and Jill lived through security curfews, bomb warnings, and other dangers. Visiting Derry just after several bombs exploded, they found themselves
close to a gunfight. Dramatic photographs of a bombed-out grocery shop and car
dealership appear in *Ireland: A Terrible Beauty*. In Belfast, they had to evacuate
their hotel because of a bomb threat, which turned out to be a car bomb that was
defused on the street. They were caught on a "border" street between Catholic
and Protestant neighborhoods in Belfast when a gunfight broke out, and they
had to hug the walls while Jill photographed the scene.[3]

A letter from Colonel M. A. J. Tugwell at the British headquarters in Northern Ireland, dated 27 September 1972, acted as a calling card. Noting the visit by Mr. and Mrs. Leon Uris during 2–3 October, it states that they want to see as much as possible of the army and its functions in Northern Ireland. They also want to meet officers and soldiers. Permission was granted, and a colonel from the General Staff was assigned to accompany both of them.[4]

In Derry, Uris met with representatives of the Irish Republican Army (IRA), among them the militant Martin McGuinness, who was commander of the Derry Brigade and a major force in the Provisional IRA, the paramilitary arm of the IRA. Jill had also given Uris a small Rolleiflex 35 mm camera, which he used to take some photos without anyone noticing (*ITB*, 287). After Derry, they were with British paratroopers in Belfast and then interviewed Ian Paisley, a Protestant paramilitary as well as a frightening figure, according to Jill.[5] However, people began to notice them, especially Jill, an attractive female photographer. Suspicions were roused because they were talking to all sides (*ITB*, 286). Uris and Jill then decided to return to the southern part of the island (the Republic of Ireland) and did not reenter the North.

The violence surrounding them influenced Uris's writing, and was captured in Jill's photographs. The daily strife they witnessed played a large part in Uris's understanding of the political struggle in Northern Ireland, which he would highlight in *Trinity* and *Ireland: A Terrible Beauty*. It is clear that what he had earlier seen of Israel's fight for independence in 1948, as well as its participation in the Suez crisis of 1956, was being replayed in Ireland. This renewed his sense of urgency to express history in his soon-to-be-written Irish novel. It was exactly the alchemy that intensified his creativity and energy. He had found not only a story to tell but also a society to celebrate.

More specifically, Uris interviewed sources, traveled the country, and helped Jill, all the while absorbing Irish life. His journeys and talks gave him credibility as an author. As he told an interviewer after *Trinity* was published: "I don't sit here in Aspen" and "dream of what's happening in Ireland," adding, "I work harder than any coal miner in the United States," and the "hard work" was what made him convincing as a writer, he believed.[6]

In Ireland, Geraldine Kelly, chief researcher and assistant, knew where to go for the most interesting material and whom to ask for interviews, especially IRA members and political contacts in the North. Uris and Jill often witnessed calamity and misfortune. In Ulster, sensitive areas became danger zones scarred by urban guerrilla warfare. Photographing from a speeding car became an art that Jill mastered. Pictures of Kilmainham Gaol (jail) or bombed-out Londonderry streets were equally harrowing.

Jill, who was twenty-five at the time, assisted with a good deal of the research for both *Trinity* and *Ireland: A Terrible Beauty*. In turn, Uris helped Jill, lugging equipment, driving, and even acting as a bodyguard. On one occasion, two young toughs spotted Jill taking pictures and took off after her. Uris and the cabbie who was with them stood their ground; miraculously, nothing happened. There were also no problems interviewing people—most, including Ulstermen, were eager to talk. But photographs were a different story, and the tensest moments were always in the Protestant districts.

And as he had done with all of his novels, Uris started his Irish research with a definite idea of which side was right and which was wrong. He also admitted in an interview that he had no desire to return to Northern Ireland, noting that the constant bombings "'played havoc with their sex life' (though the usually earthy Uris didn't put it quite so delicately)."[7] In the interview, he pessimistically said that the British wanted out and there would be a civil war.

In *Ireland*, Jill's photographs moved "from photo journalism under fire to portrait photography of the celebrities, to a treasury of scenery and most importantly a social concept of a people."[8] And the proposed chapter titles for *Ireland: A Terrible Beauty* tell a story clearly expressing Uris's point of view, as politics alternate with natural beauty: "An Unconquerable Spirit Endures Through a Tragic History," "A Mystic Land and Seascape," "The Red Hand of Ulster—Plantation and Genesis of Conflict," "May God Have Mercy on Belfast," and "The Victims," the last focusing on families on both sides who lost members to the bombs and assassins. "Friday's Children" is a poignant, final photo essay of children on both sides surviving in the ravaged streets. A transcript of children's accounts of the loss of parents provided a moving document.

IRELAND: A TERRIBLE BEAUTY

When they eventually returned to Aspen, at the end of January 1973, with their research notes, photographs, and tapes, Uris and Jill began to work intensely. At first, Uris concentrated on his novel, but after three months of sifting material, he turned to the narrative needed for Jill's book. He had written several hundred pages of *Trinity* when he took a break from the novel to write the text for *Ireland: A Terrible Beauty*: "It was helpful for me to do it that way. By the time I was finished with *Ireland: A Terrible Beauty* I was a walking encyclopedia of Ireland."[9]

Ireland: A Terrible Beauty is an unusual book. The political nature of its subject is apparent on the title page, with its quotation from Yeats's poem "Easter, 1916." It is not just a travel account or a photographic essay. It is an opinionated account of the abuse of Catholics at the hands of Protestants and the effect of British colonization on the country.

While focusing on the present in Ireland, the book does not neglect the past. In his characteristic style of condensing history while maintaining narrative interest, Uris retells the brutal history of the country from its earliest beginnings. From the outset, several themes emerge, one of the most prominent being the parallel between the Irish and the Jews in experiencing a diaspora and a fight for survival against the British (and others, in the Jews' case). The influence of Gaelic on Irish culture and literature is seen as being much like the influence of Hebrew and Yiddish on Jewish culture. Uris also predicts the inevitable end of British control of the North. In fact, Uris ends the first page of the first chapter with a prophetic glimpse of the future: the cycle of imperialism "is coming to a close after four hundred years in the same place it started. Ireland, England's first colony, is destined to be her last" (*ITB*, 11).

The issue of social and religious freedom is paramount in Uris's account. Even though he divides the text into accounts of the Republic and Ulster, the importance of liberty is the focus of each. For the Republic of Ireland, independence from the invading Vikings, Norsemen, and those associated with the Protestant Ascendancy was key. For Ulster, the independence of the Irish from the British, and more specifically the Catholics from the Protestants, is essential. Images of war and destruction overpower the second part of the book. Jill's photographs capture bombed-out stores and streets, at one point recording a gun battle that took place before her on Crumlin Road (*ITB*, 256–257). In the first part, she records the effects of the abuse and exploitation of the Irish by the British. Part II, however, with its personal accounts of Bloody Sunday and the families who lost their sons and, in some cases, daughters, is visceral in its tragedy. One of the accomplishments of *Ireland: A Terrible Beauty* was its immediacy: the Troubles were still ongoing when it appeared, in November 1975. The discussion of the fighting had an urgency and importance for readers.

Ireland and its history captivated Uris, and the result was more incisive thought than he usually displayed in his work. Writing about Ulster, for example, he summarizes its history and the institution of the Penal Laws, which debased the Irish Catholics. He then traces the decay of the Penal Laws under the beneficiaries of the Ascendancy, who wanted Ireland as their own country. The Act of Union of 1800, he writes, added "the cross of St. Patrick to the cross of St. George and the Scottish cross of St. Andrew to form the Union Jack, signifying a United Kingdom" (*ITB*, 170). But he also writes that the Protestant community was close-minded and bigoted.

Ireland: A Terrible Beauty was the workshop that allowed Uris to treat Irish history and politics from a certain point of view, which was an essential rehearsal for constructing a novel with a specific set of characters who defined the history and conflicts of the time. In writing *Ireland: A Terrible Beauty*, Uris got everything out of the way that would distract him from the novelistic enterprise of *Trinity*.

A crucial step was Uris's decision to tell the history of Ireland through its people. He would carry this over to *Trinity*, in which relationships and characters define the historical moments, not the reverse, as in his other books. He did not skimp in the research, stating at the outset that he and Jill traveled 10,000 miles in Ireland during their nine-month stay (*ITB*, 7). His talent for interviewing and learning the stories of the well known and little known is also apparent in his accounts of individual lives. Yet he does not omit criticisms. While providing a portrait of Cardinal William Conway, the 111th successor of St. Patrick, Uris is harsh on the cardinal's failure to institute much-needed Catholic reforms. His combination of "doctrinaire behavior and elusiveness" resulted in little progress (*ITB*, 35). By contrast is his praise for the MacBride family, especially Maud Gonne MacBride (nationalist, feminist, and Yeats's muse) and her son Seán MacBride, who became a lawyer and then politician. He became foreign minister in 1948 and then a champion of human rights and a founder of Amnesty International. He received the Nobel Peace Prize in 1974 (*ITB*, 151). Another hero for Uris was John Hume, a politician and expert negotiator (*ITB*, 214).

The second half of *Ireland: A Terrible Beauty* is distinctly more upsetting. It records battles and contains some of Uris's best writing and Jill's most dramatic photographs. His account of Easter Monday, 1916, is dramatic. His story of Father Edward Daly's account of Bloody Sunday is intense and emotional: he narrates how Father Daly risked his own life by trying to comfort a dying and unarmed seventeen-year-old who had been shot in the chest (*ITB*, 222–224). The paragraph on (and photograph of) the Ulster Defense Association, the largest militant organization of workingmen, is frightening. Its members had sometimes gotten rid of their own leaders through gangland-style executions (*ITB*, 253).

For some subjects, Uris's prejudices or fixed opinions create barriers. Sex is one: "Irish sexual appetites are generally low key" is perhaps his most egregious statement (*ITB*, 27). His logic could be equally suspect: Irish women, "who have found little or nothing from sex, see no wrong in urging their sons into a life of celibacy in the church" (*ITB*, 27). The "moral dictatorship" of the church was responsible for this stunted female sexuality. Uris also too readily refers to brainwashing by Catholicism, claiming its dogma and "moral ponderousness" overwhelm the Irish, unlike the French or Italians (*ITB*, 27). And again he blames the British: they were "Johnny on the spot in establishing an Irish theological institution along lines they could control" as the effectiveness of the Penal Laws receded (*ITB*, 27). He later claims that "as a subject race, the Irish have had much of their ambition knocked out of them" (*ITB*, 135).

Despite such strongly voiced views, reaction to *Ireland: A Terrible Beauty* was positive. Although initially seen as a travel book, the work revealed its political nature through the photographs and text. Additionally, Jill's photojournalistic style, coupled with her ability at portraiture—and Uris's interpretative text— added a luster to the work that made it more than a simple indictment of one side or the other. A photograph of the stone carver Seamus Murphy reveals a dedicated artist (*ITB*, 106). A shot of a young couple stiffly sitting below an equally formal accordion player at a weekly ceilidh (social gathering) is a probing social comment on the life of young adults (*ITB*, 128–129).

Isolation, geographic as well as social, is an important visual theme preparing the reader for the political isolation of the sectarian violence between the IRA, the Ulstermen, and the Republicans. Searing photos of funerals and destruction dominate the second half of the book, beginning with a two-page spread containing ten photographs of Ulster bombings, followed by double-page spreads of slogans found on Ulster walls, Derry street scenes, and an uncaptioned two-page spread of a destroyed grocery store (*ITB*, 218–219). All the photographs express a human tragedy generated by deep-seated political and religious rivalries.

A review by Andrew Greeley in *Irish People* represents the generally favorable reception of the book. Noting that it was wrong in only a few minor details (one of the photos in the Slea Head area is described as being part of the Ring of Kerry, but is actually in the Dingle Peninsula), he emphasizes that the Urises were the first Americans to point out "how deeply betrayed many of the Ulster Catholics feel about the lack of support for the people and the government of the republic."[10] Others, however, felt that while Uris was good on history, he was misguided in his political analysis. His strength—and his weakness—was that he was never dispassionate.[11]

The importance of this book and *Trinity* was as much personal as professional. Jill felt that while working on *Ireland: A Terrible Beauty* and *Trinity*, they were exceptionally close: "We talked over every story and every photo. The extraordinary success of *Ireland: A Terrible Beauty* was really the marriage between the photos and stories, it really hadn't been done like that before."[12] Months later, she would read back each day's draft of *Trinity* to her husband.

Uris felt this connection also, writing an appreciation of Jill, titled "Jilly," which followed a chronology at the end of *Ireland: A Terrible Beauty*. Accompanied by two striking photos, the personal essay recounts her recovery from her Long Island beach accident and the subsequent trauma. Uris outlines their union: how he met her after his own life "had bottomed out with the death of his [second] wife," and how Jill restored him to wholeness (*ITB*, 285). Eighteen months after her accident, she was leaping out of helicopters in Belfast and working under gunfire to take pictures for their book. And through it all, there was never a conflict between her roles as wife-partner and professional photographer (*ITB*, 285). Her calmness stabilized a sometimes-excitable Uris. In this personal appreciation of Jill and their closeness, Uris reveals a private side he had often hidden.

Ending the book is Jill's short essay "Photographing Ireland," in which she expresses her own love of the country, beginning with her visit in 1971, when she traveled from Cork to Shannon. The blending of expressiveness and remarkable scenery overpowered her. Of her trip with Uris, she tells of their encounter with the political factions, alternating between Catholic and Protestant gatherings. The Republic was satisfying, but Ulster was a challenge, not the least because she was a woman and a photographer. At one point, she almost had her equipment confiscated when she photographed a parade, not realizing her camera was aimed at an IRA leader on the run. Camouflaging the camera was a necessity, as street photography became the only way for her to capture scenes: quickly and without planning and always with natural light.

WRITING *TRINITY*

Writing *Ireland: A Terrible Beauty* had gone quickly; work on *Trinity* was slower, and Uris soon reported that he had done three drafts.[13] *Battle Cry* and *Exodus* had been clear in his mind from the start, but *Trinity* was different: it had to come out a day at a time and a page at a time: "I didn't know exactly where I was going—the book controlled me more than I controlled it."[14] Uris's view of the Irish, however, was clear: "The Irish are in love with life because they live a lot with death. They are a very persistent people."

He had returned to Aspen in 1973 with massive amounts of material that would form the foundation of his novel, as well as his belief that "any decent novel has a basis in fact."[15] Among the titles he valued was Robert Keating's *The Green Flag*, "the greatest volume ever done on Ireland."[16] He claimed to have read a hundred histories of Ireland, concluding that if "you show me an historian . . . I'll show you a guy who practices fiction." History, he emphasized, "is not a science; it is an interpretative art," although historians try to be objective.[17] He, however, did not. Research, which might stagger others, was how he made a living.[18] He would conduct research and organize material from noon until four and then usually write between four and eight.[19]

From such persistence emerged *Trinity*, a novel that follows three families from the 1880s to 1915, concentrating on religion and politics. The title refers to the three groups that caused political trouble for three centuries: Irish Catholics, the Protestant Anglo-Irish gentry, and Presbyterian Scots, who make up the dominant Protestants of Ulster. Uris personifies the friction through successive generations of the earls of Foyle and their Hubble family line, the Scottish MacLeods, and the Irish Catholic Larkins. Action begins just before the potato blight. Big moments are brought off in a series of big scenes that show a surprising grasp of Irish character and customs. The novel begins with a description of a wake and then a confrontation between the Earl and Countess of Foyle over the former's refusal to let his son and heir marry an Irish Catholic girl he made pregnant.

The smuggling of arms into Ireland from Germany during the First World War and the early preparations for what would become the Easter uprising of 1916 follow. The religious antagonism dividing Catholics and Protestants runs through the narrative. Uris summarizes the clash with a couplet from Alexander Pope: "Religion, blushing, veils her sacred fires / and unawares Morality expires." He opens and closes the novel with the same lines from Eugene O'Neill's *A Moon for the Misbegotten*: "There is no present or future—only the past happening over and over again—now."

Uris's use of language was one reason for the novel's success, the result of a carefully thought-out strategy. Unfamiliar with Ulsterisms yet determined to get them right, Uris found a source. While staying at the Europa Hotel in Belfast, around the corner from the *Belfast Telegraph*, he visited the paper almost daily to photocopy seven or eight years' worth of columns from the journalist Frederick Gamble, who signed himself "John Pepper" and regularly wrote on Ulster language. Back in Aspen, he had them filed under categories like weather, food, or health, establishing a master chart of Ulster expressions. This illustrates Uris's detailed method, which he applied also to place names.

Uris researched thoroughly, in Aspen as well as Ireland. Diane Eagle, his assistant at the time, located further books and details. She had first met Uris when she typed a portion of *Ireland: A Terrible Beauty*, and her background as a paralegal prepared her for his daily research queries. As Uris earlier said, "Research to me is as important, or more important, than the writing. It is the foundation upon which the book is built."[20] Nonetheless, Eagle had to remind him constantly that he was not writing history but a novel, as a sign she tacked to the wall declared.

Working in a study below Uris's in the two-story cabana building adjacent to the pool area at the Red Mountain house, Eagle had numerous details to follow up on, including the differences among Irish whiskeys, the size of Charles Parnell's hands, and the nature of certain rifles used by the British in the Boer War.[21] Another topic was furniture, particularly what sort was most likely to appear in Protestant, as opposed to Catholic, homes. Eagle "designed," or rather furnished, all the houses in the novel: she did the research and chose the items that defined domestic life in each.[22] Uris would often imitate an Irish brogue as he became immersed in the book, and Irish idioms became part of his daily exchange with Eagle.

The day would begin with Eagle retyping or correcting pages Uris had finished the night before and answering queries. They would then work together from one to three in the afternoon, Uris most often wearing a favored outfit: a plaid shirt with two front pockets or a velour pullover with jeans and slippers.[23] Uris would then continue to write until six, when he would knock off to relax with Jill in the Jacuzzi or pool. Drinks would be mixed (double vodka martinis were favored), and the occasional joint smoked. Jill also read the first-draft pages and made notes; at night, she would read the day's work back to him. They also acted out scenes in the novel, including Lady Caroline's first meeting with Conor Larkin at his forge before he visits Hubble Manor to examine the great screen in the Long Hall (TR, 353–355; 356–362).

Eagle became so involved with the project that she "walked about Aspen with Conor and Seamus on each shoulder."[24] Strict adherence to routine made it possible for Uris to progress through the mass of notes he had collected and fashion the story. But he couldn't stop thinking about details when he left the pool house: four-by-six-inch notepads and pens were left throughout the house. Uris, an insomniac, would often get up at night to make notes when sleeping pills did not work.

Other sources also helped: Francis Whitaker, the Aspen blacksmith who had made the freedom fighter gate to Uris's home, became the source of blacksmithing information that informed the character of Conor. The famous Triangle Shirtwaist Factory fire in New York City, which killed 146 mostly immigrant Jewish women in March 1911, became the model for the Londonderry shirt-factory fire (TR, 384–392).[25]

Once on a project, Uris was committed. Deadlines and writing remained paramount. He and Jill, in fact, had to cancel a winter holiday to Acapulco in December 1974, telling Ken McCormick that "three weeks away from the desk at this vital juncture would be cutting things too thin."[26] He gave his children the same explanation: "After looking at the number of words yet to write on the novel and what with a deadline and a publication date staring me in the face," the planned trip simply did not make sense.[27] He complained to his travel agent: "I'm into my third year on my two Irish books and when the publisher set the publication date in 1975, I thought I would be home free with room to spare . . . Things haven't turned out that way. The novel is the longest and most difficult I've ever attempted and it is simply going slower than I anticipated."[28]

Despite the canceled trip, Uris was happy, immersed in his project, with Jill at his side. To his former mother-in-law in Iowa, he wrote that he received a motorcycle as a fiftieth-birthday present, and so he didn't "really feel all that old. Life has been extremely good, peaceful and productive in the last five years."[29]

But how to narrate *Trinity* remained a problem. The length and variety of the events, plus the vastness of the story, created challenges. Uris, with Ken

McCormick's aid, created the character Seamus to frame the tale.[30] As both a participant and a friend and admirer of Conor, he became a legitimate device through which to filter the events. His becoming a journalist further established his credibility. However, Uris also introduced a second, omniscient narrator, who tells salient parts of the story, including Seamus's own death in the explosion at Lettershanbo Castle at the end. This narrative inconsistency is a flaw that critics noted, one that altered the realism maintained by Seamus.

Uris had trouble finishing the novel, and he and Jill, along with Diane Eagle, took a condominium at Coronado Beach, near San Diego, hoping that a new perspective might help. When a reporter visited, he noted unfinished manuscript pages stacked unevenly in a corner of the high-rise condo.[31] He had a hundred pages to go, and his publisher was asking every day when it would be ready. Uris made it clear to the reporter that he and Jill were not making dinner engagements or tennis plans, nor were they seeing friends. Yet the conclusion eluded him: "*Trinity* doesn't end. It dies." Nonetheless, Uris impressed the reporter with his "remarkable sense of history, tenacity for research and ability to tell convincing stories."

When he finally finished the book, in Coronado, Jill read out the ending while Uris listened, dressed in a brown caftan, and Diane Eagle cried. It was done, and they celebrated with champagne. At a party to mark the book's publication, held at the Red Mountain house, name cards for each character were at the table, and Jill gave Uris a Celtic cross, which he wore constantly.[32]

THE STORY

The success of *Trinity* originated from several sources. The clarity of history dramatized through character contributed strongly to the unity and momentum of the novel. People in the book are dominated by ideas, and by telling history through character rather than the reverse—explaining character through history—Uris pulled readers into the story. This was an important literary shift for the author. And a plot that explored the claims of institutions and warring groups through the lens of character made the historical conflicts comprehensible.

Uris's ability to write dramatic scenes was also effective. Some of the most powerful include the wake for Kilty Larkin, which begins the novel and features such details as the tying of the big toes of the corpse together to prevent him from returning as a ghost; the first visit of Conor to Hubble Manor to view the wrought-iron screen by the great artist Jean Tijou (TR, 353–361); and the dramatic trial of Conor Larkin in a rump court held secretly by the British military (TR, 606–613), anticipating a scene in *Redemption* in which Desmond Fitzpatrick, using British common law, presents the case for Irish rights (RD, 126–129).[33]

Uris also mixes myth with history and politics, allowing the storyteller Daddo Friel to set an ongoing narrative pattern in which invention offsets fact. Imagination and fact, or storytelling and history, establish a successful exchange throughout the text. Folk myths act to counter events, yet both possess the truth. History, however, is never far away, and Uris imaginatively moves back and forth in time, extending a technique, used in *Exodus*, in which the present can be understood only through the past. But history, here, remains condensed and concise.

Dialogue is similarly restrained, allowing the reader to experience character in more depth through inference rather than exposition. An early example is an argument between Sir Fredrick Weed and his daughter Caroline. Fearful that he will have no heirs, Sir Frederick pressures his headstrong daughter to consider marrying Roger Hubble. That union will give him the chance to extend his railroad to Londonderry in the west because of the Hubbles' holdings. The father, however, recognizing his daughter's independent streak, is candid:

"I'm not asking you to fall desperately in love with him for God's sake. Just marry the bastard, produce a few heirs, then bugger off to Paris and orgy with the entire bohemian colony for the rest of your life."

"You are a low, filthy, shocking, disgusting man," she replies. He shouts, "Horseshit!" (*TR*, 124)

The two understand each other perfectly, and the practical wins out: the marriage occurs, and Sir Frederick finds a son-in-law as ruthless as himself, eager for financial gain and economic stability (see Hubble's astute analysis of Sir Frederick's plan for fruits of a trans-Ulster railroad [*TR*, 134–135]). Throughout the novel, Uris shows that economics is politics, but especially in bravura scenes like Lord Randolph Churchill's visit to Hubble Manor, in which Roger Hubble wins over a crowd of six hundred and claims leadership of the Unionist cause and maintenance of the Protestant Ascendancy (*TR*, 201–205).

But if Uris manages dialogue and scenes in *Trinity* better than in his previous efforts, he still finds description a challenge—or, rather, something to overdress. Chapter Six begins with "Rathweed Hall sat candescently opulent on a high knoll in the Holywood Hills just beyond the grasp of East Belfast" (*TR*, 125). Rugby is presented as a gladiatorial sport of massive heroics and effort (*TR*, 498–499). But when it comes to action, Uris is clear. Attacked by four constables as Fenian upstarts in Bogside, "Mick struggled to his feet as a boot slammed into his stomach, choking off his breath. He gagged and vomited. Conor reeled up . . . and sagged away but as they turned on the fallen Mick McGrath . . . he [drove] his fist into an attacker's belly so hard it lifted the man off his feet" (*TR*, 311). A later scene in which Conor is beaten at the train-engine works during a

Catholic riot is equally vivid. Tied to the spoke of an engine wheel, he is almost killed (TR, 566–569).

Conor's beating follows a dramatic account of rifles being shipped to Liverpool in coffins and then placed in bronze containers inside a rejigged locomotive tender that was sent on to Ireland. The explanatory detail is characteristically Uris: "The large numbers of coffins had been decided upon so the weight of each was kept close to that of an average corpse" (TR, 532). The drama of preparing the tender car to carry the rifles in a false compartment is as gripping as the irony that the tender is part of Sir Frederick's train that is being shipped to Belfast (TR, 534–538). Only the scene of the final rifle drop—some 2,000—at Sixmilecross is more powerful, especially with its surprise ambush by the British (TR, 590–595).

As the political maneuvering becomes more intense, strategies become clearer. Analyzing the British reaction to the arrest of Larkin and other members of the Irish Republican Brotherhood, the barrister Robert Emmet McAloon outlines British concerns in this year of the story, 1907. Most importantly, with the arming of Protestant Ulster (accomplished with British complicity), the Protestants will defend the British flank from the Brotherhood, which was obtaining arms from Germany. As early as Lord Churchill, it was understood that Britain's justification for the occupation of Ireland was that because the island straddles British sea-lanes, its control was necessary for Britain's defense (TR, 599). But if the British give the Sixmilecross smugglers severe prison sentences, they will have to do the same to the gunrunners in Ulster. Legal maneuvering takes over, leading to Conor's secret trial in the Wicklow mountains, one of the most moving scenes in the novel (TR, 606–613).

Conor, after being arraigned in front of a tribunal in the basement of Dublin Castle in accordance with a new emergency-powers act, is sentenced to fifty years and twenty lashes. Shelley MacLeod is horrifically murdered, tied to a post with her arm cut off and then stabbed more than fifty times (TR, 631). The humor of Conor's escape in the disguise of a priest (suddenly, after thirty years, he agrees to attend and serve mass) is pointed. Surprisingly (and romantically), he makes it to America, where he raises money and arms (TR, 637, 654). But after he returns to Ireland, he tells Seamus that little has changed: "Nothing ever happens here in the future. It's always the past happening over and over again," echoing the book's epigraph (TR, 664).

Conor then devotes himself to the IRA, training recruits, establishing commands, and manufacturing pistols. He finally learns to love Atty Fitzpatrick as a new conflict emerges: battle with the increasingly powerful Unionists. The novel moves inevitably to the tensions between the Ulstermen and the Catholics, who are manipulated by the British aristocracy. Offered the leadership of the

Brotherhood because Long Dan Sweeney has cancer, Conor refuses, saying, enigmatically, that he "keep[s] seeing truths that destroy my illusions" (*TR*, 701). The Irish trilogy of Catholics, Protestant Ulstermen, and the British will always suffer, largely because the Ulstermen hate and will never stop. Conor tells Atty that they should be given their province (*TR*, 702).

A final speech by Long Dan Sweeney sets Yeats's phrase in context: "There is no mystery more intense than a man's love of his country. It is the most terrible beauty of all" (*TR*, 737). But politics and armies continue to confront each other as Uris moves toward the end, letting history overtake character. The finale comes with the raiding party and destruction of Lettershanbo Castle—and the deaths of both Conor and Long Dan Sweeney. Conor, in one of his last statements, tells Long Dan, after Seamus has been killed, that the cruelest joke has been to allow himself "to believe that . . . there was a life before death" (*TR*, 747). Dan acknowledges the feeling and tells his subordinate to retreat with the few remaining rebels. Only he and Conor will stay and fight the British: "Mr. Larkin and my good self have had our fucking fill of terrible beauties" (*TR*, 747).

An epilogue inadequately completes the novel. After a summary paragraph on the bloody Easter Rising of 1916, the final sentence repeats the theme of little hope: "In Ireland, there is no future, only the past happening over and over" (*TR*, 751). Uris concludes by reprinting the epigraph from O'Neill: the past in Ireland can only repeat itself.

PUBLICATION AND RESPONSE

Enthusiasm ran high when advance copies of *Trinity* arrived at the Urises' Aspen home. Jill became so excited when she grasped a copy in her hands that she cried, "This is the best book I ever wrote." A droll Uris put his arm around her and said, "I know Jill, but please don't go around saying that."[35]

The book launch for *Trinity* took place at the Denver Playboy Club in April 1976 (the publication date was 5 March 1976). Attending was the mayor of Denver, the chancellor of the University of Denver, and William E. Barrett, best-selling author of *The Left Hand of God* and *The Lilies of the Field*. Charles Goldberg, to whom Uris codedicated *QB VII*, and Barbara Taylor, the manager of the Playboy Club, old friends, talked him into it. The club picked up the tab for the fifty lunches, while Doubleday provided first editions at each place setting. Interviewed that morning—just after the report of another London underground bombing by the IRA—Uris was candid and sympathetic: how do oppressed people fight against their rulers? That was the issue. And "despite the author's current feud with Doubleday [he was unhappy with the promotion of the hardback version of *Ireland: A Terrible Beauty*], Uris says [*Trinity*] will outsell anything he has yet produced."[34] He estimated that the initial print run would be 450,000 copies.

The public quickly welcomed the novel. Conor Larkin soon became a hero to readers, who began to name their children after him (as did Uris, who named his youngest son Conor). Searches began for the origin of the name, which Uris revealed came from a street. In San Francisco, he had lived just off Larkin Street, named for James Larkin, an Irish labor organizer who moved to San Francisco.[36]

Eight months after publication, 320,000 copies were in print. "Trinity did for the Irish what Exodus had done for the Jews," wrote one critic.[37] *Trinity* became Uris's fifth novel to reach number one on the *New York Times* best-seller list (after *Battle Cry*, *Exodus*, *Topaz*, and *QB VII*). However, the climb was slow. By 25 April 1976, after five weeks on the list, *Trinity* was second, behind Gore Vidal's historical novel *1876*, but ahead of *The Choirboys* by Joseph Wambaugh. Three other best-seller lists from May 1976, however, showed *Trinity* in the top spot. But on 13 June 1976, after twelve weeks in second place, *Trinity* became first on the *New York Times* list. It held that position thirty-three weeks, until 7 November 1976, when it slipped to number two, behind Agatha Christie's *Sleeping Murder*, her last book.

Uris's reputation at the time of *Trinity*'s release was tenuous. His earlier books had established him as novelist of fact; he had had one unprecedented success, *Exodus*, and a series of equally dramatic but less artistically successful works, notably *Mila 18* and *QB VII*. *Topaz* had been a disappointment, and his reputation was in decline. *Trinity* changed all that. First reactions by critics, however, were unsupportive, many calling the work rambling and disorganized in its attempt to clarify sixty years of complicated Irish history in 751 pages. William C. Woods attacked the enormous theme expressed in an enormous book: "Uris, like most writers little interested in words, uses a great many of them."[38] He conceded that the subject matter pressed Uris to display a power not previously suspected, yet literary problems remained. Uris falsely believing that the challenge of construction could be overcome by length. Furthermore, historical material was delivered in improbable speeches and distracting, discursive essays.

Some reviewers found the novel's frank depiction of prejudice to be its most powerful feature. The characters' strong beliefs jolt them out of their meager characterizations to reveal their historical backgrounds and political views. "In his historical prejudices, Uris strikes one of his few notes of authentic Irishness," Christopher Hudson wrote in the *Chicago Tribune*.[39] But after the first half of the novel, characters drop all pretense of speaking in period style, or even in character. Twentieth-century Americanisms fall regularly from their lips. Hudson further noted that instead of presenting history through the plot, readers were given first- and third-person narratives broken up by chunks of undigested history.

Pete Hamill, writing in the *New York Times*, emphasizes that Uris is primarily a storyteller, although the form of his stories is always secondary.[40] He often writes crudely, his dialogue can be wooden, and his structure occasionally groans under "the excess baggage of exposition and information"—but none of this mattered in *Trinity*, because its narrative sweeps readers along. Hamill claims that Uris is a better storyteller than Thomas Pynchon or Donald Barthelme or Vladimir Nabokov, although not as good a writer. Uris audaciously dives into the sectarian fighting of Ireland and tries to understand it, producing a novel that "sprawls, occasionally bores, and meanders like a river." But when the reader finishes, he has been "in places where he or she was never before. The news items from Belfast will never seem quite the same again." And if "the family is a fiction, the times they lived through are not."

Through the story of Conor, we see the makings of a revolutionary: "Uris is writing for the gallery and he clearly wants everyone to understand what he is saying." Hamill admits that it is easy to find barbarisms or ludicrous passages (one of the major Protestant characters says, "I sometimes think we are slowly getting strangled in the web of our own intrigue"), and that many of the female characters appear to have been cast rather than created, but asserts that there is still muscle in the story. And even though the book ends with a dying fall, as if the subject had exhausted the writer, "the story has a kind of relentless power, based on the real tragedy of Ireland and Uris's achievement is that he has neither cheapened nor trivialized that tragedy."

As expected, the British were negative. June Southworth's review in the *Daily Mail* was titled "Pompous, Old Hat and Very, Very Dangerous."[41] Nastily, she begins with "the last thing Ireland needs is an overwrought biography of itself by an American Jew of Polish-Russian extraction who writes big themes out of a big ego about big wrongs. But that wouldn't stop Leon Uris." When he was seven, she notes, he wrote an operetta about his dead dog and then advanced to grand opera with *Exodus*. *Trinity* is tedious and overwritten. And worst of all, he has "cannibalized Ireland's history." In closing, she notes that *Exodus* was read by the Provos (members of the Provisional Irish Republican Army), who admired the Stern Gang (an extremist Zionist organization). Philip Howard, writing in the *London Times*, was no less critical, emphasizing the anachronisms and inaccuracies of the story as well as "undigested chunks of superficial and tendentious 'history.'"[42]

This stringent criticism, however, raises an interesting contrast: *Ireland: A Terrible Beauty* presents a country at odds with the one Uris portrays in the novel. The visual catalogue of Irish despair and joy, expressed in the harsh civil strife offset by the landscape, demythologizes and contradicts what *Trinity* seems to sensationalize or sentimentalize in its quest for popularity. *Ireland: A Terrible Beauty* is free of the conventions of best-selling novels. In it, Uris presents suffering stripped of romanticism. The text unhesitatingly supports the direct revelations of Jill's photos—but both aspects stress the fight against oppression, embodied by the British. The denial of freedom is the foundational theme of Uris's work; as Long Dan Sweeney dramatically tells the Irish Republican Brotherhood: "If you remember nothing else, remember this. No crime a man commits in behalf of his freedom can be as great as the crimes committed by those who deny his freedom" (*TR*, 430). It's also the cry of Uris.

The Irish received *Trinity* more positively than the English, believing that the novel had brought together a number of factions. Both the IRA and the bishop of Derry agreed that the book was good for Ireland. An influential Northern Irish politician, John Hume, who was highlighted in *Ireland: A Terrible Beauty*, wrote a strongly positive review in *Hibernia*.[43] In it, he emphasizes the novel's harsh presentation of the Unionist cause and its anticlerical stand toward Catholics. Uris's prejudices are clear, especially against the cynical alliance between the Unionist landed gentry and the Northern Irish industrialists, who were aided by British politicians. It is also clear that Uris is sympathetic to the militant republican tradition in Ireland—until the end, when Conor Larkin recognizes the futility of the effort. Yet the people, with whom Uris has the greatest sympathy, are ground down by the Ascendancy, on one hand, and the Catholic Church on the other.

Uris enjoyed Hume's comment that he must have lived in Ireland all of his life. Hume also said the dialect was incorrect in only one place in the novel. "I not only used Irish dialect but Derry dialect, Donegal dialect," Uris emphasized, "and nobody could believe that an American Jew could write a book about Ireland."[44]

Charles Haughey, who became the Irish prime minister in 1979, also wrote a sympathetic review of the novel, emphasizing the honesty of Uris's portrait and diversity of the social classes he included.[45] He admires Uris's representation of the struggle between the Irish peasant farmer and the rich landed gentry, a conflict presided over by Britain. Again, he praises the telling of the story through three families: the Larkins of Ballyutogue, a stone's throw from Derry City; the Protestant MacLeods of Belfast, working-class and respectable; and, dominating both, Sir Frederick Weed and the landlord family of the Earl of Foyle. The abuse of political power mingled with sectarianism is evident in the Weeds, and the callousness of the landed gentry is personified in the Foyles.

Regarding Irish critics of every stripe, "Uris himself waxed lyrical . . . 'Every Jewish shopkeeper is a literary critic, just as every Irishman is. I walked into a bookstore in Dublin. There were 500 books piled up in the store and people coming in and buying them like candy. And the manager had one comment:

"You made a terrible mistake in *Trinity*. You named such and such as the highest mountain in Ireland, and there is one sixteen feet higher.""[46]

An era is as important as a character, Uris said in a 1976 interview, and he believed that he had shown that with *Trinity*.[47] But in this novel, his characters are stronger and his history less dominant than in previous works. This, he recognized, was both a departure from his usual style and a sign that he could trust the story to contain its own dynamic without the scaffold or support of history. For his ninth novel, *The Haj*, he let the story control.

Overlaying *Trinity*, of course, were the current Troubles. Or, to put it differently, his novel, set between 1885 and 1915, was to be read against the present-day conflict in Northern Ireland. Theoretically, Uris writes against Ireland, against the romanticized and clichéd view of its mythical and historical past. His Ireland is immediate, violent, and emotional, although an alternate Ireland also appears at times in the text: one that is romanticized, mythologized, and urbanized.

Uris remained opinionated and passionate. Rather than treat the tragedy of Ireland as a box score—three Catholics died today, three Protestants will die tomorrow—he sought to tell the story from his point view, which he made clear: "The Irish Catholics have been screwed for a thousand years. I start with that premise."[48] He also claimed to have "been off and on that book since 1968," suggesting that the idea of a novel about Ireland had been brewing for some time.[49]

LEON URIS: THE PRICKLY HERO

When Uris wrote, he was focused, but when not writing, he often displayed insecurity and jealousy, especially of other writers who received recognition. He was livid when Norman Mailer won a Pulitzer Prize for *The Armies of the Night* in 1969; he also had little time for the self-conscious writings of Saul Bellow or Philip Roth. And he would become verbally abusive if things were not done his way. He also had a ribald sense of humor, loved practical jokes, and was generous with those around him. However, some thought he bought friends' loyalty. At parties, he veered from graciousness to misbehavior, encouraging Jill to greet guests at the door with a silver tray of marijuana-laced brownies. Cocaine would also make an occasional appearance, and its ingestion would only intensify his imperial, commanding behavior. He liked to think of himself as a hero; he loved his fans and liked to be recognized in public by people that counted. When the violinist Isaac Stern came up to him at the House of Lum (a Chinese restaurant) in Aspen to compliment Uris on his work, he was stunned: not so much by the praise as by the similar appearances of the two men.[50]

Uris, however, had tenuous relationships with women. He would put them on pedestals and then knock them down. This might have been part of his insecurity and need for control. He wanted to avoid abandonment, so he took command of the situations, preempting any action by the other party. He distrusted those who loved him, which was likely a result of his difficult relationship with his parents. His father constantly criticized him, and his mother constantly questioned him; both made him feel inadequate. He seemed to combat this by glorying in suffering. But he could not stand to be wrong. Often abrasive, stubborn, and arrogant, Uris was always purposeful. To forestall the possibility that those close to him would leave (he abhorred loneliness), he became the one who left, either on research trips or vacations alone. With Jill, he found someone as adventurous and determined as himself to experience a new country or environment—up to a point. But Uris couldn't stop from leaving the drama of his life and entering its next scene, whatever that might be. Within eight years, such actions would mark the beginning of the end of his marriage.

Throughout the 1970s, his readership continued to expand. In one letter, he deputized the Israeli ambassador to Thailand to act on his behalf to arrange a Thai-language translation of *Exodus*. He expected no royalties, but wanted ten copies of the edition. He told the ambassador that there was an Indian translation, but not one in Chinese, adding, "you have my permission to pursue the matter with Chinese or any languages you might consider fruitful."[51]

Uris's literary reputation, however, had long been questioned. As early as 1959, critic John Coleman of the *Spectator* noted that in *Exodus* Uris incredibly devalued his heroic material by the vacuity of his interpretations and that he deserved the title of a "gifted writer of hard core trash."[52] Others suggested that Uris's novels took their form directly from the movies they were meant to become. He, of course, denied it: "I don't see how a serious novelist can write with an eye to a movie sale. It just can't be done. *Trinity* is a perfect example. I've been trying to get that thing made into a movie since 1975."[53] *Topaz* was turned down by everyone except Hitchcock.

SELLING A BEST SELLER

When he wasn't working on *Trinity*, Uris worried about the promotion of *Ireland: A Terrible Beauty*, which he felt Bantam had badly handled. In February 1975, he wrote to Ken McCormick about how he wanted to use *Ireland: A Terrible Beauty* to establish Jill with the public as a genuine talent; he was determined to keep her "in the big leagues, so to speak, and avoid the grind of magazine assignments which would be somewhat alien to our lifestyle."[54] He suggested that Doubleday exploit her youth and beauty for its public relations potential: she could model a fashion layout in *Vogue, Glamour,* or *Esquire.* Displaying something of his less than admirable view of women, he told McCormick that Jill could model skiwear easily "as a motorcycle mama and of course we can't overlook the stirring aspects of the string bikini." Also, Doubleday should play up either the women-and-career angle or their lifestyle as a couple in Aspen; he and Jill would agree to do a "couple's" interview for *People* or *Parade* and would "be amenable to a town and country type layout of the house." He then offered advice on selling *Trinity* with *Ireland: A Terrible Beauty*: each should advertise the other on the back of the book. And the Doubleday sales force should ensure that displays of *Trinity* should always have *Ireland: A Terrible Beauty* nearby.

His letters also indicate that he was thinking of his next work, possibly returning to the Middle East and Israel. On Valentine's Day 1975, he told McCormick that negotiations with the Israelis were going well and that they should be traveling to Israel by October or April.[55] He envisioned "a shorter book about the length of *Topaz* with not more than a few months of research required." He was also thinking of another joint photo-book project with Jill—but wanted to keep the possible project under wraps. He then added, "I stubbed my toe slightly on Part IV [of *Trinity*] nothing major, but a reworking of several chapters that will set me back about a week. I think we're going to be able to hold our June 1 delivery date."

In Israel in early October 1975, he wrote to McCormick that a deal to film *Trinity* had fallen through and that he planned to be in New York on 15 November to read galleys of *Trinity*.[56] That overseas trip began in Ireland, and the end of their stay there "was bittersweet, the sudden death of Seamus Murphy, our sculpture friend and the reality of the situation in the north was painful but otherwise it was idyllic . . . We had a blowout in Copenhagen for a weekend . . . Jill got her China and silver and [we went] on down to Israel."

He next described being a guest of the city of Jerusalem in a nine-apartment complex restored from a centuries-old Arab-style project overlooking the walls of the Old City. Called Mishkenot Sha'ananim, it was for visiting musicians and other artists, and it was offered to Uris and Jill if they returned next year. He also outlined a series of possible projects, beginning with a photo book on Jerusalem, which, although less ambitious than *Ireland*, would cover the "full scope of the story past and present." For his other project, a possible novel, he was in consultation with government, hoping to gain their support. He and Jill also planned to head off to the desert "for a week to bake the Irish mist out of us."

In another note, Uris lays out the schedule he planned to follow after finishing work on the galleys: he would stay in New York until 21 November; move on to Tampa, Florida, for a speech by Senator Henry "Scoop" Jackson, of Washington (Uris supported his candidacy to lead the Democratic Party); and then go to

Denver, where he hoped to be by December 1975.[57] He also pointed out an error in *Ireland: A Terrible Beauty* regarding Jill's birth year (it is 1947, not 1974), and he asked that the publisher add a line about Seamus Murphy, now that he had died.

On 29 December 1975, he requested three hundred tip-in sheets and labels from McCormick for the personal copies of *Trinity* he would send out to family and friends.[58] He then thanked him for the nomination for the Nobel Prize, which was "just a little awesome." Apparently, McCormick had sent in a recommendation, and Uris was grateful: "We may never get it but I'll never forget that one of the most important men in American literature thought I deserved it."

In writing *Trinity*, Uris found constant parallels between the Irish and the Jews, the Great Famine standing in for the Holocaust. He also found similarities between their languages, religious influences, diasporas, terrorism-filled histories, and the need to liberate themselves from the British. Two small countries and two great leaders resulted: David Ben-Gurion and Eamon de Valera.[59] Uris noted that in "Northern Ireland both the Catholics and the Protestants considered themselves the Israelis in the battle, considered themselves the Jews."[60] He assumed that they felt this way from reading *Exodus*. They both identified with the Israeli side, largely because the Jews are fighters: "You have to have Jews who also hit people in the mouth, along with their Bible quotes."[61]

In a later interview, he remarked that he was moved when he learned that Bobby Sands, an Irish hunger striker, had memorized portions of *Trinity* and recited it to his fellow prison inmates.[62] Sands had become the symbolic martyr of the Irish cause. He began his hunger strike on 1 March 1981 in H-block of Maze prison. Born in Belfast in 1954, he joined the IRA as a teenager and was in and out of jail. In 1976, he was sentenced to fourteen years in prison for bombing a furniture store. In jail, he became an enthusiastic reader, first of political revolutionaries but then poetry, works of Irish nationalism, and Leon Uris. He apparently memorized large chunks of the novel and shouted out the story down the locked corridors of H-block.[63] *Trinity* suddenly took on a political currency unequaled since *Exodus* was clandestinely smuggled into Russia.

In prison, Sands found a vocation, writing Republican articles for the press and successfully running for Parliament in a by-election in April 1981, despite his imprisonment and hunger strike. His campaign slogan was "His life and his comrades' lives can be saved if you elect him." After Sands won, Margaret Thatcher would not allow him to be released to sit in Parliament. Protests continued, as did his hunger strike, which ended with his death after sixty-six days on 5 May 1981.[64] One hundred thousand attended Sands's funeral; the British flew in six hundred extra troops to reinforce their contingent of eleven thousand along with seven thousand members of the Ulster Defence Regiment. Sands became a symbol of the sacrifices made for Irish justice. And as the low-intensity conflict continued in the early 1980s, worldwide sales of *Trinity* surged.

Uris believed he was persuasive in his work, convincing readers of the moral right of the Irish cause.[65] He was critical of the popular media, such as *People* and *Time*, for criticizing the mistakes and sloppy writing in the novel, as well as the familiar charge that his characters were stereotypes, except for those in *Trinity*. He proudly cited a twenty-eight-hour nonstop reading of the novel in California on St. Patrick's Day; a mixed audience of Irish, Jews, Italians had listened to English Shakespearean actors read through the night. And he reasserted his self-confidence: "I know I'm a puncher, I have certain styles. I know what I can do and I work within that framework. You can't say that I'm controlled, but I'm disciplined to the thing that I can do best."[66] He believed, as well, that *Trinity* was a better novel because he had a more peaceful home life while writing it: "I don't have fights when I come into the house like my two other marriages."[67]

TRINITY, THE MOVIE?

To capitalize on the success of *Trinity* and to fulfill one of his dreams—a return to screenwriting—Uris began to pitch a screenplay of the work, and he had no trouble in finding interested parties. By September, after the book had been a number one best seller for several months, a news release announced that Uris and a Canadian group would produce a twelve-million-dollar film based on the novel.[68]

Unique to the deal, and characteristic of Uris, was that he was to retain complete artistic control of the film, share in its profits, and exercise veto power over its distribution—as well as write the screenplay. This was a first; no writer had been guaranteed all these features for one venture. Public relations material noted: "In addition to a percentage of the profits Uris will be paid 1 million in cash for the property."[69] *Trinity*, according to the release, had sold over 500,000 copies, including 300,000 to subscribers of the Literary Guild. Production of the film, to be shot in Ireland, Newfoundland, and Nova Scotia, was to begin in the fall of 1977, and the projected release was scheduled for a year later. No director or cast members had been chosen. At a press conference announcing the film, Uris comically remarked that he had been fired as a screenwriter from both *Exodus* and *Topaz*—"not mind you over the writing but because neither Otto Preminger nor Alfred Hitchcock could stand a mere screenwriter as their peer."[70]

Uris had first met Frederick Brogger, the lead producer, who was known for making feature-length television films, including *Jane Eyre* (1970) and *The Red*

Pony (1973), when they planned to film *Mila 18*. The success of *Trinity*, however, pushed that project ahead. The financing group included Norman Esch, a Canadian industrialist associated with communication ventures. Press material suggested that Delbert Mann, a veteran of several Brogger productions who was perhaps best known for directing *Marty* (1955), was to direct.

Casting for the project was, of course, critical. To generate buzz and to keep up press and trade interest, Gene Kelly hosted a reception for Uris at Chasen's restaurant in Los Angeles to celebrate the initial news of the film. This took place in January 1977. The A-list guests included Carl Foreman, Cary Grant, Samuel Goldwyn, Danny Kaye, Delbert Mann (confirmed as director), Robert Mitchum, Olivia Newton-John, Nick Nolte, Brenda Vaccaro, Burgess Meredith, Robert Wagner, Irving Wallace, Lew Wasserman, John Wayne, and William Wyler. Additionally, William Peter Blatty, George Burns, George Chasin, Irving Stone, Max Shulman, Karen Uris, Herb Schlosberg were there, along with Uris and Jill.[71] George Christy reported all the action in the *Hollywood Reporter*.

Rumors began to fly almost at once—one claimed that John Wayne would play Long Dan Sweeney. Nick Nolte was a favorite to play Conor: Uris wrote to the publicist Warren Cowan that Nolte was to receive a copy of *Ireland: A Terrible Beauty* as well as *Trinity*. "Confidentially, he has gained the inside track on the leading role. Also send Olivia Newton-John a copy with Jill and Lee's compliments," he added.[72] Liam Neeson, Daniel Day-Lewis, and even David Caruso were also considered.

At the same time, international interest in *Trinity* was growing. Uris reported to his publicist in January 1977 that he just learned from David Raphael in Paris that the opening reviews of *Trinity* in France were fantastic and that "the book is being compared with GONE WITH THE WIND. As you know, a run away in France generally has the effect of igniting the entire continent."[73]

But despite his success, Uris felt compelled to get on with another book: he had little choice. He had a commitment to Doubleday because of his last three-book deal. His letters reveal his anxiety about the stress of meeting publishing deadlines and commitments, a task that was essential to sustaining his income. The responsibility began to wear on him, a harbinger of the difficulties that would plague him in later years and force him to undertake projects that he would have difficulty completing.

But the success of *Trinity* allowed Uris to complain. On 16 July 1976, for example, he told Ken McCormick and Sam Vaughan that there had been a foul-up in not shipping enough copies of *Ireland: A Terrible Beauty*.[74] He then criticized their cancellation of an expensive paperback edition, so he asked that Bantam be allowed to publish *Ireland: A Terrible Beauty* and *Trinity* together and merchandize them jointly. Since he had just concluded the deal for the film rights of *Trinity*, which gave him complete artistic control as well as a full partnership with the distributors, he felt he could emphasize his authority to his publisher: "Brogger and the terms of this [picture] deal are the only way I would ever return to films." There was also the possibility that Brogger would pick up the option on *Mila 18* again, so Uris notified McCormick and Vaughan that he might soon have to go into screenplay mode with both properties, especially if the *Trinity* deal went through. If the deal collapsed, he would do *Mila 18* first. That outcome would slow down his fiction writing: he wouldn't be able to return to the promised novel (the suggested Israel story, which, ironically and eventually, would become his Arab novel, *The Haj*) until late 1977 or 1978.

Uris's cavalier attitude—putting the proposed Israeli novel on hold because of his possible new film deals—began to sour his relationship with Doubleday. Pushing off the third novel of his current contract began to look like either postponing or reneging on his commitment. He tried to assuage his publisher by tempting him with another subject, an autobiography: "I think there are aspects of my life that out-fiction some of my wilder plots."[75] This, too, would not come to pass, or at least not until 1988, when he wrote the novel *Mitla Pass*. Consequently, he asked that his last book under contract "be my option of either a novel or the autobiography." And he agreed to add a protection clause for Doubleday that would either guarantee minimum sales or impose a penalty if they felt that the difference in sales was significant.

The idea of an autobiographical work appealed to him. On 3 August 1976, he wrote to Sam Vaughan: "There you go underestimating another Uris scheme. If my letters don't sell 250,000 hardback, I'll kiss Otto Preminger's something or other in the middle of Broadway."[76] McCormick was worried about Uris not going back to Jerusalem because of the interim film scripts. But Uris agreed to make the journey—he owed it to his relationship with Doubleday, to Israel, and mostly to Jill, because "more than anything she wants to photograph Jerusalem and there's no way I could deny this."[77] But realistically, he expected to be in the film business for the next two years.

Uris began work on the screenplay of *Trinity* in the winter and spring of 1977, when he and Jill were in Marina del Rey, California. The timing coincided with Jill's thirtieth birthday. He worked closely with the director, Delbert Mann, although the project would not go ahead, partly because of costs. Throughout 1978 and part of 1979, Uris tried to get the novel filmed, but the deal soured and the project went on the shelf. A major reason was the lack of cooperation and investment from the Irish government.[78] In 1981, there would be another attempt to film the novel, and he would work with the director Dan Petrie (*A Raisin in the Sun, Fort Apache the Bronx*). In the mid-1990s, Uris would unsuccessfully attempt to dramatize the work for Broadway. The film was never made, although interest in the work continued: in 2005, HBO green-lit a production to be directed by Jim Sheridan, which at the moment remains in development.

With the film project stalled, Uris again turned to Israel, partly to capitalize on the success of *Ireland: A Terrible Beauty*, Jill's reputation as a photographer, and his own wish to see the country again. As early as 1974, he was thinking about the country, telling his father that "Israel is virtually alone except for America," since all of its other allies were totally dependent on Arab oil.[79] (Major Arab oil producers embargoed oil shipments to countries that supported Israel during the Yom Kippur War; the United States was the only country affected.)

On the same day he wrote to his father, Uris wrote to Yohanon Behan in Israel, saying his concern for the country was his major worry: "It is terrifying to see you virtually without allies."[80] The increase in oil prices had not yet been blamed on the Israelis, but it was likely to happen, and a "Munich like appeasement toward the Arabs" was beginning to "creep into some minds." He feared an isolated Israel would be the result of America and Israel's friends becoming totally dependent on Arab oil, a theme he will treat in *The Haj*. He hinted that with *Ireland: A Terrible Beauty* at the printer's and work on *Trinity* underway, he would not be against exploring an Israeli-Jewish theme, "if I felt that I could be effective." He added that *QB VII* had been recently televised across six hours and been seen by an audience of upward of fifty million people. He disliked the production, but it definitely had an impact on sales. He ended with reference to his failure to get financing during the ten-year effort to film *Mila 18*.

The letter is prophetic. Following *Trinity* and a few detours would be *Jerusalem: Song of Songs* (1981), with photos by Jill, and then *The Haj* (1984), both codas to Uris's earlier experience with the Promised Land.

RETURN

10

I'm no Solzhenitsyn . . . but I'll rest on my titles. I've written
*two novels—*Exodus *and* Trinity—*that have had some*
world impact. Things could be worse.
—LEON URIS, WASHINGTON POST, 2 MAY 1978

U RIS'S SELF-ASSESSMENT was not entirely wrong, acknowledging his
successes while admitting his shortcomings. By the time this article appeared, *Trinity* had already sold more than 1.6 million copies. He could
afford to both criticize and praise himself. And *Trinity* was an important book
because it "destroyed an essential myth: that I am a Jewish writer."[1] Implicitly,
he meant that he was also an Irish, even a world, writer.

Uris's reputation, however, was still ambiguous and partly undermined by his
divorce from his literary contemporaries. A long interview in *Writer's Digest* summarized his attitude, expressed through disdain for writers like Norman Mailer:
"He's not a novelist at all. I think he's a public masturbator."[2] On the Nobel Prize:
"If Norman Mailer wins it, I'll probably kill myself. I mean, I don't expect to win
it because I am too popular." But he admired some American writers, notably
Tennessee Williams, James Michener, and John Hersey. Steinbeck was also a
hero. He summarized his own work by declaring, "My basic material deals with
injustice in this world and the striving for that thing we call freedom."

Uris's pseudoclaim to being Irish was confirmed in February 1978 when he
received the John F. Kennedy Medal, awarded by the Irish American Society of
New York. It was a gala evening at the Waldorf-Astoria Hotel in New York, and
the key Doubleday people were invited: Ken McCormick, Sam Vaughan, John
Sargent, and Joan Ward, Ken McCormick's assistant. Later that year, Uris received
the gold medal of the Eire Society of Boston.

Leading up to this event, however, was a period of distraction and confusion.
He was unsure of his next book, switching topics from Israel to South Africa,
showing again that travel, research, and politically charged cultures were what
he needed to stimulate his creativity. But first came sales. At the end of 1976, he
had told Ken McCormick that he did not want to deal with the Literary Guild

(a Doubleday reader's club) any longer. Its offer for *Trinity* was paltry and could put the book in competition with what the Franklin Library had done (a special member's-only edition).[3] And he hated the Literary Guild for how it had tossed off *Ireland: A Terrible Beauty*—offered for free as an inducement for membership, even though it had sold 50,000 copies in the retail trade. A postscript takes a swipe at Doubleday: "After all we went through with *Ireland: A Terrible Beauty*, we are numbed with disbelief that this book is now going out of stock again all over the country."

Six months later, however, he asked Ken McCormick for help, this time for getting into South Africa.[4] He needed to be certain he and Jill could spend a few months there; he was reading a great deal about the country and its government in preparation. However, nothing was going into motion until a *Trinity* movie deal was either completed or shelved. "In the meantime," he wrote, "I am reestablishing myself with a new Begin govt. in Israel in the event the South African project does not seem feasible." A month later, he told McCormick that getting in and out of South Africa would not be easy. The *Trinity* project was also a hair closer to some sort of resolution.[5]

On Labor Day weekend that year, he began a long note to McCormick with news that he was hobbling on crutches as a result of a knee operation.[6] His oldest son and wife had visited for a week, and he admitted that it was "still difficult to realize my kids can be around the house day and night and I actually enjoy it enormously. This change of relationships has really been my greatest reward of recent years." But the proposed film of *Trinity* continued to dangle, and he couldn't go forward with new work until the film was resolved. The latest proposal was for a ten-hour television movie. But the main problem that summer had been "too much time to think and too little drive to dive into reading and research. I simply am unable to turn myself loose on another project until the fate of this [the movie] is known." He was in the doldrums, staring into space, partly from "the mental exhaustion that came with the publication of *Trinity*." Getting the book made and to market had wiped him out.

He again mentioned a possible novel set in South Africa, but it was looking "more and more difficult."[7] "Not only my getting into the country but the saturation coverage in the world press and on TV takes an awful lot of starch out of the freshness of the subject," he wrote. Another thought was Venice, perhaps something on the demise of Venice in parallel with the demise of the Western world. But he needed a change: "I'm getting bored with Uris in his present state and really don't enjoy living with him." Three months later, he asked Joan Ward at Doubleday for a copy of the historian Walter Laqueur's new study, *Terrorism*.[8]

Jill Uris compactly summed up the 1978–1979 period: "After *Ireland: A Terrible Beauty* and *Trinity*, Lee was again looking for a new novel to write. He's always wanted to do another Jewish based book and began inquiring more about the Arab perspective. He read Alan Patai's *The Arab Mind* and we visited the foremost Arab historian, Bernard Lewis at Princeton. We had visited Israel on our honeymoon in 1970 and had returned once or twice since to see old friends from Lee's *Exodus* days."[9] She went on to say that she had been eager to do another photo book and was "very taken with the city of Jerusalem as the place to do it. Doubleday agreed and gave us another contract."

JERUSALEM: SONG OF SONGS

They followed a familiar pattern: travel and an extended stay, going to Israel in the spring of 1978 and remaining for nine months, leaving in February 1979, an "appropriate gestation for a book."[10] They first lived in a guest suite that was part of the Jerusalem Foundation, Mishkenot Sha'ananim, which was below the King David Hotel with a magnificent view of the Old City. But it was too public for Uris; they relocated to an apartment in the western part of the city that had a view of the Knesset and the Monastery of the Cross.

Uris still had many friends in Jerusalem, and many of them would be profiled in *Jerusalem: Song of Songs* (see *JSS*, 314–315). Teddy Kollek, then mayor of Jerusalem, was a close ally. His office was their main support; in particular, he took Uris and Jill to all parts of the city and gave them contacts in the varied communities. The Urises dedicated the book to him. Other friends and contacts were Moshe Arad, in the Foreign Ministry; Ezer Weizman, who later became president; Moshe Safdie, the architect of most of the New Quarter, and Wolf Blitzer, then just starting his journalism career. Uris also still had some family there, mainly his cousin Yossi Yerushalmi and his family. Their Jerusalem assistant was Betsy Rosenberg, who set up appointments and generally helped out.

Jill Uris again summarized their activities and their working relationship:

> It was a very intense time with Lee holding extensive interviews, visiting Arab families and neighborhoods and my photographing. We weren't working as closely as in Ireland partly because we traveled less, being based in one city and we each had separate jobs. I was often up at 3:30 am to photograph the city with no traffic and at dawn. I was on my own with guides and translators much of the time. Lee had such a good grasp of the history from *Exodus* that he drew on that much of the time for *Jerusalem, Song of Songs*.[11]

They returned to the States to work on the book, only to find that they had "entertained" an unexpected guest. According to the Aspen police, a Palisades,

Colorado, man was arrested for allegedly trespassing at Uris's Red Mountain home early one morning. He was found in Uris's bathrobe in the pool house, typing a letter to President Carter. Sheriff's deputies said the intruder told them he was a friend of the caretakers. Neither Uris nor the caretaker knew him.[12] In August–September 1980, they were again in Ireland and Israel, Jill photographing for a series of Irish calendars she produced, Uris finishing up research for their Jerusalem project.

Fourteen chapters plus a chronology form the oversized (eleven-and-a-half-by-ten-inch) *Jerusalem: Song of Songs*, which contains more than a hundred color and black-and-white photos by Jill. Uris again supplied a detailed and personalized history informed by a persistent theme: Jerusalem was, from its inception, meant to be ruled by Jews. The theme is stressed as insistently as his presentation of British repression of Catholics in *Ireland: A Terrible Beauty*.

The challenge for Uris was to avoid being too adulatory in telling the story of Jerusalem. The city itself would not permit it. A sentence in the third paragraph of the book sets out the ambiguous nature of the place: "Her location, off the commercial beat, difficult for agriculture, in a constant search for sufficient water, without natural wealth, tells us that she should not have a place among cities considered as great" (*JSS*, 9). But it nonetheless does, and his prose celebrates its prominence: "She rises and rests on hot windy crests of omnipresent stone of which she is made" (*JSS*, 9). The difficulty for Uris is to rein in his celebratory prose as he surveys three thousand years of political, cultural, and religious turmoil.

One way to control the writing was to rely on facts and figures, starting with the various place names associated with Jerusalem, which were matched by the 103 varieties of Jews in the city (*JSS*, 11). Their survival alongside Arabs, Armenians, Greeks, Russians, Bedouins, and others was part of the wonderful mélange of the city. And yet for all its cosmopolitan background, the city remained provincial, partly because the diversity of languages, with their contrasting alphabets, never quite blended. The cultures and religions remained distinct, coexisting but not uniting. Stunning photographs, some of them double-paged, underscore the points Uris presents.

As Uris tells his sweeping history of the Jews, he tries not to whitewash the tale. Ancient Hebrews "lied, cheated, pillaged, slaughtered, thieved, burned and conspired" (*JSS*, 20). But as he charts their movement from Mesopotamia, Canaan, and Israel, he cannot resist using a heroic tone and celebrating a sense of achievement. Throughout, Uris provides analogies to modern Israeli history, which constantly overlays the past (*JSS*, 31, 37, 60). Uris's Jerusalem is a resilient city that has both suffered and triumphed.

Uris also has a second story to tell, beginning a digression on anti-Semitism and how the Jews had been victims of persecution and punishment since the time of the ancient pagan powers (*JSS*, 123). The "crime" of being born a Jew was always a cause of suspicion and danger (*JSS*, 124). By clinging to the idea of God, however, the Jews sustained their belief and their determination to return to Jerusalem. This is the focus of the second part of the book. Uris emphasizes that had the Jews given up, religions like Christianity or Islam would not have come into being. He claims that resentment at Jews' relationship to God is the source of anti-Semitism (*JSS*, 124). Turning to theology, Uris explains that in Judaism, "judgment is not imposed by teaching guilt or by terrorism, but by man's ability to redeem himself." The purpose of judgment is to encourage change here on earth (*JSS*, 125).

Uris then addresses the advent of the other Abrahamic religions, devoting a chapter to Christianity and one to Islam—this last was important as a prelude to *The Haj*. Uris's prose about Islam is energetic and colorful: "Binding this vast, semi-charted, blisteringly arid land, was a crisscross bloodline of caravan routes" (*JSS*, 149). However, an undercurrent of violence dominates Arab social patterns—the only way one could resist and survive within the system was "to destroy the man above and dominate the men beneath" (*JSS*, 149). Stereotypes soon take over his representation of this world: Arabs rely on violence, blend fantasy with reality, and passively accept everyday life (*JSS*, 149–151, 162–165). They were foreordained to follow a religion based on fatalism. Emphasizing the absolute obedience to God's will called for in Islam, Uris unsympathetically stresses submission, calling it a form of "mental sterilization" (*JSS*, 152). He then outlines the life of Muhammad, drawing parallels between Muhammad and the Hebrew prophets before surveying the relation of Islam to Jerusalem.

Uris respects the reach of Islam, noting that a century after the death of Muhammad, Arab armies ranged from Spain to India—and this was in AD 711. Functioning as a political as well as a religious symbol, the Dome of the Rock reigns over everything in the city, in many ways acting as the symbolic centerpiece of Jerusalem (*JSS*, 161). Its location on the Temple Mount reinforces its authority. Ironically, the Jewish "shrine," the Western Wall, is part of Herod's Temple, which sits beneath the Muslim holy place. In the brief history of Islam that follows, Uris traces various religious sects and rivalries.

Uris next moves on to British financier and philanthropist Moses Montefiore (1784–1885), the first of a series of Jewish heroes who reclaimed the city for the Jews (*JSS*, 204–206). He negotiated the right to buy land from the Turkish sultan and soon built his well-known windmill (for grinding flour) and some rudimentary housing, the first for Jews outside the Old City. There was concern, however, about letting Jews live outside the Jewish Quarter. What would happen? Gradually, communities formed outside the walls of the Old City, and by the end of the nineteenth century, there were sixty separate quarters outside the walls (*jss*, 206). Mea Shearim, especially well photographed by Jill in color, receives comment before Uris discusses the importance of the Jaffa Road, built in preparation for a pilgrimage by the Emperor Franz Joseph en route to the opening of the Suez Canal in November 1869 (*jss*, 216).

A quick survey of Jewish equality (or its lack) in the individual communities in Jerusalem, including the Russian, German, and American, precedes Uris's summary of Zionism, which, he believes, was "inevitable" (*jss*, 223). The roles played by the Rothschild foundation in securing land, by Theodore Herzl in providing theoretical justification for Zionism, and by European oppression in dispossessing Jews all played their part in the Jewish reclamation of the land of Israel, a movement accelerated by Arab nationalism (*jss*, 225). The Balfour Declaration of 1917, the emergence of Syria and Jordan, and, finally, the misdeeds of Britain in setting aside only 17 percent of the Palestine Mandate for what would become the state of Israel are all detailed.

A condensed history of the formation of Israel focuses on individual heroes: David Ben-Gurion, Golda Meir, Menachem Begin, Moshe Dayan, and Teddy Kollek. Uris reports on the battles waged by the Irgun and the more violent Stern Gang (*jss*, 240–241). In his most intense chapter, "Siege," he recounts the threats to independence and the anxiety between the passage of the plan for the partition of Palestine in November 1947 and the 14 May 1948 Israeli declaration of independence (*jss*, 243–246). The attack by the Arab League and the ensuing battle for Bab el Wad, the steep twisting ravine road leading to Jerusalem, which the Arabs cut off, absorbs Uris (*jss*, 249–250). He also writes effectively detailed accounts of the battles west of Jerusalem, then the massacre of Arabs at Deir Yasin by the Irgun, and, in reprisal, the massacre of a Magen David convoy of medical personnel (seventy-seven unarmed Jews, mostly doctors and nurses) heading to the Hadassah enclave on Mount Scopus (*jss*, 254).

He then moves into dramatic high gear as he narrates the battle at Latrun and the effort to save Jerusalem (*jss*, 257–262). Descriptions are vivid: the Ben Zakai Synagogue, for example, turned into a hospital, has a makeshift operating room lined with bullet-riddled prayer books (*jss*, 261). The destruction of the Jewish Quarter follows in his text.

Truce, negotiations, and an unstable détente between Israel and the Arab countries emerged as the country confronted Gamal Abdel Nasser in Egypt and terrorists from Jordan. By the 1950s, the country was growing, and Uris mixes in his own experiences in researching *Exodus* with the Sinai campaign (*jss*, 273–278). He continues with an account of the Six-Day War, celebrating the retaking of Jerusalem. He breaks his story into three days, 5–7 June 1967, offering a dramatic account of the battle (*jss*, 280–288). The reconstruction of the Old

City and the Jewish Quarter is followed by a short account of the Yom Kippur War of 1973. He then mentions terrorism, which leads to a further analysis of the Arab world. He claims that Arabs' only contribution to the twentieth century has been international terrorism and a corrupt attempt to gain financial control of the West. Their fanaticism is a threat to all democracy, their religious intolerance the danger (*JSS*, 294–295).

A chapter on Teddy Kollek ends the book. To Uris, Kollek is unquestionably both a hero and a sign of the future of a revitalized and modernized city where competing cultures can coexist—at least as understood in 1981. Biography then mixes with history as Uris ends his story with comments on his own lifelong interest in the city.

If there is a single theme that unites the disparate history of Jerusalem and explains the Jewish ingathering and eternal need to return to this place, it is the need to resist persecution. This theme dominates Uris's fiction and nonfiction, whether in *Mila 18* or *Ireland: A Terrible Beauty. Jerusalem: Song of Songs* and *The Haj*, his next novel, continue its presentation.

Although treated largely as a photo book, *Jerusalem: Song of Songs* has a critical and detailed text that reflects Uris's habitual research, strong opinions, and determination to celebrate both historical and contemporary individuals whom he believes to have shaped the life of the city and country. Its message is as much political as it is photographic, as was the case with *Ireland: A Terrible Beauty*. Marketed, however, as a travel book rather than a history, *Jerusalem: Song of Songs* had only modest sales. It did, however, provide the grounding for *The Haj*, allowing Uris to research, interview, and reexplore Israel from a new perspective, that of the Arabs. *Jerusalem: Song of Songs*, however, did receive major recognition in the country that mattered: Israel. It won the Scopus Award for the most important contribution to Jewish culture in 1981, awarded by Hebrew University to both Jill and Leon Uris.

Behind the scenes, Uris expressed unease about the project. In 1983, Sam Vaughan told Ken McCormick that Uris privately had complained about *Jerusalem* involving more work than he had imagined.[13] He underestimated the amount of time it would take to write the book, which stretched to three and a half years. He originally thought he could "knock it off" quickly, but every time he came across a name, he had to do research.

Looking ahead to the pressure that would soon emerge in Uris's trying to meet deadlines, Vaughan told McCormick that "we have to be careful that he [Uris] doesn't get sucked into a big job that keeps him from fulfilling the contracts he has with us" and that Uris and his wife should, from now on, operate separately. He also alluded to a brief breakup between the two because Uris was "spaced out on the novel [which would become *The Haj*] and resented almost any interruption." They had also apparently argued over how committed he was to promoting his wife's career. They seemed to have worked it out, but Vaughan believes that despite Uris's love for his wife, she was "making some demands on him that weigh heavily on this creative time. He must have blown up on the subject one day," adding that if she could have a child, it would "cool this subject down a lot."

WRITING *THE HAJ*

Returning to Aspen from Israel, Uris had trouble getting started on his new novel, working only fitfully on the manuscript. Excited by the perspective he was going to present—that of the Arab world, a pendant to *Exodus*—he had difficulty with organizing the story. "False start" is written over the early drafts; the earliest draft, dated December 1981, he titled *Beirut*. Its opening sentence: "Before the phone had completed its first ring, Sabri swept the sheet off and his feet thumped on the floor in an automatic movement."[14] A woman tells him a package from Belgrade has arrived. Politics immediately intrudes, leading to overwritten sentences like "Syria had once again become the apple of Moscow's eye . . . al Fatah could benefit vastly by securing more potent weapons just from Syria's overflow."

Opus Nine became the new title in late December 1981. An entirely new version, begun in April 1982, was first called *My Father, My Enemy* and then *Haggar's Family*. The next month, it had become *Ishmael: A Novel*.[15] At one point, Uris was convinced that the novel had to be split between two volumes. In October 1982, Ken McCormick summarized the two-volume structure for Sam Vaughan: volume I would be about an Arab family up to the time of their entry to Beirut, and the story would concentrate on the hero's maturity from boyhood to manhood. It would end in 1971, when the hero turns forty, and would include a flashback to 1924 of family life.[16] Volume II would start with the hero's decision to join the PLO and the consequences of this act. Uris would also stress that the Koran is viciously anti-Semitic and that Muhammad tried to convert the Jews, but with no more success than Jesus.

McCormick thought that having an Arab hero was "an absolutely great idea—a Jew writing a book from an Arab point of view." McCormick saw it as analogous to the *Winds of War*, which was split into two volumes (the second was titled *War and Remembrance*), "except we won't have to drag the ms from his [Uris's] typewriter the way Little Brown had to do with [Herman] Wouk . . . six or seven years between those two books." McCormick was excited by the two-volume idea because Uris could do justice to the big theme. Doubleday should expect to receive five hundred pages by the end of December 1982; the paperback edition of the first volume would be printed by Bantam, but volume two could go to Dell. Of course, that much writing would mean another trip to the Middle East for Uris, but McCormick thought the expense was justified: "We definitely ought to respond positively to Lee's report on the growth of what he's doing. He's sure that this is his best novel to date." The abrupt ending of the published *Haj* supports the idea that there had been a planned second volume, which was never written.

By late December 1982, Sam Vaughan could tell his Doubleday staff that the first part of Uris's new novel would be received in the second week of January 1983—"we'll do a fast read and save any heavy edit for later"—the object being to get the novel out in nine months, for the fall of 1983.[17] Vaughan added that Uris had been busy and that the strife in the Middle East was driving him on. Anticipation was high because of the unusual point of view, although one could expect controversy over what he had to say about the Koran. Also, Jill was trying to get pregnant again.

On 24 January 1983, after reading the first five hundred pages of *Ishmael*, Sam Vaughan told McCormick it was a mixed bag. There were too many long passages that were "not fiction but history, or Lee's version of it. The writing is very rough, thin in places, and the whole is like a full outline rather than a full mss."[18] The history was not smoothly integrated, descriptions were scant, and the dialogue was weak. The structure and point of view remained problems, and it was definitely not told from an Arab point of view. The story was also spasmodic, although if Uris developed the bond between Ibrahim and Gideon, it could take off. But Ibrahim had to become more likable in order to deserve Gideon's friendship. The material was still in the *Exodus* period, and it had to move forward. The manuscript needed richer details. It had something of a fabulistic quality at the outset. However, Uris probably turned this version in to get some money and be encouraged. The biggest problem other than technique was that his "one sidedness . . . weakens credibility . . . And if he didn't finally arrive at something some of the Jews did wrong, we'd have to urge him to invent it (the Irgun's massacre)." But Uris needed to supply more than the names of new players: "They have to come through as characters in their scenes."

As he worked on *The Haj*, Uris faced an unexpected personal crisis. During a routine checkup in 1982, required by his new contract with Doubleday, doctors found a tumor in his chest between his lungs and his aorta. An operation occurred almost immediately with no assurance that the tumor was benign. On 14 July 1982, the night before he went into the hospital, Uris and Jill went out and had what he later called a real "Marine Corps. blowout": a topless club, a cheap motel, drinks.[19] In case the prognosis was bad or something tragic occurred during the operation, Uris at least wanted a last night of indulgence and pleasure. Happily, the surgery was a success: the tumor was benign, and within a month or so he was fully recovered and able to get back to work on his new novel.

Understanding the difficulties with his manuscript, Uris set aside time to revise while completing the story, but by March 1983, he was also occupied with Jill's first pregnancy, which required quiet: no travel and limited physical activity. After nearly fifteen years of marriage, she wanted children; Uris was not so sure. Some friction developed, but he acquiesced, although the pregnancy ended in what became the first of several miscarriages. To McCormick, however, Uris explained that his and Jill's life would revolve around the incipient pregnancy and that he planned a new nursery wing for the Red Mountain home.[20] They would also slip down to Jamaica for a short holiday before the beginning of March. The island just might contain material for a new novel. Part Three of *The Haj*, he added, was improving. He realized he was "on a roll" with the Jaffa sequence, and when he tried to recall another such complete "creative surge," he had "to go back to the final hundred pages of *Mila 18*. By some strange quirk, the back end of this book is already starting to dictate what revisions must be made in the front end." The success of the third part convinced him that he would have no problem in cleaning up any difficulties in the first two parts.

He admitted to being worried when he heard about a new John le Carré novel, but decided it wouldn't conflict with his own. The novel was *The Little Drummer Girl* (1983), in which an Israeli spymaster, Martin Kurtz, tries to kill a Palestinian named Khalil, who bombs Jewish-related targets in Europe. Le Carré would only "tease the readers into what I'm going to tell them." Besides, he has not yet read a le Carré book that "ends on a note of triumph for the human spirit." His endings were all downbeat. He then outlined a schedule, adding that writing the final parts of his novels always went the fastest; he hoped to finish the novel on his birthday, in early August.

Four days later, Vaughan told John O'Donnell, the Doubleday treasurer, that Schlosberg would be calling in a few weeks about money.[21] He then gave a summary of the 1,200 pages he had read so far: middling, partly because Uris has packed too much history in, "sometimes failing to make it fiction, [but] when he's rolling and telling a battle scene, the old Uris fire and flair is there." Sir Walter Scott came to mind. Uris did not get an extension on delivery (which he hoped Schlosberg might achieve), only an agreement that neither he nor Ken McCormick would begin seriously editing the novel until the entire manuscript had arrived. Uris was in full flow: "If we can keep him going, it should work out," Vaughan reassured O'Donnell.[22]

In July 1983, Uris tried to assuage the Doubleday treasurer, explaining that knee surgery following his earlier chest surgery had hindered his progress; "accordingly,

I have asked Herb [Schlosberg] to draw monies from Doubleday as I sent pages along."[23] He then outlined the schedule that he had proposed to McCormick and Vaughn, feeling confident that with time for revision, the entire work could be at Doubleday by the end of December. There was a confident postscript: "Incidentally, I believe that *The Haj* is in a class with *Trinity* and *Exodus*."

A possible explanation for the solicitous tone of Uris's letter was that he had renegotiated a deal for the British rights to his work. He would receive advances totaling $280,000: $75,000 up front, $55,000 for signing the new contract, $75,000 for delivering *The Haj*, $25,000 when the hardcover was published, $25,000 when the paperback was published, and $25,000 six months after paperback publication.[24]

The title of the novel was still a problem. A test of "Ishmael" resulted in negative responses at Doubleday because, according to McCormick, Uris was being presumptuous in using that name.[25] It would give reviewers an easy opportunity to flippantly ask, "Who does he think he is, Melville?" "Actually," McCormick wrote to Vaughan, Uris "has never read *Moby Dick* and didn't know the quote that leads off *Moby Dick*." However, pronunciation of "haj" might be difficult. As McCormick wrote to Uris: "The worse thing you can do to a customer is to embarrass him on the pronunciation of a title. He'll go for another book rather than humiliate himself by mispronouncing the title."[26]

In the same letter, McCormick praises Uris, declaring that he gets "into the Arab mind far, far better than Le Carré," although there were inconsistencies and problems. All chapters needed to be assigned dates. Ten-year-old characters shouldn't have the thoughts of twenty-year-olds. McCormick liked other things: the scene with Gideon and the doctor who was prevented from aiding the ailing infant of Ramiza, Uris's way of expressing the Jewish point of view through the newspapers Ishmael reads aloud to his father. He urged Uris to stick with the Arab approach: "the strong point of the book is to view the whole through Arab eyes, [although] once in a while you get disgusted with the idea and abandon it, but please don't." McCormick also proposed some changes to the ending, but thought it was a terrific book, especially the Jaffa section at the end of Part Two.

Sam Vaughan was less ebullient but equally optimistic, especially on the matter of sales. His comments were only suggestions, and so could be ignored, but Vaughan tended "to be fussy about minor details of language" because he hated to see "an author with enormous gifts have his work undermined here and there with small and inevitable awkward sentences or perhaps mis-use of words or whatever."[27] In a nine-page letter, Vaughan first addressed the proposed titles. The key question was whose book is it? The answer: the haj's. Gideon comes on strong, but then he drops out—a problem. Other problems: Ishmael never really takes over from his father, and the book is not shared by the haj and Gideon, or by Ibrahim and Ishmael. This confusion is apparent from the mixed-up point of view: it is not immediately clear who is narrating each chapters.

Vaughan urged Uris to do more with Gideon and to keep the emphasis on the haj: his outsized character animates the book, dwarfing others. Vaughan's general assessment: "We are overdone on history and on Arab madness. We are short on a richness of description. At places the narrative seems to be almost an outline. It needs less invective and more of your own good authoritative, intimate knowledge of the people and places."

The women were also a problem, Vaughan noted. Even though their role in Arab life was diminished, more characterization of them was needed. Nada is fine but Hagar is not. Ursula, the German mistress, has potential, but at times borders on parody. And the ending is a "downer." Even though things are hopeless, Uris gave no sense of the Israelis' triumph. At the end there is only the maddened haj, an insane Ishmael who murdered his sister Nada.

Finally, Vaughan pointed out that Uris showed no real understanding of the Arab viewpoint, although he managed to create sympathy for least a couple of Arab characters. Doubleday couldn't say that the novel was written from the viewpoint of an Arab or Palestinian, "because that would set us up for a punch in the chops." Vaughan urged Uris to look at each scene in each chapter to see whether he had given it enough "character, color, incident." Although the book wouldn't have "the advantage . . . of the Irish melody and music of the language," Uris did well "with the Arab gift for overstatement." The writing "marches and moves when it is not . . . bogged down in historical detail."

Uris took the criticism with surprising equanimity, noting that he and Jill, on completing the first draft, went to Victoria, British Columbia, where she again became pregnant.[28]

In the midst of this exchange, Uris couldn't resist some humor. A letter to McCormick begins with his worry that he hasn't yet received any criticism for his "overuse of the word FUCK" in *The Haj*.[29] But he now has, and the note will join similar letters sent to him when he was writing *QB VII* and *Trinity*. He then reveals that he has always put five times as many "fucks" in a manuscript as he intends to use, just so that he could "be utterly magnanimous when I get your FUCK letter." He promised to examine each "fuck" carefully and keep only the ones necessary "for the advancement of the plot and characterizations."

But difficulties with the manuscript persisted. He had problems deciding on its voice and audience. He was also radicalizing and splintering the Israeli-Palestinian narrative, isolating one from the other in an attempt to underscore Arabs' rejection of their own people, the Palestinians, and the deep-seated, long-held anti-Semitism of the Arabs, which predated the birth of modern Israel. He also chose to have a narrator who begins the story, in its final form, at age eight and hardly seems to age beyond ten in the first three hundred pages, speaking and reporting events in a kind of surprised, naïve, and uninformed manner.

Uris sent the finished manuscript to two close friends in Israel, Moshe Pearlman and Joan Comay. Each had published a dozen or more books of nonfiction on Israel and Jewish topics. They found only two errors in the manuscript. In a letter to McCormick, Uris quotes from Pearlman, who said, "You've another WINNER!" adding that the book was both "absorbing and new in its treatment of subjects never discussed in fiction."[30] The Israelis seem spellbound.

Uris explained that *The Haj* dealt with the Palestinians at the hands of the Arabs, as well as the centuries-old Arab anti-Semitism.[31] Research, he argued, justified this view. He drew on not only his 1978–1979 visit to Israel but also his meetings with experts like Bernard Lewis and his study of works like Alan Patai's *The Arab Mind*. This last, a right-wing, simplistic, and unsympathetic view of the Arabs, emphasized a tradition of distrust, both among themselves and the outside world. There was also a chapter devoted to Arab sex, which Uris used. Lewis was a conservative historian at Princeton, a coeditor of the four-volume *Cambridge History of Islam* (1978), and author of *The Jews of Islam* (1984), among many other books on the Middle East. Like Patai, Lewis stressed a negative view of Arab culture. As Uris later stated, "The Arabs have a long, tormented history of tribal warfare, blood feuds, and repression. Western democracies have been naive about the Arab world. I knew I might be called a racist, but I had to tell the truth. Too many writers duck the hard stuff."[32]

Jill was this time less involved in writing the book, preoccupied by the task of starting a family. She explained: "I was involved with *The Haj*, but not to the extent of *Trinity*. I read pages back to Lee, but I was trying to get and was pregnant with a miscarriage and then Rachael during that time. I had some issues with the way Lee handled the Arab situation with the book and wasn't as big a fan as earlier. I did some research, I have a copy of *The Arab Mind* that I made notes for Lee in which I know was a huge influence on the book."[33]

THE STORY

Uris dedicated *The Haj* (1984) to his eldest son, Mark. It opens with an allusion to *Moby Dick*, replacing "Call me Ishmael" with "I am Ishmael" (*HJ*, 5). Organized into five parts with titles like "The Valley of Ayalon," "The Scattering," and "Jericho," the book moves linearly from 1922 to 1956, with occasional flashbacks that focus on Ishmael, who was born in 1936. His father, Haj Ibrahim ("haj" is the title of one who makes the pilgrimage to Mecca), grows up befriending the leader of a nearby kibbutz and Haganah fighter, Gideon Asch. The novel mixes politics, history, and romance in unequal doses.

History clearly dominates the story, but it is viewed through a set of Arab stereotypes, drawn partly from Patai's *The Arab Mind*, beginning with the idea that hate is the prime motivator of Arab life, seconded by mistrust. As Ishmael says early in the novel: "Never trust anyone, especially your best friend. I didn't trust my brothers. . . . I didn't even trust my mother even though I loved her very much" (*HJ*, 123). Characters readily turn against one another, as the novel shows, especially when land, money, and false promises of victory are at stake. Furthermore, the Arab is depicted as a prisoner of his society who will not accept help, because to do so is humiliating. At one point, the Arab narrator asserts: "Humiliation is the ultimate punishment," and this idea is reinforced in the dramatic scene when Haj Ibrahim refuses to let Gideon and a Jewish doctor help his gravely ill infant son, who dies as a result (*HJ*, 133, 150–152).

Arabs resent the Jews because they have jolted them "from their delusions of grandeur and shown them for what they are—a decadent, savage people controlled by a religion that has stripped them of all human ambition" (*HJ*, 81). Early in the novel, the omniscient narrator confirms this: "Arab fighting Arab was an established way of life . . . to be saved by the Jews and the British was a new humiliation" (*HJ*, 90). Even Arab sexuality receives the Uris treatment: "No women in the world can say more with their eyes than Arab women . . . They made their eyes do the work for them" (*HJ*, 128). These overstatements and simplifications indicate how easy it was for Uris to alienate readers and critics of the book.

The Haj alternates between a family story of distrust among fathers and sons (as well as brothers) and the story of the Jewish settlement of Palestine. Arab displacement and geopolitical competition among world powers vie for the reader's interest. Uris attempted to show that the roots of Arab displacement lay in their behavior toward one another, not in their mistreatment by the Jews. They were responsible for their own fate. But when not offering his family saga, Uris blankets the book with a detailed history of British deception, Arab violence, and Jewish strength. Entire chapters read like generalized history books, an effect that distances the reader from the story. There is little personal drama.

When relying on the expository rather than the dramatic, Uris outlines the history of Islam and Judaism, frequently describing sections of the Koran and the Bible. Historical figures also appear: Orde Wingate, a British soldier and Zionist sympathizer who organized the special Night Raiders of the Jews; David Ben-Gurion; the mufti of Jerusalem; Yigdal Allon. But pronouncements substitute for dialogue. When Haj Ibrahim visits his uncle Walid Azziz for advice, he gets doctrine: Palestinian nationalism will end as it always ends, "with the personal desire of one man to gain power" (*HJ*, 111). A fight with the Jews is inevitable because "they are infidels and we are Moslems. No infidel can be allowed to rule one inch of land where Islam exists" (*HJ*, 111). But the Jews must be fought carefully: unlike other foreigners who came to Palestine to exploit the Arabs, the Jews have come to stay.

The story of Israel's fight for independence takes over the second half of the novel as Uris defends Jewish aggression. While recognizing the Israelis' need to protect themselves from the attacking Arabs, Uris also makes it clear that Israel will struggle to be fair. Arabs will not be forced out of Palestine or a Jewish state if they choose to remain, Ben-Gurion tells his cabinet (*HJ*, 206).

But the doctrinaire elements of the novel work against the effectiveness of its message. In retelling the story of Israel's existence and in taking the *Exodus* story up to the Suez crisis of 1956, Uris lets his ideas overtake his narrative, ideas that often border on the slanderous ("evil . . . emanates from the Moslem world" [*HJ*, 228]). The novel is atmospheric, but the urgency with which he pushes his argument and interpretation reduces the literary impact of the work. The competition among the Arab leaders to divide up Palestine overshadows the Jewish fight for survival, which dominated *Exodus*. But Uris cannot be compassionate about his characters, only romantic. The result is an uneven work that distances rather than engages the reader. Even the battle scenes lose their impact. The attack on the kibbutz Kfar Szold by Kaukji, the Arab military leader of the Army of Liberation, is told without intensity, as are the unsuccessful attacks by the army on other enclaves. Fighting by Abdul Kahar's Army of the Jihad is similarly undramatic. Indifferent action rather than character dominates.

In a special preface to the Franklin Library edition of the novel, Uris defends his treatment of the Arabs, calling it a warning. He links his anxiety about the Arabs to the oil crisis of the 1980s and the need for the United States to accommodate Arab goals. Yet the Arabs remain an enigma to the West, mysterious and remote. Their drive for self-determination after the Second World War has created intense pressure in the West for acceptance of them as equals, as well as an acknowledgment of the emergence of oil politics, terrorism, fanaticism, and fundamentalism. Attacks on U.S. embassies in Tehran and Islamabad, followed by the terrorist bombing of a U.S. Marine Corps barracks in Beirut, indicated the extent of the threat as Uris understood it in 1984. Fear of a nuclear holocaust creates even more worry. Uris stressed to his readers "the cold fact that we share this fragile planet with a billion adherents to Islam," whose priorities are "different than our own." He hopes that his novel furthers an understanding of these people, who are "other."[34]

The setting shifts to Zurich for a UN-sponsored refugee conference that sees the unity of three refugee leaders disintegrate. This theme is carried through the final chapters as the constant story of Arab deception and self-betrayal continues.

In this sense, the novel never progresses; locations and names may change, but the story repeats itself. Arabs throughout history have imprisoned other Arabs with no hope of regaining anything that was lost (HJ, 453).

A final sign of Uris's attempt to redeem the story is Herr Schlosberg—the name, of course, of his lawyer and business manager—who, in the novel, makes jewel movements for Swiss watches and arranges a meeting in Zurich between Haj Ibrahim and Gideon Asch (HJ, 455). The only act left for Ibrahim, whose people have been abused and whose life is threatened, is to seek revenge on Effendi Kabir, who acts for a Saudi prince. His murder, carried out with the assistance of Effendi's drug-addicted German mistress, Ursula, is a Jacobean mix of fantasy and violence (HJ, 462–467). Its graphic quality is equaled by the grim account of Jamil's death by a Jordanian colonel, which, ironically, turns him into a martyr (HJ, 468–469).

Nearing its end, the novel shifts to 1953, when Ishmael, by then a seventeen-year-old teacher, pins his hopes on UN efforts to begin re-creating self-esteem through education and industrial projects. But again, "tribal avarice moved in," and the project was aborted as demonstrations became more violent (HJ, 502). Because the Arabs do not trust each other, they cannot work together. Increasingly, Ishmael's powerful father begins to weaken, something the son cannot accept. The authority of the father, tested throughout the novel and marked by his inability to protect his family, his clan, and his tribe, suddenly loses its potency.[35] Then, as Nada becomes active in the fedayeen, Ishmael tries to talk some sense into her and correct her distorted vision of victory over the Jews—but it does not work (HJ, 509).

The plot gains further momentum when Ishmael becomes an archeological assistant at the Mount Nebo dig and has an affair with Sybil, an English volunteer. A penultimate restatement of the Arab situation—"Islam is unable to live at peace with anyone" (HJ, 545)—precedes the final chapters. These involve the Suez crisis, told in a reportorial style with an almost list-like set of events but with the emotional upset of Ibrahim, who believed in Nasser and his rhetoric. In a dramatic final scene, the violent Colonel Zyyad asks Ibrahim to convince the near-rioting Palestinians from Jericho to stop their attempt to cross the Allenby Bridge. If they don't, they will be slaughtered by his Arab Legion (HJ, 552). Ibrahim succeeds. The last event is to repair the rift between Ibrahim and his daughter Nada. It fails; she humiliates him; he kills her. Told then by Ishmael of the rape of his two wives and Fatima (his sister), Ibrahim suffers a heart attack and dies. Ishmael has avenged his sister, but the family has been destroyed; Ishmael loses his mental balance and the ability to speak. Arab justice, one might expect Uris to have said.

Doubleday nixed the second volume of The Haj, which was to carry the story beyond 1956. As it stands, the novel ends abruptly and unconvincingly with

Ishmael's mental breakdown. Uris likely felt compelled to bring the Israel story up to date, perhaps feeling a need to highlight the state's importance by retelling its accomplishments on and off the battlefield up to the 1980s. The protection of Israel was also uppermost in his mind, and he wanted to alert the country and the world of the dangers of Islam (his recent health scare compounded his urgency). However, poor sales of *The Haj* validated Doubleday's decision not to publish a second volume. He would not repeat the success of *Exodus*.

Uris was worried about the book just before publication, and Doubleday did not offer much confidence. It seemed unsure of how to market the work, especially after the initial reviews. Advance comments were indifferent at best. Doubleday's plan was to go on the attack and run large editorial ads in New York and Los Angeles. The ads would try to provoke a reaction, and Uris himself wanted a forum to counter what he believed to be an Arab campaign at the UN against Israel. An op-ed piece was suggested, but Vaughan confided to McCormick that with new distractions (Jill had given birth), it would be difficult for Uris to meet a deadline.[36]

A CRITICAL AND COMMERCIAL FLOGGING

Reviewers were critical of Uris's extremism and unreceptive to his depiction of the poverty, despair, and anger that led the displaced Palestinians to embrace terrorism. In a review in its house publication, the American Library Association offered a general criticism, noting that neither Uris's compassion nor his art could mold all the material into an "appealing narrative. The result is a dutiful rather than an inspired pastiche."[37] The material seemed underexplained and often superfluous, as if pulled undigested from a reference book. By contrast, the *Chicago Sun Times* gave it a positive review, the author, Gerald Green, writing that if he had the power, he "would make *The Haj* required reading for the entire membership of the United Nations."[38]

At a launch party at Denver's Oxford Hotel, Uris was in a celebratory mood, explaining to journalists that promotion was part of the author's job: "You write it, then you help sell it," adding, "I have enjoyed being famous. I don't like being a celebrity."[39] Attending the party was Ken McCormick, described wearing a subdued grey suit, his white hair combed straight back, and sitting out of the way. McCormick praised *QB VII* as Uris's greatest book, calling *The Haj* a "tremendous undertaking." His only criticism was that Uris tended to digress as he works through a project: in a draft of *QB VII*, he had written 40,000 words about what it was like to be a film writer. The passage had to go. An editor, McCormick added, does not make a writer better but brings out the good that is in him.

The novel stayed on the best-seller list for some thirty weeks, despite, as Uris later put it, a "critical blasting, especially from the so-called liberal Jewish press."[40] "Jews have always turned on their heroes," he added in self-defense. He also claimed that the book had become a standard reference for U.S. officials dealing with the Middle East and that it could be more easily purchased in Arab countries than in the United States.

Disappointing sales soon matched the often-devastating press. Readers were mystified. Rather than recapturing the excitement of *Exodus*, *The Haj* alienated Uris from many of his core fans, Jewish and non-Jewish. He seemed unable to create characters that readers could identify with. His most sympathetic market, ironically, was among Arabs, despite his critique of Arab mistreatment of the Palestinians and an extreme view of Arab society, which was presented as one of betrayal and distrust. As he later noted: "Ironically, the Arabs were more tolerant than the Jews. The novel was sold in Egypt (as was *Exodus*)."[41] He also received many letters from Arabs who "saw a lot of truth in *The Haj*." Uris went on to claim that "no one" had been "able to point out a single error in the book" and that British and American officials serving in the Middle East had praised the work.

Others criticized the book for being dominated by a youthful narrator whose passions were out of alignment with his experience. Although he is eight when he begins the story, he improbably veers into history, political intrigue, and insistent exposition. Thematically, the main concern is only betrayal and conflict. Uris's typically well-researched presentation could not overcome reaction to his extremism. Readers rejected his simplistic view that the Arabs could not be trusted and that Jews were democratic heroes who had become a race of "Jewish Tarzans" (EX, 604). Such politics would even effect the reception of his next novel, *Mitla Pass*, his last work to be published by Doubleday.

By July 1984, however, Uris was concentrating on something else: trying to sell *Mila 18* to the movies. He "toured" the studios seeking a deal, but didn't have much to report to Doubleday.[42] Sam Vaughan had recently visited him in Aspen and told him sales of *The Haj* had been uneven. More than 300,000 copies had been printed, and most had shipped, but there had also been returns.[43] In a memo to McCormick, Vaughan went on to note three projects then underway: a screenplay of *Trinity*, then in second draft; further work on what Uris called "the *Exodus* 'Pageant,'" a musical play that was not a rewrite of his failed Broadway effort, *Ari*, but a new, slightly sentimental musical; and a movie deal for *Mila 18*, which he was working on with David Sontag, an independent movie producer and former Fox executive vice president.[44] The three projects represented approximately a six-month involvement, which meant that he wouldn't be starting a new novel until, realistically, 1 January 1985 (although Uris thought it would be July 1984, while he was trying to film *Mila 18*).

Illustrating the importance of deadlines and obligations, Vaughan told Mc-Cormick they should pressure Uris to get started by the January date. Uris had admitted that he wanted to avoid another eight-year gap, which had existed between *Trinity* (1976) and *The Haj* (1984). In fact, Uris should be thinking about two novels, not one, which would put too much pressure on a single subject.[45] But Uris had rejected a variety of subjects, from a prison novel to one about the Caribbean. He told Vaughan: "This is a period without heroes."[46] An American novel still appealed to Uris, but it was time, Vaughan emphasized, for Uris to write a novel "in which he likes somebody and doesn't just come out against the aggressors."[47] Vaughan concluded that Uris had "paid his dues on THE HAJ," and now "doesn't want to travel as much, doesn't want to invest in the same kind of research, is 'tired' of seeing starvation and blood and misery."

In a letter to his paperback publisher, Uris noted the odd sales pattern of his books: after an initial burst, they entered a period of calm, like a runner in the middle of race positioning himself until the final push at the end.[48] He claimed that *Trinity* was on the best-seller list for a year before it became number one (in fact, it was just a little over three months). After initial sales, *The Haj* sat in warehouses, but now, in July, it was picking up again, becoming number one in Philadelphia, Denver, and other cities. It was clear that "with a Uris book we sometimes require a full year to get our maximum hardcover sales. Likewise, EXODUS wasn't in full stride for a year but we obviously couldn't hold up the paperback." He told Doubleday to keep pushing *The Haj* in hardback and not to let a paperback edition supplant hardcover sales.[49] If paperback publicity began too soon for *The Haj*, hardback sales could drop by 100,000 to 150,000 copies. Clearly, involvement in the promotion of his work was something Uris took seriously.

FINANCIAL AND MARITAL PRESSURES

The novel's poor reception, however, marked the beginning of an unstable relationship between Uris and the marketplace. And declining sales soon created a financial strain between Uris and his publisher. On one hand, he needed more money to maintain his lifestyle, and on the other, inadequate sales did not justify increased advances. His publisher began to exert pressure on his productivity, subject matter, and financial support. As Doubleday became more reluctant to offer larger advances, Uris and Herb Schlosberg had to come up with more attractive "packages" and better paperback deals to increase his financial security. This, in turn, forced Uris to rethink his projects: he had to find topics that would be commercially appealing and potential blockbusters. Being a popular writer with a large following meant having to select subjects that blended the slightly esoteric or unknown with the saleable. Writing in an accessible and dramatic style was not enough; the topic had to have commercial appeal. And after *The Haj*, Uris could not risk another failure. No one would back him.

The files of Herb Schlosberg reflect these concerns. Under the terms of a 1982 contract, Uris had to deliver a new work every three years. This proved to be impossible, and by 1989, he was at least a year behind schedule. A new contract had not yet been signed, because he wanted to renegotiate due dates and add a late novel—one previously contracted for but yet unwritten—to the new arrangement. Traditionally, he could earn bonus payments by meeting delivery times, but more often he received advances before delivering a manuscript. Until the late 1980s, Doubleday leniently disbursed his advance royalties in a timely way even if he had not delivered a manuscript, knowing that he needed money to live on. On several occasions, according to his business manger, he had received a million dollars when there was no problem with delivery. When Doubleday was taken over by the German publisher Bertelsmann, however, such leniency changed.[50] Complicating Uris's negotiating power was Schlosberg's illness: in 1986, he suffered a series of strokes.

Nevertheless, by 1984, the year *The Haj* was finished and his daughter Rachael born, Uris had been paid a $3.5 million guarantee from three works, *Trinity*, *The Haj*, and *QB VII*, and his royalties to be received that year were $526,000. By comparison, eight years earlier Uris's royalties had been, according to Schlosberg, $1.53 million.[51] As part of the 1982 contract deal, Doubleday had offered Uris an annual income plan of $90,000 a year for the next seven years. Apparently, he did not accept it, leading Schlosberg to remark that with the exception of one year, all the income of the Urises was spent before the end of each year. He would often have to borrow money each November so they could get through the last two months of each year. No new monies would appear until the start of the next year, Schlosberg testified in May 1989.[52] In short, money troubles plagued Uris during the last nineteen years of his life, from *The Haj* (1984) through *O'Hara's Choice* (2003).

These problems coincided with difficulties with Jill. The tenor of Aspen life was beginning to change as Uris preferred to live in a more isolated fashion, becoming more protective of his time. He declined to meet visitors or friends who admired his work. His 1982 illness and his growing detachment from Jill, brought about largely by disagreements over children—he already had three and was unsure about starting a new family—meant friction. Feeling the pressure to write, he needed time and ideas; a young child would be a distraction. But Jill had wanted children since the early 1980s, and part of him, perhaps, wanted to prove that he could still father them, even at sixty. He had always been ambivalent about children, however, and his relationships with his first three were often strained and distant. Reluctantly, he agreed, although Jill's miscarriages in the early eighties, while intensifying their emotional relationship, began to destabilize their marriage.

Uris remained under increasing pressure from his publisher to produce. His reputation with his public was diminishing, and he knew he had to reestablish it. This meant he had to get to work even as his disillusionment with his relationship was increasing. Even after Jill gave birth to Rachael Jackson on 24 May 1984 and then Conor Twain on 22 March 1986, the marriage began to crack.

Nineteen eighty-four, however, had happier moments. In August, Uris turned sixty, and Jill held a black-tie birthday party for thirty on the upper deck of their new two-story pool house (some guests wore tuxedos with sneakers). A plane flew overhead with a banner announcing—to the PLO, as Uris sarcastically reported—the location of his house and that it was his sixtieth birthday.[53] The banner read "HAPRY 60TH LEE," the misspelling a comment on his sloppy typing. A harpist "wearing red, white and blue sneakers and little else" played for the guests. In a tent on the pool patio, Jill unveiled a large lion sculpture, "and for the first time in living memory," Uris reported, "I was speechless, that is until the belly dancer came in and did her thing." Competing with the belly dancer was the car-bumper sculpture of a lion, crafted by the Aspen artist Lou Willie and meant to suggest the Lion of Judah. But the highlight was not the roast of Uris that followed, celebrating his immodesty, nor the comic account of "life with father" by his eldest son, Mark, but the telegram from Paramount, read by producer David Sontag, stating that the studio would go ahead with *Mila 18*.

More generally, however, his life was less positive. While he still enjoyed the outdoors—walking his dogs in the woods, playing tennis, and even trying dirt bikes—he became lonelier, following a pattern of rejecting those closest to him while he rededicated himself to his idea of the life of a writer. But he refused to seek out a literary community in Aspen or elsewhere. Only his readers mattered to him, and they seemed to be turning away. He had to get them back and renew his love affair with them. Writing was what he did, how he made his living, even if he did not identify with the traditional life of a writer and was jealous of his competitors. "Down with the *New York Times Book Review* section! Down with Philip Roth!" he wrote to Vaughan and McCormick.[54] His closest friends were an insurance broker, a musician, and a doctor. Although there were almost no writers in his circle, he was jealous of the literary awards given to his peers. But when the *New York Times* invited him to participate in a literary brunch several years later, just before the release of *Mitla Pass*, he was thrilled, realizing that he was being accepted by the literati as part of a popular literary culture.[55]

Governor Richard Lamm proclaimed 10 April 1984 "Leon Uris Day" in

Colorado. The date coincided with the publication of *The Haj*. On 13 August that year, Uris, along with Louis L'Amour, the western writer, and Clive Cussler, the action-adventure author, were feted at the Governor's Mansion. All three were best-selling Coloradans who sat around the governor's office telling dirty jokes.[56]

RUSSIAN RENEWAL

You spend the second half of your life getting over the first half.
—LEON URIS, 1988

IN THE LATE 1980S, Uris's life was overturned. From Aspen, where he had lived some eighteen years, he found himself in New York and then Eastern Europe. It was an unexpected journey that led to self-discovery and a renewal of his identity as a writer. But the process was difficult, more so for one who had spent hardly any time reexamining his past.

Relations with his publisher began to deteriorate in 1984 as soon as Uris started his new project, which would be his last for Doubleday. Under pressure to produce another title, Uris decided to revisit his past. Although not an intro-spective writer, he nonetheless thought it worthwhile to review letters and other materials he had deposited at the University of Colorado at Boulder. This would be an opportunity for him to look back and reconsider his story, especially his difficult relationship with his father. Earlier, he had taken the challenging step of encouraging his father to write an autobiography. The 1975 document became a crucial source in formulating the new novel, which Uris began to plan.

Doubleday tried to discourage an autobiographical work. McCormick told Sam Vaughan that when Uris mentioned it, he should put it off unless it had "a really pulsing theme," adding, "He is best when he is mad and he's terrific when he comes to grips with something great."[1] McCormick suggested terrorism as a topic, some sort of account of those who band together to kill themselves in attempts to blow up embassies. Months earlier there had been a variation of this: the Hezbollah truck bombing of the U.S. Embassy in Beirut, and the response of the State Department to the crisis.[2]

Later that month—October 1984—Vaughan told Uris that it was time to focus on his next novel, undistracted by work on musicals or movies.[3] He hoped that Uris would find a topic both important and attractive and explore it through one or more characters he would like to live with, adding, the novel "should be fun for you to write." He also didn't want Uris to run into money problems.

When Uris began planning what would become *Mitla Pass*, William Uris's autobiography proved useful. Supposedly written for the benefit of his grandchildren, it is an episodic account of his life (see the account in Chapter 1 of this book) and became a sourcebook for Uris. Ironically (or perhaps characteristically), Uris never refers to it in the published version of *Mitla Pass*—in fact, he does not even cite his father in the acknowledgments, only Priscilla Higham, his assistant, and Jill. And yet the autobiography became the origin of Uris's own semifictionalized story in the novel.

The new work introduced a more explicitly autobiographical style for Uris, opening what he would refer to as the closed doors of the self.[4] The combination of rereading his old letters, grappling with his health scare of 1982, facing up to the disappointing sales of *The Haj*, struggling with the worsening difficulties with Jill, and again becoming the father of two young children resulted in an uncertain reconsideration of his past. His father's autobiography accelerated the process. The result was his most autobiographical novel, and the one most difficult to write.

"I have always treated my past as the enemy," Uris confided in an essay for the *Franklin Mint Almanac*, a publication of the Franklin Library, in advance of its limited edition of *Mitla Pass*.[5] But new strains on his personal life made him realize he might be better equipped to face the present if he understood his past. In the essay, titled "Old Letters Never Die" in draft, but published as "Old Letters, New Life," he writes: "I have a heavy duty thing about my past. I've always treated it as the enemy" because of "accumulated pains of childhood, stormy relationships with my parents." He then notes his two failed marriages, the suicide of his second wife, and a "catastrophic career" as a Hollywood writer. But he knows he has to confront his past. The article is an unusually self-conscious assessment of his life, and he admits that "even as I wanted to forget, I was making a counter-effort to preserve all of what had happened to me."

Uris had in fact saved much from his past, including correspondence, unpublished manuscripts, theatre programs, travel logs, and even menus. "Obviously, I was in conflict with myself," he wrote, noting how he wanted to both preserve and yet never revisit the past.[6] Being part of a second family with young children gave him the courage to open the vault of his past, and he spent nearly six months going through the material on deposit in Boulder. What he found was an unexpected happiness in a past he had thought of only as cloudy. He also understood that he had done his "share of . . . lying and cheating": "I use to think of myself as a very sad little Jewish boy isolated in a Southern town, undersized, asthmatic. When I read all my correspondence again, I realized I was a hustler," he later stated.[7] In the end, he found a man he liked very much and discovered that his writing had made a difference to many.

A rough outline of "Lullaby," which became *Mitla Pass*, is dated 6 May 1986.[8] Reading more like an antagonistic autobiography than a novel, it begins in 1956 with a criticism of his two early literary agents, Willis Wing and Ned Brown. It then moves to late 1956, when Uris was in Israel, gathering material for *Exodus*. A love affair with a woman named Eva, which likely happened before his wife, Betty, and the children arrived in Israel, is described, along with the Suez crisis. The work is a candid autobiography, undisguised and unliterary. Many passages had to be cut.

Uris hoped the work might fill two volumes; McCormick typed on the draft, however, that book one would sell like mad, but not book two. His suggestion was to "write it [the autobiographical novel] and hold it. Do Mexican novel and then Volume two, is my suggestion." Uris was, in fact, contemplating a border story about Mexico and the United States at this time.

FAMILY SOURCES

In June 1986, Uris told McCormick that his half-sister Essie would be visiting Aspen for almost a week and would provide a great deal of personal detail he could use in the novel (he would dedicate *Mitla Pass* to her).[9] After Essie's visit, Uris wrote "Rough Outline and Ramdom [*sic*] notes for Lullaby—the Life Story of Gideon Zadok," a thirty-one-page treatment of the new novel, which mixes character with narrative and Uris's actual life events.[10] In it, he does not withhold commentary on the characters, all thinly disguised members of his family. Wolf, a character given his father's actual name, "evolves as a humorless, ill-tempered, anger filled person who despises American affluence and American democracy" ("Rough Outline," 1). He is entirely negative, "immersed in permanent self-pity," but possesses a false sense of superiority because he is rooted in Jewishness ("Rough Outline," 1).

The next section deals with Gideon's mother, named Anna Blumenthal (Uris's mother's name was Anna Blumberg), and then the years in Norfolk, where Gideon (aka Uris) has moved. This account, too, is painful, since the hero realizes his mother has "tried to castrate him psychologically by making him believe he had incurable asthma and was not able to breathe without her" ("Rough Outline," 4). The second of Anna's two previous marriages, before she married Wolf, led to a daughter, Essie (which was Uris's half-sister's actual name). In this outline, Uris disguises little, although there are some romanticized elements, such as a halfhearted suicide attempt and the respite and friendship he found in the Young

Communist League in Philadelphia. He also overemphasizes the infidelities of his mother, who took "lovers into her late seventies" ("Rough Outline," 5). He credits her with teaching him a love of literature, however.

Uris's mother, Anna Blumberg, wrote an autobiography in 1970 (under her final married name, Anna Abrams), intending it to be read by Essie and Leon; it is not clear whether Uris ever read the document. Titled "Won't Somebody Please Hold Me!" the sixteen-page manuscript condenses a chapter from a work that she had written in 1968 but that was lost in a flooded basement.[11] She had shown part of her account to her sister Esther, who prohibited her from continuing because she thought it would harm her health ("Hold Me!" 1). But she persevered with recording her difficult life, although she had talked little about the account because of her age.

Her account exhibits self-pity alternating with Uris's own style of aggression; she writes at one point that death "would have saved me a horribly [sic] life of woe" ("Hold Me!" 6). She describes a move with her older brother Maurice and their parents to Havre de Grace, Maryland, where six more brothers and sisters were born. She remarks that although she never saw a psychiatrist, she has heard that they can correct wrongs by tracing back childhood experiences. That is what she wants to write about, beginning with the "cruel" behavior of her father to her mother and his children. At one point, he attacked her in the backyard, damaging her back so badly that she had to wear a brace for years ("Hold Me!" 6). Her father would in anger tear the clothes off her brother Maurice, who later died in a train accident at twelve. Her father tied another brother, Bill, to a bed and whipped him. He broke free and smashed every window in the room. "Every day there was murder in our house," she writes ("Hold Me!" 7). Her mother rented a private house, where the father would come to eat and sometimes sleep; before that, they lived over the store he ran. She herself was so fearful of him that she could not live anywhere near him. She studied music, but became so ill that she had to leave home and stay with relatives in Baltimore and then with an uncle, Dr. Buckman, in Philadelphia, where she took a business course.

The abuse continued. After she returned home, her father threatened to kill her if she left again, so she wasn't able to finish her education, which meant she was unable to work and make a living for herself—"my *greatest tragedy*," she writes ("Hold Me!" 8). But one day, after eighteen years of marriage, her mother put seven children and herself on a train to Baltimore and left her husband. She opened a small store, but it did not succeed. So she kept moving from place to place with the children, each stop worse than the last. Anna was fifteen. Soon, she joined a relative from Virginia who owned a small department store, and several months later he married her off to his son. She adjusted to a better life, although she missed her mother and siblings. She even worked in the store, which she enjoyed—until her father discovered where she was and rushed in and tore off most of her clothes and jewelry ("Hold Me!" 11). He threatened to sue her in-laws with kidnapping if they would not let her go. She was forced back to her family, and shortly afterward her husband died.

Another uncle insisted she return to Philadelphia to finish her schooling. She did, and while there, she met an older man, Benjamin Bernhardt, an engineer, who fell in love with her and her singing and piano playing. Her uncle then married her off, and her daughter Essie was born, named after Benjamin's mother, Esther Diana.

The personal narrative pauses at this point as Anna comments on the anti-Semitism and ethnic discrimination she experienced in Philadelphia—worse than even her unlucky marriages. Every New Year's Eve, for example, Gentiles would shoot bullets into their bedroom windows. She also notes that she had won several awards for short-story writing when she was going to school in Havre de Grace, although first place went to another girl because her handwriting was neater. When she won a spelling contest in grade five, she was beaten by another girl on the way home. Such acts, possibly relayed to her son, and combined with his father's communist sympathies, contributed to his hatred of injustice and social abuse. Uris's idea of the "tough Jew" likely originated in these early experiences of his parents, who encouraged him never to accept similar treatment. Anna closes her autobiographical account with the hope that her son will read it in order to understand her past.

William Uris died on 5 July 1988 in Philadelphia. His son did not attend the funeral, underscoring the intensity of his anger at his father. But the death may have deepened Uris's great fear of loneliness, which Gideon Zadok shared.

In an autobiographical amalgam of his father's story and his own, sent to Mc-Cormick as "Gideon's Early Childhood Memories," an idealized Uris emerges. After Gideon served in the marines, for example, his first wife found him appealing because of his "madness, street fighter background and his flaming ambition."[12] Reflecting Uris's ego, Gideon, a writer, announces that "'the author' was the game and everyone else was a bit player" ("Gideon's Childhood," 13). Uris notes: "The most important thrust here is not the inner workings of the first family but Gideon's drive for recognition and fame" ("Gideon's Childhood," 13). The writer as hero, driven by a fierce commitment to his work, was Uris's focus.

In writing about the end of his first marriage in the outline, Uris is candid, admitting, "Everyone brings into a marriage the elements that can later destroy it" ("Gideon's Childhood," 15). While his wife "believes in his ambition," she understood it less and less, never coming to terms "with the price that has to be paid" ("Gideon's Childhood," 15). Her own self-esteem becomes compromised when she later realizes that she has neither the talent nor the drive to pursue an independent career and that her "original awe for Gideon is now tempered with resentment" ("Gideon's Childhood," 15). She fails to support him in battles with studios or publishers. Gideon's infidelity soon follows, the story seemingly overtaken by Uris's romantic view of his own life: "At home [he] prowls the tenderloin district, visiting prostitutes, hanging around the fighter's gym, always relentlessly searching the underlife for another story" ("Gideon's Childhood," 15, 16).

In "Author's Reflections," Uris recounts the excitement of receiving the telegram telling him that his first book has been accepted. It is a triumph buttressed by smug self-satisfaction: "With it comes the dubious pleasure of spitting in the eye of everyone who has ever hurt or disparaged you," a somewhat extreme, even vengeful, reaction ("Gideon's Childhood," 14).

Uris writes that Gideon "always served as his father's alter ego," and after Gideon achieves fame, that was their relationship "in spades" ("Gideon's Childhood," 17). The father becomes a critic and celebrity. At this point, Uris quotes from several letters, written by a friend, concerning his own father and himself. One passage is telling: "Your father is a classic study of a narcissistically deprived being who, learning that his child is the one being who does attend to him, demands that this attention be total—and *his* attention to *you* be whimsical, mean and entirely self indulgent" ("Gideon's Childhood," 17).[13]

An incomplete account of Uris's career comes next, from his early publishing success to his declining marriage. *Battle Cry*, Uris's first book, is here called *The Raid*, and like the actual novel, it is made into a movie. Gideon writes the screenplay, which provides some much-welcomed money. Uris admits that Gideon's insecurity as a novelist, partly promoted by his publisher, led to his attraction to Hollywood. When Gideon declines a regular contract with the studio, friction develops with his wife—but he is determined to write his second novel. It fails to meet sales expectations (as did *The Angry Hills*). Uris then digresses to offer a critique of his first agent, Willis Wing, who, according to him, never stood up for his writers ("Gideon's Childhood," 20).

While describing Gideon's career as studio writer, drifting from project to project, Uris interjects that he—Uris—had worked on *Boy on a Dolphin*, *Rebel Without a Cause*, and *The Court-Martial of Billy Mitchell*, as well as films that were shelved. By now, Gideon has become a "hard drinking libertine" despite still being married, a reflection of his intense fear of being alone ("Gideon's Childhood," 21). But Hollywood saves the day: Gideon is invited to write a western. *Gunfight at the O.K. Corral* is the result, although in the outline it is called *The Gringo*.

Next, an overdramatized scene sees Gideon reject the blandishments of fame in favor of going to Israel to "resolve his pent up Jewish fury" ("Gideon's Childhood," 24). Details drawn from Uris's experience of writing *Exodus*, retitled *The*

Galilee in the outline, are next, including a femme fatale named Natasha, from Hungary. Gideon finally leaves the country, returning to America to write his novel. References to Otto Preminger and his brother Ingo, the agent, now appear. Chronology jumps about, but Gideon's dislike of "Bruno Ludwig," the Preminger character, also called "The Prussian," stays constant. Uris recounts how his fear of MGM turning down the option on *Exodus* (it was too critical of the British to get released in England) led him to press Ingo into securing the option for his brother.

The outline of what would become *Mitla Pass* combines autobiographical fancy with a skeleton plot based on events in Uris's life. The comments he offers, however, reflect his thoughts on various matters, and the document is helpful for understanding his outlook in the mid-1980s. McCormick, however, wanted Uris to fictionalize more, disguising the actual people more thoroughly.[14] And "the long war" with his father needed to be better integrated with the story.

MITLA PASS, A THINLY DISGUISED AUTOBIOGRAPHY

By December 1986, Schlosberg had negotiated a new payment arrangement. Doubleday would provide Uris with $250,000 in the first week of January 1987, and then another $550,000 in payments by 10 September 1987. These amounts were to be charged against a 28 June 1982 contract for "Lullaby" and a second title, now due on 31 July 1992. The deadline for "Lullaby" was extended until 31 December 1987. The full amount Uris was to receive from the June 1982 contract was $1.4 million. The second book mentioned would be further delayed until 1994, to be published in 1995 as *Redemption*, a sequel to *Trinity*.

Composing *Mitla Pass* was difficult: "Writing the book was the most painful experience of my life," he said later in an interview.[15] Previously when he would go into his office, "a book would just sort of begin writing itself" on his typewriter. Not so with *Mitla Pass*. But, he added, "at a certain point, I stopped fighting this book. After 60 years I finally stopped fighting this book and a funny thing happened. You can call it manic depression or whatever but I'd go into fits as in pure ecstasy while I was writing." He then cites Faulkner as an authority for the idea that the resolution of fear is the greatest challenge for any writer: "You're dealing with your fears or other peoples fears all day long. You're going into dark rooms that other people stay away from, because you're a writer." A writer has to absorb pain in order to enter these other worlds, and "if you're a Jew, it seems you have to face the history of the world all over again, everyday." Gideon's grandfather tells this to his father daily, and it becomes a message repeated throughout the novel and the rest of Uris's later works (*MP*, 185).

In published form, *Mitla Pass* differs from Uris's extensive outline, although it keeps the broad autobiographical elements and romanticized adventures. In fact, the generally poor reception of the novel was due to the exaggerated story of Gideon Zadok, who was a hero, lover, and superman, both on the battlefield and in the bedroom. Critical responses ranged from quasi approval, "imaginative fodder for the mind at rest," to the claim that the novel was yet another demonstration of how Uris could personalize history and make it immediate.[16] But the difficulty for many readers was that Uris could not decide whether he was writing a war story, a family saga, or a case history, and so his prose style veered between the breathless and the reportorial. Stereotypes stand in for character. Roger Jaynes, writing in the *Milwaukee Journal*, complained that there were too many stories: Uris should have limited it to Gideon and Val.[17] Nevertheless, at its release on 6 November 1988, *Mitla Pass* debuted at number eleven on the *New York Times* best-seller list. Anne Rice was first, with *The Queen of the Damned*, and James Michener's *Alaska* was sixth, still on the list after nineteen weeks.

One of the themes that Uris wanted to explore again in the novel was that of the Jewish hero, tough, unflinching, and resolute. He had defined such heroes with Ari Ben Canaan in *Exodus* and the fictionalized real heroes in *Mila 18*. He thought of himself that way in *QB VII*, but he was still plagued by the perception of the Jew as weak. Faulkner, one of Uris's heroes, offered a psychological insight that was applicable to this aspect of Uris's character. In a letter to his stepson, Faulkner wrote, "It is a strange thing how a man, no matter how intelligent, will cling to the public proof of his masculinity: his courage and endurance, his willingness to sacrifice himself for the land which shaped his ancestors."[18]

In *Mitla Pass*, Uris again addresses the stereotype of the miserly, withdrawn, fearful Jew. In the novel, Hannah Balaban, of Baltimore, explains that for some two thousand years, Jewish men suffered "nothing but humiliations and defeats," having lived through pogroms and massacres without being able to defend their families (*MP*, 258). The persistent anti-Semitism in the old country gave them no opportunity to resist. The situation crushed their manliness, causing Jewish men to hide inside their religion. Cowardice crushed them and left them with no release for their frustration—except in the family: "If you have no country to fight for, you have no heroes to copy" (*MP*, 258–259). Becoming a Jewish fighter was the only answer to such a history of defeat.

In a 1989 interview, Uris expanded on the frustration of the Jewish men who were robbed of their self-esteem by the harshness of shtetl life and the strict, uncompromising discipline of the Talmudic schools.[19] Many reacted by taking out their frustrations on their families. As a result, wife beating was common, and many men deserted their families. He said that in New York in the early twentieth century there were more than 25,000 cases of desertion by husbands on the Lower East Side (most of them Jewish, presumably). But this was not only a Jewish problem: the subjugated often take out their aggression on someone weaker in the family. Men become angry but lose their efficacy at home. A similar situation existed in Ireland, resulting in women's emergence as figures of strength in the family. Uris suggests that similarities exist between Jewish, Irish, and black women in this regard.

Uris rejected the idea of a Jewish coward. In the post-Holocaust world, Jewish heroes reign, larger-than-life figures like Shlomo Ben Asher, the warrior leader of the Lion Battalion in *Mitla Pass*. But Gideon, a marine who lived through Tarawa, as Uris did, and who tries to be a hero, has a dark secret. The source of his anger and behavior is not the abuse from his father or his difficult upbringing, but an event in the war that revealed him to be a Jewish coward, not a hero.

On Tarawa, his aide was hit by gunfire after getting a radio message out. A captain and corporal rushed to help him, but they, too, were shot. Gideon froze, failing to help any of the three men, an act counter to the marine principle of *Semper Fidelis* (MP, 426–427). This secret, he believes, makes him a fake, as he tells Natasha, his mistress, late in the novel. But she insists he was a hero anyway: he could not have helped the dead Pedro, but he stayed on the generator to ensure that the message got out. She convinces him to give up his guilt, just as he had earlier advised her that "you can't be guilty because you lost everyone in the gas chamber" (MP, 428).

In many ways, *Mitla Pass*, though flawed, was a necessary book for Uris to write, a project undertaken at a time of intense self-scrutiny and upheaval. He no longer had to prove to others the value of what he did, but he had to prove things to himself. And because he could not free himself from past grievances, *Mitla Pass*, even if it was a literary tangle, was an important personal effort.

One self-conscious way Uris enhanced the literary importance of the novel (and himself) was to incorporate references to other writers. Uris begins with his hero, Steinbeck. He mentions *Tortilla Flat*, one of Uris's earliest reading experiences, as well as *In Dubious Battle*. Other early influences cited in the book are Jack London, Hemingway, and Eugene O'Neill (MP, 350–351, 343). Hemingway, perhaps the epitome for Uris of the romantic writer–war hero–author, appears in the book when Gideon's youthful English teacher goes off to be a pilot in the Spanish Civil War and reports having met the American writer in Madrid, where he interviewed her for a story. In an ironic aside, Uris has the woman comment that whenever another person is with Hemingway, "he has to put on a show of his bravado. He has created an image that sometimes makes him as a person larger than his writings" (MP, 367). Deep down, he is probably quite insecure, she adds. This could be Uris commenting on himself. To solidify his identification with Hemingway, Uris has him pen a letter to the young Gideon, telling him that writing "a novel takes the courage of a marathon runner" (MP, 367; the language of the letter is too formal to be Hemingway's).

Faulkner enters indirectly when Gideon discovers that he is using Faulkner's office in the writers' compound at a movie studio—as Uris had done when he began his screenwriting career at Warner Bros. A conversation with Faulkner's former secretary reaffirms Zadok's (and Uris's) admiration of his work (MP, 78–79). The dilemma of remaining a novelist in the face of the money offered by the movies is one of the early themes of the novel, but Uris is realistic: "This town [Hollywood] is stacked against the writers" (MP, 84). A collateral theme is that a writer can write successfully only if he is angry. Writers have to be mad to write well. The price of being a writer is high: "Everyone's blood ends up hidden in the pages" (MP, 349, 28).

The autobiographical element of *Mitla Pass* surpasses the fictional, especially in the hero's resentments, anger, and guilt. One notable incident from Uris's youth is prominent because it reminded him of repeated parental denials. In the novel, it takes the form of a letter from Nathan to his son Gideon (dated 10 March 1940), with this classic opening: "Finally I received from you a letter after a week of an empty mailbox. Do you know what that can do to a father, especially a sensitive, loving father like myself?" (MP, 138). He then goes on to explain that his son's request for a tux—he at first didn't know what one was, because "all my friends are working people who likewise have no knowledge of a T-U-X"—cannot be honored. Did his son want to become a hotel porter or a servant for a millionaire family or work in a nightclub? "For what purpose do you strive for a T-U-X? To become a Charlie McCarthy dummy?" (MP, 138–139). Or is it, writes the father, because "you are intending to go every night to a party"? (MP, 139). As a father, he works hard for what his son wants, but "the tux alone is not the end of it but the beginning. With a tux you will be asking for more money to go with girls to those places where a tux is required" (MP, 139). The father begs Gideon not to ruin himself with such clothes. The incident was one Uris could not forget.

The trope of the western also runs throughout the novel. The genre and its expectations remain part of the story, from Gideon's introducing himself as a cowboy to the costume party late in the novel, which he attends dressed as a cowboy. Even later, as Gideon recovers from the battle of Mitla Pass, Natasha greets him with the words "I love mean little five-foot-eight, Jew, cowboy, writers" (MP, 421; Uris was five-nine). Mitla Pass itself is called "Apache country" (MP, 137). The loneliness of the writer was an extension of the heroic loneliness of the cowboy, fighting evil on the prairie.

When asked in October 1990 to name the most influential books he had read, Uris answered with four titles by John Steinbeck. He added, "Knowing that one is not alone in the world and shares the same fears as everyone else, can be imparted to you by great writers."[20] In *Mitla Pass*, the writer-hero Gideon Zadok tells a teacher he wants to be a writer because "writers know when a person is lonely" (*MP*, 349). And when citing other books that made an early impact on him, Uris celebrates Michael Gold's *Jews without Money* because it deals with individual suffering in an urban Jewish family.[21]

"The resolution of fear is one of the writer's greatest reasons for being," Gideon says in *Mitla Pass* (*MP*, 80). Uris faced many fears in his life, from the fear of failure (his father constantly reminded him of this danger) to the fear of lacking courage. But what he feared most was loneliness, which troubled Uris throughout his life, even though he chose a profession in which loneliness was necessary. At the same time, he desperately needed companionship, which he often found through marriage. The constant companionship of Jill Uris in particular—not only did they travel and write together but they shared domestic duties—speaks to how he combated loneliness. Yet he spoiled those marriages by fighting against the intimacy they required. At the core of Uris's insecurity, masked by his narcissistic behavior, temper, aggressiveness, and self-confidence, was a gnawing fear of loneliness, which may have been initiated by the early divorce of his parents and his constant shuttling (often alone) between Baltimore, Norfolk, and Philadelphia as an adolescent and teenager. Correspondingly, his lifelong identification as a marine, and the pride that instilled in him, originated in the comradeship, brotherhood, and unity that the marines upheld at any cost. *Semper Fidelis* became an ideology, as well as a motto, for what Uris sought throughout his entire life.

As a writer, Uris repeatedly needed to prove that he was a success. His best sellers, works that gained him immense public approval, lucrative contracts, and steady royalties, deal with overcoming failure. And he demonstrated the same kind of courage as his characters, whether in a crisis he survived (the fighting in the Pacific), an experience he sought out (going on desert patrols in Israel), or a challenge he met head on (a potentially ruinous libel trial).

Uris also transposed the idea of loneliness to a country and a culture. Israel, both in *Exodus* and *Mitla Pass*, is constantly presented as isolated, lacking the support of the world powers. In the novel, when the Anglo-French forces attack the Suez Canal, and Jordan and Syria appear to form an alliance to aid Egypt's response to Israel, the Israelis again understood that they must defend themselves without help (*MP*, 409). Its citizens and soldiers are shown to be cut off, and they must turn to a variety of strategies to overcome such isolation.

Uris's need for absolute moral clarity, demonstrated by his characters but tested in his life, is another expression of his fear of loneliness. He thought that to know what was right and to fight for it would provide insurance against the ambiguities and confusions of life while insulating him. Such objectivity was both his strength and weakness in the construction of character. On one hand, his heroes are unmistakable, as are his villains, but they can also appear simplistic and one-dimensional.

For Uris, to be a writer is to "prove you can bear your loneliness," the publication of every novel another sign of success (*MP*, 89). Uris constantly tested himself, pushing the barrier of loneliness by seeking assurances that he was loved by his readers. Strong sales were the simplest measure—not reviews, which he increasingly dismissed. When *Exodus* finally became number one on the *New York Times* best-seller list on 17 May 1959, more than nine months after its publication, Uris had at last objective proof that he was admired and respected. But the paradox remained. As Gideon explains, although he became a writer "so that [he] could work alone," he needed constant affirmations that he was loved and rejected any action that might, in fact, isolate him (*MP*, 82).

In *Mitla Pass*, Gideon asks his father to recognize him for what he has accomplished and to welcome him for it, knowing that the "conquest of loneliness was the missing link that was, one day, going to make a decent novelist out of me" (*MP*, 100). Not surprisingly, perhaps, Uris would later explain that parents form the attitudes of a writer, the act of writing being a constant search for approval and the replacement of loneliness with love. The motivation to write could come "from the normal human urge to win acclaim. But more than likely, the drive to write is simply to make our mother and father love us."[22] Poignantly, he added: "There comes that awesome day in all of our lives when we realize for the first time that our parents are not infallible and that our relationships with them are flawed. How often is it that we must spend the second half of our lives trying to get over the first half?"

In September 1989, a statement made during his divorce proceedings reiterated the "the awesome fears and loneliness demanded of the [writing] profession."[23] Uris never overcame this anxiety. The statement also details his financial crises and the pressure to produce works that will earn money. He gives speeches to "keep out of debt," lives off royalties from past works, and is "fearful" about future earnings.

THE CRITICS ARE AGAIN UNKIND

Reviews of *Mitla Pass* overseas were less kind than those in North America. Doubleday UK launched a new line with *Mitla Pass* (Uris had formerly published with William Kimber). Critics, however, were candid. The reviewer in the *Sunday Times* referred to the wretched writing, hackneyed plot, and tortuous themes. No character engenders empathy. The reviewer also noted that since Priscilla

Higham did the research, she, too, should be blamed, since the research was manhandled in the leaden saga. Because Uris's name was clearly placed above the title, his "presence" took precedence over any story. The only thing that could be honestly praised was the clear type.[24]

In an interview with Uris for an Edinburgh newspaper, Julie Cockcroft observed that "Jewish grief is Leon Uris's trademark."[25] At one point, Uris said that he was going to write a book set on the Mexican border, but with two young children, he felt "a bit old for border hopping." In the States, he added, reaction to the book focused on his sexist presentation of women, the result of the current war between the sexes. He then referred to his 1982 surgery and how he had spent the night before enjoying a good binge in "real Hemingway style." Later, when crossing a Denver street, he asked himself if he could change places with anyone in the world, who would that be? "Nobody."

Writing the novel renewed Uris's persistent and proud view of himself as a marine. This took on visible form on 1 July 1988, when he spoke at the dedication of the Tarawa Monument at Long Beach, California. He opened the speech with "Fellow Marines and Fellow Americans" and spoke of his honor in representing his "buddies on this hallowed occasion."[26] A quick and self-mocking summary of his education preceded a retelling of his marine experiences on Tarawa. He identified himself as "neither hero or coward," but someone who had been able to do what was expected of him. He was in the last reserve battalion, which drew few casualties as it chased the remaining Japanese garrison across the small linked islands. After coming down with dengue fever, he was sent home; afterward, his group, the Second Battalion of the Sixth Marines, was "cut to pieces on Red Beach on Saipan." He was filled with remorse for not being there.

For Uris, writing *Mitla Pass* was a necessary kind of writing out of his life, an engagement with the past that he had long avoided. His difficulties with Jill, as much as his monitoring of his past through his review of correspondence, prompted this reencounter. But where would he go after its appearance, personally and professionally? His immediate plan was to visit the Soviet Union. His next novel would again take him to his past—his literary past. He would revisit the world of *Trinity* and, in *Redemption*, take it forward into early twentieth-century New Zealand. But before he went anywhere, he had to face a divorce.

THE END OF A THIRD MARRIAGE

The period between *The Haj* and *Mitla Pass* was a stressful time in Uris's relationship with Jill. The effort to have children constantly upset the romantic energy that had defined their marriage since 1970. A series of miscarriages beginning in

March 1983 undermined their relationship. Jill needed bed rest and was less active, although Uris was at first keen to adapt to the new situation. In 1983, he told Ken McCormick and Sam Vaughan about her happy pregnant state, her eagerness to "help me through the next couple of novels," and the possibility of a new joint project.[27] An addition to their house was also underway. A trip to Jamaica was planned, and there was the possibility of using that experience as material for a future novel and a photography book. Work on *The Haj* continued, and he began to see its structure more clearly.

Jill, however, gradually became unhappy over the distance that was growing between the two, brought about not only by her restricted activity but also by less than loyal behavior on Uris's part. This in turn led to disloyalty on Jill's part, beginning in 1984. In December 1987, she told Uris about an affair that had gone on for some time several years earlier. During the rather difficult divorce proceedings that would follow, she acknowledged having had another relationship in 1987, which led to further anger. Such knowledge incensed Uris, although he himself was not a stranger to such behavior.

Their relationship deteriorated, each accusing the other of angry responses and constant misunderstandings. As Jill put it in a bitter letter: "Whenever my thoughts run counter to yours and things aren't going your way, you resort to angry name calling and lashing outbursts." Having admitted her guilt, she expected some reconciliation. But "when I say things that don't fit your script, you seem to take this as an attack . . . Revenge and hatred have not left you."[28]

The growing estrangement took a toll on both of them. Jill tried to grapple with the hurt and outbursts, admitting that when they argued, she seemed to want "to force you into being my daddy and if I cry loud enough you'll love me again."[29] But she also believed that she was strong enough to come out of this struggle more mature. For his part, Uris felt betrayed. In his mind, she had cheated on him, and he was not going to relent, even if it meant the end of his family and a financial crisis: "It takes two people to trash a marriage. I am very sad, but things just don't seem mendable."[30] Jill resented his attitude.

A ten-page letter from Uris to his lawyers in the fall of 1988 highlights their antagonism, itemizing past and present grievances and difficulties.[31] In it, he vents his hurt at her undoing of their marriage yet celebrates his impending liberation. The letter formalizes his decision to seek a divorce, partly recalling his divorce from Betty, which took almost six weeks in court. He felt particularly protective of his children: "These children are what is really left of my life." Although he felt that time was growing short, he was ready to take on New York, where he has now moved: "I tried to whip it twenty years ago and fell flat on my ass . . . so I've got a score to settle and man, I'm ready."

But money had become an even bigger problem, since neither seemed to be too concerned about saving. When asked in May 1989 at the divorce hearing what would be an appropriate budget for the Urises, given their lifestyle, Schlosberg said that if they had $10 million a year, they would spend it: "They adjusted their lifestyle to the amount of money that comes in."[32] Uris always traveled first-class, but as a result of his separation and the poor reception of his current work, his "earning capacity has plummeted from moderate wealth to attempting to keep even." Questions about his health led Uris to admit that "given the emotional Auschwitz I have undergone in the last twenty months, [there was] a distinct possibility" that his health would collapse.[33]

Uris filed for divorce in November 1988 and anticipated a need for extra money. He then asked Schlosberg to attempt to negotiate a new contract, with a new advance, from Doubleday. But the publisher was hesitant, aware of how the distraction of a divorce could interfere with the completion of a new set of novels (Uris's contracts were always for two or three new works). Additionally, Uris thought *Mitla Pass* would shoot to number one. It didn't; in fact, it hardly came close, which restricted Schlosberg's ability to ask for a revised contract and more money. In addition, Uris also still owed Doubleday a book, a commitment from his *Mitla Pass* contract. The last of the $350,000 payments related to *Mitla Pass* had been distributed by January 1989. There was no more money, new or old, available.

Uris had, in fact, begun work on the second proposed novel in his *Mitla Pass* contract, an immigrant narrative about Jewish families on the Lower East Side of New York. Their histories and European background would be the focus. After two months of research, however, his editor, likely Ken McCormick, convinced him that the topic was worn out. They decided on a new subject: the Chinese of New York. This would not be a *Good Earth* type of story, but one about "Chinese people and the American Chinese here and their roots back in China."[34] Various organizations in Chinatown in Manhattan were already doing research for Uris, who had also gone to Boston to meet with communities there and was supposedly preparing a trip to China. His assistant, Priscilla Higham, was currently doing additional research. But distracting him at this time was the possibility of a Broadway play based on *Trinity*.

His divorce proceedings disclosed a great deal of financial information, since Uris was seeking joint custody of Rachael and Conor. Various threats and counterthreats were made as the acrimony increased: at one point, Uris succeeded in having Jill undergo a urine test for cocaine; the results were negative, although an initial mix-up had suggested the reverse, which Uris thought he could leverage. Similarly, while he was prepared to pay for her health coverage, he would not pay for any psychiatric treatment. The Red Mountain home was also now for sale.

The case dragged on through the summer of 1989, and when Uris responded

to written questions from Jill's lawyers, he was candid, even if slightly overdra-
matic, about his financial status: "Over the past two years my financial structure
has virtually been destroyed and I anticipate a drastic drop of income due to
my inability to resume my career as a novelist for the foreseeable future."[35] He
cited the abnormal expense of keeping his family in their Aspen home after he
relocated to New York City in 1988 and then to Shelter Island, off New York, in
May 1989. He also kept an office in New York City, which was necessary if he
were "to resume any kind of writing activity at all."

Uris also outlined the state of his health, which was alarming: high blood
pressure, asthma, arthritis, dental problems, sleep apnea, lower back problems,
ongoing residual pain and swelling, and immobility from knee surgery. He also
had occasional attacks of gout. He claimed he could not be fully self-supporting,
citing almost no income, although he had received $10,000 as an advance for a
stage adaptation of *Trinity*, but that would not be ready for Broadway until 1992.
The only extra money he earned came from making speeches. He recounted their
first separation—six weeks, beginning on 20 February 1988—and acknowledged
that Jill was entitled to half the money earned during their marriage, but not to
anything from contracts before or after their marriage. He admits that she twice
contributed to the acquisition of property adjacent to their Red Mountain home:
the first lot cost $25,000 and a second cost $50,000, of which Jill paid $16,000.
The listing agreement to sell the house was dated 9 December 1988. Price:
$2.6 million.

Uris tried to explain the financial burden of being a popular writer. He added
that at the start of his career, he had actively participated in his financial affairs.
But he soon realized that writing and finance did not mix, especially as his income
sources became more complex (foreign contracts, film options, etc.). Financial
meetings distressed him, broke his concentration, and detracted from his work:
"Oftentimes after a financial session, I would be unable to write for several days."[36]
From the mid-1950s on, he turned to an accountant, lawyer, or literary agent, and
soon Herb Schlosberg played all three roles, and Jill oversaw all their personal
finances. But his current financial situation was dire. One document from the
divorce hearing shows that from 1968 to 1988, his total sales, including those of
Mitla Pass, of all his books, films, and lectures produced an income of $6,136,035.
The amount from his books written before his marriage to Jill in 1970 exceeded
$2.3 million.

For Uris, the truth of narrative, especially his own, ruled. His researched stories
had to be accepted as reliable, and he believed that others should accept even the
story he told of himself. Similarly, he believed his appeal and dominance over
women should be unquestioned. Hence, his anger when they disobeyed him or
left; even shooting themselves was no excuse. Uris believed his own story, even

when opposed by fact. Unwilling (or unable) to admit his own weaknesses, he remained arrogant, stubborn, and abrasive.

Supporting himself now also meant supporting his children, but he worried about whether he could do this in the future or even depend on past royalties. He worried about his age—he was sixty-five—and his deteriorating health: "After half a century of work, I am tired and tired of carrying other people on my back ... yet in the twilight of my life and career, I am facing a financial disaster that is going to force me to work."[37] Allowing for a degree of overstatement, Uris was offering an objective assessment of the state of a popular writer no longer popular. Expectations from his publisher and reading public were high, but his productivity was flagging. He also offered a somewhat self-serving evaluation of himself as a popular American novelist: "Of all the major writers out of the second World War, only myself, Herman Wouk and Michener have survived in America and Wouk no longer writes and Michener, at last report, is gravely ill."[38]

In a draft will of October 1989, he left Priscilla Higham $25,000, established a trust for his children, with Rachael and Conor getting the bulk of it, and left nothing to Jill. She did, however, receive a portion of the proceeds of the sale of 5 Wrights Road, Red Mountain, which brought $2 million. A condo in Denver also had to be sold. Their marriage officially and legally ended on 2 January 1990, a formal separation agreement entered in the court on 14 December 1989 remaining as a guide.

MANHATTAN AND SHELTER ISLAND

Looking back on this period and his move east, Uris later said, "I do everything bass-ackwards. I lived in the mountains for 25 years and came to retire in New York City, which is not the way you do it."[39] Uris moved to New York in the spring of 1988 to get away from Aspen and find stimulation for a new work, his separation from Jill becoming official by 7 October that year. He first moved into the Surrey, an uptown, East Side hotel at 20 East 70th Street. New York, he says, "is gritty, but, by God it's LIFE and I'm so alive I can't believe it."[40] Aspen had become "a graveyard of bitter memories." After five months, he rented an apartment near Lincoln Center at South Park Tower, 124 West 60th Street, apartment 28E (he later moved to 44D), and then rented a house on Shelter Island at the end of Long Island.

He first visited this small island, which is protected by the North and South forks of Long Island and was settled by the English in 1652, at the invitation of Bill Reily, one of the producers of the proposed Broadway version of *Trinity*. Reily owned a vacation home there, and the setting and isolation appealed to

Uris. For a year, he tried to live in both Manhattan and Shelter Island. He was unsure about settling in Manhattan (in a larger apartment), and Shelter Island might work best as a weekend getaway. He also wanted to keep the Denver condo and share it with Jill. He could return there if life on the East Coast didn't work out.

In the end, he decided in favor of the isolation and rural life of Shelter Island, converting his lease of the modest but modern home that backed onto Chase Creek into a purchase in April 1990. The moves to New York and Shelter Island, however, worried Jill: she felt he was spending all their money. A year earlier, he had blamed her for spending too much, reminding her of his "fears of being alone and particularly in New York hotels. Yes, I took a nice east side apartment [a suite at the Surrey Hotel] when I came here. I needed it to get through my nightmare."[41] He claims to be reducing his expenses, moving to a smaller West Side apartment and taking a house on Shelter Island at the tip of Long Island— he needed "sanctuary." He had taken on "piles of extra work to hold up my end." Regarding an impending trip to Ireland, England, and the Soviet Union, he made it clear he was being sponsored by B'nai B'rith International. Finally, resentment mixed with indignation overcame him: "You'll get what is yours but you're not going to be rewarded for what you did to me and our children."

In the course of the acrimonious breakup, Jill brought up Uris's past: "Remember the feeling you used to get when there was a letter from your father? That's the feeling I now feel when I see your stationery. The needles, sarcasm, and self pity are recognizable."[42] She added, "I only pray that some day you will take responsibility for your own life and cease blaming me and your mother for your unhappiness." Eight months later, she complained that he continually attempted to make her feel guilty for causing him pain: "I don't buy that . . . Your self pity is evident and I pity you for that. When you choose to let go of the blame, I will gladly let go of responding."[43] Uris always deflected her efforts at informal psychoanalysis; he just went for a complete break. During the worst part of the breakup, he told a friend that when he had recently seen Jill in New London, Connecticut, and then at LaGuardia Airport, "it was the final step in my liberation because I realized I never wanted to see her or touch her again."[44]

An Aspen lawyer, Andy Hecht, who knew Uris well, offered a different view of their breakup. Uris put the attractive and youthful Jill on a pedestal (as he did with most women); it reflected well on him that he had improved her, helping her with her career and reputation.[45] When she disobeyed or became disloyal, he resented it. When she had an affair, a symptom of their unraveling relationship (drugs, sex, and drinking were inadequate panaceas), Uris felt betrayed. He was deeply angered by such deception because he believed no one should ever question or leave him.

One New York expense Uris did not mention in any of his statements was his attractive research assistant, Priscilla Higham. Originally from South Africa, Higham had worked for him in Aspen and accepted his invitation to continue in New York. She soon became invaluable, assisting him with research on the proposed Lower East Side novel, the Chinese American novel, and, finally, what became *Redemption.*

Life in New York mixed mirth with melancholy. An incident with a black prostitute put him temporarily in the hospital (she did not respond well to his overly aggressive acts, he proudly explained to his son Mark on the phone from the emergency room). A feeling of loss from being cut off from his family brought unhappiness. Riding around Manhattan in his large Chrysler, which he had driven from Aspen, emphasized his awkward adjustment. But when women began to contact him, unaware that Priscilla Higham and another assistant had (on a bet) placed ads in *New York Magazine*'s personal columns, he found it flattering.[46]

Nonetheless, in the midst of his personal upheaval, he managed to think about literature. In an interview conducted at his New York apartment, he was asked whether there were any tricks of the trade he could reveal. He answered, "Know what your curtain line is."[47] A writer should always know where he was going in his novel, geographically and thematically: "That is the major flaw in most plays and writing, that you start out with a good idea and somewhere in the middle of the sea the writer gets lost. Knowing before you go in what your curtain line is, would be the major trick to writing."

BEHIND THE IRON CURTAIN

As a distraction from his personal problems, Uris accepted an invitation from B'nai B'rith International to participate in a trip to the Soviet Union in October 1989. He invited his half-sister Essie and her husband to accompany him. Michael Neiditch, of B'nai B'rith, and Priscilla Higham would also join him.

Before he left, Uris noted a report that a Hungarian publisher was planning to print 100,000 copies of *Exodus*, the first translation of the novel to appear behind the Iron Curtain. He planned to visit Budapest after the Soviet Union. Uris was almost a mythic figure to Eastern European Jews, but confusion over his identity persisted. The book jacket of the Hungarian-language *Exodus* identified Uris as an Irish Catholic, the mix-up a result of his success with *Trinity*. Nonetheless, the largest Jewish minority in Eastern Europe was eager to read *Exodus* in Hungarian.[48]

Uris began his trip on 10 October 1989, flying Finnair to Helsinki, where he was met by his Finnish publisher, Pekka Salojarvi, and the Israeli ambassador,

Asher Naim. He held a press conference at the airport, and by the evening, he had done interviews with every print outlet and television station in Finland. Reindeer and venison were featured at a dinner in his honor. The next day began with a visit to Stockmann, Finland's largest bookstore; one woman left with four signed copies of his work. In an interview with a Swedish newspaper during his stay, he played up his aggressive attitude, stating, "I am something of a hawk. I am not a diplomat," and remarked that his next novel would deal with immigration and New York.[49]

He and the others took the train from Helsinki to Leningrad, crossed the border without incident, and arrived at the Hotel Moskva, "grey, monstrous, bleak," with "greenish yellow lights in the hallways," as Priscilla Higham noted in "USSR," an informal record of the trip.[50] The Soviet Union was not welcoming, and Uris and his party were constantly watched by supposed key ladies in the hallways. The next morning there was a tour to see the graves of Dostoevsky, Tchaikovsky, and Pushkin, but Uris did not go. That evening, the group met two refuseniks for dinner, but there were "bad vibes" ("USSR," 1). The B'nai B'rith event was located far from the center of the city, and only about forty people attended, all "sad, dejected and dispirited" ("USSR," 1). The next day, 14 October 1989, there was a city tour led by a student from Leningrad State University who had read *Armageddon*. At noon, they had drinks with the U.S. consul general. Lunch followed, but during the afternoon, Priscilla's suitcase was stolen. That afternoon, the police moved a meeting of the Leningrad Jewish Cultural Association from a hall seating five hundred to one holding only fifty. Fear of disruptions by Pamyat, an ultranationalist group, was the reason given.

The next day, Sunday, they flew to Riga, the capital of Latvia. The Hotel Latvia was bright and relatively comfortable; its restaurant boasted a long menu, but there were only two items in stock: chicken and fish ("USSR," 1). Uris and Neiditch then got calls from some women, and Uris decided to go for a massage, believing the woman was a prostitute. He was mistaken: he returned with several dark bruises and a welt on his arm, which were unrelated to a massage. She got tough with him when he disobeyed a prominent sign reading "Do Not Touch."[51] That evening, they met with four hundred Jews in the Hall of the Communist Party, the hammer and sickle in gold above the stage. This was a relaxed audience, which gave Uris roses and a strong reception to this speech. There were also many copies of *Exodus*, in all shapes and sizes, to sign.

His Riga speech (15 October 1989) is autobiographically revealing for its shifting of earlier emphases.[52] He begins with his family's political background. In Baltimore, where he was born, there were active communist or workman's circles, which were left-wing organizations. He claimed to have been involved with the Young Pioneers and in training to be a young communist, the only group in the country then fighting for the rights of the blacks and the underprivileged. They picketed against the arrival of German ships and opposed fascism, but being an American, he never fully embraced communism. Two brothers, friends of his, (Joe and Sam Brockman) died as volunteers in the International Brigade during the Spanish Civil War, which posed a dilemma for him, since America did not support Loyalist Spain. At the beginning of the Second World War, he was not strongly supportive of U.S. involvement in the conflict, but Pearl Harbor changed all that.

He enlisted in the marines, noting the small number of Jews in the corps: out of eight hundred in his battalion, there were no more than half a dozen. Although isolated, they never suffered violent anti-Semitism. He was accepted as a marine but not always as a Jew, although he kept quiet about it. Because he had not been bar mitzvahed, his Jewishness did not really mean much to him, except during his four years in the marines. The day he became a Jew was when he learned about the Holocaust, which had "the most damaging, long lasting impact on my life" ("Riga," 2).

After a summary of his career as a Hollywood screenwriter and a potted history of his time in Israel, he stressed how he returned home broke, but a new contract enabled him to write *Exodus*. The success of the book, he said, was due to its unprecedented story and because it "broke a 2,000 year misconception that Jews would not fight" ("Riga," 2).

He recalled the story of Moshe Sharett's son, Yaacov (Sharett the second prime minister of Israel), who was the Israeli consul general in Leningrad and who left a copy of *Exodus* with a Jewish family; that may have started the entire samizdat craze for the novel, which was copied clandestinely throughout the country ("Riga," 3). Stories emerged of many who had found their Jewishness through *Exodus, Mila 18*, and then *QB VII*. He continued to write about the Holocaust, but allowed himself to turn to other subjects, although his writing always confirmed his Jewishness. He then cited a comment of Jill's after her conversion to Judaism: "I don't feel any different." Uris answered: "Don't worry, sooner or later someone will come up to you and call you a dirty Jew and you'll know you're Jewish" ("Riga," 3). He concluded with a celebration of the feeling of being a part of a worldwide Jewish community and of knowing that after having been denied entry into the Soviet Union for twenty years, he was there now, and it was "one of the proudest moment[s] of his life" ("Riga," 4).

The next day the party toured Riga and saw the Star of David Monument in a park, the only Jewish monument in the USSR. But the pressure of politics and coercion hounded Uris and his group. They were told that their flight the next day had been cancelled and that they would have to leave earlier, which prevented him from giving an interview on Riga Television. They were surprised—the more so when they later found out the flight had departed on time. Nonetheless, that night Uris spoke to five hundred people.

On 17 October, they flew from Riga to Moscow, arriving at a filthy and crowded airport. They proceeded to the new Savoy Hotel, which had been open only a week and was a mere ten-minute walk from Red Square. But there was confusion over Uris's reservation, and he threatened to take his party elsewhere unless the suite he had reserved was located. The protest succeeded (with help from Neiditch and Higham). Within fifteen minutes, he had his rooms ("USSR," 2).

A meeting with the heads of Jewish organizations in Moscow took up the next morning, and representatives of the U.S. embassy came by, including, at one point, Ambassador Jack Matlock (ambassador from 1987 to 1991). At seven that night, Uris spoke at the Shalom Theatre, which was forty-five minutes from the city center, to a friendly and large audience, but they were not prosperous like the Latvians. Uris was presented with a samizdat translation of *Exodus*, which became one of his most prized possessions. On Friday, 20 October, Uris had lunch with Ann Blackman of *Time* and her husband, Mike Putzer, who was chief of the Associated Press bureau. She spoke about the fear that the USSR might be on the brink of starvation. Later that day, Uris was interviewed by Walter Ruby of the *Jerusalem Post*.

In the Kremlin Armoury on the 21st, Uris saw the jewels and gifts of the tsars. And at six that night, he attended the Simchat Torah celebration at the Moscow Choral Synagogue. There was great excitement in the crowd of several thousand over Uris's presence, and he was repeatedly urged to dance with the Torah. He was reluctant, but Mrs. Joseph (Connie) Schmuckler, an active promoter of the tour, shouted, "Just because you didn't write it, doesn't mean you can't carry it!"[53] After he did, he was besieged by the crowd. Later, after dinner at the Savoy, Uris was visited by the Israeli liaison team, which was housed in the Dutch embassy. Part of his reason for visiting Moscow was also to see about an official Russian-language translation of *Exodus*. Twenty years earlier, Connie Schmuckler reported, she had secretly carried in copies of the novel ("USSR," 3).

A final event on the tour was a showing of *Gun Fight at the O.K. Corral* at the House of Cinema (Dom Kino) in Moscow before an audience of "Soviet cinematographers, screenwriters and Russian friends of the American western."[54] To get a print, Neiditch had had to give assurances that Uris would personally carry the print from the United States Information Agency office to the screening and then return it. Paramount was concerned about piracy. Uris would also speak to the audience on the topic of "the American Western and Hollywood."[55] The screening went ahead on 22 October, but Uris and his party had to miss it in order to catch a three o'clock flight to Copenhagen.

Michael Neiditch, who at the time was the associate international director for program services and director of education for B'nai B'rith International, published his own account of the trip in the Israeli paper *Ha'aretz*.[56] Stressing the efforts of Mikhail Gorbachev to reform Soviet society, Neiditch records how the Soviet fabric was tearing in the midst of nationalist movements, and the Soviet Jews were caught in the middle. He expressed apprehension over the rise of anti-Semitism. Little glasnost (openness) was evident in the cultural lives of the Jews of Leningrad and Moscow. He reports the sudden cancellation of the hall for five hundred in Leningrad, which was intended to send a clear message to Jews: don't come to hear Uris. Similarly, he recounts the fiasco of the cancelled television interview in Riga as a form of Soviet pressure.

One of major events Neiditch recounts was a lecture by Uris in Moscow at the Michoels Center, a Jewish cultural center that had opened a year earlier. They arrived at a building of neoclassical design with a grand entranceway and were met by an official from the center. Walking through the lobby, however, Neiditch was struck by the absence of any artwork or announcements relating to Jewish topics. They had, in fact, been taken to the "Center for Anti-Religious Propaganda and Hall of Atheism." Their host still insisted it was the Michoels Center. When Neiditch then said that he would take a photograph of Uris in the center and send it to the Australian Jewish philanthropist who had led the effort to build it, the host, named Zeitsev, took Neiditch by the arm and walked him out to confirm the switch in venues. A heating problem had forced them to move, he weakly explained. The audience of some two hundred knew where they were, and none of them seemed surprised by the move. Uris chose to give his talk, a memoir of his life and how he came to write *Exodus*, out of respect for their attendance.

But why did the Soviet Union allow Uris to visit, knowing he would be a flash point for refuseniks and Soviet Jews? Neiditch believed it was a bureaucratic mix-up. There was no connection between the decision to let him in and the subsequent decision to disrupt his schedule. Uris had declined an invitation to appear at an event sponsored by the Soviet Peace Committee, depriving this KGB front organization the chance to host "the great Zionist novelist."[57] Upset at his decision, which had been taken on the advice of U.S. and Israeli officials, others may have sought to upset and harass Uris during his stay. The entire experience made Neiditch suspicious about the success of perestroika and the democratic processes occurring in the Soviet Union.

Uris's own account of the visit ("Helsinki-Leningrad Express") is less political and more personal.[58] He moves from describing the titular train, which he calls a "downgraded Amtrack [*sic*]," to his traveling party, including his "closest friend and confidant," Priscilla Higham, a "tall, striking, peaches-and-cream English lady of forty." He states that trip would be "a victory lap that I thought I'd never live to see" ("HLE," 1).

The Hotel Moskva reminded him of a subway station under Times Square, and he compared the dining room to a derelict, run-down music hall with a nightly cabaret, a "macabre setting of three hundred soiled, off-white table cloths holding a fallen regiment of empty vodka bottles" ("HLE," 3). Dinner, of a sort, followed, and it included currency being exchanged while groups of prostitutes paraded through. Foreign goods at a Berioska in the lobby, a hard-currency store for foreign guests, were of interest. They found a decent hard-currency restaurant, but dinner for six cost $400. Priscilla had her room broken into, and her shoes, cigarettes, and a couple of sweaters were taken. Uris believed that glasnost meant only that the authorities had lost control ("HLE," 5). The local mafia controlled everything from black-market money to caviar, break-ins, and prostitution. From the three refuseniks who drove Uris to his meetings, he learned that when they became too strong or vocal, the authorities let them emigrate, in order to weaken the movement. The country was run-down; cars, except those assigned to party members, lacked windshield wipers. Uris's report breaks off after his description of the Pamyat, young Russian fascists.

Essie offered a further perspective on Russia in a short essay ("Notes"), and her remarks contain some small insights.[59] At the Hotel Moskva in Leningrad, she discovered that no Soviet citizen could enter a hotel unless accompanied by a guest. A visit to a Jewish music club on the night of 12 October revealed much sadness, frustration, and hopelessness. The sense of despair was strong, but she records how Uris and Neiditch tried to convince their audiences that Jews in the United States and Israel were concerned about their safety and status. She later observed long lines of people waiting for bread, milk, or vodka, but there was little food on the shelves. She called Leningrad "a magnificent city planned by the exploiters and built by the oppressed" ("Notes," 2).

In Riga, she met a Jewish theatre director who had formed a Yiddish theatre and a Yiddish school. Four hundred children attended. She then walked to a square where a synagogue had once stood, but it had been torn down. There was also a Jewish cemetery, but it had been desecrated. She retold the story of Uris's protest when his hotel reservation in Moscow was lost. Service soon improved, and one night they even had a ballet dancer dance up and down the dining room for them.

Uris and his party returned to Copenhagen on 22 October, relieved to leave. But he was not idle for long. He was about to participate in a United Jewish Appeal mission to Poland and appear at the *Mila 18* ceremony in Warsaw on 24 October, part of the Dor L'Dor ("Generation to Generation") project.[60] Ernie Michael, a friend, joined him.

In a later talk about his trip to Eastern Europe, Uris noted that twenty-five years earlier, when he had visited Poland to do research for *Mila 18*, the only place he could find a map of prewar Warsaw was at the Library of Congress.[61] He then recounted his visit to the Mauthausen death camp near Linz, Austria. There, he noted the uneven steps at the Mauthausen quarry, which made it impossible for a prisoner carrying rocks and stones up and down to do so without stumbling.

On 24 October 1989, in Poland, he visited a Jewish cemetery for a ceremony on the site of a mass grave. There was then a gathering at the former location of Mila 18 and a presentation by Uris, typed on a Polish typewriter (which presented challenges), followed by a walk to the Warsaw Ghetto Memorial for wreath-laying and candle-lighting ceremonies. An ambassador's reception, with brief remarks from the U.S. and Israeli ambassadors and Polish representatives, followed. The next day, he flew to Krakow and then drove to Auschwitz and Birkenau and saw the barracks where Ernie Michael had been imprisoned. They had held one thousand prisoners in a space built for fifty horses. On the 26th, the tour ended in Warsaw, and the group, but not Uris, flew on to Israel.[62]

On 27 October, Uris, with Priscilla Higham, departed for Budapest, where there was a lavish reception at the airport. The welcoming party was largely from Fabula, his publisher. Television and news interviews followed, and he met Anna Szasz, his translator. He stayed at the Atrium Hyatt Hotel in Pest, overlooking Buda. Interviews and sightseeing followed, and there was a press conference at the Club of Hungarian Artists on the 29th. Higham then left, but Uris stayed on for a meeting on 31 October with the Hungarian cultural minister, Ferenc Glatz, and an evening performance of Prokofiev's ballet *Romeo and Juliet* at the opera house. Feted and praised, Uris then left for New York.[63]

REDEMPTION, OR AMERICA REDUX

12

I'm over 70 now. I don't know how many 800-page novels I have left.
—LEON URIS, 1996

HIS TRIP TO EASTERN EUROPE rekindled Uris's writerly identity and sense of self-importance. Ambassadors, ministers, fans, and the press had turned out to greet him. Given the personal difficulties he was facing at home, it was reassuring for his image and ego to receive the attention he found in Finland, the USSR, Poland, and Hungary. He was seen throughout Eastern Europe as a writer of importance who had revived the Jewish identities of hundreds of thousands. His confidence returned, and he identified himself as a Jewish Hemingway. Shortly after he returned, he told an interviewer: "I am mainly a man's writer. I write about war, violence, sex . . . the type of things that men like to read about."[1] He drove the point home: "None of my books can be called a woman's book. I do think that my female characters are getting better. In the beginning, women weren't a strong part of my writing." In *Mitla Pass*, the character of Ben-Gurion makes this into a joke, telling his adviser Jacob Herzog that "we are entitled to a poor man's Hemingway" when permitting the writer Gideon Zadok to join the Lion Battalion: "God knows he doesn't write like Hemingway, but I hear he drinks as well" (*MP*, 9).

Uris returned to New York at the beginning of November 1989 rejuvenated and ready to write, although he needed cash. He decided to try the lecture circuit, giving talks about his Soviet adventures for Jewish organizations in Mexico, Canada, and the United States. He was eager to restart his writing, although his first effort was as unexpected as it was unplanned: a children's story, the first he had attempted.

The story is set on Shelter Island, where Uris had gradually been spending more and more time. He rented a house owned by Ralph Kast on North Ferry Road for $25,000 a year, but soon bought it. The small, modern, three-bedroom home had a study for Uris upstairs in the back, facing Chase Creek. A small dock led to his boat, *Kitty's Wake*. This became the setting for "Secrets of Forever Island," a barely disguised allegory of his children's time at Shelter Island. It grew out of long letters to Rachael and Conor, which were filled with stories he made up.

Channing Thieme was to illustrate the work. Uris had met her in 1989, and by the early nineties, she had become a vital part of his life. She saw the film *Exodus* at thirteen and learned the song by heart to play on the piano. In her early twenties, she decided to read the novel, and it awakened her to the horrors of the Holocaust. She then went on to read everything Uris wrote. At dinner parties in the 1970s, when playfully answering the question of whom would she like to have dinner with, her first response was always "Leon Uris." In the late 1980s, she read *The Haj*, and on a whim she wrote to Uris, offering to do a pencil portrait in gratitude for his books. She and her then husband were planning a visit to Aspen, and she wrote to him there.[2]

Some months later she received a phone call from Priscilla Higham, Uris's assistant. He wanted to speak to her, and he got on the line to tell her how amusing he found her sample sketch: a drawing of the back of her head holding a pencil. Uris, by then in New York, agreed to meet her, and what had been scheduled as a two-hour meeting lasted for six. Soon to be divorced, she found in the intense, exciting Uris a natural friend. She took a series of photographs at their first session, and a wonderful pencil portrait of Uris emerged, which he admired. They remained friends for a year or so, and then for the next four enjoyed a relationship described as very great when it was great (more than 80 percent of the time) and very bad when it was bad. Although she never moved in with him, she did visit him almost every other week in New York—Boston was her home—and spent long periods with him on Shelter Island. She also became very close with Uris's young children, Conor (four) and Rachael (six). Her own two sons also became part of the extended group, all six traveling at one point to Cancun.[3]

Once Uris had the idea of a storybook, he enlisted Channing to illustrate the semiallegorical adventures. Lengthy and often hilarious phone calls took place between the two as Uris outlined the arabesque-like plot to Channing. She would then fax drawings to him to illustrate the adventures, something new for her, since she was essentially a portrait artist.[4]

Channing found the time with Uris stimulating, partly because he had such a high regard for her art. He constantly encouraged her and often had articles and essays for her to read when she arrived at his New York apartment. His intensity was unavoidable and magnetic, and he had a way of looking right through you, into the depths, she said. He also loved to be shocking, although he was reluctant to do so. And even in New York, he was recognized on the street, which was both a bother and a compliment. One night at the end of a meal at a Long Island restaurant, the entire kitchen staff came out to greet him.[5]

In "Secrets of Forever Island," Uris is Barnaby Appleseed who had recently moved from Colorado to New York and who wrote "books about war, injustice, tyranny and other miserable subjects because some one had to . . . let people know these things existed" ("SFI," 1). Atty and Luke are his children. Their adventures during the summer and on vacation make up the bulk of the text, and they are aided by several fantasy machines, such as a fancy car with an "Automatic Trip-Tracker" (like a GPS) and voice-activated directions. Following their first and not entirely happy summer in Manhattan, the children return for a trip to Forever Island, Uris's Shelter Island home.

Forever Island is special because it encourages people to be what they want to be. But it is also a world of temptation, and in Chapter 2, the children disobey their father and cross the bridge onto the Orange Trail, where they are captured. Uris employs a simple style that is strong on imagery and supported by his characteristic sense of detail. Action, however, trumps character, and the work thins out as the story progresses and the children explore the green part of the island, Peekaboo Preserve, a wildlife sanctuary. *Kitty's Wake*, Uris's small motorboat, is rechristened *Rosebud* in the story, and Chase Creek becomes Izzupada creek. And the animals talk to the children.

But danger lurks, and escape from a water buffalo occurs only after Atty and Luke find the courage to punch the buffalo in the nose. They return to their father and tell him the truth about their adventure, but he doesn't believe them. They are grounded but soon meet a friendly, "effervescent" swan, Ernestine, from the Isle of Primavera. Other figures appear, like One-Note Rodman, the singing pirate; Mr. Beachfront, a real estate agent; and Angelo Crescendo, who owned an Italian grocery and gas station. The secretary of the yacht club is F. Liberty Endeavor III. Uris is remarkably playful with the characters but not his lesson: the importance of always telling the truth ("SFI," 30).

Later adventures include a hurricane that threatens the island, and a performance of *Swan Lake* in San Francisco in which Ernestine has to substitute for the principal dancer. There is also a battle with a group of outlawed mosquitoes in Jordan Springs, Colorado. The story ends with the children arriving for another summer at Forever Island and learning that their father has finished a new "war and justice novel" but is now thinking of writing a "mature kid's novel" about a brother and sister whose parents are divorced but who get to visit their father on an enchanted island ("SFI," 99).

The writing in "Secrets of Forever Island" is simple and affectionate. Details like the Grapefruit Blossom ferry, commanded by a female pirate, capture reader interest. Even the comments on divorce in the story are gentle, emphasizing that both parents love the children so much that they feel thankful. There is a wistful moment when the children, misled by parental affection, contemplate the parents reuniting—what "all divorced kids dream about. But if it happened, they'd just be unhappy again. Both of them are happy now" ("SFI," 90).

"Secrets of Forever Island" projects Uris's own self-image in the early nineties, a figure who enjoys the isolation and peace of Forever Island. It is a place to feel good, where difficult times become easier to endure. He also portrays himself writing, talking out both the male and female parts of a story ("SFI," 22). The illustrations by Channing are natural and lively, reflecting the fanciful and imaginative text, an example of what Uris could do when freed from fact. The book was an interlude from his other writing obligations, but it remained unpublished, despite the efforts of his new agent, Nancy Stauffer. The problem was how to identify its target audience. Editors could not determine whether it was for six- or sixteen-year-olds, and Uris was typically reluctant to alter any part of the text.

GROWING OLD ON SHELTER ISLAND

Despite his residences in New York and Shelter Island, Uris missed Aspen, and on two or three occasions he took Channing there to see the area. Once, they even went to look after Rachael and Conor. During this period, there were also important moments of recognition for Uris. The first took place in New York at a literary-awards dinner when James Michener presented Uris with an honor. Michener paid him a supreme compliment when he said that after *Trinity*, it would be impossible for him to write about Ireland because Uris had done it so well. Washington, D.C., was the site of the second event. At an evening ceremony for the 150th anniversary of B'nai B'rith, held at the Jefferson Memorial, President Bill Clinton introduced Uris, the featured speaker. Uris was deeply honored. Mrs. Clinton—as well as Channing—was also present.

At the ceremony, Uris addressed the question of life on the Lower East Side of New York. His remarks reflected his current interest in immigration, which would become a key theme in *Redemption*. More than a thousand people attended the Havdalah service, which marks the end of the Jewish Sabbath, at the Jefferson Memorial. In a comic footnote to the event, after the pageantry and ceremony, Uris and Channing could not get a ride back to their hotel. They had taken a cab and did not realize there would be no cabs available when they needed to return. They had to flag down a bus and join a surprised group of travelers. The next day, they had a private tour of the U.S. Holocaust Museum from the director, who told Uris that his books were a catalyst in the drive to establish the institution.

In 1990, Uris replaced his longtime lawyer and business manager, Herb Schlosberg, with Michael Remer, a New York attorney, and hired Nancy Stauffer as his literary agent. She was the former director of foreign rights at Doubleday. In April 1990, he became upset over layoffs as Doubleday dismissed editors and marketing people who had aided various best-selling writers. The beleaguered publisher was under pressure from Bertelsmann, its corporate boss, which was disappointed in the U.S. bottom line—in 1989, Doubleday supposedly lost $5 million–6 million.[6] Stephen Rubin soon replaced Nancy Evans as president, and Uris and others publicly expressed their unhappiness with changes at the company. Uris was particularly upset at the dismissal of Joan Ward, an administrative assistant to Harry Gollob, a senior vice president and editor at large who worked with Uris after Sam Vaughan moved on. Ward had worked with Uris for twenty-four years as an assistant and adviser to his editors and publisher.

Uris's status with his publisher, however, created its own problems, because there were sizeable time gaps between the publication of his works. There were eight years between *Trinity* (1976) and *The Haj* (1984). Four years later, *Mitla Pass* appeared (1988), and seven years later, *Redemption* (1995). *A God in Ruins* was published in 1999, and *O'Hara's Choice* appeared posthumously in 2003. These lengthy breaks meant publishers were hesitant to offer large advances: Uris's ability to deliver became uncertain, and his sales were uneven.

For Uris, this was a period of both renewal and strain. His divorce, the trips to the Soviet Union and Eastern Europe, and the attempt to write a theatrical version of *Trinity* overtook his obligation to complete a new novel for Doubleday. Distracted from immediate work, he concentrated on Broadway, his children's story, and also a possible screenplay of *Mila 18*, while considering potential new subjects for his fiction. But finally, and perhaps in desperation—the children's book could not find a publisher, the *Trinity* play failed, and the movie version of *Mila 18* collapsed—he turned to a sequel to *Trinity*. His work on the play probably renewed his interest in Ireland as well as the possibility of revisiting the novel. *Trinity* provided the spark for a new story, appropriately titled, given its personal connotations, *Redemption*.

His life now mixed self-promotion with an effort to write. He lived mostly on Shelter Island, having given up the New York apartment, and found new momentum in preparing what would become *Redemption*. His relationship with Channing Thieme continued, although it began to hit a few snags: he was hesitant about any permanent association, and she maintained her independence. Two new research assistants—Jeanne Sillay Jacobson and Jeanne Randall—replaced Priscilla Higham, and they would be followed by a third, a Shelter Island resident, Marilynn Pysher, who worked with him on his last two novels, *A God in Ruins* and *O'Hara's Choice*. Fees for lectures supplemented a dwindling income, although declining health limited his productivity. By the time he was writing his last novel, his eldest son, Mark, assisted in providing both physical comfort and literary advice. But while working on his new project, originally called *Father, Son, and Holy Ghost: An Irish Novel*, Uris continued to speak out on Jewish matters.[7]

For his seventieth birthday party, held at Shelter Island, Channing Thieme organized a lively affair that was attended by Michael Neiditch, Michael Remer, neighbors, and a former New York Jets football player. The group of twenty-five or so enjoyed the "roast," which comically exposed Uris's foibles. But despite his youthful manner, Uris was not aging well: he was becoming overweight and suffering from the ingestion of excess alcohol and occasionally soft drugs. He turned to such remedies as Rolfing (a system of soft-tissue manipulation intended to align the body), although he did not follow a diet or even eat proper meals. A housekeeper came one day a week to cook for him, but he preferred packaged, frozen food. He also did little reading, nothing more than newspapers, and watched television. The only books on display, as was the case in his New York apartment, were ones he had written.

Rachael and Conor continued to visit, and he installed an intricate jungle gym for them, as well as a swimming pool. He also hired a captain for his small boat to guide the children about the island. They also loved Channing and enjoyed being with her when she visited.

REDEMPTION

In preparing his new novel, he again relied on research assistants, as he had done throughout his career. For *Redemption*, he had two, and they did everything from locate source material and confirm details to provide summaries of the story and characters as it proceeded so that duplication could be avoided. Uris loved doing research and would spread books, maps, letters, and even ledgers around his second-floor study as he wrote. His models, he later told another researcher, Marilynn Pysher, were the military campaign books that outlined detailed plans before a battle. Preparedness was everything: it would determine whether you won or lost—or in Uris's case, whether you had a best seller.

Uris called *Redemption* "an unplanned pregnancy." He did not initially antici- pate a sequel to *Trinity*, but a question emerged: what happened after the end of that novel, which covered only the years 1885–1912? The Easter Rebellion was no more than a postscript, but as time passed, Uris realized he had not done justice to the uprising, which "was the beginning of the end of colonialism."[8] He began to draw a parallel between the impact of this "small uprising" and that of the Warsaw Ghetto, noting that the meaning of the Easter Rebellion came to him only years after *Trinity*. He wanted to present the uprising more clearly and reengage with the same characters, not so much from a historical perspective, "but as they related to each other."[9]

As he worked on *Redemption*, he consulted multiple drafts of his stage version of *Trinity*. Working intently on the play, which had two elaborate readings in New York in anticipation of a Broadway production, had renewed Uris's interest in the characters from the novel and the possibility of another epic account.

The setting for *Redemption* is New Zealand, not Ireland, although the novel extends the story line from the earlier book. The book opens in 1895 as Irish immigrants sail to New Zealand, courses back to Ireland, and then moves on to the outbreak of the First World War. It ends in 1916, first with a postscript on the Easter Rebellion, delivered by his character Theobald Fitzpatrick (son of Atty and Desmond Fitzpatrick), and then a final section on Roger Casement and treason, set in August 1916. Historical figures appear or play a role—notably the young Winston Churchill, Arthur Griffiths, and Prime Minister Herbert Asquith—as well as a cast of characters from *Trinity*. The Gallipoli campaign is one of several historical events presented in the story, and Uris treats it empathetically. He also cites incidents and battles in Cairo, Dublin, and Belfast. Such a mix of the historical and fictional was now a Uris trademark.

Redemption became his first novel written for HarperCollins. After years with Doubleday, Uris found the publisher unwilling to postpone his contractual obligations, because of his persistent involvement with the proposed Broadway production of *Trinity*. He broke with them unforgivingly, defending his actions as a response to their new bottom-line attitude, the reshuffling of senior editors, and the new sense of corporate oversight exercised by their German owners, Bertelsmann.[10] HarperCollins, by contrast, was eager to publish Uris, seeing him still as a bankable popular writer. It expected large sales of *Redemption*, which was given a marketing budget in excess of $200,000 and a print run of 350,000 copies, partly based on the assumption that the novel would become a Literary Guild selection.[11] As a gesture to his youngest children, Uris dedicated the book to Rachael and Conor, "with love from Daddy."

Sections of *Redemption* expand on particulars in *Trinity*. For example, details on Jean Tijou, the late seventeenth-century French Huguenot ironworker who designed the great screen at Hubble Manor, were fleshed out in *Redemption*. His presence signals that Uris gave attention to artists, as well as to politicians and rebels, in the novel. Tijou arrived in England around 1689 when William and Mary, his lifelong patrons, began their reign. His notable gates and railings adorn the grounds of Hampton Court (1689–1700), and he fashioned the screens and grilles of St. Paul's Cathedral for Sir Christopher Wren.[12] Uris transposes Tijou's work to Ireland, where, in *Redemption*, it is treated as inspired art (RD, 152).

"Research to me is as important or more important than the writing," Uris said just before *Redemption* appeared.[13] The comment is apt because it identifies his skill but also his weakness. His earlier novels established their authority through such detail, but it generally stayed subordinate to character and drama. This is clear in *Exodus, Mila 18,* and *Trinity.* But with *Redemption* and *The Haj,* his research dominated character, narrative, and plot. And at 827 pages and ninety-one chapters, *Redemption* is Uris's longest work. Its anticipated success, however, did not materialize, and he was caught again in a cycle of work and debt.

In *Redemption,* Uris offers a series of remarks about art and artists, something absent from his earlier writing except for *Mitla Pass.* Characters discourse on the theatre, the logic of art, and, quoting Uris in an interview, the importance of the "curtain line." Ironically, Seamus O'Neill, a childhood friend of Conor's and now a journalist, gets a lesson from Conor on writing. Essentially, Conor tells him that he has to know where he is going and that there has to be a logic to his art. In addition, he needed to know his "curtain line," what the dramatists call the through-line in a play. Uris had made the same point in talking about novel writing to a Columbia University journalism student shortly after *Mitla Pass* appeared.[14] Another passage repeats a favorite Uris expression, which appeared in *Mitla Pass* and in various interviews: "We all seem to spend the second half of our lives getting over the first half," Georgia Norman, a nurse, tells young Rory Larkin (RD, 49). A variation of the line appears later in relation to a soldier's experience (RD, 431).

Uris's concern with art was not a surprise. *Mitla Pass* suggested some of this in Gideon's discussions about becoming a writer and the motivations of his art. But there is always a high price. Caroline tells Conor in *Redemption* that "no man has ever taken on a greater work of art without paying a terrible price and creating terrible pain for those he loves the most" (RD, 190). In *Redemption,* the sacrifice demanded by art receives new prominence, a kind of self-conscious awareness of the surrender required, as well as the importance of aesthetics and artistic direction. Furthermore, references to Beethoven's Fifth Symphony, Shakespeare, and Cezanne in the novel allude to the theme of the inspired artist. The title of the novel might mean, indirectly, Uris's acknowledgment or redemption of his sense of aesthetics and art, which he previously had consciously avoided. Earlier, he had distanced himself from the idea of the artist, preferring to be identified by the more workmanlike term "writer," a kind of journeyman who accomplishes a task. But at this stage of his career, he seemed ready to accept, and seek, an identity as an artist.

Uris was also ready to acknowledge the ambiguities of art. Andrew Ingram, the Scottish schoolteacher, reminds Lady Caroline at the great screen in the Long Hall of Hubble Manor that while it may be a masterpiece by Tijou, it is also a symbol of oppression to Catholics (RD, 133). It was used as a prison, and almost five hundred women and children died of torture and hunger behind it. She responds, "That's in the long past." "There is no long past in Ireland," he replies, articulating a historical thesis to which Uris had long subscribed (RD, 133).

Redemption dispenses with a logical chronology, which might be surprising given the numerous statements by characters about the validity of logic in art. Time shifts backward and forward, revisiting the past from different angles. Events in *Trinity* find expansion and development, as if Uris now wanted to take his time with the experience. He starts with dramatic suspense, opening with a memo from Winston Churchill in 1894 that seals his papers until 2050 (although they reappear in Chapter 34).

The novel proper opens in 1895 with the arrival in New Zealand of Liam Larkin, the outcast son of Tomas and the brother of Conor. We follow his adventures and successful marriage and rise to become owner of a sheep station, and a reference is made to a visit from Conor in 1904 during a period of exile from Ireland. There is also a reminder of Conor's martyrdom in the raid against Lettershanbo Castle at the end of *Trinity*. At that point (RD, 341), Liam's son Rory flees his father and goes off to fight in the First World War. He ends up at Gallipoli and, in one of many improbable coincidences, finds himself serving with Lady Caroline Hubble's two sons. After the war, Rory makes his way to Ireland, where he joins forces with Lady Caroline to battle the British again and also undermines the efforts of the Protestant Orangemen to stamp out the Catholics. Uris's sympathies for the republicans are again restated. Uris also continues to attack the British, showing the middle class and the Ulster aristocracy to be hypocritical and senseless; they order Anzacs (Australian and New Zealander soldiers) to their deaths at Gallipoli, destroy rural Irish villages, and pursue young boys in Hong Kong.

Big scenes interrupt the novel's progression. Two of them are the rebuilding of the impressive Tijou screen at Hubble Manor and the Gallipoli campaign, one of Britain's greatest military blunders in the First World War. Uris cannot resist the opportunity to dramatize crucial moments of personal or national history. Neither does he forget lines from the earlier novel that reinforce the nationalist cause. "The Brits have the guns and we have the words, and now the stage to shout them from," Atty tells Jack Murphy early in *Redemption* (RD, 91). Uris also makes sure that the title is explained. Andrew Ingram, the Scottish teacher who educates Conor and Seamus, tells Lady Caroline that he must finally leave Ireland: redemption is "the greatest of all human qualities," and he must redeem himself in Scotland (RD, 131). Furthermore, he explains to her that everything that happened in the past is with them in the present (RD, 133). Later in the novel, Lady Caroline hopes that "a redemption" might be possible between herself and her husband, whom she is disowning, and her sons (RD, 365).

Individual sections are definite successes, but the novel ends up being fragmented into parts that do not form a whole. The fight between Rory Larkin
and the Australian boxing champ aboard ship is effective (RD, 418–420), as
is the socially engaged life of Lady Caroline when she goes to London to run
her father's expanding shipbuilding empire in Belfast. A private meeting with
Churchill in her office, which involves political blackmail, is especially dramatic
(RD, 379–386). Similarly, a chapter set in Cairo, where the Anzac troops train and
where pleasure and anger intermingle, exhibits convincing detail, another Uris
hallmark. But stylistic fluency, seen most effectively in the dialogue, contrasts
with the disjointed overall structure. Sections seem out of place or tacked on or
thrown in to explain the historical past.

The recounting of the Battle of Gallipoli, 115 pages long, moves almost step-
by-step through the briefings, errors, and deaths. Uris tells readers the locale is
the site of ancient Troy and the *Iliad*, as well as of the *Odyssey* (RD, 567), but then
vivid and graphic scenes of mayhem and death quickly replace history. Despite
a British naval bombardment, the Turks decimate the Anzac force. Ill equipped
or underequipped, the troops face a slow but steady slaughter; the description
is supplemented by graphic details of a truce to recover bloated and bloodied
bodies (RD, 620–621). The discovery of Rory Larkin's identity by Christopher
Hubble precedes his encounter with Dr. Calvin Norman, Georgia's husband (RD,
630). Coincidence, once more, reigns, followed by insurrection as some of the
leaders refuse to allow their men to be massacred (RD, 670). The blunders by
the general staff lead to further deaths until the final evacuation order and the
execution of an original plan to divert the Turks (RD, 679–680).

But jumps in the plot deflect the emotional intensity of the concluding Gallipoli section. What follows is, first, "A Retrospective on the Easter Rising of
1916," written by the son of Atty and Desmond Fitzpatrick; it is essentially an
account of the nationwide wake held for Conor Larkin. Then comes a condensed
history of Ireland, leading to the drive for independence and the introduction of
Sir Roger Casement and his secret plans to gain money from America and arms
from Germany. Easter Monday, in April 1916, then receives the treatment it did
not get in *Trinity*, as Uris details the unprepared Home Army's determination
to face down British authority, including the seizure of the General Post Office.
The deaths of the arrested leaders follow.

The fifth and final part of the novel shifts supposedly to Roger Casement's
treason (Chapter 87 dramatizes his imprisonment and hanging), but it is a
pretext for the characters to take revenge on General Brodhead, who was sent
to pacify Ireland after bungling the fight for Gallipoli. Rory Larkin, living in
Dublin and honored with the Victoria Cross, joins Brodhead's staff, although
his Larkin roots lead him to play a new role. With the help of Lady Caroline, he

plots to kill the incompetent general, who was responsible for the deaths of Lady Caroline's two sons in battle. Here, content and character are again in conflict, creating an extra plot twist that acts more as a postscript than a conclusion to the novel. In a prolonged chapter, the general meets his end with the assistance of Rory Larkin. A chapter in which Lady Caroline confronts Churchill with the mistakes of the preceding decade lends a political, even if not historical, stamp to the book—and confirms Churchill's aid in expunging evidence of Rory's presence in Ireland and ensuring his return to New Zealand, which the final chapter rather sentimentally sums up.

Response to *Redemption* was surprisingly modest; the Uris formula of history and grand romance seemed to be losing its appeal. The confusing plot and lack of focus led one critic wittily to declare that with its contrivances, digressions, and shifting time lines, *Redemption* "resembles the Irish countryside—full of twists and turns, replete with bogs and quagmires."[15] Other critics treated the book as just another Uris blockbuster with history rather than character as the central subject. Exaggeration from the Associated Press—"Uris is to the twentieth century what Charles Dickens was to the nineteenth"—did little to boost sales. Ireland again? Critics felt Uris had done that better in *Trinity* and that the new novel was just a recycling of earlier material. Nevertheless, *Redemption* debuted on 2 July 1995 at number twelve on the *New York Times* best-seller list, but within two weeks it fell to fourteenth, and by the end of the month it was gone. Competition included *The Bridges of Madison County* by Robert James Waller and *The Rainmaker* by John Grisham. However, the appearance of *Redemption* as a mass-market paperback in May 1996, where Uris traditionally had strong sales, saw its numbers soar. Hardback sales were 167,000, but nearly 400,000 copies of the paperback were sold (although 700,000 copies were shipped).[16] Respectable but, for Uris, disappointing numbers.

INCREASING ISOLATION

Uris was unsure of his next step. He had by now given up his New York apartment and was spending most of his time on Shelter Island, becoming more reclusive than social. Only a small circle of nonliterary friends formed his network; his relationship with Channing Thieme had unraveled by late August 1994. He then invited Ray Diffley, the former wife of his Irish friend, to join him, but she declined. Difficult relations with his older children, who rarely if ever visited him, continued. Mark Uris described his father at one point as a "one way street": he made the rules and you agreed or not.[17] And if not, you were out. He could not understand or even accept other peoples' weaknesses. His younger children came for their summer vacations, but as they grew older, they became anxious at his quick-tempered behavior. He did, however, turn up unexpectedly at Rachael's bat mitzvah in Aspen but had health difficulties because of the high altitude. He took little action to resolve them, which upset Mark and his wife, Pat, a nurse.[18]

The paradoxes of Uris's character became more apparent as he grew older. He could be gracious or mean. He would repay those who helped him generously, but act frugally toward those closest to him. He had a temper and angered quickly. For over a year, he and his son Mark did not talk. However, as he grew more infirm, Uris tried to make amends, calling each of the children to say good-bye as his health declined. "I think I'm checking out tonight" was how he started the conversation with one of his children.[19] Many demons plagued him, according to his New York literary agent, beginning with his father, who had always seemed to compete with him and whom he could never satisfy.[20] Other demons included the memory of his failed marriages and his lack of respect from the literary establishment, which he, of course, despised.

Even Uris's Judaism was contradictory. He did not celebrate the Jewish holidays and was nonpracticing, yet he accepted the pedestal Jews put him on and used it. And while he had a wide readership and received plenty of popular attention, he never won a major literary prize, which angered him. He wanted to be the center of attention, but found himself shunned by critics and the literati. On one hand, he felt in competition with this group and those historical novelists taken seriously, like Gore Vidal, but, on the other, he rejected their company and society. Even though his signature gestures, notably travel and research, became dormant in the last few years of his life, politics continued to interest him, as did his favored Denver Broncos football team.

A GOD IN RUINS

Uris soon began to pay more attention to what he saw as the social and political deterioration of the United States, becoming increasingly concerned about its future. Though a patriot, he had, since adolescence, hesitated to acknowledge the existence of oppression in his country. Approached by blacks and women to address such issues, he refused, explaining in a colorful phrase to his son Mark that "you don't shit in your own backyard."[21] But anxiety over the state of America led to his first novel to be set in the United States, *A God in Ruins*. The novel, he predicted, would create a reaction in the country because of its dire forecast of violence and upheaval.

A God in Ruins (1999) deals with a presidential election in 2008 in which an Irish candidate for the presidency discovers he is, in fact, Jewish—a fantasy

Uris had long nurtured. To him, all Irishmen were Jews, echoing some fanciful eighteenth-century histories of Ireland (the Irish were supposedly a lost tribe of Israel). This discovery is set in a plot driven by the effort to repeal the Second Amendment to the Constitution, which guarantees the right to bear arms. The hero, appropriately, is a marine, a subject Uris returns to in his final novel, *O'Hara's Choice*, a historical work ranging from the Civil War to 1900. Uris's return to the marines as a theme in these last two works, especially the second, may have been stimulated by the gift, from his son Mark, of a coffee-table book on the marines, a picture history of the service. Both of these late novels also continue the moral clarity that shadows all of Uris's work.

Uris wrote *A God in Ruins* throughout 1998, a period when the United States was awakening to the danger of terrorism, international security threats, and the dominance of computers. In the novel, he combines a series of stories in an unbalanced but urgent way: an all-American-style marine hero of remarkable talent, who grew up on a ranch in Colorado, has a series of love affairs and succeeds, however improbably, in becoming the governor of Colorado and then a candidate for the presidency. The initial setting is days before the 2008 election. However, Quinn Patrick O'Connell, who seems headed for victory because of his campaign of moral integrity, unexpectedly learns that he was the orphan of Jewish parents. The book opens as he prepares to announce this revelation to the nation, unsure of its impact on his candidacy.

This summary does not do justice to several overarching Uris themes in the book, including genealogy, fathers, Jewish heroism, and the need for social reform. Two persistent themes stand out: the need to know one's past, and the troubled relationship between fathers and sons. As one character notes, we are all looking for something to make our fathers proud (*AGR*, 139–140). Jewish military accomplishments also receive praise. When Jeremiah Duncan, a rugged marine major general, presents the president and others with a plan to strike back at Iranian terrorists—this is the Tom Clancy portion of the novel, which stresses the use of a new lighting strike force and an ultralight fighting aircraft—he cites the tactics the Israeli Air Force used when attacking Egypt in the 1967 war (*AGR*, 149). A few pages earlier, he celebrates the work of the Mossad in tracking down the Iranian terrorists responsible for blowing up a U.S. Air Force Learjet carrying an ambassador and a NATO general (*AGR*, 142, 150). He then parlays the certainty that the United States will be perceived as weak if it does not strike back against Iranians into the action plot of the novel.

Another theme is the decline of the arts in America and the need for their constant support. Here, Uris cites the "Disneyfication" of 42nd Street as the sanitized ideal of America (*AGR*, 129). Uris had witnessed the very cleanup he criticized. The novel also manages to address both the decline of writing and the importance, for every writer, of working everyday and to working hard, the core of Uris's own professional practice. When the hero's wife recognizes her failings as writer, she espouses Uris's solution: "A large part of the writer's being, of his talent, could only emerge through hard, hard work" (AGR, 242). Uris referred to this as learning by the seat of one's pants.

In some ways, however, the novel is eerily prescient. Reference is made to a terrible massacre that occurs when a militant group of white supremacists repel an attack on their fortification by what they believe to be a group of invaders. The "invaders" turn out to be a troop of Boy Scouts, who are mercilessly mowed down. The government covers up the incident by claiming it was a rare natural disaster, since the explosions in the canyon in which the boys are killed cause an immense rockslide. The Four Corners Massacre, as it was known, nearly unseats the incumbent president. Uris uses the issue to argue for gun control, which he strongly supported, while the action chimed with such events as the school shootings at Columbine High School in Colorado, which occurred just a few months before the book was published. Uris also refers to the likelihood of the United States being subject to a severe terrorist attack, since so many of its overseas facilities and citizens were being targeted. By 1999, the U.S. had already suffered the first World Trade Center bombing (1993) and the destruction of the federal building in Oklahoma City (1995). The narrator predicts that it will only be a matter of time before an even worse event occurs, a prediction some two years before 9/11 (AGR, 142).

A further disaster scenario involves the violence unleashed across the country when O'Connell announces that he is Jewish, just before the presidential vote. The backlash, fueled by belief in a Jewish conspiracy, leads to Kristallnacht-like actions (Uris uses the term), which the sitting president does nothing to stop until his top aides threaten to leave him. The outbreak of virulent anti-Semitism across the United States, which only a few groups, notably blacks, oppose, anticipates the fears and events depicted in Philip Roth's novel *The Plot Against America* (2004) and Roberto Bolaño's *Nazi Literature in the Americas* (2008).

Uris, however, cannot resist inserting the autobiographical into the story, beginning with the life of the protagonist's father, Daniel Timothy O'Connell. A few of the details taken directly from Uris's life: Dan O'Connell is a marine veteran who fought at Guadalcanal and Tarawa. He comes down with dengue fever on Tarawa. Quinn O'Connell, the adopted son, admires John Steinbeck's *Of Mice and Men* for its depiction of loneliness (AGR, 431). Uris also includes a disguised reference to his son Mark when he has Rae, Quinn's daughter, work at the Atmospheric Research Institute in Boulder, Colorado. Mark Uris, a computer specialist like the character, worked at the similarly named National Center for Atmospheric Research in Boulder. Uris also includes a brief section (in Chapter 14) on the history of the marines, which would become the foundation of his last novel, *O'Hara's Choice*.

But unlike *Mitla Pass*, *A God in Ruins* is not a disguised autobiography. O'Connell was a policeman from Brooklyn who, after returning from the war and recovering from his wounds (though he is left with a limp), marries his Catholic girlfriend and then heads west, settling in Colorado. Perhaps the biggest nonautobiographical detail is that the O'Connells, father and son, love each other.

The need for moral reform and a restoration of the humane in a world dominated by computers, information, and impersonality are additional concerns. The hypocrisy of the response to the Monica Lewinsky–Bill Clinton affair receives repeated criticism by Uris when certain elements of Quinn's past are dredged up but do no harm. The two-year affair of President Thorton Tomtree's wife (he is a computer billionaire who manages to become elected) is seen as a sordid reminder of the Clinton past. O'Connell's commitment to honesty and decency is intended to provide a new direction for America, the claim for a new "Moral Imperative" reflecting Uris's own hopes for a decent society, one also freed from racial bigotry. The irony of his protagonist's claim is that Uris's own personal life did not support such a position, his own moral behavior being frequently more hypocritical than ethical.

The replacement of personality by computer-generated information is another bête noire of Uris's. A reliance on data rather than people, which is the key to the incumbent president's success, receives strong criticism throughout the novel. The success of Quinn's challenge, despite his revealed Judaism, shows that, for Uris, character and morals can overpower sheer information and polls.

The Second World War and, more specifically, the Warsaw Ghetto uprising also appear. To trace the true origins of Quinn O'Connell, who is actually Alexander Horowitz, the narrative moves back to 1945 (in another of the quick chronological shifts) in order to reveal the child's origin. The son of the Russian Zionist Marina Geller, who married a hero of the Warsaw Ghetto, Uri Sokolov (who was sent to Siberia and is presumed dead), Alexander is the product of Marina's affair with a Russian professor in New York, David Horowitz. When, after more than five years, she learns that her husband has survived the Gulag, she gives up her son for adoption to a Catholic agency that she is put in touch with by a rogue priest who is a close friend of David Horowitz. She then leaves her partner and returns to Israel, where she had first gone after the war, to meet her formerly lost husband. This condensed story, which forms Chapter 43, unites Uris's traditional themes of loss, resistance, and Jewish identity.

The possibilities of the story, which blends romance with politics, and warfare, sink under an improbable plot involving the question of race (the president's success depends on a black adviser; Quinn's wife is a Mexican American), and wooden, often awful, dialogue. Characters speak awkwardly, in a style that manages to be both overwritten and tired. Women are predictably formulaic and unimaginative, and sex is only referred to, never enacted. The language is exhausted and clichéd: "Hearing his voice was like eating chocolate" (AGR, 217). Uris is at his stylistic best when writing swift, action-filled scenes, as when a small team of marines rescues an Iranian double agent from a mountain hideaway (Chapter 16). The combination of macho military behavior and action results in tense, tight writing.

One sign of the undisciplined mix is the presence of poetry in the text. On two occasions poems appear, although they were not written by Uris. He commissioned work from the New York poet Anna Stoessinger, although she received no credit in the novel, despite an agreement stating that she would. Uris blamed his publisher for the slip. He did pay her a thousand dollars, however.[22]

A God in Ruins—the title is taken from Ralph Waldo Emerson's essay "Nature"—was Uris's first novel set entirely in the United States, and it suffers because he tries too hard to make it American. Although he strives for accuracy, the authenticity that marked his earlier work is absent. It is as if he only skimmed the culture and its contemporary history. Replacing in-depth research, a strength that dominated works like *Exodus* or *QB VII*, is an almost glib knowledge of American life, which is treated generally and superficially. Yet he is attuned to, and disturbed by, new developments, especially the growth and power of the computer industry. The need for encryption and new security systems only intensify the paranoia dominating America. But beneath the questionable plot and characters, a moral urgency remains. With his strong criticism of the gun lobby and the power of corporations to control government, which encourages greed, not morals, Uris manages to maintain a powerful tone of calamity.

Reaction to the novel was predictably cool, the complaints ranging from poor characterizations to fearmongering and an exaggeration of the dangers of the computer age.[23] Yet despite lukewarm reviews, *A God in Ruins* did reasonably well as Uris's name still attracted readers. Printed hardback copies numbered 127,000; paperback copies numbered 336,000.

In an interview shortly after the novel's publication, Uris, then seventy-four, felt depleted and let down, since he had to let go of characters he had been living with for some five years (his last book, *Redemption*, had come out in 1995).[24] His ailments were under control, and he had started to lose weight and feel better. Pugnacity, however, still characterized his attitude as he listed obstacles he had encountered, including a difficult childhood, his daughter Karen's bout with polio, and the suicide of his second wife. Yet his passion for heroism in the face of injustice remained. The absence of gun control and acts of terrorism by American militias are at the heart of his new novel, he explained. He repeated

the story of how he had stood by the original version of *Battle Cry*, again inton-
ing his mantra: "Once you compromise your integrity, you can never go back."
He also emphasized the necessity of a purpose, a mission, when writing: "You
have to get mad and stay mad, and then write from your guts." The need to write
A God in Ruins had emanated from his sense of the millennium and a desire to
write out what troubled him at that moment in American history.

THE LION IN WINTER

A God in Ruins, dedicated to his brother-in-law Harry Kofsky, was the second
book due under the lucrative HarperCollins contract negotiated by Nancy
Stauffer. He approached the work confidently while enjoying the paperback
success of *Redemption*. He continued to live well and travel in style and did
not seem to be too worried about money. He thought matters would just work
themselves out and that he could sustain what his son Mark called "the Imperial
Roman habits of living large," his grandiose manner a mixture of entitlement
and success.[25] According to his children, he behaved more like a proconsul
than an author. He also continued to take people on, remaining argumentative
and passionate, almost belligerent. He felt deeply about things, so if the wrong
button were pushed, he would explode. When Nancy Stauffer was unsuccessful in placing his last novel, *O'Hara's Choice*, with a publisher, they parted. He
went to Owen Laster, at the William Morris Agency, who negotiated a modest,
single-book deal with HarperCollins. Laster was experienced: his client list
included James Michener, Robert Penn Warren, Gore Vidal, and the estate of
Margaret Mitchell.

Uris was by now known to be cantankerous, difficult, and demanding to work
with. He also still carried on his misogynistic ways, at one point telling the editor
Marjorie Braman at HarperCollins to procure him some women. "Those days
are over for people like you," she answered. He tried to reassert his macho image,
but it didn't work, even when he reminded her of his pleasure in getting roughed
up by a black prostitute in New York.[26]

But Uris, who never undertook a book without a contract, was finding writing itself difficult, his physical ailments distracting from and even interfering
with the task. His pleasure in research diminished. Earlier, he had taken great
pride in being accurate and knowing all the key works that might provide an
understanding of historical conflict and detail. His approach was more an assault
than a study. Now, he became impatient with the work, relying increasingly on
others. But he was bothered by the question of how could one have ownership
over information without bothering to read it. Errors in *A God in Ruins* caused

him to rewrite two chapters; his new editor, Gladys Carr at HarperCollins, who had worked on *Redemption*, demanded the changes.[27]

His insomnia also increased, and he would often rely on sleeping pills, wine, or even marijuana to help him rest. A psychologist visited several times to teach him self-hypnosis, and it seemed, for a while, to work.[28] When it didn't, he would sleep late and often not descend from the study-bedroom on the second floor of his house. His flirtatious, even outrageous interest in women, however, did not abate. On one occasion, he startled a substitute nanny by coming downstairs in bikini underwear and making suggestive remarks. She ran shrieking out of the house. He often competed with his Denver friend Charles Goldberg as to which was the bigger "joker and stroker." He always seemed to proposition the most inappropriate women, who were usually married and entirely uninterested in him.[29]

As his mobility lessened, he stayed in bed more, although the bed was now on the first level of his house. With pulleys and a ski towrope, his son Mark arranged a system by which Uris could swing up and out of bed to sit upright. It was laborious but welcome. For amusement, he watched sports on television (mostly tennis, which he had once avidly played); he read little except for the newspapers and rarely kept up with his literary contemporaries, although he constantly felt overlooked, and deprived of a Pulitzer Prize. He considered himself "the people's writer," a streetwise author who offered more reportage than creativity. Storytelling was his trade, not writing in any literary sense. Despite his ailments, he considered moving to Switzerland, largely for tax reasons, and had Rachael and Conor study French in anticipation of a possible change.[30]

O'HARA'S CHOICE

He continued to write, now on his first love, the marines. He expanded references and details in *A God in Ruins* into a historical novel about the evolution of the corps. *O'Hara's Choice* blends a history of the marines with a renewal of their purpose: to be an effective and essential amphibious landing force that combined prowess at sea with extraordinary fighting skill on land. Chronology organizes his story: he begins in 1888, although other sections are set as early as 1861. It concludes thirty years later, in 1891.

Zachary O'Hara, the hero, is a true marine, committed to the discipline, brotherhood, and the command structure. Sounding much like Uris, he says, "I never felt a weight of orders and discipline because the Corps was my life" (*OHC*, 389). His personal conflict, however, is his love for Amanda Blanton Kerr, the daughter of an industrialist who is a fierce opponent of the corps. Echoing some of the conflicts outlined in *Trinity*, Uris traces in parallel the history of the marines and the way personal feelings conflict with military obligations.

O'Hara, Uris stresses, is not an extraordinary man but simply a well-disciplined and organized thinker who understands that the future of the corps resides in amphibious warfare. His senior officers grudgingly admire him, and one tells another: "A twenty-four-year-old Marine captain who won't bullshit. That's a hell of a piece of personnel for the Corps. Don't lose him" (OHC, 354). The conflict in the novel becomes how to preserve a separate corps, a political as well as a military challenge.

The writing is again flaccid and displays an especial fondness for romantic clichés: "The lovemaking, from fierce to subtle glance across the room, did not begin or end but was in motion all the time. . . . Bold and shy, they answered the curiosities of rich minds. Bold and shy they loved each other's raw naked beauty" (OHC, 345). Even the battle scenes seem tired. Uris writes that a soldier preparing for the raid on Fort Sumter "girds for battle with fear and fantasy" (OHC, 30). The confusion in the battle that follows, however, emphasizes the need for a disciplined, well-organized strike force, which only the marines can offer. History is Zachary's teacher, and one of the more effective scenes occurs when Zachary explains to Major Boone the tactics used at the Battle of Marathon in 49 BCE. Here, the writing becomes dynamic and active (OHC, 201). Uris is also strong on setting, especially Newport, Rhode Island, in the 1890s, which he carefully researched.

Uris faced the usual narrative conflict, however, between history and character, fact and fiction. He found the history and men of the Marine Corps irresistible, (recalling his first novel, *Battle Cry*), but he still had to balance personality with information. He remained conscientious about facts, but inadequate in detailing relationships. As a group of Civil War veterans tries to propel the marines forward, Zachary O'Hara rises from the enlisted ranks to become an officer. Bright and educated, he writes a report on the future of amphibious warfare; he also marries the daughter of a shipbuilding robber baron and enemy of the marines. The lines are drawn. Class conflict—O'Hara is a Catholic and a marine—dominates his life, and the choice becomes one between love and duty, while the Uris themes of loyalty, honor, and comradeship, evident since his first work, persist. Uris maintained a steadfast attachment to the marines and tried to attend one of their events every year.

Age and illness made the writing difficult, and his health prevented him from pursuing research with the gusto that marked his earlier books. The first draft of *O'Hara's Choice* read like a Harlequin romance, and Mark Uris repeatedly urged him to add more battle scenes.[31] But unable to travel to the sites he described, and relying on secondhand observations, he was reluctant. Uris was also uncertain about the ending and changed it numerous times.

His researcher corrected his text, both spelling and facts, and supplied him with details such as the scheduled stops of a boat traveling on the St. Lawrence river, the details of the major tennis clubs in Newport, and, of course, the manner of dress in the late nineteenth century. But he still objected to corrections, and Marilynn Pysher had to negotiate each change with tact.[32]

O'Hara's Choice appeared in October 2003, some three months after Uris died. Reception of the work was predictably low key, many critics acknowledging that the book lacked the typical Uris energy and relied too extensively on history. It sold poorly for a Uris title: 68,000 hardcover copies in 2003 and 273,000 paperback copies when it appeared in April 2005.

THE END

Leon Uris died on 21 June 2003, his death the result of continuing heart problems complicated by diabetes (he refused to give up drinking, for example). Severe arthritis caused by various knee operations prevented him from walking. The eventual cause of death was kidney failure, worsened by a weakened heart. At one point while in intensive care in a Stony Brook, Long Island, hospital, he became delusional and insisted on calling various marine generals and Hillary Clinton. After suffering a partial stroke, he refused to pursue rehabilitation or to spend time at a convalescent home. The severe arthritis in his legs increased. Throughout this period, his relations with his children remained difficult. He could never understand the foibles or shortcomings of others, repeating his earlier, intolerant behavior. According to his eldest son, he was a good father to begin with, but as his publicity and fame increased, so, too, did the pressure to behave like a celebrity. This meant he was around less and had little time for his family. "He wasn't much of a father," Mark Uris once remarked.[33]

Until the end, Uris loved the physical act of writing, and for most of his career he undertook research with enthusiasm. He loved to learn and to let his knowledge inform his fiction. But when he was working on a book, he isolated himself, though his demands on others did not diminish.

The Uris paradox was that although he found people difficult, especially when they disagreed with his opinionated ideas, he couldn't do without them. He remained passionate, argumentative, and belligerent if he had to be. He used language effectively but at times in a devastating, harmful manner. He was hard on his family, and it was only in the last few years of his life that he reconnected with his older sons. He found greater difficulty with his younger children. And his patronizing attitude toward women did not change. The inscription in Marilynn Pysher's copy of *A God in Ruins* reads "To a Great Broad."

From the first, Uris felt he had to establish his authority as a writer. He needed to make his credentials clear, but all he had were his experiences, beginning with the marines. Consequently, he wrote only from them. He also used the experiences of others, such as those of his uncle who fought in Greece in the Second World War. Then he hit upon a method that would provide authenticity for his writing: foreign travel, which would be the foundation of his research. Trips to Israel, Poland, Germany, Ireland, and New Zealand became essential for establishing credibility for his work, which readers valued. His confident tone and storytelling skill originated in his physical encounter with the past, whether he found it in the Irish countryside, the Negev, or the remains of the Warsaw Ghetto. And he loved to draw parallels between classical texts and his own: the first five books of the Hebrew Bible parallel the five books of *Exodus*.

The reading public loved Uris, making him one of the wealthiest and most popular American novelists of his time. This occurred when such writers such as James Michener, Herman Wouk, Irwin Shaw, and Norman Mailer—who would be superseded by Harold Robbins, Irving Wallace and Jacqueline Susann—were beginning to climb the best-seller charts.[34] Uris made many promotional appearances on television and at book signings, conventions, and shopping malls; he also made frequent demands for high advances. He was as marketable as his titles, and his career coincided with the explosion of the mass-market paperback. Sizeable print runs of paperback books and new steps in their promotion, including the author tour, became standard. Tie-ins began to define the new links between books and other media, marked by the early connections between his first novel, *Battle Cry*, and the 1955 film of the novel produced by Warner Bros.

As a writer, Uris capitalized on the public's fascination with history, relying on fiction to tell the story of the past. Unlike contemporaries who came to popular writing through journalism, Uris approached it first through his direct experience as a marine and then through his research. The Middle East and Europe captivated him, and seven of his thirteen novels are set there. And what he wrote in the preface to *Battle Cry* still stands as a guide to all his fiction: "To do justice to a story of the Marine Corps I felt that a sound historic basis would be the only fair avenue of approach." But, he adds, there are instances in which "events have been fictionalized for the sake of story continuity and dramatic effect" (BC, 1). This was the Uris method: researched fact restructured for narrative impact.

Literature was memory for Uris, who drew from recent history to cement past experiences in imaginative worlds that drew in readers. He made history in the sense that he refashioned its presentation so that it became vivid and understandable. And he did not disguise its uglier aspects. But he was also a victim of some of its larger narratives, notably that of Zionism and the British exploitation of Ireland. For the former, he attached the memory of the Holocaust firmly to the defense of a single country—Israel. This has increasingly come under attack from the so-called new historians in Israel, who emphasize the Palestinian displacement.[35] But Uris, like his hero Ben-Gurion, remained focused, and he stated and restated his narrative. He portrayed Britain one-sidedly in *Trinity* and in *Redemption* (as he did the Arabs in *The Haj*) and allowed for no sympathies. Nevertheless, Uris's writing, despite its literary shortcomings, worked to prevent the twentieth century from becoming "a moral memory palace," a place where history could be safely enshrined and ignored.[36] The past, he reminds us, is not behind us.

Uris avoided joining the emerging school of Jewish writers of the 1960s, which was shaped by Wouk, Bellow, Roth, Malamud, or Chaim Potok.[37] He did, however, see himself in a larger tradition of moral writers such as Dreiser, Steinbeck, Dos Passos, and Hersey, blended with the adventure writing of, say, Eric Ambler or Graham Greene, with perhaps the moral concerns of Elie Wiesel. He centered most of his fiction on twentieth-century traumas: the Holocaust, the establishment of the State of Israel, the Berlin airlift, the Cold War, the Cuban missile crisis, Irish independence, the Battle of Gallipoli. His legacy can be seen in a new generation of novelists, including Alan Furst, Louis de Bernières, William T. Vollmann and Jonathan Littell.[38]

Vollmann's sense of Europe's tragic history most closely parallels Uris's: at the opening of *Europe Central* (2005), the narrator observes that "the sleepwalker gets Lithuania, the realist Finland."[39] Europe pays the price: "We'll whirl away Europe Central's wine-tinted maple leaves and pale hexagonal church towers," says the narrator. Rhetorically, he then asks, "What once impelled millions of manned and unmanned bullets into motion? You say *Germany*. They say *Russia*. It certainly couldn't have been Europe herself."[40] Covering the years 1914 to 1975, this sweeping novel charts the unstable history of Central Europe and the warring cultures of Germany and Russia. It won the 2005 National Book Award for Fiction.

Jonathan Littell's *The Kindly Ones* (2009), originally published in French as *Les Bienveillantes* (2006), is the story of the Second World War and the Eastern Front through the fictional memories of a sadistic SS *oberstrumbannführer*, Max Aue. Its themes range from incest to genocide, and an unrepentant Nazi SS officer is the hero. It describes massacres of Jews and Bolsheviks in Ukraine, the Battle of Stalingrad, the implementation of the Final Solution, and the last days of Berlin. It won the Grand prix du roman de l'Académie française and the Prix Goncourt in 2006. Like Uris, these writers treat war, history, and culture as necessary proving grounds for ideas, politics, and heroism.

Uris, however, knew his limitations as a writer, which began with the treatment of characters. He did not attempt to explore the individuality or complexity of his characters, but rather the impact of historical events upon them. He preferred to have them "carry along the plot that history has already written." His aim was simple: "to paralyze [the average reader] with a story he cannot put down," and in this he succeeded.[41] But his purpose was always moral: to show the Jew as a Eurocentric figure who heroically challenged injustice and who shared, with the narrator of Vollmann's *Europe Central*, the monumental ambition "to invade the meaning of Europe."[42]

EPILOGUE

It took all my life to become an overnight success.
—URIS, 1984

THE DAY URIS DIED on Shelter Island, his first wife, Betty, had a stroke in California. At the same time, Rachael and Conor were preparing to board a flight in Aspen to visit him. En route to the airport, Jill received word of his death. They returned home to prepare for a funeral. At first, Uris wanted to be cremated. The thought of a burial reminded him too vividly of the mass burials of the Holocaust. But he was a marine and wanted to be remembered as one, therefore the possibility of internment in a Marine Corps cemetery appealed.

Uris called the Marine Corps Historical Library two or three weeks before he died to ask about procedures for a marine funeral. He made it clear to his cousin Herschel Blumberg, however, that if being buried in a military cemetery meant that he would be taking the plot of someone killed in action, he would refuse to do so. Throughout his life, he upheld the *Semper Fidelis* code of the marines.[1]

With the assistance of his cousin Herschel, the dedicatee of *O'Hara's Choice* and himself a former marine, and Michael Neiditch, attempts were made to bury Uris at Arlington National Cemetery. Confusion over his war records prevented his internment there, but he was allowed to be buried at Quantico National Cemetery in Quantico, Virginia, home to more than 24,000 deceased members of the armed forces.[2] Uris would have approved: the land was once part of a U.S. Marine Corps training base established in 1918. In 1977, the more than 700 acres became part of a new cemetery administered by the U.S. Department of Veterans Affairs. On a hot day in June 2003, Uris had a full military funeral with honors, which meant an honor guard, a three-volley gun salute, and taps.

A rabbi and brigadier general conducted the service. The latter movingly read from the opening of *Battle Cry*. Both were unusual tributes for an enlisted man who had not risen above the rank of private first class. A letter was read from the commandant of the corps. The service, conducted in a gazebo-like shelter some distance from the burial plot, was impressive. Although it was not standard practice to go to the burial site, the group had permission to do so, since Jewish tradition required mourners to accompany the body to the grave. The party drove the half mile to the location on Jefferson Road and sat in their air-conditioned cars until the coffin arrived by forklift some minutes later. It was a grand entrance for his exit, one attendee remarked.[3]

NOTES

PROLOGUE

1. For the remark on *Exodus* outselling *Gone with the Wind*, see Otto Preminger, CBC radio interview, 24 February 1961, reprinted in Gerald Pratley, *The Cinema of Otto Preminger* (New York: Barnes, 1971), 133; the 2,500-a-day figure occurred in February 1959 (*Publishers Weekly*, 9 March 1959). *Exodus* reached the top spot on the *New York Times* best-seller list on 17 May 1959, eight months after its debut.

2. Sales figures for *QB VII* come from the president of Doubleday, John T. Sargent, in a letter dated 15 March 1971 to Herb Schlosberg, Uris's business manager (copy in the Library of Congress). In April 1974, just before *QB VII* was to be shown as a televised miniseries, Bantam Books reprinted a further 300,000 paperback copies (John Bear, *The #1 New York Times Best Seller* [Berkeley, Calif.: Ten Speed Press, 1992], 113, 137).

3. Quoted in Thomas A. Larkin, "A Talk with Uris," *Scáthán*, July 1995. This is a Celtic literary and news magazine.

4. Leon Uris to William Uris, 10 July 1957, box 137, folder 8, Leon Uris Archive, Harry Ransom Humanities Research Center, University of Texas, Austin (hereafter cited as Uris Archive).

5. Leon Uris to William Uris, 17 July 1957, box 137, folder 8, Uris Archive.

6. Ibid.

7. William S. Burroughs, "Screenwriting and the Potentials of Cinema," in *Writing in a Film Age: Essays by Contemporary Novelists*, ed. Keith Cohen, 77 (Niwot: Univ. Press of Colorado, 1991).

8. Shakespeare, *The Merchant of Venice*, act 1, scene 3, line 107. Uris opposed the view of Abram Leon Sachar, the author of *The Jew in the Contemporary World: Sufferance Is the Badge* (New York: Knopf, 1939), who wrote: "It is stupid to call upon Jews to show their indomitable fortitude by defiance in lands where all groups have been beaten and cowed into submission" (573). Tragically, given the events that were soon to unfold, he added: "He [the Jew] can bear his fate . . . very much better when he knows that he is an

innocent victim and that the tirades of detractors are vile lies, made out of whole cloth, for self gain or power" (577).

9. Quoted in Hillel Italie, "Leon Uris . . . Dies at 78," Associated Press, 24 June 2003. Uris originally made his comments in an Associated Press interview in 1988. To his satisfaction, an earlier interview began with "Leon Uris is a tough, squat, mod-haired, bluntnosed son of an immigrant paperhanger. He looks like an old street fighter and ex-Marine and he is" (Paul Henderson, "A School Drop Out, Leon Uris Knows What Success Is," *Watertown (N.Y.) Daily News,* 1977 [box 175, Uris Archive]).

10. Quoted in Bill Clopton, "Author of No. 3 Best Seller Once Flunked English," *Cincinnati Post and Times-Star,* 18 February 1959.

11. Quoted in Pearl Sheffy Geffen, "Leon Uris," *Lifestyles* 17 (1989): 16.

12. Michael Korda, *Making the List: A Cultural History of the American Bestseller, 1900–1999* (New York: Barnes & Noble Books, 2001), 108–109 and passim.

13. "Topaz," *Library Journal,* 1 October 1967; Melvin Maddocks, "The Uris School of Non-Fiction Fiction," *Life,* 27 October 1967; Anthony Boucher, "Criminals at Large," *New York Times,* 29 September 1967.

14. Ernest Hemingway, *A Farewell to Arms* (1929; New York: Scribner's, 1949), 191. "Accuracy means something," a character adds late in the novel (292).

15. Uris, speech at the dedication of the library of Mesa College, Grand Junction, Colorado, 13 October 1967.

16. Although Uris was never a journalist, reporters appear in a number of his novels: Michael Morrison in *The Angry Hills,* Mark Parker in *Exodus,* Christopher de Monti in *Mila 18,* and Seamus O'Neil in *Trinity.*

CHAPTER 1

1. Leon Uris, "The Truth Will Rise," n.d. [1940?], box 114, folder 9, Uris Archive.

2. These student compositions are found in box 119, folder 9, Uris Archive.

3. Abram Bellow to his son Saul in Mel Gussow and Charles McGrath, "Saul Bellow, Who Breathed Life into American Novel, Dies at 89," *New York Times,* 6 April 2005.

4. Arthur Liebman, *Jews and the Left* (New York: Wiley, 1979), 346.

5. Ibid., 348.

6. Leon Uris was born on the day Joseph Conrad died, 3 August 1924.

7. Isaac M. Fein, *The Making of an American Jewish Community: The History of Baltimore Jewry from 1773 to 1920* (Philadelphia: Jewish Publication Society of America, 1971), 223.

8. Sandra Featherman, "Jewish Politics in Philadelphia, 1920–1940," in *Jewish Life in Philadelphia, 1830–1940,* ed. Murray Friedman (Philadelphia: Institute for the Study of Human Issues, 1983), 288–289.

9. Earl Lewis, *In Their Own Interests: Race, Class, and Power in Twentieth-Century Norfolk, Virginia* (Berkeley and Los Angeles: Univ. of California Press, 1991), 129.

10. An article in the *Norfolk Virginian-Pilot* (27 February 1977) called attention to parallels between Ben Cady, brother of the hero in *QB VII,* and an actual Jewish athlete from

Norfolk, Sam Friedberg, who attended Maury High School. In the novel, Uris vividly describes Church and Holt streets, Colonial Place, J. E. B. Stuart Elementary School, Blair Junior High School, the old airfield with a dirt runway in Granby Street across from the cemetery, and the Bush (Boushi) Street Bowling Alley.

11. Eli N. Evans, "Southern-Jewish History Alive and Unfolding," in *Turn to the South: Essays on Southern Jewry*, ed. Nathan M. Kaganoff and Melvin I. Urofsky (Charlottesville, Va.: American Jewish Historical Society / Univ. Press of Virginia, 1979), 159.

12. A copy of the program is in box 167, Uris Archive.

13. These student compositions are found in box 119, folders 6 and 9, Uris Archive.

14. It was discovered forty years later when the brother of his teacher found it in an attic trunk and sent it to Uris. The synopsis reads in part:

> Act I. Rosett makes love to Gracia in an old garden. She tells him that she loves him too. He asks her mother for her daughter, and she tells him to be good to her always.
> Act II. The Wedding
> Act III. Six years later. Gracia, the mother of children, is very ill. The father is away from home trying to earn money.

15. Military personnel record of Leon Uris, U.S. National Personnel Records Center, St. Louis, Missouri.

16. Michael Gold, *Jews without Money*, 2nd ed. (New York: Carroll and Graf, 1996).

17. Ibid., 309.

18. Leon Uris, address to the Smithsonian Institute, Washington, D.C., 24 October 1988, box 3, folders 4–5, Uris Archive.

19. Leon Uris, address to the New York Times Literary Luncheon, 18 September 1988, box 181, folder 8, Uris Archive.

20. John Steinbeck, *Novels and Stories, 1932–1937* (New York: Library of America, 1994), 888.

21. Ibid., 897.

22. Quoted in Myra Yellin Goldfarb, "Leon Uris: A Profile," *Hakol* (Allentown, PA), November 1989.

23. Gefen, "Leon Uris," 15.

24. Leon Uris to William Uris, 20 February 1957, box 137, folder 8, Uris Archive.

25. Quoted in Leslie Hanscom, "Author of *Exodus* Tells of His Genesis," *Newsday*, 23 October 1988.

26. Gefen, "Leon Uris," 15.

27. Quoted in Hillel Italie, "Uris Taps His Own History," Associated Press, 1988.

28. Gefen, "Leon Uris," 16.

29. Leon Uris to Anna Blumberg Uris, 30 July 1943, box 136, folder 5, Uris Archive.

30. Leon Uris to Anna Blumberg Uris, n.d., box 136, folder 5, Uris Archive. The date of the letter was obliterated by wartime censors.

31. Leon Uris to Anna Blumberg Uris, n.d. [1940 or 1941], box 136, folder 5, Uris Archive.

32. In a July 2001 taped interview for his grandchildren, Uris was more direct: "I joined up because I had to get out of a difficult family situation."

33. The note is folded in a first edition of *Battle Cry* that Uris inscribed to his son Michael.

34. Leon Uris to "Uncle Eddie," n.d. [1942?], box 136, folder 6, Uris Archive.

CHAPTER 2

1. Uris was so proud of his number that he assigned it to Danny Forrester in *Battle Cry* and to Clinton Loveless in *Armageddon*. It is also became the number tattooed on Dov Landau's forearm at Auschwitz in *Exodus*.

2. Leon Uris to Esther Uris, 18 January 1942, box 136, folder 8, Uris Archive.

3. Leon Uris to Esther Uris, 8 February 1942, box 136, folder 8, Uris Archive.

4. Ibid.

5. Leon Uris to Esther Uris, 15 February 1942, box 136, folder 8, Uris Archive.

6. Ibid.

7. Leon Uris to Esther Uris, 16 March 1942, box 136, folder 8, Uris Archive.

8. See, for example, Leon Uris to Esther Uris, 19 March 1942, box 136, folder 8, Uris Archive.

9. Leon Uris to Esther Uris, 8 April 1942, box 136, folder 8, Uris Archive.

10. Ibid.

11. Harry Bioletti, *The Yanks Are Coming: The American Invasion of New Zealand, 1942–1944* (Auckland: Century Hutchinson, 1989), 195.

12. Leon Uris to Esther Uris, 13 April 1942, box 136, folder 8, Uris Archive.

13. Leon Uris to Harry Kofsky, 13 April 1942, box 136, folder 8, Uris Archive.

14. Leon Uris to Esther Uris from San Diego, n.d. [mid-1942?], box 10, folder 11, Uris Archive.

15. Leon Uris to Anna Abrams, n.d. [1942?], box 136, folder 5, Uris Archive.

16. Quoted in Julie Hutchinson, "Uris: A Life as Epic as the Stories He Tells," *ElectriCity* (Denver), June 1984, 31.

17. Leon Uris to Esther Uris, 28 May 1942, box 136, folder 8, Uris Archive. The International Workers Order, established in 1930, assumed an outlook close to that of the Communist Party. In addition to its political interests, the IWO sold insurance and offered money and other benefits to needy members and their families. It also sponsored schools, summer camps, lectures, dances, and dinners, essentially creating a social world for left-leaning, progressive Jews.

18. William Blake, *The Copperheads* (New York: Dial, 1941). The 741-page book contains a panoramic story, anticipating the sweep and history of Uris's own fiction.

19. Leon Uris to Esther Uris, 22 April 1942, box 136, folder 8, Uris Archive.

20. Leon Uris to Esther Uris, 4 May 1942, box 136, folder 8, Uris Archive.

21. Leon Uris to Esther Uris, 24 May 1942, box 136, folder 8, Uris Archive.

22. Leon Uris to Esther Uris, 1 June 1942, box 136, folder 8, Uris Archive.

23. Leon Uris to Esther Uris, 6 June 1942, box 136, folder 8, Uris Archive.

24. Ibid.

25. Ibid.

26. Leon Uris to Esther Uris, 23 January 1943, box 136, folder 9, Uris Archive.

27. Leon Uris to Esther Uris, 17 July 1943, box 136, folder 5, Uris Archive.

28. Leon Uris to Anna Abrams, 26 January 1943, box 136, folder 5, Uris Archive.

29. Leon Uris to Anna Abrams, 12 May 1943, box 136, folder 5, Uris Archive.

30. Bernard Guilbert Guerney, translator's note to Alexandre Kuprin, *Yama* (*The Pit*) (New York: Modern Library, 1932), xix. The original English edition, translated and published by Bernard Guilbert Guerney, appeared in 1922.

31. Kuprin, *Yama*, 82.

32. Leon Uris to Esther Uris, 12 May 1943, box 136, folder 9, Uris Archive.

33. Leon Uris to Esther Uris, 4 January 1943, box 136, folder 9, Uris Archive.

34. Leon Uris to Esther Uris, 1 February 1943, box 136, folder 9, Uris Archive.

35. Major John L. Zimmerman, *The Guadalcanal Campaign* (Washington, D.C.: U.S. Marine Corps, Headquarters, Historical Division, 1949), 159n12.

36. Ibid., 164.

37. Ibid., 169.

38. Leon Uris to Esther Uris, 11 January 1943, box 136, folder 9, Uris Archive.

39. Leon Uris to Esther Uris, 19 January 1943, box 136, folder 9, Uris Archive.

40. Leon Uris to Esther Uris, April 1943, box 136, folder 9, Uris Archive.

41. Joseph A. Alexander, *Utmost Savagery: The Three Days of Tarawa* (Annapolis, Md.: Naval Institute Press, 1995), 44.

42. Leon Uris to Esther Uris, April 1943, box 136, folder 9, Uris Archive.

43. Leon Uris to Esther Uris, 5 April 1943, box 136, folder 9, Uris Archive.

44. Ibid.

45. Betty Cogswell to Leon Uris, 24 March 1943, box 136, folder 9, Uris Archive.

46. Leon Uris to Anna Abrams, 9 May 1943, box 136, folder 5, Uris Archive.

47. Leon Uris to Esther Uris, 9 November 1943, box 136, folder 5, Uris Archive.

48. William Uris to Esther Uris, 17 October 1943, box 136, folder 9, Uris Archive.

49. Leon Uris to Esther Uris, 9 April 1943, box 136, folder 9, Uris Archive.

50. Leon Uris to Esther Uris, 29 June 1942, box 136, folder 8, Uris Archive.

51. Leon Uris to Anna Abrams, 26 April 1942, box 136, folder 5, Uris Archive.

52. Nearly a year later (August 1944), however, an argument emerged over who had originated and contributed the most to the show. A letter to *Leatherneck*, the marine magazine, by Sergeant Paul Smith, says that the follies, which Uris claimed to have written and produced, were one of those "returned veteran snow jobs." In fact, according to Smith, all Uris did was to sing "one very corny song" and read a few lines. Etheridge conceived the show, which Earl Hall and Smith enlarged. "Direction came from Capt. Walter and Lt. Babo," he added, "and that leaves us with very little room for PFC Uris. And that is that" (Paul Smith, "At Ease," *Leatherneck*, Pacific edition, 1 August 1944). However, Smith later apologized for having overstated the case (Paul Smith to Leon Uris in San Francisco, 18 December 1944, box 165, Uris Archive).

53. Leon Uris to Esther Uris, 29 May 1943, box 136, folder 9, Uris Archive.

54. Leon Uris to Esther Uris, 11 July 1943, box 136, folder 5, Uris Archive.

55. Leon Uris to Esther Uris, 9 August 1943, box 136, folder 5, Uris Archive.

56. Leon Uris to Anna Abrams, 13 October 1943, box 136, folder 5, Uris Archive.

57. Leon Uris to Esther Uris, 9 November 1943, box 136, folder 9, Uris Archive.

58. Alexander, *Utmost Savagery*, 206.

59. Uris, interview by the *Memphis Press-Scimitar*, 4 February 1955.

60. Uris, speech at the dedication of the Tarawa Monument, Long Beach, California, 1 July 1998, box 182, folder 1, Uris Archive.

61. Ibid., 3.

62. Ibid., 4.

63. Ibid., 8.

64. Gefen, "Leon Uris," 9.

65. Norman Mailer went to the Philippines after Uris had come home, later publishing the first important novel of the Second World War, *The Naked and The Dead* (1948). James Jones's *From Here to Eternity* (1951) appeared next, along with Herman Wouk's *The Caine Mutiny* (1951), followed by Uris's *Battle Cry* (1953). Interestingly, each was a first novel.

66. Leon Uris to Anna Abrams, 24 March 1944, box 136, folder 5, Uris Archive.

67. Leon Uris to Anna Abrams, 31 March 1944, box 136, folder 5, Uris Archive.

68. A clipping of this article is located in a scrapbook in box 165 of the Uris Archive.

69. These items are in a scrapbook in box 165, Uris Archive.

70. Leon Uris to Esther Uris, 7 July 1944, box 136, folder 5, Uris Archive.

71. Leon Uris to Anna Abrams, 11 December 1944, box 136, folder 5, Uris Archive.

72. Ibid.

73. Mark Uris, interview by the author, 20 June 2005, Boulder, Colorado.

74. A copy of the rebuttal editorial is located in a scrapbook in box 165 of the Uris Archive.

75. Leon Uris to Anna Abrams, 26 April 1945, box 136, folder 5, Uris Archive.

76. Leon Uris to Anna Abrams, 21 March 1945, box 136, folder 5, Uris Archive.

77. Ibid.

78. Leon Uris to Anna Abrams, 3 November 1945, box 136, folder 5, Uris Archive.

79. Leon Uris to Anna Abrams, 29 May 1945, box 136, folder 5, Uris Archive.

80. Leon Uris to Anna Abrams, 11 December 1944, box 136, folder 5, Uris Archive.

81. Laura Wilck to Chelle Janis (the publisher of *Opportunities on Parade* and perhaps Uris's agent), 19 January 1946, box 165, scrapbook, Uris Archive.

82. Story department to Leon Uris, 26 January 1945, box 165, scrapbook, Uris Archive.

83. For details on Israel London (1898–1968), see David Mazower, "Israel London's Life and Work," *Mendele Review: Yiddish Literature and Language* 6 (13 April 2002). The Marstin Press had its offices at 228 East 45th Street in New York City.

84. Isaac E. Rontch, foreword to *Jewish Youth at War: Letters from American Soldiers*, ed. Isaac E. Rontch (New York: Marstin Press, 1945) 1.

85. Martin Greenberg, "Jewish Youth at War," *Commentary* 1, no. 3 (January 1946): 98.

86. A copy of the protest letter is located in a scrapbook in box 165 of the Uris Archive.

87. Clippings and handbills are located in a scrapbook in box 165 of the Uris Archive.

88. Clipping in a scrapbook in box 165, Uris Archive.

CHAPTER 3

1. Norman Mailer, *The Naked and the Dead* (1948), James Gould Cozzens, *Guard of Honor* (1948; Pulitzer Prize, 1949), James Jones, *From Here to Eternity* (1951), Herman Wouk, *The Caine Mutiny* (1951), and Leon Uris, *Battle Cry* (1953).

2. Leon Uris to Esther Uris, n.d., box 136, folder 5, Uris Archive.

3. Leon Uris to Esther Uris, n.d., box 10, folder 11, Uris Archive.

4. Two decades later, Larkspur would gain fame as the home of Janis Joplin, who lived in the suitably named (for Uris) Baltimore Canyon. Other notables in Larkspur at that time included Jerry Garcia, founder of the Grateful Dead, and Ken Kesey. For a short time in the mid to late sixties, Larkspur became a hippie enclave.

5. Leon Uris to Esther Uris, n.d., box 136, folder 5, Uris Archive.

6. Leon Uris to Esther Uris, n.d., box 136, folder 5, Uris Archive.

7. Ibid.

8. Uris, *Memphis Press-Scimitar* interview.

9. Leon Uris to Esther Uris, n.d., box 137, folder 5, Uris Archive.

10. Marsh Maslin, "Leon Uris," *San Francisco Call-Bulletin*, 10 April 1953.

11. Donald Cormack to Leon Uris, 9 June 1950, box 166, folder 1, Uris Archive.

12. Leon M. Uris, "All-American Razz-Matazz," *Esquire*, January 1951, 95.

13. Quoted in Donald Kirley, "A Marine's Literary Landing," *Sunday Sun Magazine*, *Baltimore Sun*, 17 October 1954.

14. Recounted in Mark Uris interview.

15. "Newspaper Driver-Author, Local 921 Member, Writes Book while Working as Circulation Man," *San Francisco Labor*, 17 April 1953 (clipping in box 166, Uris Archive).

16. Quoted in Marylou Luther, "Don't Let Education Sanitize Talent—Uris," *Los Angeles Times*, 10 November 1960 (clipping in box 169, Uris Archive).

17. Francis Veach, "Author of Famous War Novel Tells Story of Success," *Waterloo (IA) Sunday Courier*, 2 January 1955.

18. "Cleveland Amory's Celebrity Register, Leon Uris," 1966 (clipping in box 173, folder 1, Uris Archive).

19. Uris, *Memphis Press-Scimitar* interview.

20. Quoted in Bernard Kalb, "The Author," *Saturday Review of Literature*, 25 April 1953, 16.

21. Ibid.

22. Ed Brooks, "Battle Cry Aim Told by Author," *New Orleans Times-Picayune*, 3 February 1955. The novel, he added, was out in 14 languages, and the one-millionth copy was presented to the Los Angeles Public Library. Also see Uris, "Why the Marines?" incomplete typescript, for *McClurg's Book News* (Chicago; Uris, box 17, folder 8). Article by Uris (April 1953) and Uris, "Interview, Songs of A City," *San Diego Union*, July 1954.

23. Paul Nathan, "Rights and Permissions," *Publishers Weekly* 1953 (clipping in box 166, Uris Archive).

24. A copy of the contract is located in box 155, folder 8, Uris Archive.

25. Gefen, "Leon Uris," 9.

26. Ibid.

27. Win Fanning, "Battle Cry Author Here First to Reject Own Book," *Pittsburgh Post Gazette*, 8 February 1955.

28. Quoted in Veach, "Author of Famous War Novel."

29. Interestingly, in the fiftieth reprinting of the paperback of the novel in 1980, this statement appears at the end rather than the beginning. By the sixty-third reprinting, the section was dropped.

30. Shapiro becomes heroic through his antiauthoritarian, risk-taking actions. He dies on Saipan with his two pistols firing (echoes of the Old West) as he screams, "*Blood!*" (*BC*, 498).

31. John McCormick to Leon Uris, 13 April 1953, box 166, scrapbook, Uris Archive.

32. C. S. Nichols, review of *Battle Cry*, by Leon Uris, *Military Affairs* 18 (1953): 38.

33. Merle Miller, "The Backdrop Is Victory," review of *Battle Cry*, by Leon Uris, *Saturday Review of Literature*, 25 April 1953, 16–17.

34. The citation is located in a scrapbook in box 166 of the Uris Archive.

35. The critics' poll was reported in the *Cleveland Press*, 2 December 1953; for the readers' poll, see "Year's Best," *Saturday Review of Literature*, 26 December 1953, 36.

36. Joseph Blotner, *Faulkner: A Biography* (New York: Random House, 1974), 2:1106–1107, 1120–1121.

37. Faulkner, in ibid., 2:1144.

38. Ibid., 2:1142; Louis Daniel Brodsky and Robert W. Hamblin, eds., *Faulkner: A Comprehensive Guide to the Brodsky Collection*, vol. 4: *"Battle Cry"* (Jackson: Univ. Press of Mississippi, 1985), xix.

39. Blotner, *Faulkner*, 2:1142.

40. Brodsky and Hamblin, *Faulkner Guide*, 4:xv.

41. Ibid., 4:xxv.

42. Quoted in ibid., 4:xxxi.

43. Ibid., xi. After leaving Hollywood, Faulkner received credit for only two works: collaborating on the adaptations of Hemingway's *To Have and Have Not* (1944) and Raymond Chandler's *The Big Sleep* (1946), both directed by Howard Hawks. Upset at not being able to negotiate a new contract, Faulkner walked out of Warner Bros. in September 1945, telling Jack Warner, "I feel that I have made a bust at moving picture writing."

44. Faulkner quoted in Rudy Behlmer, ed., *Inside Warner Bros., 1935–1951* (New York: Viking, 1985), 250; on the early publicity for *Battle Cry*, see Publicity Department, Warner Bros., "Trades," Warner Bros. Archive, University of Southern California [1953].

45. Script report on *Battle Cry*, n.d., 1 (Warner Bros. Archive, University of Southern California; hereafter cited as WB Archive).

46. Ibid., 1–2.

47. Paul Nathan, "Rights and Permissions," *Publishers Weekly*, 7 February 1955.

48. Leon Uris to Ted Purdy, n.d., box 1, folder 8, Uris Archive.

49. Ibid.

50. Leon Uris to Bob Amussen, 21 September 1953, box 1, folder 9, Uris Archive.

51. Bob Amussen to Leon Uris, 16 September 1953, box 1, folder 9, Uris Archive.

52. Willis Wing to Leon Uris, 21 September 1953, box 1, folder 9, Uris Archive.

53. Leon Uris to Bob Amussen, 21 September 1953, box 1, folder 9, Uris Archive.

54. Putnam catalogue, 1954, box 166, Uris Archive.

55. A manuscript copy of Aaron Yerushalmi's autobiography is located in box 1, folder 1 of the Uris Archive.

56. Bob Amussen, handwritten note on the typescript of "Hellenic Interlude," box 1, folder 9, Uris Archive.

57. Leon Uris, draft of *The Angry Hills*, 119, box 1, folder 9, Uris Archive.

58. Leon Uris to Bennett Cerf, 22 September 1955, box 168, Uris Archive. Cerf's reply is in the same box.

59. Katherine Gauss Jackson, review of *The Angry Hills*, by Leon Uris, *Harper's Magazine*, December 1955, 105.

60. Review of *The Angry Hills*, by Leon Uris, *Richmond (VA) Times-Dispatch*, 30 October 1955.

CHAPTER 4

1. Janetta Somersett, "Mayor, Marines and a Mob Help Send off Battle Cry," *Baltimore Sun*, 2 February 1955.

2. Also in the cast was a young Fess Paker (Speedy), later to become a television star as Davy Crockett, and Jonas Applegarth (Shining Lighttower), a Cree from Alberta who, when he heard he had won the part, had to take a sleigh to an airport to fly to Puerto Rico.

3. Finley McDermid to Steve Trilling, Warner Bros., 20 February 1954 and 23 February 1954 (WB Archive).

4. Warner Bros. publicity release, box 167, Uris Archive.

5. Warner Bros. publicity department, memo, WB Archive.

6. Uris to Mort Blumenstock, 1 April 1954, WB Archive.

7. Lemuel Shepherd, 9 December 1954, WB Archive.

8. *Daily Variety*, 27 January 1955 (clipping in WB Archive).

9. Quoted in ibid.

10. Herbert Pickman to Mort Blumenstock, telegram, 1 February 1955, WB Archive.

11. In a letter dated 10 October 1955, Uris told Mayor Thomas D'Alesandro that he was returning the three awards given to him in February: "You may burn them in the Civic Plaza along with all known copies of Battle Cry." He sent back the key to the city, the proclamation declaring February *Battle Cry* month, and the scroll given to him on the stage of the Stanley Theatre. In a free society, he writes, "we must live with these small-minded groups of malcontent blowhards who live in mental vacuums," but he wanted nothing to do with them (box 168, Uris Archive).

12. Warner Bros. reported that the film earned $1,250,000 in its initial thirty-three engagements and that it was "shaping up as the company's top grosser of all time" (*Variety*, 16 February 1955). Warner Bros. also reported 100 percent holdovers in movie theatres in the first dates, with the peak pace continuing in twenty-one additional dates.

13. Quoted in Ian Hamilton, *Writers in Hollywood, 1915–1951* (New York: Harper and Row, 1990), 52.

14. Uris, speech at the dedication of the library of Mesa College, Grand Junction, Colorado, 13 October 1967, 11–12.

15. Ibid., 12.

16. Ibid.

17. Ibid.

18. "I Like Hollywood Because . . . ," *Dallas Morning News*, October 1955.

19. Fred Johnson, "On the Aisle," *San Francisco Call-Bulletin*, 8 January 1955. See also passages in *Mitla Pass* in which the writer-hero's father warns him that those who go to Hollywood are soon degraded and forgotten (*MP*, 68–70). On Tab Hunter's experience in making *Battle Cry*, see Tab Hunter, *Tab Hunter Confidential: The Making of a Movie Star* (Chapel Hill, N.C.: Algonquin, 2005).

20. Betty Uris to her parents, 28 May 1954, box 185, folder 3, Uris Archive.

21. Bosley Crowther, review of *Battle Cry*, directed by Raoul Walsh, *New York Times*, 3 February 1955.

22. The memo is quoted in Lawrence Frascella and Al Weisel, *Live Fast, Die Young: The Wild Ride of Making "Rebel Without a Cause"* (New York: Touchstone, 2005), 48. The details in the next several paragraphs come from this source.

23. Quoted in Hayden White, "The Modernist Event," in *The Persistence of History: Cinema, Television, and the Modern Event*, ed. Vivian Sobchack, 17 (New York: Routledge, 1996).

24. Bruce Cook, "Did Uris Write Novel or Script?" *Chicago Sunday Sun-Times*, 25 June 1961.

25. Betty Uris, diary, 1954, box 185, folder 3, Uris Archive; Uris to William Uris, 25 February 1956, box 137, folder 7, Uris Archive.

26. Paul Joseph Gulino, *Screenwriting: The Sequence Approach* (New York: Continuum, 2004), 4.

27. Diane Eagle, "Leon Uris—The Work Day," unpublished essay dated 13 July 2005, private collection.

28. Leon Uris to Colin Robertson, 10 October 1974, box 101, folder 1, Uris Archive.

29. John Steinbeck, *The Red Pony* (1937; repr., New York: Viking Press, 1960), 7.

30. On this structure, see Philip Parker, *The Art and Science of Screenwriting* (Exeter, UK: Intellect Books, 1998), 27–29. Also helpful are William Miller, *Screenwriting for Film and Television* (Boston: Allyn and Bacon, 1998), 49–51, and Ari Hiltunen, *Aristotle in Hollywood* (Bristol, UK: Intellect Books, 2002), 19–20, 124–126.

31. Donald Freeman, "Wyatt Earp Story Stirs Up Dispute, "*San Diego Union*, 23 September 1955.

32. Quoted in *Publishers Weekly*, 29 March 1976. On the western, see, for example, Lee

Clark Mitchell, *Westerns: Making the Man in Fiction and Film* (Chicago: Univ. of Chicago Press, 1996), and Jeffrey Wallmann, *The Western: Parables of the American Dream* (Lubbock: Texas Tech Univ. Press, 1999). Flexibility might be illustrated by Nelson Nye's novelization of Uris's *Gunfight at the O.K. Corral* (South Yarmouth, Mass.: Curley, 1982).

33. Emily Dickinson titled an early poem "My Life had stood—a Loaded Gun." Faulkner's *Light in August* (1932) and Richard Wright's *Native Son* (1940) are two important modern examples of violent literary novels. Sherwood Anderson sensed the endemic nature of violence in American writing: "For a long time I have believed that crudity is an inevitable quality in the production of a really significant present-day American literature" (*Sherwood Anderson's Notebook* [1926; repr., Mamaroneck, N.Y.: Appel, 1970], 195).

34. Eastwood, quoted in Mitchell, *Westerns*, 150. This is reminiscent of Peter Ustinov's advice to a young Method actor: "Don't just do something—stand there!" (quoted in Ira B. Nadel, *David Mamet: A Life in the Theatre* [New York: Palgrave, 2008], 132).

35. Paula Mitchell Marks, *And Die in the West: The Story of the O.K. Corral Gunfight* (Norman, OK: Oklahoma University Press, 1996), 18–33 and passim.

36. Uris, author's note to *QB VII*, 9. Of course, writers of historical fiction have long followed this practice. In E. L. Doctorow's Civil War novel *The March* (2005), he fabricates a moving letter from General William T. Sherman to General William Hardee after the latter loses a son in battle, as had the former; see Janet Maslin, "Using History as a Guide, but Skipping the Details," *New York Times*, 27 September 2005.

37. Nevertheless, Uris said he learned more about motion pictures from Hitchcock in six months then he had learned before or since (Ted Bredt, "Leon Uris Retains Rugged Charm," *San Jose Mercury News*, 22 August 1976).

38. Murray Schumach, "Hollywood Prose, Studio Deal with Novelist Prompts Reappraisal of the Movie Writer," *New York Times*, 23 August 1959.

39. Quoted in Gefen, "Leon Uris."

40. Griffith, quoted in Hamilton, *Writers in Hollywood*, 9.

41. Cited in Uris to William Uris, 11 January 1956, box 137, folder 7, Uris Archive.

CHAPTER 5

1. Ezra Rusinek, "Afterword: The Samizdat," in Alla Rusinek, *Like a Song, like a Dream: A Soviet Girl's Quest for Freedom* (New York: Scribner's, 1973), 256; see 252–256 for one of the most extensive descriptions of the samizdat process for translating *Exodus*. The translation Rusinek describes occurred in 1963. Numerous accounts of these samizdat efforts exist; one of the fullest is in Leonard Schroeter, *The Last Exodus* (1974; repr., Seattle: Univ. of Washington Press, 1979), 64–68. When Uris visited the Soviet Union in 1989, one of his most cherished moments was the presentation of a samizdat translation of the novel. The inscription on the bootlegged copy read: "Thank you for reaching us." According to Michael Neiditch, who was with Uris at the time, this copy was signed by Natan Sharansky. For Sharansky on *Exodus*, see his *Fear No Evil*, trans. Stefani Hoffman (New York: Random House, 1988), xv. On the origin of the Russian dissident movement,

see Anatole Shub, "From Russia with Chutzpah: Origins of a New Exodus," *Harper's*, May 1972, 72–79.

2. Feldman is quoted in Allan Richter, "Exodus: A Ship's Hold on the Jewish Imagination," *Jewish World* (September 30–6 October 1988). Feldman told his story on 6 September 1988 at the Baltimore celebration of the *Exodus*, with Uris present. Feldman became the first refusenik ordained as a Conservative rabbi in the United States.

3. Edwin McDowell, "'Exodus' in Samizdat: Still Popular and Still Subversive," *New York Times Book Review*, 26 April 1987, 13.

4. Schroeter, *Last Exodus*, 64–68.

5. Arie Lova Eliav, in *Israel at Sixty: An Oral History of a Nation Reborn*, ed. Deborah Hart Strober and Gerald S. Strober, 168 (Hoboken, N.J.: Wiley, 2008).

6. On the role of the Mossad in bringing in copies, see ibid. Eliav served in the Haganah, the Jewish Brigade of the British army in the Second World War, the Aliyah Bet movement after the war, and the Mossad. He was also a member of the Knesset for eighteen years. The actions of Ari Ben Canaan in *Exodus* parallel Eliav's in many ways (see "Leon Uris Says," EX, 1–2).

7. Neal Gabler, *An Empire of Their Own: How the Jews Invented Hollywood* (New York: Crown, 1988), 299, 394–395.

8. Foster Hirsch, *Otto Preminger: The Man Who Would Be King* (New York: Knopf, 2007), 284. Ingo Preminger was a political progressive who had several Hollywood blacklisted writers among his clients. In a "Note of Thanks" in the first edition of *Exodus*, Uris writes that the book "evolved out of a conversation at lunch and became a tangible project because of the dogged persistence of Malcolm Stuart," his agent (EX, 5). Stuart (1928–2004) was Malcolm "Max" Sterz, who became "Stuart" when he started an agency career.

9. Uris, "About *Exodus*," in *The Quest for Truth*, ed. Martha Boaz (New York: Scarecrow, 1961), 127.

10. Details of the contract are located in box 156, folder 1, at the Uris Archive. If MGM exercised its rights to fully purchase his story, Uris would receive $42,500, assuming he met the deadline of 25 January 1957.

11. Gabler, *Empire of Their Own*, 421.

12. Leon Uris, "Notes on the Background of *Exodus*," box 25, folder 7, Uris Archive.

13. William Uris, quoted in "Uris Pere," *Philadelphia Jewish Exponent*, 11 July 1959.

14. Leon Uris to Anna Abrams, n.d. [1942?], box 135, folder 5, Uris Archive.

15. Leon Uris quoted in Jill Lai, "Uris Looking At His Past," United Press International, Washington, 4 November 1988, 331.

16. Leon Uris, quoted in George Murray, "Tough Israelis Inspire Author," *Chicago American*, February 1959 (clipping in box 11, folder 1, Uris Archive). He also says he "was made almost ill by those beatnik writers who degrade Jews. I wanted to do *Exodus*."

17. Leon Uris to William Uris, 8 March 1956, box 137, folder 7, Uris Archive.

18. Other books that retold the story of Israel at this time include Ernest Pawel, *The Island in Time: A Novel of Survival* (1951); Dean Brelis, *Shalom* (1959; the author was a passenger on a refugee ship to Israel in 1948); Lester Gorn, *The Anglo-Saxons* (1958); and James Murdock, *Ketti Shalom* (1953).

19. Leon Uris to William Uris, 10 May 1956, box 137, folder 7, Uris Archive.

20. Ilan Hartuv, interview by the author, 23 February 2007, Jerusalem.

21. In a 1959 interview, Uris remarked that when he heard his voice on playback, he felt the strong emotional effect on him at the time he recorded. This was important in re-creating the feeling that he tried to convey in the novel (Uris, interview by Yoram Vidan, "Uris's Tricks in Creating Exodus," *Yedi'ot Aharonot* [Tel Aviv], 4 December 1959 [in Hebrew]).

22. Hartuv interview. Hartuv was appointed government liaison officer for Otto Preminger's production staff during filming. But he was rebuffed when he confronted Preminger with anomalies. He pointed out, for example, that it would have been impossible to bury Karen, the young immigrant in love with Dov Landau, and Taha, the Arab friend of Ari Ben Canaan, in the same grave. Neither Islam nor Judaism condones it, and neither permits an unmarried couple to be buried together. Preminger refused to change the scene.

23. See Michalais Firillas, "Prodromos Papavasileiou," *Ha'aretz*, 3 January 2007. The correct spelling is "Papavassiliou," according to his son, who is the current managing director of Shosham (Cyprus) Ltd. The father died on 22 December 2006. Hugh Griffith played him in the film.

24. Hartuv's own life is quite extraordinary. In 1976, he was a hostage at Entebbe, and his mother, Dora Block, was the only Israeli killed by Idi Amin's men. He went on to become the Israeli ambassador to Fiji and the Solomon Islands. He also had the longest nonspeaking role in Preminger's *Exodus*, shown first listening to a radio announcement of the UN partition vote on 29 November 1947 and then standing on a balcony between Lee J. Cobb, playing Barak Ben Canaan, Ari's father, and Meir Weisgal (president of the Weizmann Institute), who was standing in for David Ben-Gurion when the news was announced to the crowd of some 20,000. Hartuv retired from the Foreign Ministry in 1993 but has taught African studies (another of his specialties) at Hebrew University for many years. Uris's appreciation of Hartuv remained long after *Exodus* was completed. He based the character of Shlomo Bar Adon, in *Mitla Pass*, on him. A fighter who also worked at the Foreign Ministry, Shlomo heroically dies in the final battle (*MP*, 302, 410–416).

25. Leon Uris to William Uris, 3 June 1956, box 137, folder 7, Uris Archive.

26. Leon Uris, "Notes on the Background of *Exodus*," box 25, folder 7, Uris Archive.

27. Ibid.

28. Leon Uris to William Uris, 3 June 1956, box 137, folder 7, Uris Archive.

29. Leon Uris to William Uris, 25 June 1956, box 137, folder 7, Uris Archive.

30. Levin's career in many ways anticipated Uris's. His early work about Palestine, *Yehuda* (1931), followed by a work on assimilated second-generation Jews in Chicago, *The Old Bunch* (1937), and then *My Father's House* (1947), the first full-scale feature film produced in Palestine, were successes. Both *Compulsion* (1956) and *The Obsession* (1973), the latter about his battle over his stage adaptation of *The Diary of Anne Frank*, illustrate how he anticipated some of the critical subjects that define Uris's work. Levin's popularity may have prepared readers to accept Uris.

31. Hartuv interview.

32. Ibid.

33. Ibid.

34. Leon Uris to Doubleday, 25 September 1956, box 137, folder 7, Uris Archive.

35. Uris quoted this exchange in his address to the West Area Conference of Hadassah, St. Francis Hotel, San Francisco, California, 7 December 1958.

36. A copy of this document is in a scrapbook in box 168, Uris Archive.

37. Leon Uris, first dispatch to the *Philadelphia Inquirer*, October 1956 (unpublished), box 25, folder 6, Uris Archive.

38. Ibid.

39. Ibid

40. Ibid.

41. Mark Uris interview.

42. Leon Uris, first dispatch to the *Philadelphia Inquirer*, October 1956 (unpublished), box 25, folder 6, Uris Archive.

43. The telegram is in a scrapbook in box 168 of the Uris Archive.

44. Leon Uris, second dispatch to the *Philadelphia Inquirer*, October 1956 (unpublished), box 25, folder 6, Uris Archive.

45. Leon Uris, third dispatch to the *Philadelphia Inquirer*, October 1956 (unpublished), box 25, folder 6, Uris Archive.

46. Leon Uris, printed notice, letter of gratitude to the Israeli public, November 1956, box 114, folder 8, Uris Archive.

47. Leon Uris, "Notes on the Background of *Exodus*," box 25, folder 7, Uris Archive.

48. Kenneth McCormick to Leon Uris, 9 May 1969, box 139, folder 8, Kenneth Mc-Cormick Collection, Library of Congress; hereafter cited as McCormick Collection.

49. Leon Uris to William Uris, 26 February 1957, box 137, folder 8, Uris Archive.

50. Leon Uris to William Uris, 29 March 1957, box 137, folder 8, Uris Archive.

51. George Haessler, "Author Tells of History without Parallel," *Daily Collegian* (Pennsylvania State Univ.), 2 March 1960.

52. Leon Uris to William Uris, 25 April 1957, box 137, folder 8, Uris Archive.

53. Leon Uris to William Uris, 17 July 1957, box 137, folder 8, Uris Archive.

54. Leon Uris to William Uris, 20 June 1957, box 137, folder 8, Uris Archive.

55. Leon Uris to William Uris, 29 March 1957, box 137, folder 8, Uris Archive.

56. Leon Uris to Ken McCormick, 22 April 1957, box 137, folder 8, Uris Archive.

57. Ibid.

58. Leon Uris to William Uris, 14 August 1957, box 137, folder 8, Uris Archive.

59. Leon Uris to Walter Bradbury (at Doubleday), 22 April 1957, box 135, folder 6, Uris Archive.

60. Leon Uris, quoted in Joe Saltzman, "The Literary Lab," *Daily Trojan* (Univ. of Southern California), ca. 1958 (clipping in Uris Archive).

61. Raymond Stross to Leon Uris, 1 May 1957, box 137, folder 8, Uris Archive.

62. Leon Uris to William Uris, 8 May 1957, box 137, folder 8, Uris Archive.

63. Leon Uris to William Uris, 29 May 1957, box 137, folder 8, Uris Archive.

64. Leon Uris to William Uris, 4 June 1957, box 137, folder 8, Uris Archive.

65. Uris was the one of several writers to work on the script, which was an adaptation of Donald Hamilton's short story "Ambush at Blanco Canyon" from the *Saturday Evening Post* (later expanded into a novel, *The Big Country*). When the film was finally released in August 1958 in North America, it grossed four million dollars in its first year. Uris, however, did not receive any screen credit. The film, with Gregory Peck, Jean Simmons, Charlton Heston, Carroll Baker, Charles Bickford, and Chuck Connors, was reported to have been President Eisenhower's favorite. *Variety* called it "a serviceable adult yarn" that "lives up to its title" (review of *The Big Country*, directed by William Wyler, *Variety*, 13 August 1958, 6).

66. Leon Uris to William Uris, 3 July 1957, box 137, folder 8, Uris Archive.

67. Leon Uris to Walter Bradbury, 24 May 1957, box 137, folder 8, Uris Archive.

68. Leon Uris to William Uris, 27 June 1957, box 137, folder 8, Uris Archive.

69. Leon Uris to William Uris, 1 May 1957 box 137, folder 8, Uris Archive.

70. Moshe Pearlman to Leon Uris, 15 July 1958, box 137, folder 7, Uris Archive.

71. Leon Uris to William Uris, 3 December 1957, box 137, folder 8, Uris Archive.

72. Uris, "About *Exodus*," in *The Quest for Truth*, ed. Martha Boaz, 128.

73. "He Went for Broke," ca. 1959 (copy in box 170, Uris Archive).

74. Uris, interview by Joseph Wershba, *New York Post*, 2 July 1959; a section of the interview is quoted in Philip Roth, "Some New Jewish Stereotypes," in *Reading Myself and Others* (New York: Farrar Straus and Giroux, 1975), 138. Roth called Uris's last statement ("In truth, we have been fighters") a simplification "so bald, stupid, and uninformed . . . that it is not even worth disputing"—although he then proceeded to do so (138). He cites Elie Wiesel's *Dawn* as a more genuine picture of the struggle for Jewish heroism (139). Roth finds disingenuous Uris's celebration of the "Hebrew Hero" and the Jew as a perpetrator of violence (141).

75. On the Israeli criticism of the sabras as Uris depicted them, see Philip Gillon, "The Image of Ari," *Jerusalem Post*, 21 May 1961.

76. Bantam promotional material, box 171, scrapbook, Uris Archive.

77. Harry Gilroy, "The Founding of the New Israel," *New York Times Book Review*, 12 October 1958.

78. David Boroff, "Exodus: Another Look," *New York Post*, 17 May 1959.

79. Herman Wouk is quoted in an advertisement for the novel (box 170, scrapbook, Uris Archive); the reviews from the *San Francisco Examiner* and the *Nation* are quoted in Boroff, "Exodus Another Look."

80. There is a copy of the poster in a scrapbook in box 169, Uris Archive.

81. *Johannesburg Jewish Herald*, 2 December 1960.

82. The British officers club at Goldschmidt House, on King George Street in the center of Jerusalem, was the object of an Irgun assault on 1 March 1947. Dressed in British uniforms, the attackers placed bombs in the compound that killed seventeen officers and injured twenty-seven. The immediate result was the imposition of martial law and the removal of all civil judicial procedures. Attacks by the Irgun and the Lehi increased (sometimes called the Stern Gang, after its leader, the Lehi was the most violent and radical of the three Zionist paramilitary groups, the others being the Haganah and the

Irgun). On 12 March, the Irgun succeeded in blowing up another British stronghold in Jerusalem, the Schneller camp.

The attack on Goldschmidt House and the debacle of martial law motivated the opposition in Great Britain under Winston Churchill to increase its denunciation of governmental policy in Palestine. This, in turn, forced the government to bring forward to 28 April 1947 a UN special session to debate the Palestine question, which had originally been proposed for September. The attack on Acre prison on 4 May 1947, which freed twenty-seven members of the Irgun and seven of the Lehi, intensified pressure on the British to revise their policy in the Middle East.

The result was a UN committee formed to study the problem. The committee arrived in Jerusalem on 14 June to meet with Jewish representatives, the Arabs having boycotted the proceedings. During this visit, the *Exodus 1947*, with 4,539 displaced persons, attempted to break the British blockade and land. The British turned the ship back, and Ernest Bevin, the foreign secretary, ordered the refugees and Holocaust survivors to return to Europe. The UN committee witnessed this event on 18 July 1947. Its report of 31 August 1947 recommended that the British mandate for Palestine be ended and that the country be granted independence. On 29 November 1947, the UN General Assembly adopted the committee's recommendation to partition Palestine. UN Resolution 181 separated the Israelis and Arabs, who, nevertheless, violently came together on 14 May 1948 when Israel proclaimed its independence. But as the British mandate ended, five Arab armies prepared to invade the new country. The United States recognized the State of Israel eleven minutes after David Ben-Gurion finished reading the proclamation; Russia and Guatemala quickly followed suit. (This account is drawn from Ahron Bregman, *A History of Israel* [New York: Palgrave Macmillan, 2003], 39–46).

83. For contemporary criticism of the novel, see "Diplomat Puts His Foot in It," *Johannesburg Jewish Herald*, 24 January 1961; for later criticism, see Jeremy Salt, "Fact and Fiction in the Middle East Novels of Leon Uris," *Journal of Palestine Studies* 14 (1985): 54–63; William Darby, *Necessary American Fictions: Popular Literature of the 1950s* (Bowling Green, Ohio: Bowling Green State Univ. Press, 1987), 93–100.

84. Roth, "Some New Jewish Stereotypes," 137–147; this was originally a speech delivered in Chicago in 1961. Robert Alter, "Sentimentalizing the Jews," *Commentary* (September 1963): 72.

85. Aziz S. Sahwell, *Exodus: A Distortion of Truth* (New York: Arab Information Center, 1960), 1.

86. Andrew Furman, *Israel through the Jewish-American Imagination* (Albany: State Univ. Press of New York, 1997), 39–40.

87. Unidentified Israelis quoted in Seth S. King, "Exodus and Israel," *New York Times*, 4 October 1959.

88. On the concept and representation of the tough Jew, see Paul Breines, *Tough Jews: Political Fantasies and the Moral Dilemma of American Jewry* (New York: Basic Books, 1990); Todd Samuel Presner, *Muscular Judaism: The Jewish Body and the Politics of Regeneration* (London: Routledge, 2007).

89. Said, "Propaganda and War," *Al-Ahram Weekly Online*, 30 August–5 September 2001;

http://weekly.ahram.org.eg/2001/550/op2.htm. More recently, the Israeli filmmaker Ari Folman, the director of *Waltz with Bashir* (2008), referred to *Exodus* as a "must-read" in Israel and the film of the novel a "must-film" (quoted in Deborah Solomon, "The Peacemaker," *New York Times Magazine*, 11 January 2009, 11).

90. Sara R. Horowitz, "Cinematic Triangulation of Jewish American Identity," in *The Americanization of the Holocaust*, ed. Hilene Flanzbaum, 155 (Baltimore: Johns Hopkins Univ. Press, 1999).

91. Ibid., 156.

92. Bernard Malamud, quoted in Leslie Field, "Israel Revisited in American Jewish Literature," *Midstream*, November 1982, 50.

93. David Ben-Gurion, quoted in Seth S. King, "'Exodus' and Israel," *New York Times*, 4 October 1959. Ilan Hartuv later questioned the remark, saying someone must have told Ben-Gurion about the book, since he "wasn't a man who cared very much about propaganda" and hardly had time for fiction (Hartuv interview).

94. Aharon Geffen, "U.N. Delegates Read Exodus," *Yediot Aharonot*, 22 September 1959 (in Hebrew).

95. Specially designed tours quickly materialized, one unabashedly called the "Exodus Tour." This twelve-day sojourn around the country, beginning at the port of arrival and led by a guide who had fought in the war of liberation, included visits to practically all the key sites in the war and the novel. Also, INBAL, an Israeli dance group, added an "Exodus dance" to its repertoire. Cyprus similarly benefited when tourists began to look for the Dome Hotel in Kyrenia, where Ari met Kitty, and sought the spot in the port where the *Exodus* had departed (materials related to these events are found in a scrapbook in box 169 of the Uris Archive).

96. United Artists publicity statement, box 169, scrapbook, Uris Archive.

97. Otto Preminger, *Preminger: An Autobiography* (Garden City, N.Y.: Doubleday, 1977), 165.

98. Hirsch, *Otto Preminger*, 165–167.

99. Chris Fujiwara, *The World and Its Double: The Life and Work of Otto Preminger* (New York: Faber and Faber, 2008), 257. Preminger would receive $160,000 for services, the first $250,000 of profits, and 75 percent of the profits thereafter.

100. A copy of the photo is in a scrapbook in box 169 of the Uris Archive.

101. Otto Preminger, *Preminger*, 166; for Uris's side, see Hirsch, *Otto Preminger*, 321.

102. Dalton Trumbo, who eventually wrote the screenplay, received $50,000.

103. Leon Uris, quoted in Hirsch, *Otto Preminger*, 321.

104. Ibid., 325.

105. Leon Uris, quoted in "Leon Uris, I'm in Every One of My Books," *Dayton Journal Herald*, 23 June 1980.

106. Preminger, quoted in Gerald Pratley, *The Cinema of Otto Preminger* (New York: Barnes, 1971), 133.

107. Otto Preminger, quoted in Ted Bredt, "Leon Uris Retains Rugged Charm," *San Jose Mercury News*, 22 August 1976. Supposedly, there is not a single word of dialogue from the novel in the movie.

108. Trumbo and Preminger quoted in Bruce Cook, *Dalton Trumbo* (New York: Scribner's, 1977), 274. On the script of *Exodus* and the working methods of Dalton Trumbo and Preminger, see Cook, *Dalton Trumbo*, 273–275, and Fujiwara, *World and Its Double*, 259–260. For Preminger's lack of interest in the script, see Trumbo's comic letters to Ingo Preminger, collected in *Additional Dialogue: Letters of Dalton Trumbo, 1942–1962*, ed. Helen Manfull, 527–532 (New York: Evans, 1970). Everything, it seems, distracted Preminger, including lunch (Pratley, *Cinema of Otto Preminger*, 135). Pratley quotes from a CBC interview with Preminger recorded on 24 February 1961.

109. Fujiwara, *World and Its Double*, 263.

110. Otto Preminger, quoted in Pratley, *Cinema of Otto Preminger*, 133.

111. Georgia Hesse, "A New Siege for the Exodus," *San Francisco Examiner*, 5 February 1961.

112. Otto Preminger, quoted in ibid.

113. Otto Preminger, quoted in Willi Frischauer, *Behind the Scenes of Otto Preminger: An Unauthorised Biography* (London: Michael Joseph, 1973), 187. For the most extensive website dealing with the film, see http://www.cine-holocaust.de/eng (search for "Exodus"). Also useful is Tom Ryan, *Otto Preminger Films: "Exodus"* (New York: Random House, 1960). This contains stills from the film and location shooting. On Newman's notes and Preminger's reaction, see Frischauer, *Behind the Scenes*, 187, as well as Fujiwara, *World and Its Double*, 265. Fujiwara also reports that Newman tried to get out of the film, deeming the script too cold and expository (258).

114. Frischauer, *Behind the Scenes*, 191–192.

115. Ibid., 186.

116. Fujiwara, *World and Its Double*, 269.

117. Hartuv interview; see also Frischauer, *Behind the Scenes*, 193. Foster Hirsch says Eva Monley, Preminger's production manager, came up with the idea of the lottery; the source is in dispute (*Otto Preminger*, 334). Hartuv and his wife were also to attend the New York premiere; Preminger conveniently forgot to invite them.

118. Geographical errors also occur. Uris put Gan Dafna in the Upper Galilee, where Arabs try to overrun it in their drive to Safed. Preminger puts Gan Dafna in the Emek, opposite Kafr Kanna (modern Cana), five miles north of Nazareth. There are many beautiful shots of the Emek, and they are mentioned in dialogue, but a contradiction emerges when the defenders of Gan Dafna say it must be held to protect Safed, in the north.

119. Bosley Crowther, "3½ Hour Film based on Uris' Novel Opens," *New York Times*, 16 December 1960.

120. Mort Sahl, quoted in Fujiwara, *World and Its Double*, 271.

121. A copy of the cartoon is in a scrapbook in box 171, Uris Archive.

122. See Yosefa Loshitzky, "National Rebirth as a Movie: Otto Preminger's *Exodus*," *National Identities* 4 (2002): 119–131. For another view, see Rachel Weissbrod, "Exodus as a Zionist Melodrama," *Israel Studies* 4 (1999): 129–152.

123. Fujiwara, *World and Its Double*, 271.

124. Capitalizing on his fame, an ambitious Uris decided to try another genre and contracted for a new project in September 1959: a children's book on the subject of Jew-

ish heroes. He was to receive a modest $5,000 advance and submit a manuscript by June 1960. It is one of the few projects he did not complete, although he hired a researcher to get the work underway and even proposed a title: "Judah's Warriors." He cancelled the contract in May 1961.

125. "The characters are firmly typecast, but their main function is to carry along the plot that history has already written and in that service they do quite well" (Dan Wakefield, "Israel's Need for Fiction," *Nation*, 11 April 1959, 319).

126. Review of a Robert Ludlum novel in the *Washington Post*, cited in the Associated Press obituary of Ludlum, who died on 12 March 2001.

CHAPTER 6

1. A report on the evening is in a scrapbook in box 170, Uris Archive.

2. On 13 February 1960, for example, the Irving Thalberg Lodge of B'nai B'rith honored Uris as "Man of the Decade." Jeff Chandler, an actor, presented the award at the Beverly Wilshire Hotel. Mel Blanc and Alan Reed were masters of ceremony.

3. Don Duncan, "Best-Seller Author Admits Flunking High School English," *Seattle Times*, 4 November 1959.

4. "Clerk Loses Case against *Exodus*," *Australian Jewish Herald* [November] 1960 (clipping in box 169, scrapbook, Uris Archive).

5. Murray Schumach, "Hollywood Prose," *New York Times*, 23 August 1959, 348.

6. Ibid.

7. Thomas M. Pryor, "Mirisch to Film New Uris Novel," *New York Times*, 7 January 1959. Also see Louella Parsons, "Fantastic Deal at Columbia for 4 Books Still Unwritten," *Los Angeles Examiner*, 13 August 1959. Stuart and Preminger could be partners with Uris because they were not members of the Artists Management Guild, which prohibited any of its agent members from having a stake in any type of production.

8. In *Exodus*, Uris depicts the lashing of Aronsohn's feet and the placement of hot stones in her armpits.

9. *Hollywood Reporter*, [March?] 1959 (clipping in box 170, scrapbook, Uris Archive).

10. Uris, interview in the *Kansas City Times*, 8 December 1960.

11. Quoted in "Uris Blasts Pasternak," *Heritage Southwest Jewish Press*, 17 November 1959 (clipping in box 170, scrapbook, Uris Archive).

12. Uris in Gefen, "Leon Uris," 15.

13. Israel Gutman, *Resistance: The Warsaw Ghetto Uprising* (Boston: Houghton Mifflin, 1994), 76. See also Gutman, *The Jews of Warsaw, 1939–1943: Ghetto, Underground, Revolt*, trans. Ina Friedman (Bloomington: Indiana Univ. Press, 1982). The most important recent and comprehensive work is Barbara Engelking and Jacek Leociak, *The Warsaw Ghetto: A Guide to the Perished City*, trans. Emma Harris (New Haven, Conn.: Yale Univ. Press, 2009). The original Polish text was published in 2001.

14. Gutman, *Resistance*, 77.

15. Ibid., 82.

16. For other photographs of the ghetto, see Gunther Schwarberg, *In the Ghetto of Warsaw: Heinrich Jost's Photographs*, trans. George Frederick Takis (Gottingen: Steidl Verlag, 2001), which includes photographs of burials at the mass graves. Jost, a sergeant in the Wehrmacht, photographed the Warsaw Ghetto in September 1941. The pictures remained unpublished until displayed at Yad Vashem (the Holocaust memorial) in Jerusalem in 1988.

17. While the Warsaw Ghetto was the largest one in Poland, it was not the first. The ghetto in Lodz, the city with the second-largest concentration of Jews in the country, was formed in May 1940.

18. Haggai Hitron, "Jewish History Museum Rises from Old Warsaw Ghetto," *Ha'aretz* (Israel), 13 January 2006.

19. Gutman, *Jews of Warsaw*, 129, 141.

20. Ibid., 197–213, 362–363.

21. Ibid., 312–323.

22. Quoted in Uris, *Exodus Revisited*, 259.

23. Uris's visit to the Warsaw Ghetto and Lublin empowered him to criticize Boris Pasternak. Uris began by sarcastically saying to Pasternak, who had given up his Jewish identity, that he was sorry, but the Jews were not giving up theirs. He then criticized the attack on Jewish survival that coincides with a celebration of the strength of the Christian faith in *Dr. Zhivago* ("Uris Blasts Pasternak").

24. David Grober, quoted in Emanuel Ringelblum, "Time Capsule in a Milk Can," an exhibition at United States Holocaust Memorial Museum, Washington, D.C., Summer 2004.

25. The surviving archives are in the Jewish Historical Institute in Warsaw, part of the state archives, and at Yad Vashem in Jerusalem. In 1999, the United Nations placed the Oneg Shabbat archives in the Memory of the World Register. For more information, see Samuel D. Kassow, *Who Will Write Our History? Emanuel Ringelblum, the Warsaw Ghetto, and the Oneg Shabbat Archive* (Bloomington: Indiana Univ. Press, 2007).

26. Hersey used the diary to frame all of *The Wall*. Uris used a diary form as a springboard for a conventional third-person narrative. Uris also preferred a broader approach than Hersey, allowing him to range freely from ghetto victims to the office of the German commander. Hersey's form gives the illusion of reality, which makes the reading deeply personal. *Mila 18* lacks the depth and intensity of *The Wall*, but has more drama and movement. For Uris on *The Wall*, see his (unpublished) interview with Sharon D. Downey, 26 November 1976, Aspen, Colorado, 36 (private collection). (Downey was a student at the University of Nevada at the time; I am indebted to the late Mark Uris for alerting me to this source.) Uris criticized Hersey's paternalism toward Jews, noting, emphatically, that Hersey was not Jewish.

27. Emanuel Ringelblum, *Notes from the Warsaw Ghetto: The Journal of Emanuel Ringelblum*, trans. Jacob Sloan (1958; New York: Schocken Books, 1974), 326.

28. Berg's account was published as *Warsaw Ghetto: A Diary*, ed. S. L. Schneiderman (New York: Fischer, 1945).

29. Korczak's diary was published as *The Ghetto Years, 1939–1942* (Tel Aviv: Hakibbutz Hameuchad, 1980).

30. Gutman, *Resistance*, 257.

31. Uris, interview by Joseph Wershba, *New York Post*, 2 July 1959.

32. Isaac Bashevis Singer, *The Slave* (1962; New York: Fawcett, 1980), 249. On Jews as fighters, see the Uris quotation in Roth, *Reading Myself and Others*, 138. On the long history of tough Jews, see Breines, *Tough Jews*, 77–167. Also see Isaiah Trunk, *Jewish Responses to Nazi Persecution* (New York: Stein and Day, 1982), and Reuben Ainsztein, *Jewish Resistance in Nazi-Occupied Eastern Europe* (New York: Barnes and Noble, 1975). On Jewish revenge in the Second World War, see Quentin Tarantino's film *Inglourious Basterds* (2009). Two novels that present tough Jews are Clive Irving's *Promise the Earth* (1982), dealing in part with Sarah Aronson and her spy network of the twenties, and Primo Levi's *If Not Now, When?* (1985).

33. Quentin Reynolds, "In the Ghetto a Battle for the Conscience of the World," *New York Times*, 4 June 1961.

34. Patrick Cruttwell, review of *Mila 18*, *Guardian*, 27 October 1961. Also see "Back to the Wall," *Time*, 2 June 1961, 94.

35. Bruce Cook, "Did Uris Write Novel or Script?" *Chicago Sunday Sun-Times*, 25 June 1961.

36. To avoid confusion with Uris's best seller, Heller's agent, Candida Donadio, suggested replacing "Catch-18," the original title of the 1955 short story and later novel, with something else. Supposedly, "Catch-22" was chosen because October 22 was her birthday (Lawrence Van Gelder, "Candida Donadio, 71, Agent who Handled 'Catch 22,' Dies, *New York Times*, 25 January 2001).

37. Quoted in "Exodus Author Tells Jewish Appeal of Warsaw Fight," *Cleveland Plain Dealer*, 20 April 1961.

38. The slides are in box 163, folders 8 and 11, Uris Archive; the photos are in box 203.

39. Uris, interview by Sharon Downey, 29.

40. Joseph P. Tustin, *USAFE and the Berlin Airlift, 1949: Supply and Operational Aspects* (1950). "USAFE" was the abbreviation for "United States Air Forces in Europe." Uris's copy is in box 12, folders 1–2, Uris Archive.

41. Display advertisement from the *New York Times*, 27 September 1964. The ad cites reviews from the Associated Press, the *Denver Post*, and *Newsday*.

42. Gefen, "Leon Uris," 10.

43. William Barrett, "Big Canvas and Small," review of *Armageddon*, by Leon Uris, *Atlantic Monthly* July 1964.

44. Herbert Mitgang, "Problems and Perils of Berlin Airlift," review of *Armageddon*, by Leon Uris, *New York Times Book Review*, 28 June 1964, 22–23.

45. Review of *Armageddon*, by Leon Uris, *Denver Post*, 1964, as cited in a *New York Times* advertisement, 27 September 1964.

46. Frederic E. Faverty, "Turbulent Times, 16 Centuries Apart," review of *Armageddon*, by Leon Uris, *Chicago Tribune*, 7 June 1964.

47. "Fresh off the Assembly Line," review of *Armageddon*, by Leon Uris, *Time*, 12 June 1964.

48. Uris, interview by William A. R. Melton, Jr., "Uris Negotiates Harper Pact," *Los Angeles Times*, 27 March 1966.

49. Ibid.

CHAPTER 7

1. Leon Uris to William Uris, 16 February 1964, box 11, folder 4, Uris Archive.

2. Leon Uris to William Uris, 6 July 1964, box 11, folder 4, Uris Archive.

3. Forty-six of the 130 experimental operations were recorded in Dr. Dering's hand. See Mavis M. Hill and L. Norman Williams, *Auschwitz in England: A Record of a Libel Action* (New York: Stein and Day, 1965), 26–27. This is a 293-page account of the trial written by two barristers. A more detailed account of the testimony appears in my chapter dealing with the novel *QB VII*.

4. Copy in box 137, folder 10, Uris Archive.

5. Leon Uris to William Uris, 15 June 1966, box 137, folder 10, Uris Archive.

6. Leon Uris to William Uris, 6 July 1964, box 137, folder 10, Uris Archive.

7. Ibid.

8. Leon Uris to William Uris, 9 July 1964, box 137, folder 10, Uris Archive.

9. Leon Uris to William Uris, 4 August 1964, box 139, folder 4, Uris Archive.

10. Mark Uris interview.

11. Betty Uris, diary, box 185, folder 3, Uris Archive.

12. Mark Uris interview.

13. The two novels he wrote before he left Aspen in 1988 (*The Haj* and *Mitla Pass*), however, did not generate the astonishing sales or attention of his earlier work. His last three novels, written after his 1988 move to New York and then Shelter Island, at the tip of Long Island, marked his continued decline in popularity.

14. Leon Uris to William Uris, 9 November 1964, box 137, folder 10, Uris Archive.

15. Bob Braudis, "On the Trail," *Aspen Peak*, Summer–Fall 2005, 300. More recent violence included the car-bomb murder of drug dealer Steven Grabow in 1985 and the suicide of Hunter S. Thompson in 2005.

16. Ted Conover, *Whiteout: Lost in Aspen* (New York: Random House, 1991), 124.

17. Hunter S. Thompson, "Freak Power in the Rockies," in *The Great Shark Hunt: Strange Tales for a Strange Time* (New York: Summit, 1979), 166. The essay documents the attempt by Joe Edwards, a young pothead, lawyer, and bike racer from Texas, to become the mayor of Aspen in 1969. Thompson added that Aspen was "full of freaks, heads, fun-hogs and weird night-people of every description" (155).

18. Jill Uris, interview by the author, 21 June 2005, Aspen, Colorado.

19. Ibid.

20. Leon Uris, "Heatherbedlam," *Ski Magazine*, February 1965. The article also summarizes some of Aspen's cultural accomplishments.

21. Martie Sterling, interview by the author, 21 June 2005, Aspen, Colorado.

22. Mark Uris interview.

23. This description comes from the author's visit to the house on June 22, 2005.

24. Off that room was a small bathroom with a finicky door that some would later say was controlled by the ghost of the woman who would become his second wife, Margery Edwards. If she chose, she could trap anyone in that small space (Jill Uris interview).

25. See Jill and Dick Durance, "A Town . . . a Mountain . . . a Way of Life," *National Geographic* 144, no. 6 (December 1973), 788–807; Nellie Blagden, "To Jill and Leon Uris: 'Our Marriage Is like the Melding of Two Generations," *People*, 12 January 1976, 40–44.

26. Quoted in Joanne Ditmer, "Uris Fills Home with Junk" [1966] (clipping in a scrapbook in box 172, Uris Archive).

27. Jill Uris interview.

28. Ibid.

29. Ken McCormick, "Leon Uris: An Editor's View," *Literary Guild Magazine*, January 1971.

30. Betty Uris, diary, box 185, folder 3, Uris Archive.

31. Ibid.

32. Leon Uris to William Uris, 15 June 1966, box 137, folder 10, Uris Archive.

33. Mark Uris to the author, e-mail, 5 March 2006.

34. Leon Uris to William Uris, 15 June 1966, box 137, folder 10, Uris Archive.

35. Leon Uris to William Uris, 27 June 1966, box 137, folder 10, Uris Archive.

36. Leon Uris to William Uris, 15 December 1966, box 137, folder 10, Uris Archive.

37. Leon Uris to William Uris, 5 August 1966, box 137, folder 10, Uris Archive.

38. Leon Uris to William Uris, 19 September 1966, box 137, folder 10, Uris Archive.

39. Leon Uris to William Uris, 9 November 1966, box 137, folder 10, Uris Archive.

40. Ibid.

41. Leon Uris to William Uris, 15 December box 137, folder 10, Uris Archive.

42. Leon Uris to William Uris, 23 December 1966, box 137, folder 10, Uris Archive.

43. Leon Uris to William Uris, 27 December 1966, box 137, folder 10, Uris Archive.

44. Jill Uris interview.

45. Leon Uris, deposition, Superior Court of California, 14 May 1969 (copy in box 84, folder 2, Uris Archive).

46. Douglas Porch, *The French Secret Services: From the Dreyfus Affair to the Gulf War* (New York: Farrar, Straus and Giroux, 1995); Roger Faligot and Pascal Krop, *La Piscine: The French Secret Service since 1944*, trans. W. D. Halls (Oxford: Blackwell, 1989).

47. Philippe de Vosjoli, deposition, 15 May 1969, before Notary Public. Box 84, folder 1, Uris Archive.

48. Leon Uris, deposition.

49. A few days later, Uris gave Vosjoli $2,500 and then a check for $22,500, money from the Bantam deal, which was supposedly worth $400,000. Schlosberg normally received 10 percent.

50. This would become the source of a 1971 California court case between the two men, Vosjoli claiming he had not been given his share of the proceeds (Uris claimed that

Vosjoli had violated their agreement by publishing some of his material under his own name in *Life*). Vosjoli said he had been paid only $65,000; Uris had supposedly received nearly $1 million. Uris testified that Vosjoli hoped that publicity for the novel would spark an official investigation, which would permit him to return to France a hero. In February 1972, Uris lost the case, one of the few legal disputes he did not win. After losing at the appellate level in August 1973, he had to pay Vosjoli $352,350 in royalties. In 1970, Vosjoli had published his version of the original autobiography as *Lamia*.

51. Vosjoli, deposition.

52. Mark Uris interview.

53. Leon Uris, deposition.

54. Leon Uris, "The Third Temple," in *Strike Zion!* William Stevenson, 121–142 (New York: Bantam, 1967).

55. Leon Uris, deposition. The details in this paragraph and the next come from this source.

56. *Topaz*, Bantam pamphlet (1968), [3].

57. Ibid., [6].

58. Ibid., [11].

59. Mark Uris interview.

60. Review of *Topaz*, by Leon Uris, *Library Journal*, 1 October 1967.

61. Review of *Topaz*, by Leon Uris, *Los Angeles Times*, 22 October 1967.

62. Melvin Maddocks, "The Uris School of Non-Fiction Fiction," review of *Topaz*, by Leon Uris, *Life*, 20 October 1967.

63. Ibid.

64. Ibid.

65. Review of *Topaz*, by Leon Uris, *London Sunday Times*, 31 March 1968. A review in the *New York Times* opined that Uris was "flagrantly unable to construct a plot, a character, a novel or a sentence in the English language—and he takes 130,000 words to display his incompetence" (Anthony Boucher, "Criminals at Large," review of *Topaz*, by Leon Uris, *New York Times*, 29 September 1967).

66. Quoted in Patrick McGilligan, *Alfred Hitchcock: A Life in Darkness and Light* (New York: Regan Books, 2003), 684.

67. Alfred Hitchcock to Leon Uris, memorandum, 18 June 1968, folder 681, Hitchcock Collection, Academy of Motion Picture Arts and Science, Los Angeles, California (hereafter cited as Hitchcock Collection).

68. Ibid.

69. Leon Uris to Alfred Hitchcock, memorandum, 24 June 1968, folder 681, Hitchcock Collection.

70. Alfred Hitchcock to Lew Wasserman, memorandum, 24 June 1968, folder 681, Hitchcock Collection.

71. McGilligan, *Alfred Hitchcock*, 685.

72. Ibid., 685–686.

73. Transcript of audiotape reel 2, section 16, Hitchcock Collection.

74. Transcript of audiotape reel 2, section 18, Hitchcock Collection.

75. Vincent Canby, "Topaz," *New York Times*, 20 December 1969. On the difficulties of filming, see McGilligan, *Alfred Hitchcock*, 684–693.

76. The information in this paragraph comes from newspaper clippings from 1968 in box 173, scrapbook, Uris Archive.

77. *Time*, 20 September 1968.

78. Newspaper clippings, box 173, scrapbook, Uris Archive.

79. Leon Uris, statement to Pitkin County Sheriff's Office, 20 February 1969.

80. Barbara Browne, "Author Uris Testifies in Death of Wife," *Rocky Mountain News*, 8 March 1969.

81. Ibid.

82. Dr. H. C. Whitcomb, 22 February 1969, case #69106, case report, Pitkin County Sheriff's Office, Pitkin County, Colorado.

83. Leon Uris, statement to Pitkin County Sheriff's Office, 20 February 1969, 2.

84. *Los Angeles Times*, 21 February 1969.

85. "Services Held Sun. for Margery Uris," *Aspen Times*, 27 February 1969.

86. Statement of Sergeant Bob Husted, Pitkin County Sheriff's Office, Aspen, Colorado, 23 February 1969, 4.

87. Quoted in "Jury Still Ponders Death of Mrs. Uris," *Aspen Times*, 6 March 1969.

88. Uris in Hutchinson, "Uris: A Life," 31.

CHAPTER 8

1. Michael Mulnix, "The Battle Cries of Leon Uris," *Writers Digest*, November 1977, 26.

2. Gefen, "Leon Uris," 16.

3. Leon Uris to Ken McCormick, 24 February 1970, box 139, folder 2, McCormick Collection.

4. Ken McCormick to Leon Uris, 16 February 1970, box 139, folder 2, McCormick Collection.

5. Ken McCormick to Sam Vaughan, memorandum, 14 April 1970, box 139, folder 2, McCormick Collection.

6. Ken McCormick to Sam Vaughan, 29 April 1970, box 139, folder 2, McCormick Collection.

7. Leon Uris to Ken McCormick, 2 May 1970, box 140, folder 7, McCormick Collection.

8. Ken McCormick to unidentified recipient, 12 January 1971, box 140, folder 8, McCormick Collection.

9. W. G. Rodgers, "Dr. Adam Kelno: Hero or Villain?" review of *QB VII*, by Leon Uris, *New York Times*, 15 November 1970.

10. Martha Duffy, "Bestseller Revisited," review of *QB VII*, by Leon Uris, *Time*, 28 June 1971, 80.

11. Christopher Lehmann-Haupt, "How to Write a Leon Uris," review of *QB VII*, by Leon Uris, *New York Times*, 2 December 1970.

12. Larry McMurtry, "Prose Isn't the Worst of It," review of *QB VII*, by Leon Uris, *Washington Post*, 6 April 1971.

13. Newspaper clippings, box 72, folders 4 and 5, Uris Archive.

14. On the differences between the novel and the miniseries, see Horowitz, "Cinematic Triangulation," 156–161.

15. Quoted in Michael C. Hodes, "The Battle Cry of Leon Uris," *Maryland Magazine*, February 1996, 23.

16. Uris in Hutchinson, "Uris: A Life," 33.

17. Gefen, "Leon Uris," 16.

18. Ibid.

19. William Collins, "'Ari' Has More Chutzpah than Inspiration in Opening at Shubert," review of the musical *Ari*, by Leon Uris, *Philadelphia Inquirer*, 1 December 1970.

20. Ernest Schier, "'Ari' Lies Becalmed in Its Own Rhetoric," review of the musical *Ari*, by Leon Uris, *Philadelphia Bulletin*, 1 December 1970.

21. Clive Barnes, "Uris's Ari," review of the musical *Ari*, by Leon Uris, *New York Times*, 16 January 1971.

22. Hodes, "Battle Cry of Uris," 23.

23. Ken McCormick to William Kimber, 9 September 1971, box 140, folder 6, McCormick Collection.

24. Ken McCormick to Sam Vaughan, 3 September 1971, box 140, folder 6, McCormick Collection.

25. Ken McCormick to Sam Vaughan, 14 September 1971, box 140, folder 6, McCormick Collection.

26. Leon Uris to Col. Robert H. Fechtman, 15 September 1971, box 140, folder 6, McCormick Collection.

27. Leon Uris to Ken McCormick, 23 September 1971, box 140, folder 6, McCormick Collection.

28. Ken McCormick to Gunnar Dahl, 21 September 1971, box 140, folder 6, McCormick Collection.

29. Ken McCormick to Mr. Sharif, Ministry of Information and Culture, Kabul, Afghanistan, 20 September 1971, box 140, folder 6, McCormick Collection.

30. Ken McCormick to Ambassador Huang Hua, 28 July 1971, box 140, folder 6, McCormick Collection.

31. Transcript of a telephone conversation between Ken McCormick and Leon Uris, 20 July 1971, box 140, folder 6, McCormick Collection.

32. Ken McCormick to Sam Vaughan, memorandum, 14 September 1971, box 140, folder 6, McCormick Collection.

33. Ibid.

34. Paul Feffer to Jack Madgwick, 28 September 1971, box 140, folder 6, McCormick Collection.

35. John Sargent to Ken McCormick, memorandum, 28 September 1971, box 140, folder 6, McCormick Collection.

36. Ken McCormick to the consul general of India, Washington, D.C., 20 September 1971, box 140, folder 6, McCormick Collection.

37. Leon Uris to Ken McCormick, 11 November 1971, box 140, folder 7, McCormick Collection.

38. Ambassador Robert Neumann to Ken McCormick, 11 October 1971, box 140, folder 6, McCormick Collection.

39. Ken McCormick to G. S. Bryant, 28 September 1971, box 140, folder 6, McCormick Collection.

40. Jill Uris to the author, e-mail, 6 June 2007.

41. Hodes, "Battle Cry of Uris," 21.

42. Jill Uris to the author, e-mails, 6 June 2007 and 9 June 2007.

CHAPTER 9

1. Paul Bew and Gordon Gillespie, *Northern Ireland: A Chronology of the Troubles, 1968–1999*, 2nd ed. (Dublin: Gill and Macmillan, 1999), 57.

2. Jill Uris to the author, e-mail, 8 June 2007.

3. Ibid.

4. The letter from Col. Tugwell is in box 175, Uris Archive.

5. Jill Uris to the author, e-mail, 8 June 2007.

6. Uris, interview by Sharon Downey, 9.

7. Quoted in Linda Zink, "Seeks Clues to Ireland's Fate," *Long Beach (CA) Independent Press Telegram*, 16 July 1976.

8. Jill Uris, outline of *Ireland: A Terrible Beauty*, box 51, folder 7, Uris Archive.

9. Quoted in Zink, "Seeks Clues to Ireland's Fate."

10. Andrew M. Greeley, "A View of Ulster," review of *Ireland: A Terrible Beauty*, by Leon and Jill Uris, *Irish People*, 5 June 1976, 11.

11. David Legate, "Foray to a Strange Land," review of *Ireland: A Terrible Beauty*, by Leon and Jill Uris, *Montreal Star*, June 1976.

12. Jill Uris to the author, e-mail, 8 June 2007.

13. Leon Uris to Sam Vaughan, 19 November 1974, box 140, McCormick Collection.

14. George D. Kane, "Leon Uris Embraces Irish Soul," *Los Angeles Times*, March 1976.

15. Uris, interview by Sharon Downey, 7.

16. Ibid., 10.

17. Ibid.

18. Uris, interviewed after the publication of *Redemption* (1995); the interview is quoted in an entry on *Trinity* on the website *20th-Century American Bestsellers*, http://www3.isrl.illinois.edu/~unsworth/courses/bestsellers/search.cgi?title=Trinity (accessed November 28, 2009).

19. Jill Uris, interview by Michael Norris; quoted in ibid.

20. Quoted in Travis Willmann, "Leon Uris's Exodus," *Ransom Edition* (University of Texas at Austin), Fall 2003; available at http://www.hrc.utexas.edu/ransomedition/2003/

fall/exodus.html (accessed November 28, 2009). In 1996, Uris criticized Gore Vidal's liberal treatment of history in creating conversations and situations that could not have taken place (Hodes, "Battle Cry of Uris," 21).

21. Uris once asked a military expert for an exact description of the British infantry rifle used in the Boer War, specifically whether it fired a bolt-operated clip containing several bullets or a single shot. And were officers' pistols automatic or revolvers? (Leon Uris to Colin Robertson, 10 October 1974, box 151, folder 6, Uris Archive).

22. Diane Eagle, interview by the author, 13 July 2005.

23. Ibid.

24. Ibid.

25. Michael Neiditch, interview by the author, Washington, D.C., 6 May 2004. Neiditch had become a close friend of Uris's through his work with B'nai B'rith.

26. Leon Uris to Ken McCormick, 31 October 1974, box 151, folder 1, Uris Archive.

27. Leon Uris to his children, 31 October 1974 (box 101, folder 1, Uris Archive).

28. Leon Uris to Topper Wilson, travel agent, 1 November 1974 (box 101, folder 1, Uris Archive).

29. Leon Uris to Mrs. Svend Beck, n.d., 1974 (box 101, folder 1, Uris Archive).

30. Uris, interview by Sharon Downey, 17.

31. Patrick Dillon, "Ireland: A Dirge Yet Unfinished," *San Diego Union*, 11 April 1976. Also see Neil Morgan's earlier report in the *San Diego Evening Tribune*, 25 July 1975.

32. Diane Eagle interview.

33. Uris liked the drama of trial scenes, as *QB VII* proved.

34. George D. Kane, "Leon Uris Embraces the Irish in Trinity," *Los Angeles Times*, 11 April 1976.

35. Quoted in Jan Golab, "Leon Uris," *Denver*, November 1976, 31.

36. Thomas A. Larkin, "A Talk with Uris: 'Trinity' Was the Seed, 'Redemption' Was the Unplanned Progeny," *Interviews with Past Masters*, http://www.readersroom.com/masters.html (accessed November 28, 2009).

37. John Barkham, "Eloquent Uris Has Made Irish Cause His Own," *San Francisco Chronicle*, 7 March 1976.

38. William C. Woods, "The Literary Scene," review of *Trinity*, by Leon Uris, *New York Post*, 11 May 1976.

39. Christopher Hudson, "Ireland, 1885–1915: Uris Insists on Present-Day Parallels," review of *Trinity*, by Leon Uris, *Chicago Tribune*, 7 March 1976.

40. Pete Hamill, review of *Trinity*, by Leon Uris, *New York Times Book Review*, 29 August 1976, 5.

41. June Southworth, "Pompous, Old Hat and Very, Very Dangerous," review of *Trinity*, by Leon Uris, *Daily Mail*, 8 October 1976.

42. Philip Howard, review of *Trinity*, by Leon Uris, *London Times*, 7 October 1976.

43. John Hume, "As It Was in the Beginning," review of *Trinity*, by Leon Uris, *Hibernia Fortnightly Review*, 8 October 1976: 20.

44. Uris, interview by Sharon Downey, 36.

45. Charles J. Haughey, "Suffering Still but the Dream Remains," review of *Trinity*, by Leon Uris, *Sunday Independent* (Ireland), 10 October 1976.

46. Uris, interview by Sharon Downey, 22.

47. Ibid., 8.

48. Ibid., 11.

49. Ibid., 2.

50. Mark Uris interview.

51. Leon Uris to Reuven Dafni, 3 April 1976, box 151, folder 6, Uris Archive.

52. John Coleman, "Proper Study," review of *Exodus*, by Leon Uris, *Spectator*, 10 July 1959.

53. Quoted in Brian Benna, "Leon Uris, Author Bristles at Suggestion of Historical Distortion," *Calgary Herald*, 9 May 1980.

54. Leon Uris to Ken McCormick, 4 February 1975, box 135, folder 8, Uris Archive.

55. Leon Uris to Ken McCormick, 14 February 1975, box 135, folder 8, Uris Archive.

56. Leon Uris to Ken McCormick, 14 October 1975, box 135, folder 8, Uris Archive.

57. Ibid.

58. Leon Uris to Ken McCormick, 29 December 1975, box 135, folder 8, Uris Archive.

59. Gefen, "Leon Uris," 10.

60. Uris, interview by Sharon Downey, 34.

61. Ibid.

62. Gefen, "Leon Uris," 10.

63. *Bergen (NJ) Record*, 1988.

64. Richard English, *Armed Struggle: The History of the IRA* (London: Macmillan, 2003), 197; J. Bower Bell, *The Secret Army: The IRA*, rev. 3rd ed. (London: Transaction, 1997), 500–503.

65. Uris, interview by Sharon Downey, 24.

66. Ibid., 19.

67. Ibid.

68. Promotional material, box 101, folder 1, Uris Archive. The announcement of 1 September 1976 noted that the production would be financed by Fred Brogger and Video Progressive Service of Toronto. Trinity Productions was the name of the company.

69. This material is in box 101, folder 1, Uris Archive.

70. Leon Uris, quoted in promotional material, box 101, folder 5, Uris Archive.

71. A copy of the guest list is in box 101, folder 3, Uris Archive.

72. Leon Uris to Warren Cowan, 31 January 1977, box 151, folder 6, Uris Archive.

73. Leon Uris to Rogers Cowan Agency, 31 January 1977, box 101, folder 5, Uris Archive.

74. Leon Uris to Ken McCormick and Sam Vaughan, 16 July 1976, box 135, folder 6, Uris Archive.

75. Leon Uris to Ken McCormick, box 151, folder 6, Uris Archive.

76. Leon Uris to Sam Vaughan, 3 August 1976, box 151, folder 6, Uris Archive.

77. Ibid.

78. Brogger reportedly backed out after negotiations between Uris and Ardmore

Studios, in Wicklow, Ireland, failed ("Trinity Film Out," *Dublin Sunday Press*, 25 June 1978). The Irish government would not agree either to invest several million dollars in the project or to provide film equipment or facilities. Apparently, no formal negotiations with the government ever occurred; Uris just met a few ministers socially.

79. Leon Uris to William Uris, 18 December 1974, box 151, folder 1, Uris Archive.

80. Leon Uris to Yohanon Behan, 18 December 1974, box 151, folder 1, Uris Archive.

CHAPTER 10

1. Uris in Paul Hendrickson, "*Exodus* to *Trinity*: The Impact of Leon Uris' Runaway Epics," *Washington Post*, 2 May 1978.

2. Mulnix, "Battle Cries of Uris," 26–27. Adding further insult, Mailer was a presenter at the Academy Awards in March 1977; the attention angered Uris.

3. Leon Uris to Ken McCormick, 31 December 1976, box 150, folder 7, Uris Archive.

4. Leon Uris to Ken McCormick, 27 July 1977, box 135, folder 8, Uris Archive.

5. Leon Uris to Ken McCormick, 24 August 1977, box 135, folder 8, Uris Archive.

6. Leon Uris to Ken McCormick, 5 September 1977, box 135, folder 8, Uris Archive.

7. Ibid.

8. Leon Uris to Joan Ward, 4 November 1977, box 135, folder 8, Uris Archive.

9. Jill Uris to the author, e-mail, 9 June 2007.

10. Ibid.

11. Ibid.

12. "Uris Visitor," *Aspen Daily News*, 13 September 1979.

13. Sam Vaughan to Ken McCormick, memorandum, 14 November 1983, box 140, folder 6, McCormick Collection.

14. A copy of the manuscript is in box 46, folder 1, Uris Archive.

15. Copies of these drafts of what would become *The Haj* are in box 46, folders 2–3, Uris Archive.

16. Ken McCormick to Sam Vaughan, memorandum, 16 October 1982, box 140, folder 6, McCormick Collection.

17. Sam Vaughan to Doubleday staff, 27 December 1982, box 140, folder 6, McCormick Collection.

18. Sam Vaughan to Ken McCormick, 24 January 1983, box 140, folder 6, McCormick Collection.

19. Leon Uris to Ken McCormick, 3 August 1984, box 140, folder 6, McCormick Collection.

20. Leon Uris to Ken McCormick, 4 March 1983, box 140, folder 6, McCormick Collection.

21. Sam Vaughan to John O'Donnell, 8 March 1983, box 140, folder 11, McCormick Collection.

22. Ibid.

23. Leon Uris to John O'Donnell, 26 July 1983, box 140, folder 11, McCormick Collection.

24. Linda Winnard to Sam Vaughan, 29 July 1983, box 140, folder 11, McCormick Collection.

25. Ken McCormick to Sam Vaughan, 8 September 1983, box 140, folder 11, McCormick Collection.

26. Ken McCormick to Leon Uris, 7 September 1983, box 140, folder 11, McCormick Collection.

27. Sam Vaughan to Leon Uris, 12 September 1983, box 140, folder 11, McCormick Collection.

28. Leon Uris to Sam Vaughan, 14 September 1983, box 140, folder 11, McCormick Collection.

29. Leon Uris to Ken McCormick, 29 September 1983, box 140, folder 11, McCormick Collection.

30. Leon Uris to Ken McCormick, 20 January 1984, box 140, folder 11, McCormick Collection.

31. Ibid.

32. Quoted in Pearl Sheffy Gefen, "From the Inside Out," *Jerusalem Post*, 28 January 1995. Ironically, the "new historians" in Israel have recently upheld some of Uris's views. In *1948: The First Arab-Israel War* (2008), Benny Morris argues that the Arabs' lack of a national identity, combined with their focus on the family, the clan, and internal struggles for power, made them vulnerable to the better-organized and better-prepared Israelis in 1948. It was no surprise that determined Israeli forces, though fewer in number, defeated the underfunded and poorly prepared Arab armies.

33. Jill Uris to the author, e-mail, 8 June 2007.

34. Uris, "A Special Message for the First Edition from Leon Uris," *The Haj* (Franklin Center, Penn.: Franklin Library, 1984), n.p.

35. The creation of such strong father figures as Ari Ben Canaan, Gideon Asch, or Haj Ibrahim compensated, perhaps, for the absence of a strong, supportive, nurturing father in Uris's own life.

36. Sam Vaughan to Ken McCormick and the Doubleday PR staff, 3 June 1984, box 140, folder 11, McCormick Collection.

37. Review of *The Haj*, by Leon Uris, *ALA Booklist*, 15 February 1984.

38. Gerald Green, "A Novel of Besieged Israel, from an 'Arab' Viewpoint," review of *The Haj*, by Leon Uris, *Chicago Sun-Times*, 15 April 1984.

39. Quoted in John Coit, "Son of Abraham Pitches a New Tent," *Denver Rocky Mountain News*, 10 April 1984.

40. Quoted in Gefen, "From the Inside Out."

41. Ibid.

42. Leon Uris to Sam Vaughan, 16 July 1984, box 140, folder 11, McCormick Collection.

43. Dick Hoffman to Sam Vaughan, 21 June 1984, box 140, folder 11, McCormick Collection.

44. Sam Vaughan to Ken McCormick, memorandum, 23 July 1984, box 140, folder 11, McCormick Collection.

45. Ibid.

46. Leon Uris to Sam Vaughan, 23 July 1984, box 140, folder 11, McCormick Collection.

47. Sam Vaughan to Ken McCormick, 23 July 1984, box 140, folder 11, McCormick Collection.

48. Leon Uris to Lou [?], 16 July 1984, box 140, folder 11, McCormick Collection.

49. Ibid.

50. Herb Schlosberg, deposition, 17 May 1989 (copy in box 135, folder 4, Uris Archive). This was testimony during Uris's divorce from Jill Uris.

51. Ibid.

52. Ibid.

53. Diane Eagle, "Ode to Leon," August 1984 (private collection).

54. Leon Uris to Sam Vaughan and Ken McCormick, 2 November 1983, box 140, folder 11, McCormick Collection.

55. See Uris, address to the New York Times Literary Luncheon, 18 September 1988 (box 181, folder 8, Uris Archive).

56. Mark Uris, who was present at the event, to the author, 20 June 2005.

CHAPTER 11

1. Ken McCormick to Sam Vaughan, 10 October 1984, box 140, folder 11, McCormick Collection.

2. Vaughan explained to Uris that the words "diplomacy," "State Department," and "foreign policy" were usually "numbing, commercially." Nevertheless, he believed that Uris's handling of the topic would be strong. And even though Uris wanted "to do an American novel," Vaughan thought that "it ought not to be a 'Washington novel.'" There was a great deal of fatigue among people in the trade about Washington novels at the moment. In any new topic explored by Uris, Vaughan wondered whether it would be something that would engage his "sympathy, power and passion? Where is the underdog?" A final suggestion was for a novel set in the American West, where Uris lived—a new American western, perhaps (Sam Vaughan to Leon Uris, 9 May 1984, box 140, folder 11, McCormick Collection).

3. Sam Vaughan to Leon Uris, 25 October 1984, box 140, folder 11, McCormick Collection.

4. Hodes, "Battle Cry of Uris," 22.

5. Leon Uris, "Old Letters, New Life," *Franklin Mint Almanac* (Exton, Penn.: Franklin Library, 1988); copy in box 140, folder 8, McCormick Collection.

6. Leon Uris, "Old Letters Never Die," box 179, Uris Archive. The scale of the Uris Archive at the Harry Ransom Humanities Research Center at the University of Texas at Austin attests to the magnitude of what Uris retained: 169 boxes, 43 oversize boxes (containing scrapbooks and other material), and 6 galley folders, filling 108 linear feet.

7. Uris quoted in Hillel Italie, "Leon Uris . . . Dies at 78," Associated Press, 24 June 2003.

8. Copy in box 140, folder 8, McCormick Collection.

9. Leon Uris to Ken McCormick, 3 June 1986, box 140, folder 8, McCormick Collection.

10. Uris, "Rough Outline and Ramdon [sic] Notes for Lullaby—The life story of Gideon Zadok" [1986], box 140, folder 8, McCormick Collection.

11. Anna Blumberg Abrams, "Won't Somebody Please Hold Me!" 1970, box 140, folder 8, McCormick Collection.

12. Leon Uris, "Gideon's Early Childhood Memories," 1986, 13, box 140, folder 11, McCormick Collection. This differs from Uris's "Rough Outline" and appears in an outline, sent to McCormick, of the new novel, then called "Lullaby." Additionally, a file in the McCormick Collection contains excerpts from the letters of William Uris, selected by Leon Uris, along with McCormick's objections to Uris writing an autobiography.

13. For McCormick's benefit, Uris excerpted a letter from his father (dated 22 April 1953), sent just after the publication of *Battle Cry*: "I received the book you sent me, but 'Oi Gewald' I am t-e-r-r-i-b-l-y d-i-s-s-a-p-o-i-n-t-e-d you didn't autograph it. I was really embarrassed, when I looked for the autograph and didn't find it" (box 140, folder 8, McCormick Collection).

14. Ken McCormick to Leon Uris, 5 June 1986, box 140, folder 8, McCormick Collection.

15. Uris in Gefen, "Leon Uris," 15.

16. "Imaginative fodder" is from Webster Schott, "Pilgrim in the Promised Land," review of *Mitla Pass*, by Leon Uris, *Washington Post Book World*, 30 October 1988; the description of the novel as a personalization of history is from "Uris' Mitla Pass," *Boston Globe*, November 1988.

17. Roger Jaynes, "Michener Syndrome: Leon Uris Writes a Masterpiece then Buries It in Words," *Milwaukee Journal*, 20 November 1988.

18. Faulkner to his stepson, Malcolm Franklin, ca. 1942; see William Faulkner, *Selected Letters of William Faulkner*, ed. Joseph Blotner (New York: Random House, 1977), 165–168.

19. Myra Yellin Goldfarb, "Leon Uris, a Profile," *Allentown (PA) Hakol*, November 1989, 4.

20. Leon Uris to Burlington Township Schools, 31 October 1991, box 133, folder 4, Uris Archive.

21. Uris, address to the New York Times Literary Luncheon, 18 September 1988, box 181, folder 8, Uris Archive.

22. Ibid.

23. Leon Uris, "Answers to Petitioner's Interrogatories," 6 September 1989 (copy in box 135, folder 5, Uris Archive).

24. Antony Delano, "Shtetls and Sweatshops," review of *Mitla Pass*, by Leon Uris, *London Sunday Times*, 7 May 1989.

25. Leon Uris, "Leon Lays Bare His Complex Life," interview by Julie Cockcroft, *Edinburgh Evening News*, 13 May 1989.

26. Uris, speech at the dedication of the Tarawa Monument, Long Beach, California, 1 July 1998 (box 182, folder 1, Uris Archive).

27. Leon Uris to Ken McCormick and Sam Vaughan, 4 March 1983, box 140, folder 3, McCormick Collection.

28. Jill Uris to Leon Uris, 16 February 1989 (box 135, folder 4, Uris Archive).

29. Jill Uris to Leon Uris, n.d., box 135, folder 4, Uris Archive.

30. Leon Uris to Jill Uris, 10 November 1988, box 135, folder 4, Uris Archive.

31. Leon Uris to Herb Schlosberg, Andy Hecht, and Robert Kendig, 3 January 1988, box 135, folder 5, Uris Archive.

32. Herbert Schlosberg, deposition, 17 May 1989 (copy in box 135, folder 4, Uris Archive).

33. Uris, "Answers to Petitioner's Interrogatories."

34. Ken McCormick to Leon Uris, 17 May 1989, box 135, folder 4, Uris Archive.

35. Uris, "Answers to Petitioner's Interrogatories."

36. Ibid.

37. Ibid.

38. Ibid.

39. Hodes, "Battle Cry of Uris," 21.

40. Uris to Schlosberg, Hecht, and Kendig, 3 January, box 135, folder 5, Uris Archive.

41. Leon Uris to Jill Uris, 10 April 1989 (box 135, folder 5, Uris Archive).

42. Jill Uris to Leon Uris, 12 September 1989, box 135, folder 5, Uris Archive.

43. Jill Uris to Leon Uris, 23 April 1990, box 135, folder 5, Uris Archive.

44. Leon Uris to Robert Kendig, 13 September 1989, box 135, folder 5, Uris Archive.

45. Andy Hecht, interview by the author, 21 June 2005, Aspen, Colorado.

46. Michael Neiditch interview.

47. Leon Uris, interview by Esther Boylan, *Columbia Perspectives* (Columbia University), February–March 1989.

48. *Budapest Daily News*, 31 October 1989 (clipping in a scrapbook in box 179, Uris Archive).

49. Pia Ingstrom, "I'm No Diplomat," *Independent* (Sweden), 12 October 1989.

50. [Priscilla Higham], "USSR," chronology, box 149, folder 6, Uris Archive.

51. Michael Neiditch interview.

52. Uris, speech in Riga, Latvia, 15 October 1989, box 149, folder 6, Uris Archive.

53. Michael Neiditch interview.

54. Michael Neiditch to E. Barnes, Motion Picture Association of America, 6 October 1989, box 149, folder 6, Uris Archive.

55. Ibid.

56. Michael Neiditch, "The Dead Hand of Perestroika," *Ha'aretz*, 10 November 1989, box 149, folder 6, Uris Archive.

57. Ibid.

58. Uris, "Helsinki-Leningrad Express," typescript, n.d., box 149, folder 6, Uris Archive.

59. Essie Kofsky, "Notes," Russia, 1989, box 149, folder 6, Uris Archive.

60. Alan L. Shulman to Leon Uris, 11 August 1989, box 149, folder 6, Uris Archive.

61. Uris's notes for the talk are in a scrapbook in box 178, Uris Archive.

62. The itinerary for the trip is in box 149, folder 6, Uris Archive.

63. Ibid.; Michael Neiditch interview.

CHAPTER 12

The epigraph to this chapter is from Michael C. Hodes, "The Battle Cry of Leon Uris," *Maryland Magazine*, February 1996, 23.

1. Goldfarb, "Uris Profile," 4.

2. Channing Thieme, interview by the author, 18 April 2008.

3. Ibid.

4. Ibid.

5. Ibid.

6. Linda Moss, "Authors Restive at Doubleday," *Crain's New York Business*, 16 April 1990.

7. Mark Uris interview; Marilynn Pysher, interview by the author, 18 May 2005.

8. Hodes, "Battle Cry of Uris," 22.

9. Ibid., 23.

10. Nancy Stauffer, interview by the author, 20 May 2005, New York City.

11. Marjorie Braman, HarperCollins, interview by the author, 17 May 2005, New York City.

12. Maxwell Ayrton and Arnold Silcock, *Wrought Iron and Its Decorative Use* (1929; repr., Mineola, N.Y.: Dover, 2003).

13. Larkin, "A Talk with Uris."

14. Uris, interview by Boylan.

15. Malachy Duffy, "In Short: Fiction. Redemption," *New York Times Book Review*, 2 July 1995, 11.

16. Marjorie Braman interview.

17. Mark Uris interview.

18. Ibid.

19. Jill Uris interview.

20. Nancy Stauffer interview.

21. Mark Uris interview.

22. Marjorie Braman interview.

23. Linda L. Richards refers to his labored and stilted writing, childish dialogue, and rambling narrative, which begins with a first-person account by O'Connell but is quickly replaced by an omniscient narrator. She goes on to say that the work reads more like a poorly executed screenplay than a novel, the plot exposition resembling set directions ("A Story in Ruins," *January Magazine*, July 1999). *Publishers Weekly* called the novel "too stylistically scattered" (July 1999).

24. Uris in Pearl Sheffy Gefen, "Among the Ruins . . . Leon Uris Struggles back," *National Post*, 17 July 1999, 9.

25. Mark Uris interview.

26. More vividly, according to his oldest son, Uris told him the woman had nearly bitten off one of his testicles. He took pride in this proof of his masculinity.

27. Marjorie Braman interview.

28. Uris provided the following blurb on the back of Stanley Fisher and James Ellison's *Discovering the Power of Self-Hypnosis* (New York: Harper Collins, 1991): "Through Dr. Fisher's self-hypnosis, I am able to revitalize myself as often as I need during the day by short restful breaks."

29. Mark Uris interview.

30. Ibid.

31. Ibid.

32. Marilynn Pysher interview.

33. Mark Uris interview.

34. Irving Wallace received the largest advance in the history of Bantam Books: $2.3 million in April 1972, although it was for a three-book deal. *Valley of the Dolls* by Jacqueline Susann became the fastest-selling novel in history: Bantam printed 4 million paperback copies the first week of publication in July 1967, and 4 million more by the end of the year. In 1973, it surpassed *Peyton Place* as the novel with the highest sales: the total was 15.8 million. Louis L'Amour, however, was Bantam's all-time best-selling author: in twenty years, the publisher sold some 42 million copies of his titles. See Clarence Petersen, *The Bantam Story*, 2nd ed. (New York: Bantam, 1975), 24, 28, 32.

35. The leading new historian in Israel is Benny Morris, whose *The Birth of the Palestinian Refugee Problem* (1998) and *1948: The First Arab-Israeli War* (2008) initiated the reassessment of the Israeli narrative.

36. The phrase "moral memory palace" is from Tony Judt, *Reappraisals: Reflections on the Forgotten Twentieth Century* (New York: Penguin, 2008), 4.

37. Uris complained to the president of Bantam Books when *Portnoy's Complaint* by Philip Roth appeared, berating the self-indulgent fantasies of the hero and the wasteful energy of the author in writing the book (Oscar Dystel, interview by the author, 20 May 2005, New York City).

38. See Alan Furst, *Dark Star*; Louis de Bernières, *Corelli's Mandolin*; William T. Vollmann, *Europe Central*; and Jonathan Littell, *The Kindly Ones* (*Les Bienveillantes*).

39. William T. Vollmann, *Europe Central* (New York: Viking, 2005), 5.

40. Ibid., 9.

41. Dan Wakefield, "Israel's Need for Fiction"; Leon Uris to William Uris, 10 July 1957 (box 137, folder 8, Uris Archive). Uris might have agreed with Mickey Spillane's claim that "I don't have readers, I have customers" (quoted in Larry Orenstein, "Even More Satisfied Customers," review of *The Lost Symbol*, by Dan Brown, *Toronto Globe and Mail*, 19 September 2009).

42. Vollmann, *Europe Central*, 10.

EPILOGUE

1. Evelyn Englander, interview by the author, 5 May 2004, U.S. Marine Corps Historical Center, Naval Yard, Washington, D.C.

2. See http://www.cem.va.gov/cems/nchp/quantico.asp (accessed 14 January 2010).

3. Herschel Blumberg, interview by the author, 7 May 2004, Chevy Chase, Maryland.

INDEX

Dreiser, Theodore, 6, 301
Dublin, 207, 224, 286
Dystel, Oscar, x, 70, 106, 183, 194, 207, 208

Eagle, Diane, xi, 208, 216–217, 218
Earp, Wyatt, 85
East Germany, 136
Eastwood, Clint, 89
Edwards, Margery, 163, 179, 188–192, 193, 194, 196, 208
Egypt, 101, 103, 111, 238, 250, 265, 292
Eichmann, Adolf, 107, 121, 123, 134, 135, 170
Eilat, 100, 101
Emerson, Ralph Waldo, 295
Encino (CA), 64, 104, 172, 175
Eshkol, Levi, 123
Esquire, 55
Exodus (ship), 12
Exodus 1947, 124
"Exodus Tour," 321n95

Faulkner, William, 2, 65–66, 76, 91, 261, 262, 264, 312n43; *Battle Cry* (film), 65
FBI, 182
Feldman, Leonid, 93–94
Ferguson, Barbara, 35
Finland, 274, 280, 301
Fitzgerald, F. Scott, 81, 105
Ford, John, 90
Forverts, 14, 19
France, 8
Franklin Library, 234, 247, 256
Freeman, Mona, 72, 154
Freiheit (Freedom), 14–15, 16, 19, 40, 49
Furst, Alan, 3, 301; *Dark Star*, 3

Gallipoli, 286, 288, 289, 301
Gann, Ernest, 196
Garvis, Red, 37, 38, 50
Gaza Strip, 103
Germany, 3, 8, 102, 103, 110, 216, 289, 300, 301

Ghetto Fighters Kibbutz, 130
Gold, Michael, 22, 24, 265; *Jews without Money*, 22, 265
Goldberg, Charles, 176, 197, 207, 221, 297
Golden, Harry, 7
Gone with the Wind, 1, 21
Gorky, Maxim, 36
Greece, 3, 68, 69, 300
Griffith, D. W., 92
Guadalcanal, 119, 293: as described in *Battle Cry* (book and film), 37, 60, 61, 62, 73, 78, 88; memorial show about, 51; Uris's experiences at, 29, 35, 36–38, 39, 40, 41, 44, 49, 50

Haganah, 98, 99, 107, 108, 110, 111, 119, 121
Haifa, 120
Haley, Alex, 174
Hamill, Pete, 223
Hargrove, Marion, 35; *See Here, Private Hargrove*, 35
Harissiadis, Dimitrios, 123, 125
Harlem, 13
Harper and Row, 140, 183
HarperCollins, 286, 296, 297
Hartuv, Ilan, x, xii, 98–99, 101, 107, 121, 317n22, 317n24, 321n93
Haughey, Charles J., 2, 224
Hawks, Howard, 65–66
Hearst, William Randolph, 47
Heatherbed Lodge, 174
Hebrew, 11, 12, 14, 95, 107, 108, 170, 212
Hebrew University, 239
Heflin, Van, 7, 72
Heller, Joseph, 7, 22, 136, 325n36; *Catch-22*, 3, 136
Hemingway, Ernest, 6, 7, 8, 76, 105, 193, 197, 263–264, 267, 280; *Farewell to Arms, A*, 8
Hersey, John, 2, 105, 131, 135, 140, 233, 301; *A Bell for Adano*, 140; *The Wall*, 5, 105, 131, 135, 324n26
Herzlia, 100

King David Hotel, 110, 235
Koestler, Arthur, 97; *Thieves in the Night*, 97
Kofsky, Essie, x
Kofsky, Harry, 31, 296
Kollek, Teddy, 98, 235, 238, 239
Krim, Arthur, 117
Kuprin, Aleksandr, 36; *Yama (The Pit)*, 36

L'Amour, Louis, 253
Lancaster, Burt, 67, 74, 86, 155
Larkspur, xii, 51, 52–53, 172, 175, 311n4
Laster, Owen, 296
Lebanon, 13
le Carré, John, 140, 242, 243; *Little Drummer Girl*, 242; *The Spy Who Came in from the Cold*, 140
Lehmann-Haupt, Christopher, 200–201
LeMay, Curtis, 137, 138
Lenin, V. I., 15
Leningrad, 274, 275, 277, 278
Levin, Meyer, 7, 25, 97, 100, 317n30; *Compulsion*, 100, 317n30; *The Old Bunch*, 100, 317n30
Lewis, Bernard 235, 245
Lithuania, 93, 127, 301
Littell, Jonathan, 301; *The Kindly Ones*, 301
Little, Brown, 183
London, Jack, 263
Look (magazine), 184
Lorch, Netanel, 95
Lubetkin, Zivia, 124, 126, 130
Lublin, 127

MacArthur, Douglas, 47, 48
Maidanek, 127
Mailer, Norman, 2, 4, 7, 57, 100, 105, 225, 233, 300; *Armies of the Night*, 225; *Deer Park*, 105; *The Naked and the Dead*, 52, 57
Malamud, Bernard, 7, 116, 301
Malone, Dorothy, 6–7, 72, 74, 75, 154
Maltz, Albert, 118

Mann, Delbert, 230, 231
Marines, U.S., 98, 119, 241, 247, 259, 263; in *Battle Cry* (book and film), 8, 35, 37, 52, 57, 58, 59, 62, 63–64, 65, 67, 73, 74, 75, 79; in *A God in Ruins*, 292, 293, 295; in *O'Hara's Choice*, 8, 292, 294, 297–299; Uris's career in, 1, 5, 6, 12, 21, 23–24, 24–25, 26, 27, 28, 29–48, 96, 123, 202, 204, 265, 267, 275, 300, 303
Marx, Karl, 15
Masada, 125, 196, 204
Massey, Raymond, 72
McCarthy hearings, 24
McCormick, Ken, 85, 208, 233, 250, 251, 259; consoles and encourages Uris after Margery's suicide, 192, 193; descriptions of Uris by, 104, 177, 205, 206, 255; Uris's correspondence with, and comments on writing by, 217, 226–227, 228, 230–231, 234, 253, 257, 261, 268, 269; and the writing of *Exodus*, 104, 195; and the writing of *The Haj*, 239–240, 241, 242, 243, 244, 249; and the writing of *QB VII*, 196, 197, 204
McGraw-Hill, 183, 184
McMurtry, Larry, 201
Meir, Golda, 98, 99, 123, 238
Melville, Herman, 243; *Moby Dick*, 243, 245
MGM, 71, 90, 95, 117, 140, 171, 178, 261
Michener, James, 4, 233, 262, 271, 283, 300
Miller, Arthur, 24, 105
Miller, Merle, 63
Milton, John, 135; *Paradise Lost*, 135
Mineo, Sal, 121, 122
Mirisch Productions, 91, 124
Montefiore, Moses, 237
Morton, Henry, 7; *The Cardinal*, 7
Moscow, 94, 136, 276, 277, 278
Mossad, 316n6
Murray, Ray, 43
Mussolini, Benito, 95

Dream," 95; "The Billy Mitchell Story," 82, 178; "Blood My Battle Cry," 57; "Blood on the Beaches," 48; *Exodus*, ix, x, 1–2, 3, 4, 5, 7, 8, 9, 10, 20, 23, 24, 35, 62, 69, 70, 71, 78, 81, 82, 83, 86, 88, 89, 90, 91, 93–122, 123, 125, 126, 130, 132, 133, 135, 139, 140, 169, 170, 172, 176, 183, 194, 195, 196, 200, 202, 215, 218, 222, 226, 228, 233, 235, 238, 240, 241, 243, 247, 249, 250, 251, 257, 260, 261, 262, 265, 266, 273, 274, 275, 277, 287, 295, 300, 305n1; *Exodus* (film), 3, 91, 99, 116–122, 229, 281, 322n113; *Exodus* (geography), 322n118; *Exodus* (musical), 179; *Exodus* (samizdat), 276; *Exodus Revisited*, 81, 25, 126; "Fair is my Gracia," 21, 307n14; "The Fighter," 82; *Fourragere Follies*, 41, 45, 50, 309n52; "Gideon's Early Childhood Memories," 259–260; *A God in Ruins*, 2, 185, 284, 291–296, 299; "The Gringo," 90, 91, 169, 179, 260; *Gunfight at the O.K. Corral*, 3, 70, 71, 82, 85–90, 91, 106, 260, 276; *The Haj*, 2, 3, 90, 225, 231, 232, 237, 239, 240–251, 252, 253, 256, 267–268, 281, 284, 287, 301; "Heatherbedlam," 174; "Helsinki-Leningrad Express," 277; "Hellenic Interlude," 68, 69, 70; *Ireland: A Terrible Beauty* (with Jill Uris), 81, 208, 209, 210, 211–215, 216, 223, 226, 227, 228, 230, 232, 234, 236, 239; *Jerusalem: Song of Songs* (with Jill Uris), x, 81, 126, 208, 232, 235–240; "Lullaby," 257–258, 261; *Mila 18*, 3, 8, 23, 24, 33, 62, 70, 78, 81, 83, 84, 86, 88, 90, 91, 104, 126, 129, 130, 131, 132–136, 139, 169, 202, 222, 231, 232, 239, 242, 250, 275, 278, 279, 287; *Mila 18* (film), 171, 179, 250, 284; *Mitla Pass*, 2, 5, 6, 21, 22, 23, 25, 26, 56, 58, 62, 66, 70, 82, 87, 91, 100, 193, 195, 207, 231, 250, 253, 255–260, 261–268, 269, 270, 280, 284, 287, 294, 314n19; *O'Hara's Choice*, 1, 2, 8, 29, 86, 88, 252, 284, 292, 294, 296,

297–299, 303; "Old Letters, New Life," 256; *The Parent Spark*, 45–46; *QB VII*, 2, 6, 8, 19, 32, 58, 81, 84, 86, 88, 188, 193–202, 205, 208, 209, 221, 222, 244, 249, 252, 262, 275, 295, 305n2; *QBVII* (TV), 3, 201–202, 232; *Rebel Without a Cause*, 79–80, 82, 260; *Redemption*, 2, 3, 193, 218, 261, 267, 273, 283, 284, 285–290, 295, 296, 297, 301; "Ringside," 40, 82, 88; "Russian novel," 204, 208; "Secrets of Forever Island," 281, 282–283; *Situation Out of Hand*, 41, 45, 49, 51, *145*; *Strike Zion!*, 183; "This Is My War— Personally," 49–50; *Topaz*, 3, 7, 8, 24, 81, 82, 86, 87, 140, 178, 179, 180–185, 193, 194, 222, 226, 227; *Topaz* (film), 91, 229; *Trinity*, ix, 2, 3, 6, 8, 10, 23, 35, 81, 82–83, 84, 86, 88, 89, 91, 173, 174, 207, 208, 209, 210, 211, 213, 214, 215–225, 226, 228, 229, 230, 231, 232, 233, 234, 243, 244, 245, 251, 252, 261, 267, 269, 270, 271, 273, 284, 285–286, 287, 288, 289, 290, 298, 301; *Trinity* (film), 229–232, 234, 250; *Trinity* (play), 203, 284; "The Truth Will Rise," 10

Uris, Mark, ix, 57, 100, *155*, 182, 184, 273, 292, 293, 296, 298; comic account of at sixtieth birthday party, 253; assists Uris late in life, 285, 297; birth of, 54; difficulties of, with Uris, 178, 290–291, 299; *The Haj* dedicated to, 245; during the Suez crisis, 102–103

Uris, Michael Cady, 54, 58, 100, 102, 174, 180, 189, 191, 206–207, 308n33

Uris, Pat, x, 291

Uris, Rachael, x, 180, 245, 252, 253, 269, 271, 281, 283, 285, 286, 291, 297, 303

Uris, William Wolf (father), 139, *142*, 172; autobiography of, 75, 256; death of, 259; life story of, 11–22; meeting of, with Margery Edwards, 188; difficult relationship of Uris with, and criticism of Uris by, 5–6, 10–11, 25–26, 107,

226, 255, 259, 260, 291; politics of, 7, 24; Uris's correspondence with, 35, 40, 49, 97, 105, 107, 171, 173, 178, 232; and Uris's enlistment, 27

USSR. *See* Soviet Union; *see also* Russia

Vaughan, Sam, 205, 230, 231, 233, 253, 255, 268, 284, 336n2; and *The Haj*, 239–240, 241, 242, 243–244, 250, 251

Vidal, Gore, 291, 296

Vogel, Joseph, 117

Vollmann, William T., 301, 302; *Europe Central*, 301, 302

Wallace, Irving, 3, 4, 185, 230, 300, 340n34

Wallis, Hal, 85, 106

Walsh, Raoul, 66, 72, 73, 75, *153*, *154*

Ward, Joan, 233, 234, 284

Warner, Jack, 75

Warner Bros., 64–67, 73–76, 77, 82, 178, 264, 300

Warsaw, 12, 125, 127–128, 278, 279

Warsaw Ghetto, 23, 84, 87, 88, 90, 105, 110, 123, 124, 126–136, 279, 285, 292, 300, 323n13

Washington, D.C., 27, 28, 86, 180, 182, 184, 186, 203

Wasserman, Lew, 186, 187, 230

Wayne, John, 78, 230

Weidman, Jerome, 7, 25

Wells, Orson, 37

West, Nathanael, 77

westerns, 3, 71, 86–90, 95, 116, 119, 264, 277

Whitaker, Francis, 217

Wiesel, Elie, 301, 319n74

Wilde, Oscar, 185

Williams, Tennessee, 169, 233

Wing, Willis, 68, 104, 257, 260

Workers Party, 14, 15, 16, 17

Wouk, Herman, 4, 7, 25, 105, 113, 240, 271, 300, 301; *The Caine Mutiny*, 52, 57, 58; *The Caine Mutiny* (film), 82; *Marjorie Morningstar*, 4, 7, 100; *War and Remembrance*, 240; *Winds of War*, 240

Wyler, Billy, 106

Yad Vashem, 130

Yeats, W. B., 211, 213, 221; "Easter, 1916," 211

Yemen, 99, 111

Yerusalimsky, Wolf. *See* Uris, William Wolf

Yerushalmi, Aaron, 67, 68, *142*

Yiddish, 11, 12, 14, 16, 212, 278

Zionism, 11, 12, 97, 114–115, 116, 119, 122, 238, 300

Zuckerman, Mort, 176

Zuckerman, Yitzhak (Antek), 124, 126, 130